THE WESTERN FRONT

European History in Perspective
General Editor: Jeremy Black

Benjamin Arnold *Medieval Germany*
Ronald Asch *The Thirty Years' War*
Christopher Barlett *Peace, War and the European Powers, 1814–1914*
Robert Bireley *The Refashioning of Catholicism, 1450–1700*
Donna Bohanan *Crown and Nobility in Early Modern France*
Arden Bucholz *Moltke and the German Wars, 1864–1871*
Patricia Clavin *The Great Depression, 1929–1939*
Paula Sutter Fichtner *The Habsburg Monarchy, 1490–1848*
Mark Galeotti *Gorbachev and his Revolution*
David Gates *Warfare in the Nineteenth Century*
Martin P. Johnson *The Dreyfus Affair*
Peter Musgrave *The Early Modern European Economy*
J. L. Price *The Dutch Republic in the Seventeenth Century*
A. W. Purdue *The Second World War*
Christopher Read *The Making and Breaking of the Soviet System*
Francisco J. Romero-Salvado *Twentieth-Century Spain*
Matthew S. Seligmann and Roderick R. McLean
Germany from Reich to Republic, 1871–1918
Brendan Simms *The Struggle for Mastery in Germany, 1779–1850*
David Sturdy *Louis XIV*
Hunt Tooley *The Western Front*
Peter Waldron *The End of Imperial Russia, 1855–1917*
James D. White *Lenin*
Patrick Williams *Philip II*

European History in Perspective
Series Standing Order
ISBN 0–333–71694–9 hardcover
ISBN 0–333–69336–1 paperback
(*outside North America only*)

You can receive future titles in this series as they are published by placing a
standing order. Please contact your bookseller or, in the case of difficulty, write
to us at the address below with your name and address, the title of the series
and the ISBN quoted above.

Customer Services Department, Palgrave Ltd
Houndmills, Basingstoke, Hampshire RG21 6XS, England

THE WESTERN FRONT
BATTLE GROUND AND HOME FRONT
IN THE FIRST WORLD WAR

Hunt Tooley

First published 2003 by
PALGRAVE MACMILLAN
Houndmills, Basingstoke, Hampshire RG21 6XS and
175 Fifth Avenue, New York, N.Y. 10010
Companies and representatives throughout the world

PALGRAVE MACMILLAN is the global academic imprint of the Palgrave
Macmillan division of St. Martin's Press, LLC and of Palgrave Macmillan Ltd.
Macmillan® is a registered trademark in the United States,
United Kingdom and other countries. Palgrave is a registered trademark
in the European Union and other countries.

ISBN 0–333–65062–X hardback
ISBN 0–333–65063–8 paperback

This book is printed on paper suitable for recycling and made from
fully managed and sustained forest sources.

A catalogue record for this book is available from the British Library.

Library of Congress Cataloging-in-Publication Data
Tooley, Hunt, 1955–
    The Western Front : battleground and home front in the First World
    War / Hunt Tooley.
        p.   cm. — (European history in perspective)
    Includes bibliographical references and index.
    ISBN 0–333–65062–X — ISBN 0–333–65063–8 (pbk.)
    1. World War, 1914–1918—Campaigns—Western Front.   2. World War,
    1914–1918—Europe, Western.   I. Title.   II. Series.

    D530.T63 2003
    940.4′144—dc21

                                                            2002044811

10   9   8   7   6   5   4   3   2   1
12   11   10   09   08   07   06   05   04   03

Printed in China

CONTENTS

PREFACE AND ACKNOWLEDGMENTS

In this book I have tried to achieve several, perhaps too many, goals in the span of a single volume. First, this study is an introduction to World War I. Second, it is an interpretation, an attempt to make sense of this catastrophic conflict in a certain way – by looking at connections between activities and places we usually think of as separate: the battle front and the home front. Third, the book is also an effort to focus on the experiences of the countries fighting across No Man's Land from 1914 to 1918 and to compare these experiences.

I may have tried to do too much in this work, but some things I have not tried to do. This is not an attempt to present a complete and coherent account of every, or indeed, any Western Front country's situation on the home front, or on the battle front. Such a goal would have been impossible, such a work either volumes long or so general as to be of little use or interest. For such a comprehensive picture, of one front/one country, we can consult a number of excellent books: Roger Chickering's *Imperial Germany and the Great War* or David Kennedy's classic account of the American home front, *Over Here*, or any number of histories dealing with the terrible battlefields of the war and the human beings who fought over them.

Instead, I intend this comparative work to be more suggestive than exhaustive. One can, I think, find in this account a coherent and understandable narrative of the major elements of World War I, from the viewpoint of the (mostly) advanced industrial countries that fought on the Western Front. But my hope is that even those for whom this book serves as an introduction to First World War studies will find it helpful in developing a critical approach to history, not only about this passage of history, but about others as well. I have tried to demonstrate here that "History" is not a closed subject, that people still debate with each other, sometimes furiously, over the past, even a past that is now more than 80 years behind us. Yet I have not hesitated to take positions: no honest historian can hold that all past historical writing, all past historical views, can somehow produce a single synthesis, a single coherent account. Historians, like everybody else, *will* disagree.

Those who are knowledgeable about the First World War – scholars, teachers, and students at all levels – will doubtless find that some of their favorite topics, perhaps facets they regard as essential, do not receive treatment in this book, or receive too little. I apologize in advance because any Great War student or scholar will be sure to perceive gaps, missed opportunities, themes unexploited. Indeed, I see several myself, but space must be limited in a book of this nature.

I have tried to keep to English-language sources in the documentation, since readers for whom this serves as an introduction will be predominantly English-speaking, and since scholars will be able to work out bibliographical references for themselves. In some few cases, I have used French or German sources to help with the comparative treatment or to make a special point.

It is a pleasant task to thank those persons and institutions who helped make this book possible. I teach at Austin College, a fine institution which works its faculty hard but values scholarly work and provides many kinds of support for it, all of which I have received in abundance. My colleagues in the History Department have been especially supportive of my efforts to examine all kinds of ideas about World War I, and I thank Light T. Cummins in particular for making available to me a recording of his collection of World War I-era popular songs. The Abell Library staff (in particular Larry Hardesty, Carolyn Vickrey, and Ilene Kendrick) have been cheerful and resourceful in finding needed items in the library and through Interlibrary Loan. They have also allowed me some grace in the iron laws of book circulation, for which I am grateful. My colleagues in the Psychology Department, Jane Ellington and Howard Starr, conducted a very helpful sort of "consultation" (without fee) through me with two individuals unable to be present and on the couch, Moltke and Ludendorff. And for similar consultations concerning the environmental and microbial profile of the Western Front, I am grateful to my colleagues in Biology, Peter Schulze and Kelly Reed.

I have worked on many of the ideas in this book in the framework of the Austrian Scholars Conferences of the the Ludwig von Mises Institute at Auburn University. I have gained much from the scholarship and discussions that the Institute generates.

My series editor, Jeremy Black, has been more than patient with me as I extended what appeared to be a simple project far beyond what was reasonable and took far more time doing it than he ever imagined I would. To my editors at Palgrave Macmillan – Terka Acton in particular – I extend my gratitude for their kindness and their patience with me as I struggled to finish this project. I am most grateful to Juanita Bullough for her excellent work copyediting the manuscript.

I owe a very special collective thanks to the several hundred members of the email discussion list WWI-L, specifically over the years from 1996 to the present. To me, this list is the exemplar of what modern electronic communication can do: it connects a specialized community of interest in an immediate way – in this case, those interested in World War I. "The List" has supplied much help on this book without knowing it. Very enriching and erudite discussions have made me think long and hard about many historical issues. And not only in discussions but in matters of detail, the List can be downright amazing. I thank everyone involved for all these contributions. In particular I am indebted to Jane Plotke and the other owners of the List. They run it with aplomb, as well as maintaining the finest historical site on the Web, *The World War I Document Archive*.

Lewis Ray – bibliophile, connoisseur of World War I history, and my dear friend – volunteered to read this manuscript. His suggestions have been most helpful, and our long discussions about the war have contributed materially to this book. I must also thank Major Gordon Corrigan, who has taught me much about World War I and military history in general, quite apart from his excellent book on the Indian Corps.

I was unusually lucky, while I was in college, to encounter two outstanding teachers of history, Professors Arnold Krammer and R. J. Q. Adams, both of Texas A&M University. They became the pillars of my early history education and started me out on my professional study of the subject. Their enthusiasm and learning have influenced me more than I could have comprehended at the time. It was they who introduced me to World War I and the Western Front. Professor Adams is to be found in the notes and text for his extensive work in British politics and social history in the World War I period. Both men encouraged me in the writing of this book, and in some measure the idea for it goes directly back to them. If they disagree with some parts of it, I hope at least that they will not be disappointed with their student.

I have to say that any mistakes are mine and not theirs, but they would have to bear at least some of the blame!

My family has been a special inspiration to me on this project. Harris, Austin, and Calvert Tooley have buoyed me up time and time again by their interest and encouragement. They are my best students and my most faithful supporters. They also accompanied me on a once-in-a-lifetime adventure: our discovery and exploration of the Western Front, or what is left of it. Karen Calvert Tooley ramrodded that trip and together with me navigated across the difficult Belgian and French roads that carry one to the landscape of the Western Front, and she has encouraged me and shown interest in the project without fail. Few historians can be so lucky in their families as I am. I dedicate this book to them.

H.T.

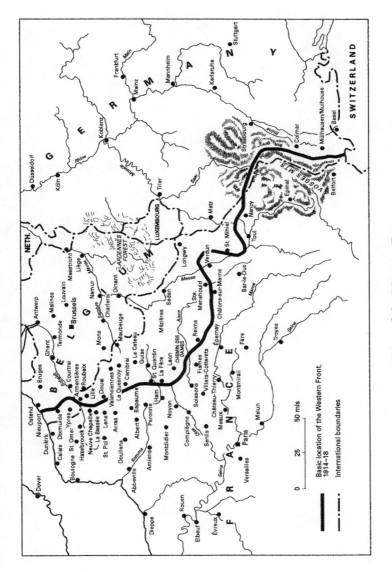

Map of the Western Front

Basic location of the Western Front, 1914–18

International boundaries

0   25   50 mls

1

ORIGINS, PRECONDITIONS, OUTBREAK

World War I broke out during the late summer of 1914 as the result of a crisis in the diplomatic relations between two antagonistic states: the rambling, jaded multinational Austro-Hungarian Empire, and the young but proud country of Serbia, the most dynamic of successor states to the Ottoman Empire in the Balkans. The antagonisms were both long-standing and real, and the interconnected nature of European power relations brought the two basic prewar camps into open hostilities in the first days of August 1914.

Historians and diplomats have argued about the origins of World War I intermittently, and frequently heatedly, since 1914. Even as late as the 1960s and 1970s, scholars carried on an acrimonious debate about who started the war and how it started. Since this book is about the war itself, we need to look at these historical discussions only enough to make sense of them and in particular, to relate trends in the prewar period to the theme of this book, the relationship between the battle front and the home fronts among the Western Front powers. We shall indeed find some important background to wartime behavior and wartime events in the run-up to the war.

In the wake of World War I scholars in Europe and North America fell into two different camps as to how the war had started, both of them influenced by contemporary events. On the one hand, Germany was seen as the brutal aggressor, a view related to wartime propaganda about "the evil Hun," but moderated somewhat for calmer consumption. The Germans still came out as the side of evil, though increasingly Austria-Hungary shared the blame, in some cases even eclipsing Germany. Yet by the mid-1920s a number of Western historians began to "revise" the old wartime view by pointing out that

1

all the belligerents had contributed in some way to the outbreak of the war.[1] By the 1930s, this revisionist view had for the most part won the field, and in a sense it comprised one of the bases of thinking about the appeasement of Hitler's Germany: if the first war had not ended so harshly and unjustly for the Germans, this argument ran, and if they had not been forced to sign a treaty which condemned them alone, the Germans would not have followed so vile a person as Hitler.

Of course, World War II intervened. This time there was no doubt as to war guilt: the Germans, it was said – or rather, Hitler himself – had started the war in spite of enormous efforts by Britain and France to appease the Germans and rectify their just complaints. New histories about the First World War were relatively few in the wake of the Second World War, and they tended either to utilize new sources to condemn German foreign policy before 1914 and after,[2] or to approach the problem with interpretations that reflected current world problems, in particular those of alliance and international organization.[3]

Hence, one opinion which enjoyed currency among historians in the 1950s was that the war was caused by the alliance systems dating from the last third of the nineteenth century. In this view, alliances became so tightly knit that they eventually, and blindly, gave up their own decision-making powers and plunged into war. Other historians of the post-World War II period, perhaps in response to contemporary desires for an international order guaranteed by the new United Nations or some other structure, argued the reverse: that the years before World War I represented "international anarchy," in which the brute interests of each state dominated their behavior to such an extent that all plunged into war together.

Neither of these structural interpretations held together very well after the Fischer Thesis came to dominate discussions about war origins in the 1960s. The German historian Fritz Fischer had in effect combined a structural view of origins with an analysis of the historical contingencies, or "real" events and records. Fischer drew tremendous fire from his fellow-German historians by asserting not only that Germany started the war, but that German elites had consciously brought on the war as the solution to domestic problems (rising working-class dissatisfaction) and the attempt to become a "world power," as opposed to merely a continental one.[4]

After a decade of scholarly strife and a second decade of calmer analysis, historians in Europe and North America tended to accept at least the idea that Germany had started the war, though many historians in the end thought that the Fischerites had stretched interpretations farther than the evidence warranted. Another principal criticism was that Fischer and his followers had generated their whole thesis with very little reference to the other powers. Fischer had adopted as a rule of thumb that domestic politics enjoyed "primacy" when national leaders made diplomatic decisions. But he and his followers seemed to recognize this principle only for Germany. Could the British, French, and Russians have had similarly aggressive designs in 1914? The reexaminations which criticized the Fischer school approach did a great deal, if not to rehabilitate Germany, at least to indicate that all the powers nursed aggressive ambitions.[5] Scholars on both sides of the Atlantic used the opportunity of this kind of intellectual flux to examine anew many older views of war origins and many new issues, in particular the kind of "mentalities" which characterized the social and political cultures on both sides of the Atlantic. Moreover, by the 1980s the return of the interest in the contingencies of events, and in narrative itself, led to new perspectives on the outbreak of the war and fresh work on many of the older, purely military or diplomatic issues involved.[6]

What follows is an attempt to incorporate many of the newer, post-Fischer perspectives into a coherent framework for understanding the war's outbreak. We will be very interested here in such recently emerging issues as the aggressive-mindedness which characterized military planning in the heyday of Social Darwinism. One would also expect that ideas about combat, community, and killing from before the war impacted the shape of the war once it started. We will also review the internal conflicts and financial disruptions (attendant upon modernization and the growth of the state) which made war appear as a viable solution to domestic crises, and not least the whole complex of technological changes which influenced not only the training and tactics of European armies, but their relationship to the policies of their governments as well.

The European System and War

We might begin by looking at the commonplace assertion that Europe experienced 100 years of relative peace after the Napoleonic Wars ended in 1815. Scholars have tended to explain the war as an aberration from a relatively long peace, the result of a "powder keg" waiting to

explode, then exploding. More recently, some historians have pointed
out that the century from 1815 (the settlement of the Napoleonic Wars)
to 1914 was after all something of an aberration; since at least the
fifteenth century, the "normal" mode of Europe during any given few
decades was war at some fairly virulent level.

This view serves as a useful corrective to the exaggerated picture of
a peaceful Atlantis sinking under the weight of war. A related, and
more "global" view likewise qualifies our ideas about "100 years of
peace." Organized violence in Europe had perhaps been alleviated
during the period 1815–1914, but one could still count well over
a dozen major wars in which one or more European powers participated, even if none of them turned out to be the benchmark
"general" war, one including most of the Great Powers. Hence, in
this period, all European Great Powers experienced warfare, and not
just in border skirmishes or colonial pacifications, but in real wars
resulting in large numbers of casualties and great public expense.
It is true that many of these wars were fought between European
and non-European powers, but the bulk were not. It is less accurate
to say – as is sometimes asserted – that after the war-intensive period
from 1848 to 1871, no two European powers fought each other. This
would only be true in the limited sense of the word "powers," since
European states fought each other in two Balkan wars in 1912 and
1913, and Spain fought the United States in 1898. In any case, after
1871 large-scale European military forces were deployed in three
major wars, not counting the Balkan wars or the Spanish-American
War. In this period of imperialism, minor wars and "pacifications"
fought by European armies would number in the dozens. Qualified
as the term "general peace" needs to be, it is clear that Europe experienced much less war in the 44 years after 1871 than in the 57 years
before it.

Indeed, in this year Great Power relations reshaped themselves
dramatically when the north German state of Prussia stepped into the
leadership of the confederated German states and defeated France in
a short but very violent war. Even as Paris was under siege, the architect of German unification, Otto von Bismarck, was able to convince
the various German princes to swear allegiance to the Prussian king
and to add to his titles that of German Emperor in a new, united
Germany. Italy had followed a similar path of unification a decade
before, creating from several disparate states a single Italy under the
kingship of the ruling house of northern Italian Piedmont.

The club of large, powerful European states had changed significantly: before 1860, Britain, France, Russia, and Austria formed the membership (with a weak Prussia on the side); after 1871, Britain, France (now weakened and humiliated), Russia, Austria-Hungary, Italy, and Germany. The expansion of the number of Great Powers complicated international relations considerably. The British Prime Minister was exaggerating only a little when he declared the balance of power "entirely destroyed" in 1871.[7] The idea of the "balance of power" had never meant that all Great Powers should be equal, but that they should line things up so that no dominant combination was likely. The new configuration could have been "balanced" along the lines of the old thinking, and Bismarck, the preeminent international statesman of his day, created something like a balance during the 1870s and 1880s by keeping France isolated, by keeping Britain unthreatened, and by keeping Russia friendly.

The technical aspects of this system need explaining here only in outline. And one must start with the hatred that the French felt for the new Germany. The victory of 1870/71 had been a crushing, humiliating blow to a country accustomed to humiliating others during 400 years of warmaking and aggression. During the war, France's emperor was captured and imprisoned, the capital was surrounded and shelled, and government members had to escape Paris by balloon. The Germans declared their Empire in Louis XIV's spectacular Hall of Mirrors at Versailles. In the peace settlement, the French lost the eastern province of Alsace and a part of Lorraine. On top of everything, France had to pay Germany five billion francs by way of indemnity. It is hardly surprising that the French were full of rancor toward the Germans in the wake of 1871. Bismarck predicted, "France will never forgive us," and ordered Europe accordingly. The Iron Chancellor did attempt to help France toward an expanded colonial empire which would engage French energies and renew French pride. One might also point out that many of France's homegrown social, demographic, and political problems might have provided distraction from the wounds of 1871. Yet a substantial school of French political and military leaders tended to nurse a smoldering sense of *revanchisme*, a systematic desire for revenge, during the next 40 years.[8]

Bismarck made much of Germany's status as a "saturated" power, one with no territorial desires in Europe. France hoped fervently to regain lost territory. The centerpiece to Bismarck's diplomacy was thus the diplomatic isolation of France. He achieved this isolation by entering into a series of alliances with France's potential suitors.[9] During the 1870s, Bismarck worked out a "three emperors' alliance" designed to keep both Austria-Hungary and Russia friendly to the new Germany and on guard against France. Yet during a crisis which drew Germany and France close to war in 1875, the Russians proved unreliable, and indeed the British also demonstrated that another German attack on France would not be acceptable. Bismarck's role, moreover, in scaling down Russian gains at the expense of the Ottoman Empire after the 1877/78 Russo-Turkish War led to bad feelings on the Russian side. Bismarck dealt with this problem at both ends. First, in 1879 he created a new bond with Austria-Hungary, the Dual Alliance, which would remain in effect through World War I. The goal of the Alliance was to arrange for aid from the other partner in case one was attacked by Russia, or benevolent neutrality in the event of an attack by any other country. This Dual Alliance was made Triple when it was expanded eight years later to include Italy.

Yet the great chancellor was always concerned about keeping the Russians on his side, from long-standing association with St. Petersburg (as ambassador years before), from his fear that a France backed by Russia would be able to carry out a war of revenge, and from his hope of keeping solidarity among the three authoritarian European empires: Germany, Russia, and Austria-Hungary. Hence, after a number of desultory attempts to keep the Russians friendly, in 1887 Germany concluded with Russia the Reinsurance Treaty, whereby each side agreed to remain neutral should the other engage in war with another party (though this agreement was not to apply should Germany attack France or Russia attack Austria-Hungary). Secret clauses indicated that Germany would support Russia in gaining access to the straits which contained Russia in the Black Sea, a long-standing Russian goal. The treaty, potentially renewable of course, was to last for a period of three years.

Meanwhile, a new emperor came to power in 1888, 31-year-old Wilhelm II. Wilhelm's personality turned out to be an important factor in European international politics, and the first major international episode he would influence was at hand. Having suffered through two years of Bismarck's irritated and irritating tutelage, the young emperor – with extensive but haphazard knowledge and a vain and overbearing personality – accepted Bismarck's resignation, hoping now to run his country from the throne. Disliking Bismarck's Russian orientation, he favored shoring up flagging relations with the British, whose distrust of Russia bordered on mania. Advisors in the German Foreign Office likewise downplayed the importance of the Russians. Hence the Reinsurance Treaty lapsed.

Like much German policy during the reign of Wilhelm II, this decision reflected an unwillingness to contemplate the potential ramifications of a given measure. In this case, the lost link to Russia had an immediate impact. If Bismarck had managed to keep France in isolation, as a kind of diplomatic pariah, the Russians were in a sense preoccupied with the terrible prospect of becoming a diplomatic pariah themselves. This diplomatic problem was exacerbated by the economic problems of the country. Worried that their country was lagging far behind Western and Central Europe in industrial development, Russian leaders from the time of the Crimean War onward feared that Russia would not be able to hold its own as a great power. From the 1860s onward, they attempted to foster industry, but they needed capital accumulation (typical of the great middle classes of the Western European countries). Sergei Witte, a railway executive who became Minister of Finance in 1893, proposed a dramatic program of "industrialization from above"; and the commitment of the Russian state to this meant that at the same time the Russians were searching for a diplomatic partner, they were also in need of massive loans to fuel the ambitious industrialization program. Russia found both in France. For their part, the French could gain security by making friends on Germany's east. The Russians could gain not only a diplomatic partner, but the French market of saving consumers, who in fact bought into Russian industrialization by purchasing the Russian loan issues floated in France. Almost incidentally, the French middle class, that class which formed the saving and investing public, came to have a close interest in the industrial development and general economic well-being of the Russian Empire.[10]

The Alliance was a fact by January 1894. Each partner would be obliged to join in the war should the other be attacked by Germany, and to mobilize should any member of the Triple Alliance marshal its military forces. Where the Dual Alliance had formed the first link that would become part of the belligerent coalitions in the Great War, the Franco-Russian Alliance formed the first link of the coalition that would become the Entente powers.

Though historians have frequently blamed the "alliance system" – these partly secret, partly open treaties and agreements arranged by Bismarck – for increasing the tensions which led to World War I, in fact this system worked quite well in keeping European powers out of wars with each other during two decades and even beyond. The problem with Bismarck's "system" was that his successors cut Germany's ties with Russia. Thus, where Bismarck had effectively kept France without close allies since the 1860s, the rebuff of the Russians sent them into the arms of France. This Franco-Russian connection now produced in reality the threat that had haunted Bismarck: should European powers go to war, Germany would find itself with formidable enemies on both the west and the east. Germany could probably defeat France or Russia singly, but together, the team of backward but well-endowed Russia and industrialized and bitter France produced nightmares for German strategic planners.

Finally, one might supplement this somewhat mechanical reading of the European system with new interpretations which emphasize the shifting of the world balance of forces, not just the European system itself. One would expect that the rise of the new powers, especially the United States and Japan, would impact upon European diplomacy, which was, after all, hardly a hermetically sealed world. Scholars utilizing a global approach to the history of the prewar period have shown that this rapid rise of non-European powers made for tremendous instability within the world subsystem of Europe, as did dramatic changes within the economic and demographic structure of Europe itself. Yet in a sense, Europe never held such a sway over the rest of the globe as it did at that time, politically, militarily, and economically.

In the economic sphere, European world trade skyrocketed at the end of the century and enjoyed the unique advantage of the international gold standard. Until 1914, all countries tying their currencies to gold (which could be cleared through the world's greatest banking center, London) could rely on fixed exchange rates and the self-regulation of international exchange. Since an unhampered market operates as a huge communications network, allowing buyers and sellers to agree on prices, the communications capabilities of the international market at the turn of the century was a tremendously efficient system of distribution. Yet liberal economic policies in Western countries which allowed this system to spread began to be eclipsed by the end of the century, as economic nationalism and neo-mercantilism dictated beggar-thy-neighbor economic policies of protective tariffs. By 1900, Britain and Holland stood alone as the practitioners of free trade. Steep protective tariffs in all other great trading countries made not only for inefficiencies in the international market, but for frictions among countries as well.[11]

Social Conflicts and the Origins of the War

Industrialization had a transformative impact on the shape of societies which the European powers would lead to war. By the end of the nineteenth century, over half of the populations of Western Europe and Germany lived in urban settings. The growing working class had been on the minds of most social and political theorists and activists since early in the century, especially after the revolutionary outbursts of the 1840s. Though it seems clear that most working-class people were seeking a better life for themselves and their children individually and not as a part of some broader, altruistic behavior, "working-class" movements did indeed spring up around mid-century in Western and Central Europe, including many led by uprooted middle-class intellectuals, like Karl Marx, who hoped not for gradual improvement in the condition of the working class, but for the overthrow of "bour-geois" society and the establishment of the dictatorship of the working class, or "proletariat," as Marx called the class of urban workers. After the spectacular class confrontations in the 1840s (the Chartist movement in England, and some phases of the 1848 Revolutions on the Continent), social conflict in this sense relaxed a great deal toward the end of the century.

The question then becomes: Did the new shape of industrialized society in some way destabilize Europe or contribute to the origins of the war? Standard views of the social dynamics of this period have changed a great deal since the 1960s, an early heyday of social history. Inspired to a great extent by Marxist theory, early social historians tended to agree that the main distinctions in Europe were class distinctions that cut across international boundaries, that the great movement of history in the decades before World War I was a world crisis involving capitalist overproduction and the manipulation of European and, indeed, worldwide working classes. "Alienation," as Marx called it, eased somewhat by the early twentieth century as a result of habitual accommodation by the working class with the capitalist class. But the clash of classes nonetheless led European elites to decide that only war could solve the social crisis at home. Some historians adopted a more sociological view in seeing the discontents as arising from "modernization," a sociological model designed to give depth to some of the cruder Marxist assumptions of social history.[12] In the intervening years, a number of new approaches have tended to move away from a class interpretation of society (and the coming of the war), many of these interpretations employing Marxist mechanics but with some motor other than class, gender, for example. In these views, the oppression of the underclass is still at issue, and the principal story is still the suppression of the underclass and its relation to war, but the identity of the underclass is changed.[13]

Two problems presented themselves for the social historians of the 1960s and 1970s, as for the hardline Marxists of the 1890s. First, as recent work has shown, the kind of unified proletariat described by Marx never existed; there were many working classes, and the goals of working people were anything but homogenous. Second, class conflict of the sort that aimed at overthrowing systems was rare indeed and was waning rapidly in Western and Central Europe, except for the artificial class consciousness of leftist intellectuals. The vision of workers as primitive revolutionaries in squalid, polluted cities was simply not working out to be the case. Instead of the dramatic bluebook conditions with which Marx and Engels had filled their imaginations, the Europe of the decades before the war was turning out to be a workers' state of another sort. Real wages rose steadily. Life remained rigorous for working-class Europeans; family budgets were low, housing was cramped, factory discipline was harsh by later norms. But by most measures for which one can find clear data – infant mortality rates, for example – living standards in Western and Central Europe were improving in the years before World War I.[14]

Many European workers were voting for workers' parties, but the old revolutionary vanguard of uprooted intellectuals had a difficult time persuading workers – given the possibility of upward social mobility – that what they should really do was to overthrow the system instead of moving on up the socioeconomic ladder. To European workers who had by choice sacrificed a great deal in order to provide more comforts and a good start in life for their children and grandchildren, the words of bourgeois radicals emerging from their Victorian libraries to advocate workers' revolts did not always find resonance.

Indeed, socialist parties in Europe began to pick up steam in the last decade of the nineteenth century only as the party leadership became increasingly "reformist" as opposed to "revolutionist." The most successful European socialist parties, Germany's in particular, managed to ally themselves to the trade unions, which had always called for reform rather than revolution. Naturally, the 1904 Congress of the Socialist International duly condemned the siren calls of reform socialists who proposed to cooperate with bourgeois governments instead of overthrowing them. Hence, in the late 1890s the German Social Democratic Party, already dominated by union activists rather than intellectual firebrands, more or less dropped Marxist revolution in favor of a "revisionist" program of gradual social reforms. The great gains of the German Socialist Party in 1912 put into the German parliament, the Reichstag, mostly socialists who dressed, spoke, and acted like good German patriots. In the United Kingdom, it took the gradualist appeals of the "Fabian" intellectuals to make an alliance with the political forces of the union movement and form the Labour Party after the turn of the century. In France, the various socialist parties took the rebuff of the Socialist International to heart and, under the extraordinary leadership of Jean Jaurès, united to form a single party, whose name even reflected devotion to the radical Socialist International. But the new French Socialist Party was not always pre-pared to mount the barricades. Its constituency increasingly included civil servants, schoolteachers, and peasants, who hoped for reform, not revolution. Jaurès himself seemed to link socialism and bourgeois democracy, and the new party increasingly reflected the reformist tendency. It is true that immediately before the war, strike activity rose rapidly in industrialized Europe, and that much violence occurred. Yet the goals of almost all of the strikes, even those which turned ugly indeed, were those of higher pay, shorter hours, and better working conditions – in short, something like bourgeois improvements. In the decade and a half before the war, it is clear that class conflicts among the future Western Front belligerents were gradually approaching a stage of compromise worlds away from Marx's calls for violent revolution. European socialists were experiencing the greatest political gains they would see for many decades, but the gains tended to be in the communities of mainstream "democratic" socialism, which combined the demands of the trade unions with a call for enhanced systems of social welfare.[15]

The United States

On the outside of the immediate power competition among the European powers stood the United States. Before 1898 the American Republic counted little on the world scene, since on the one hand the republic had been designed to avoid any "entangling" alliances not absolutely necessary, and on the other since the United States had, like

Germany and Italy, been absorbed with its "national question" from the
1850s through the period of the Civil War and Reconstruction. From
the lofty heights of the European Great Powers, observers could admit
by the last decade of the century that the United States had achieved
a breathtaking rate of industrialization. Indeed, in the last two decades
of the nineteenth century, the American level of industrialization
doubled, and it doubled again in the first decade of the twentieth.
Already in 1880 the United States had stood second behind Britain in
terms of economic productivity, but by 1913 it had for some years been
the most industrialized and productive economic unit on the globe. By
that year, it was producing about a third of the world's manufacturing
output. In the area of iron and steel production, so relevant to modern
war, the United States produced more steel (31.8 million tons) in 1913
than the next three leading steel-producing countries, Germany (17.6
million), Britain (7.7 million), and Russia (4.8 million). With a population
greater than that of any European power, the United States had by any
measure a significant place in calculations of international strength.[16]

Europeans might have seen some clues as to America's future
emergence as a world power, even before the USA's conscious step in
that direction in 1898 in the Spanish-American war, a war fought out in
two hemispheres (Cuba and the Philippines) and utilizing the kind of
coordinated land-based and naval power which stood as the ideal for
most European strategic thinkers. Actually, as will be seen below, the
Americans had amassed a great fund of military knowledge during
the Civil War, the frontier wars against the American Indians, and a
number of imperialist conflicts after 1898. Recent research has begun to
indicate that some European biases against all things American stood in
the way of realistic planning for some future European war.[17]

In any case, it will be seen below that in spite of the Spanish-American
War and new urges of the United States to become a world power,
traditional tendencies to avoid "entangling alliances" and stay out of
European conflicts formed a powerful hurdle to those who hoped to
engage the country more in the international system.

War, the Nation, and the State in 1900

The emergence of industry-based warfare in the Western world signaled
a new stage of thinking about the nation-state, a European political form
which had taken its earliest shape – amid constant warfare – in the

period between 1450 and 1650. Against the brutal aspects of these centralizing tendencies of the European state (mostly in the form of dynastic rule) over the next centuries, Europeans developed a number of defense mechanisms. But the most prominent ones were the maintenance of regional rights and individual autonomy. In expanding this defense against the unlimited power of the centralized kingdom, with its absolute monarch and his bureaucratic representatives, European anti-absolutists also revived the classical ideas that law ought to operate as a contract, and not as an administrative tool, and that the natural order of things confers autonomy, or natural rights, upon individuals. These ideas coalesced in the eighteenth century in the doctrine called liberalism.

Not limited to liberal thinkers and politicians themselves, liberalism had a great impact on leaders from many parts of the political spectrum, and liberal policies were indeed in operation throughout Western and Central Europe in one form or another during the nineteenth century. Long tarred by enemies from many directions as the representatives of mere business interests, classical European liberals were much less concerned with the form of government than with its size and aggressiveness. Liberals throughout Western and Central Europe tended to work against the growing size and reach of centralized governments. In this they had their work cut out for them: all European bureaucratic states grew relatively rapidly from the eighteenth century onward, though it is necessary to say here that the degree to which central governments could control populations, or even divert their wealth into government coffers, was severely limited by modern standards. Still, the size of governments was increasing, their activities expanding. Looking at the simple comparison of per capita government expenditure, one finds that France's spending per person almost doubled from 1850 to 1875; the ratio of spending for the years 1850, 1875, 1900, and 1913 works out as 1, 2, 2.5, 3.1, respectively. In the years from 1875 to 1913 alone, German government spending per capita multiplied by a factor of 3.65. Among the three Western Great Powers, liberal Britain maintained the lowest growth in spending, which increased between 1850 and 1913 by a factor of only 1.7.[18]

It is important to recognize that thinking about society in terms of the collective or group was likewise potent during the nineteenth century – indeed, more collectivist ideologies, like that of Marx, were being created all the time. Yet in spite of much competition, the dominant European collectivist ideology was the idea represented by the abstract term "state" or less abstractly by the ethnicity-oriented "national state"; that is, the centralized national state in which the citizens were united by fraternal (especially linguistic) and civic ties.

The result of the revolutionary period beginning in the late eighteenth century had been to forge more and more group identification among populations. For this purpose, the Romantic myth of the mystical ties of linguistic and "blood" relations was borrowed. To achieve this program, which we call "nationalism," European power centers had to do away with competing loyalties as well as to exalt or glamorize the administration of the state and the state's monopoly of violence. We must keep in mind that this program formed the background to most discussions of politics and international relations after the mid-nineteenth century. And after the 1860s, a harder-shelled, more aggressive (and often more ethnically exclusive) kind of jingoism represented an intensification of the movement for power and success by centralization. Indeed, though rationalist, individualist liberalism was in most ways diametrically opposed to irrational, collectivist nationalism, during the great nationalist convulsions of the mid-nineteenth century, even many liberals had defected from the cause of freedom, seduced by the attractions of national power, and had supported much growth in the size and intrusiveness of government.

In a classic study, American historian Carleton J. H. Hayes identified late nineteenth-century Europe with the reign of the "national liberals," a reference not only to the National Liberal Party which played an important role in German politics, but to the simultaneous mixing of nationalist and liberal goals throughout Western and Central Europe. Similar attempts to harmonize mostly opposing systems led to "national liberal" camps in all the major European states, and these parties tended to be influential in party systems which had a kind of static quality, since both the class politics of the old order (the various aristocratic parties) and of the rising socialist left (the various social democratic parties) had constituencies which were physically limited by class. These national liberal governments introduced state compulsion where it had not existed before, especially in schooling and military recruitment. From the 1870s onward European governments accelerated measures of economic nationalism as well. Hence, French officials burnt the midnight oil in the effort to make true patriotic Frenchmen out of the peasants in remote rural France. Germans were educated about the glories of their national state in both schools and the military, which was increasing its size and influence regularly.

Where insufficiently homogenized ethnic groups stood in the way of national cohesion, programs designed to "nationalize" the offending groups were put in place, though by the end of the century, the problem was becoming increasingly difficult, since many of these recalcitrant ethnic groups – German Poles and Danes, and the Irish, for example – developed national identities and national movements of their own. The same was true for regions with long-standing traditions of autonomy or even independence. The results were apparently "seamless" national states, but the stresses of World War I would reveal that many seams still existed.[19]

Hence, all conceptions of planning for eventual war in the years before 1914 took place against not only the background of industrial growth and concomitant social changes, but against an equally important tension between two of the defining tendencies of modern Europe, and indeed, the Western world: that between centralized, powerful, and efficient sovereign governments on the one hand, and the autonomy and integrity of the individual on the other. And yet the enthusiasm of nationalism, or merely national pride, could cover a host of sins. Again and again during the late nineteenth century, European governments showed that where rational arguments failed in support of a given policy, the national argument rarely misfired, whether the issue was taking over tropical real estate to create a new colony, erecting a stiff tariff barrier which would raise the price of goods to "protect" home industries, or building a navy of threatening battleships whose existence would turn friends into enemies.

Superiority, Aggression, Technology, and Violence

By the end of the nineteenth century, another factor which increasingly cut across the social and political segments, permeating public discussions and private attitudes, was the doctrine of Social Darwinism. Deriving from the widespread discussions occasioned by the publication of Darwin's *Origin of the Species* in 1859, Social Darwinism emerged when a number of Darwin's champions – most importantly the British social philosopher Herbert Spencer – extended Darwin's evolutionary principle of "survival of the fittest" (Spencer, not Darwin, coined the term) to society and eventually world history. Hence, where Darwin assumed that the mechanics of nature depended on natural selection based on what succeeds best (the fittest), Social Darwinists assumed

that individuals, institutions, and even nations operated on the same
principle: the fittest would survive, and those which survived were
clearly the fittest.

It is difficult to isolate the multifarious ramifications of Social
Darwinism in the Western world in the century after Darwin wrote his
book: these ramifications are indeed many, complex, and frequently
contradictory. Social Darwinism could cut across the political spectrum
easily. For conservatives, it seemed to justify elitist social position; for
old-style liberals it seemed to argue for freewheeling competition
within society; for national liberals and social imperialists it gave a
scientific patina to imperial conquest; for socialists, it could work well
as a secondary (and materialist) explanation of historical evolution. In
science and the academic world, Social Darwinism gave impetus to the
whole field of behavioral studies. Management science, Taylorism at
the start, was an outgrowth of the Social Darwinist view, as were many
schools of thought hoping to "direct" social evolution by one scheme or
another. It also gave rise to the related movements of eugenics, birth
control, and scientific racism. Social Darwinism was nothing like
a coherent philosophy and only a very blurred set of doctrines, but it
had at its core a few powerful ideas which influenced the attitudes of
millions of people in the Western world who had never read Darwin
and never heard of Spencer.[20]

The influence of Social Darwinism on both the outbreak and course
of World War I has been only superficially studied by historians
and deserves much more attention. In the confines of this overview,
three important influences should not be passed over. First, Social
Darwinism was, when intermixed with nationalism, a potent impulsion
to the foreign conquests we call imperialism. And it may not be merely
coincidence that the renewed and feverish imperial activity that historians call the "new imperialism" after the 1860s was concomitant to
the percolation of Social Darwinism throughout European society.
Those pushing for imperialist ventures in the 1870s and 1880s already
had a powerful argument in the appeal to national pride: "let us take
this tropical region, lest our national rival take it first and exclude
us from our place in the sun." A number of ingredients could be added
to this argument. Naturally, some businessmen added economic and
fiscal ingredients; and religious people could add missionary ingredients. But the double-sided Social Darwinist contention was a powerful
one: European states had the *right* to conquer peoples because they
were inferior and needed organizing for the good of the human race,

and advanced states had the *duty* to conquer these peoples in order to pull them upward (at least some distance) toward the civilized level already achieved by the Europeans. This appeal was not limited to industrialists and merchants, or to church leaders or churchgoers. Indeed, in the ongoing work to create stronger and more powerful national identities in Europe and its appendages this kind of argument contributed to the kind of secular civic ethos which European states hoped to create. As British imperialist Cecil Rhodes put it in 1877: "I contend that we are the finest race in the world and that the more of the world we inhabit, the better it is for the human race."

Hence, the Great Powers and lesser powers of Europe launched an outburst of imperialist activity after the emergence of the new Europe of 1871. To take the busy imperial field of Africa, in 1875 a Conservative British prime minister engineered the British purchase of the Suez Canal, though little else in Africa was ruled by Europeans; in 1884–85, the imperial powers met in Berlin to lay ground rules for the rough-and-tumble scramble for Africa; by 1895 nearly the whole of Africa was under some form of European sovereignty. The same process, with variations, was replicated across the globe. From 1876 to 1914, the colonial powers of the world annexed over 11 million square miles of territory. The new imperialist outburst was characterized by the planting of European flags and occupation of whole hinterlands, rather than informal control of a few coastal areas. By the 1890s, even the United States, a state born in the fight against empire, had gotten into the act in the Pacific region: in 1898 American troops, having "liberated" the Philippines from Spain, were sent in to "pacify" local groups and leaders and, all, as President Taft said at the time, to help protect "our little brown brothers." Indeed, in a speech at this time an American legislator, Albert J. Beveridge, managed to assert that the Social Darwinian justification of "might makes right" was actually intertwined with providence: "God has not been preparing the English-speaking and Teutonic peoples for a thousand years for nothing but vain and idle self-admiration. No. He made us master organizers of the world to establish a system where chaos reigned . . . . He has made us adept in government that we may administer govern-ment among savage and senile peoples."

The rivalries of imperialism helped lead to World War I in two ways. First, and most evidently, the various rivalries kept the European powers at each others' throats, or at least on their guard, since in most cases at least two powers were in competition for the same territory.

In the end, as will be seen below, imperial rivalries can hardly be said to have led directly to World War I, since the opponents in most of the imperial competitions later fought together in alliances after 1914. This was certainly the case with the most spectacular of these competitions: the Anglo-Russian rivalry in northwestern India–Central Asia, the Anglo-French rivalry in North Africa, and the Russo-Japanese rivalry in northeastern Asia. Precisely these powers would make up the core of the Alliance that won the Great War.

Yet these imperial clashes had a less direct, but quite significant, influence in bringing Europe to war simply by generating military emergencies and, indeed, the occasion for keeping large armies and large navies. These tensions, moreover, kept states aggressive and military in outlook and posture, and the availability of military personnel, equipment, and material made it seem natural for European powers to contemplate war in connection with any international crisis in the decades before 1914. The soldiers, moreover, were trained for war in these imperialist adventures, as the listing of late nineteenth-century wars above indicates.

Social Darwinism was again embedded in thinking about military matters, whether imperial or not, and indeed whether it was a matter of current clashes or planning for future war. Here Social Darwinist doctrine was reflected in the new, heightened insistence on aggressive behavior and an aggressive attitude. In practice this attachment to the offensive combined with new technologies of war to create a new doctrine of attack.

One of the effects of the military–technological revolution of the nineteenth century was the ability to deliver higher levels of metal and more powerful explosives to a given target than ever before. During the short span of one or two decades, most Western armies dropped the smooth-bore musket (essentially the same weapon in use since the late seventeenth century) and adopted, by stages, rifled, breech-loading (as opposed to muzzle-loading) weapons which enabled regular infantry soldiers not only to load and fire more rapidly, but to do so without standing up. Moreover, the newer weapons had a rifled barrel, with spiraled grooves inside, which could shoot both farther and more accurately.

Hence, infantry alone could produce enough firepower to make advancing on the battlefield, or even standing up, a much more deadly proposition. Recent work in the history of the American Civil War emphasizes that this change alone altered some of the fundamental dynamics of battlefield behavior as early as the 1860s. Observing that they had a much greater chance of being shot, soldiers clearly tended to stop advancing and find cover more often, and to spend more time under cover. Within a given battalion or regiment, this kind of individual behavior multiplied by 500 or 1,000 could decide the outcome of a battle. All in all, the effectiveness of troops on the *attack* seemed to be blunted; *defensive* tactics in a battle could prove capable both of lessening casualties and of winning the battle. And rifled, fast-shooting infantry weapons were only a beginning of this trend. By the end of the century, all Western armies were experimenting with machine guns, which could deliver rates of fire which were higher by magnitudes. Hence, even more lead could be hurled across the battlefield to stop attacking troops.

Still, lessons which seem clear to us today were less clear to students of warfare in 1900 or 1914, in part because few wars of the period pitted one European-style army against another. Indeed, advances in artillery production and utilization would prove to be the most decisive factor in creating a new battlefield dynamic in World War I. But the tactics of artillerists did not catch up to the technology until the war itself. It was not clear at all from any contemporary war experience that artillery would become the primary weapon of the next war.[21]

In sum, no one could be certain about the effects of the new advances. Among the few instances of fighting which incorporated at least some of the new technology were the Cuban battles of the brief Spanish-American War in 1898 and the longer Russo-Japanese War of 1904/1905. In the former, the most publicized action was the charge of Americans up the heights above the San Juan River. One could hardly say that it was a victory for the defense. Earlier in the battle, the Americans had used Gatling guns, an early machine gun, in the process not of defending against an enemy onslaught, but in taking Spanish positions. Six years later, the Russo-Japanese War incorporated much more of the new technology, and ferocious land battles developed in the Amur River region, fighting in which trenches screened with barbed wire and protected by machine guns were components of the battlefield. Still, though the Japanese lost extraordinary numbers of killed and wounded in the course of the great battles, ultimately, the human waves overwhelmed the entrenched Russian defenders. If one could also find evidence for the contrary in both of these wars, generally, most European military experts chose what they regarded as the psychologically sounder position that offensive-mindedness would win battles and wars.[22]

From the beginning of these developments strengthening the defensive in the 1860s, military thinkers began to analyze what it meant to attack and to receive attack. One of the earliest of these analysts was the French officer Charles-Ardent du Picq (who died in action in 1870). In battle, said du Picq, men rarely fight hand to hand; the "clash" of battle rarely occurs. Instead, one side or the other tends to give way before the actual clash. It was morale, not numbers or accurate shooting, which counted. Further, since it is such a terrible and nerve-racking thing to await attack, and since attackers have the psychological advantage of being able to see their own forward progress, the attackers will have the advantage in most battles. The attack gives, du Picq wrote, a "moral superiority": "The moral effect of the assault worries the defenders. They fire in the air if at all. They disperse immediately before the assailants who are even encouraged by this fire now that it is over. It quickens them in order to avoid a second salvo." Du Picq did add, however, that an unprepared attack could indeed be defeated by a prepared defense, and he was not so dismissive of physical factors in battle as to dismiss the need for as heavy an artillery and rifle fire as possible, right up to the point of the final bayonet charge.

Du Picq thus articulated what many military officers in the nineteenth century thought anyway. Indeed, his psychological arguments were especially taken to heart in France, where military training at all levels increasingly emphasized "morale" over mere technical advances. At the level of military doctrine, perhaps the most convincing of the theorists of the "morale" movement was Ferdinand Foch, later, of course, Commander-in-Chief of Allied armies during World War I. As a teacher of officers at the French War Academy (Foch was born in 1851) and a military theorist in the years before the war, he was perhaps even more significant to the attitudes and events that made the First World War.

In lectures and writings Foch began, around the turn of the century, to enunciate a carefully reasoned doctrine of the offensive as the preferred military mode. A defensive posture can keep the enemy from accomplishing some aim, he wrote, but this kind of "negative result" will never achieve victory. Even a successful defensive battle merely postpones the outcome of the war: "A purely defensive battle is like a duel in which one of the men does nothing but parry. He can never defeat his opponent, but on the contrary, and in spite of the greatest possible skill, he is bound to be hit sooner or later." It also follows that the goal of winning the battles, and therefore the war, does not mean that the victorious army will always be the one with the fewest casualties. An army might be physically decimated, Foch insisted, and still maintain the attack, put the defenders to rout, and win the battle. In any case, he points out, soldiers on the battlefield have no way of knowing who is losing more men, their own army or the enemy. Foch was only one of the teachers of this inspiring doctrine of the offensive, and most writers on the French generalship of World War I associate this offensive-mindedness most directly with Colonel Louis de Grandmaison, operations chief of the general staff in 1914. Hence, the whole mode of thinking is sometimes spoken of as the "Grandmaison school."[23]

Though one recent interpretation of World War I holds that tracing links between "war and society" confuses us by connecting what is in reality hermetically isolated,[24] the "war and society" historians from the 1970s to the present have much expanded our analytical weaponry for understanding the Great War. In the case of planning for war, we see a critical connection between war plans and the great shift in European intellectual development which began in the 1890s, a shift away from purely positivistic or rationalistic ideas and toward approaches to the problems of life involving depths of will, psychology, and "creative forces" within the human mind. In this connection, and from various directions, European thinkers and writers, from Nietzsche to Freud to Bergson, emphasized – each in a different way – an interest, an enthusiasm for the darker forces within human beings and human society.

A new interest in violence and aggression lay very close to the core of the new thinking. Though the great Nietzsche was institutionalized for mental illness by 1889 and dead by 1900, his complex philosophy could be popularized by lesser thinkers, who gave to increasing numbers of readers in the West views of self-assertion and power of the will which could verge on glorifying brutality. Freud, whose work began to gain notice in the 1890s, was not in any sense glorifying violence, but he was certainly interested in violence and aggression as important components of the makeup of any individual. French philosopher Henri Bergson hung his ideas on a beneficent "vital force," which determined the course of "creative evolution" (the title of his famous 1907 book), but Bergson's contemporary Georges Sorel used the same somewhat mystical style (or "intuitionalism") to raise social violence to the level of a necessary and cleansing force, especially when carried out by the working class in general strikes and other workers' revolts.

Through these thinkers and their popularizers, Europeans were increasingly attuned to an intellectual response to violence which could easily mesh with older mental constructs, such as patriotism. And indeed, on the popular level, it is important to remember that most of the millions of men who would eventually be in uniform during World War I had never heard of Freud and Sorel. They also had no clear information about the experience of recent wars. For one thing, popular information during the period before World War I was carefully sifted, not by governments for the most part, but by public sensibilities.

The vast new hordes of lower- and lower-middle-class readers (the result of expanded state schooling) now avidly read the penny press and formula, escapist fiction, in which wars and violence, to be sure, were present in large measures. But both newspapers and fiction, while they sensationalized violence and disaster, nonetheless sanitized them, avoiding graphic depictions of the results of violence. In general, the European wars around the turn of the century reached the public in mediated forms, which emphasized *esprit* and heroism, the virtues of the "stiff upper lip" and self-sacrifice, and did so in an elevated language borrowed from Romantic poets of the mid-nineteenth century. Hence, as the literary historian Paul Fussell has pointed out, before the war Europeans tended to think of battlefields in terms of "sacrifice" and the dead in terms of the "fallen." In popular fiction, the deadly confrontations in South Africa, Cuba, and the Philippines seemed more like dangerous larks. This image of heroism and sacrifice combined with fun was especially prominent in boys' fiction, a genre in which – from the 1890s right up to wartime – familiar heroes in numberless serial episodes faced evil foes and won through pure grit. Many readers of these novels became, of course, the young men who stood in the long lines at recruiting stations in Europe under the sunny skies of August 1914, just as did a large number of young intellectuals who welcomed the coming of war as a kind of cleansing of a generation.[25]

Further, even in staid Europe itself, the quiet years of the *belle époque* began to give way, offering examples of violence at home. The enormous industrial strikes of the prewar period – in France, Germany, and Britain – displayed organized violence by the workers, when in the attempt to gain higher wages and better conditions strikers used physical violence to take over workplaces, fight non-union workers (scabs), and the like. Authorities also used violence to quell many of these strikes. Hence, both elements of the strike could create large-scale violence. Violence was a regular feature of collective action in the prewar world, and strikes were practically everyday matters, at least to the newspaper-reading public. Hence, Europeans knew something about violence even at home.[26]

Oddly, two sources of prewar European public violence were the more striking because they issued from traditionally staid, calm, phlegmatic England. The first came in the form of a branch of the women's movement. Generating perhaps more headlines than the hundreds of thousands of striking workers in the years before the war was the spectacular and often destructive movement of the "suffragettes." The women's movement in Britain had, since the 1860s, called for the vote for women. Two main approaches emerged in the campaign for women's suffrage in the decade before the war: a constitutionalist movement (the National Union of Women's Suffrage Societies – called "suffragists") which was based on working primarily by means of education and at the local level, and a small but violent movement which adopted the Sorelian approach of violent acts of protest which would frighten politicians into national change. The latter group was the Women's Social and Political Union (WSPU), usually called "suffragettes," founded by socialist feminist Emmeline Pankhurst, the wife of a Manchester barrister, and her daughters, Sylvia and Christabel. The movement organized heckling and disruption of Liberal Party speeches from 1905 onward, and beginning in early 1912, after the failure of one of several women's suffrage bills, Pankhurst and over a hundred other women marched on Number 10 Downing Street with hammers and rocks, smashing the prime minister's windows. They continued on throughout the West End of London, breaking the windows of thousands of shops and department stores. "The argument of broken glass," commented Pankhurst, "is the most valuable argument in modern politics." Despite arrests, the suffragette "arguments" continued, becoming increasingly violent: members chained themselves to railings in public places, dropped acid in mailboxes, slashed paintings in public art galleries. In hiding in Paris, Christabel Pankhurst organized a campaign of arson which succeeded in burning a good many public and private buildings. At the 1913 Derby races, veteran suffragette Emily Davison – who was, perhaps, suicidal – rushed onto the track in front of a racehorse owned by the king, injuring the jockey and killing herself. These violent activities were criticized by "suffragists," the more moderate workers for the vote for women, who pointed out that reason and education made more sense for the cause than the politics of violent confrontation. Some gains were, indeed, made in minor issues, but constitutional reform in the matter of the vote for women would only come about after the war.[27]

Still more in the minds of most Britons on the eve of the war, the Irish problem reached the level of a really violent outbreak. Since Ireland had been dominated by England in a colonial relationship for several hundred years, the nineteenth-century movement for Home Rule, autonomy within the British system, had occasioned an inordinate share of political maneuvering since the first Home Rule bills were voted down in the 1880s and 1890s. The central problem of the "damnable question" was that the northern counties, called Ulster, had roots that were to a large extent Scots Presbyterian. For historical and social reasons, many considered the large majority of Irish Catholics throughout Ireland as a whole as the real problem – certainly an implacable foe should Ulster find itself submerged in a Catholic polity run from Dublin. The Liberal cabinet of Asquith introduced a Home Rule bill on the heels of significant parliamentary and consti-tutional reforms in 1911, and the bill was to become law in 1914. The Protestant Unionists in Ulster, led by Sir Edward Carson, proceeded to prepare for armed resistance to incorporation even into a autonomous Ireland. George V, king since 1910, found himself caught in the middle and at the mercy not only of events, but of the Liberal cabinet. He wrote to Asquith in August 1913, "I cannot help feeling that the Government is drifting and taking me with it." After seeing several compromises rejected by both sides, the cabinet tried armed force in the north, ordering the army to suppress the Ulster Volunteers. This too backfired, when a number of officers resigned rather than face the prospect of ordering soldiers to fire on the pro-Empire Unionists. This "Curragh Mutiny" made it clear that the army could not be relied on in this civil conflict. Meanwhile, the Irish nationalists in the south created their own fighting force and looked for weapons. A month before World War I would break out, Britons were expecting a war, but a civil war in Ireland. As writer Alec Waugh later wrote, "There were no clouds on my horizons during those long July evenings, and when the Chief in his farewell speech spoke of the bad news in the morning papers, I thought he was referring to the threat of civil war in Ireland."[28]

Planning for War

At the level of national planning, the strategic level, we can begin to see the threads of the various preconditions and origins of the war coming together. The technological changes in warfare that seemed, paradoxically, to make aggressiveness both more necessary and more deadly offered the consolation that the next war would be, if violent, at least short. Social-Darwinist ideas about great climactic struggles led many military intellectuals to assume that the next war would consist – like the Austro-Prussian War of 1866 – of short preliminaries and a colossal battle of decision. For another, close observers predicted that the next war would be a storm of steel involving weapons and ammunition so expensive and casualties so great that no government could sustain it either physically or spiritually.[29]

The national budgets of the eventual belligerents in World War I were not only not up to the task of financing modern, industrialized, total war: they were many times too small to collect the revenues needed to fund it. Hence, the short-war prediction was an illusion, but still a very good guess. The war states of the twentieth century – one thinks automatically of Soviet Russia and National Socialist Germany, but we might include many "democratic" states as well – which achieved ratios of wealth transfer from private to public coffers previously unheard of, were still in the future. The self-generating powers of the modern state during World War I are still surprising in retrospect: they could hardly have been guessed at in advance.

Hence all grand strategies among the prewar belligerents tended to be based on rapid, relatively cheap victories. And these strategies inflated the meaning of the gearing-up stage for each national plan, that is, "mobilization." One of the "lessons" taught by late nineteenth-century wars was that only the richest armies could fight much more than one or two battles without "reorganization," a process analogous to retooling, rebuilding, and reloading a weapon. With the ponderous millions of troops necessary to modern warfare, and the enormous stocks of supplies and materials needed for the briefest of campaigns, gearing up for war meant a whole range of activities, including manning forts, calling up reserves, stockpiling material, declaring martial law for certain regions, commandeering rolling stock, and hundreds of other activities. As historian Laurence Lafore pointed out, the prewar dictum that "mobilization equals war" was not strictly true, but mobilization was certainly more than a slight threat.[30] The expenses of mobilization were so great, that if a state mobilized its military forces, it had to mean it.

All of these elements are seen in the great war plan of the Germans. Named after the German Chief of the General Staff Alfred von Schlieffen, the plan emerged in the War Department as a direct result of the altered international politics of the Franco-Russian Alliance of the early 1890s. With potential enemies now linked, Germany's strategists had to plan for precisely the case which Bismarck had seen as the worst. Hence, the new staff chief devised a plan by which Germany could come to grips with two enemies at once. The basic outline of the plan came from the calculation that the French could put their army on a war footing, or mobilize it, in about two weeks, while the Russians would take up to six weeks to do the same. Schlieffen therefore proposed, first of all, that France must be defeated first, before the Russians could mobilize their full forces.

A major problem was that France, though perhaps weaker than Germany militarily, was nonetheless a prime military power whose defeat was in no way assured. To solve this problem, Schlieffen relied on surprise and high technology. The surprise was dependent on geography. The Franco-German border is for the most part marked by high, forested hills, and even mountains, in any case serious obstacles to early twentieth-century armies. The exception was the "Lorraine Gap," a relatively flat passage from northeastern France to southwestern Germany, defined by the Ardennes/Eiffel forests in the north and the Vosges mountains all the way to Switzerland in the south. But the French army was likely to close this gap. Schlieffen therefore proposed to put only a relatively small holding force in front of this French army. The bulk of the German army would form a line which was to pivot, something like a gate. The key to the plan was the decision to send the bulk of this swinging gate through Belgium and the Netherlands, flat countries which could accommodate a planned human wave a million strong (the Netherlands part of the invasion was eventually dropped by Schlieffen's successor).

The greatest problem with this plan was the political one: the major European powers had signed the London Treaty of 1839, in which Belgium's existence, borders, and neutrality were all recognized. Hence, to violate the internationally agreed-upon neutrality of Belgium by invading the country on the way to France would hand to any other possible allies of France (we may read "Britain" here) the opportunity to declare war, the *casus belli* in the legal phrase. It was not certain that Britain would declare war in such a case, and at the period when the plan really adopted the Belgian invasion, Britain and Germany had been experimenting with a short-term friendship, or *rapprochement*. Still, Schlieffen knew that this political problem could well result in bringing the British into the planned war. He simply decided that there was no other way to effect the rapid destruction of France's armies required in the desperate case of fighting two powerful enemies in two different directions at once.

The second element in the French defeat would be technology. Since the Prussian military reforms of the 1860s, the Prussian army had prided itself on the use of telegraphy, railroads, and advanced weapons. Schlieffen now tapped into this tradition by having his staff plan in detail the precise movements of the invading army, utilizing rail transport as far as possible and using the network of roads in such a way as to allow minimum delays. Naturally, horse transport was still a significant means of moving supplies and heavy weapons in 1914, but the whole "timetable" style of coordination was characteristic of the plan and gave it a very modern air.

The strategy of defeating France first was of course dependent on the slowness of the Russians and Germany's ability to hold off any offensive the Russians could mount until France was defeated, and until German troops would board trains in France, make their way east as rapidly as possible, and reinforce the fairly small holding force which the Germans had stationed in East Prussia.[31]

This was the Schlieffen Plan in the form it had from about 1905 onward, though the general staff was constantly updating and upgrading (and, some would have, weakening certain aspects of) it. Apart from the significant political problem associated with routing the offensive through Belgium, the plan seemed sound when viewed as a whole. Its efficiency, its rapidity, and its sweeping mobility certainly represented qualities called for by the great theorists and practitioners in military history. Yet it did not take into account the problem of what the nineteenth-century German strategic Karl von Clausewitz called the "frictions" of war. Schlieffen and his officers did not allow enough for human error and machine breakdown. They did not worry enough about a British expeditionary force, which was at least a distinct possibility in the wake of the swing through Belgium. Indeed, they did not allow for Belgian resistance either. As we shall see, the plan also relied too heavily on intelligence estimates that Germany would have a six-week window of time before the Russians could mount a real

invasion of Germany's East. Yet as will be seen below, at moments
during August 1914, the Germans in fact would come very close to
executing it.

Of course, as a causative factor, one must inquire into the extent to
which the Schlieffen Plan was held secret. Schlieffen himself at times
discussed aspects of the plan in public. German maneuvers – often
carried out with observing officers from other countries on hand – might
give away some aspects of the plan. Yet, by and large, British and French
intelligence analysts did not comprehend enough of the general picture
to overcome their own ideas about what they should do when the next
war broke out. All major powers had their strategic plans for the next
war, and all the plans were based, like Schlieffen's, on the premise of
intensive mobilization and a knockout blow. The French Plan XVII
envisioned mobilizing the bulk of the army opposite the Lorraine Gap,
and with the onset of war driving through the Gap into central
Germany. By wedging the army between Prussia in the north and the
lesser German states in the south, the French hoped to talk the less
aggressive south Germans into a separate peace, and eventually perhaps
an existence separate from Prussia. In this way, Plan XVII, highly
charged politically, would not only regain Alsace-Lorraine in the first
stroke, but undo 1870/71 completely.

Perhaps the most fateful war plans apart from the Schlieffen Plan,
however, had to do with planning in the context of the Anglo-German
naval rivalry after 1898. Here again, military thinking reflected trends
of thought in European society at large. By the mid-1880s, it has been
seen, Europeans were increasingly preoccupied with oceans, navies,
and exotic places overseas. This preoccupation was both cause and
consequence of the "new" imperialism. Navies were necessary to
maintain colonies and sea routes to them. The shining example was, of
course, the British Empire, whose opening of the Suez Canal in
late 1869 shortened the distance between London and the Indian
subcontinent and signaled the heyday of the Empire on which the sun
never set. France got into the scramble in the 1870s, Germany only
in the 1880s.

Providing a different support for "navalism," in 1890 American
naval officer Alfred Thayer Mahan published *The Influence of
Seapower Upon History, 1660–1783*. In it, Mahan "demonstrated" that
the greatness of empires (the British in particular) rests on the
potency of their "seapower." Hence, in each of the great military and
commercial struggles he considered, Britain came out ahead because

it controlled the seas. Since the battle of Trafalgar played a decisive role in Mahan's construction, a corollary to his basic premise came to be the necessity of maintaining a potent fleet which could triumph in a decisive battle (like Trafalgar, according to Mahan).[32]

Not only did Mahan's work harmonize with popular Social-Darwinist modes of thinking; it also spoke to the imperialist factions in all the countries of the West (the United States included). But nowhere did the book have the direct impact it did in Germany. The Kaiser reported that he was "not reading but devouring it," and the German Colonial Society put out 2,000 copies of the book. Their activities coincided with the arrival of a new and dynamic head of the German navy, Admiral Alfred von Tirpitz, in 1897. Supported by numerous pressure groups and politically influential individuals, Tirpitz called for the construction of a German battle fleet. Tirpitz justified the massive expenditure by asserting, first, that the fleet would pay for itself by the returns on German colonies; and, second, that the building of a great navy would woo working-class sons away from the Social Democratic Party and engage them instead in the great national work of achieving "world," as opposed to merely continental, power. Tirpitz and his allies were successful, and as the result of the two great German Navy Bills, of 1898 and 1900, Germany set out to build a battleship-heavy fleet.[33]

Like the Schlieffen Plan, Tirpitz's creation contained a terrible political liability, in that, in reality, a German battle fleet could be aimed only at Great Britain. The results were spectacular. Alienating the previously ambiguous British, the Germans had driven them into the arms of the French within five years. Domestically, expenditures on the fleet spiraled nearly out of control in the decade before the war, making German leaders more desperate for success. Irony haunted the program in its main goal. Germany did indeed jump from fifth to second as a naval power by the time of World War I, but the British not only retained the lead, but in 1906 introduced a new class of battleship in the form of the *H. M. S. Dreadnought*, a ship of larger size, more firepower, and increased firing range. The *Dreadnought* and the other dreadnought-class ships which soon appeared could destroy their counterparts before they could use their guns. Hence, the Germans set about, within months, appropriating funds for even greater ship expenditures.[34] It should be added here that if the German plans seemed to be technically adept and politically inept, it is nonetheless true that all the eventual belligerent powers harbored plans which resembled those of the Germans in relying on rapid and massive mobilization for a knockout blow and in their tendency to preempt a great deal of political decision-making.[35]

The Formation of Opposing Camps

Overall, the effects and dynamics of these aspects of the European world led to a situation in which war could occur, indeed, one in which war was expected in many quarters. Yet after all, the two "camps" which seem in retrospect to have been quite clear-cut were in fact not as rigid as we might think. Between 1890 and 1914 Europeans were engaged in at least a dozen major attempts to head off conflict, and in many ways, international cooperation and contacts increased. While historians have tended to emphasize the frictions between future enemies, there were in fact many instances of close relations and diplomatic cooperation between powers which would oppose each other in war in 1914. Moreover, international business ventures flourished, and the still largely open markets of Europe worked for the most part to make peace a project of producers and consumers throughout Europe. A lively international movement promoted the peaceful resolution of conflict, and as one of its many manifestations, the Nobel Committee started giving its peace prizes in 1901. Regional European fairs and exhibitions, and indeed world fairs, brought peoples of many stations of life together across borders, and European states devoted significant efforts to promoting such exhibitions and making a good showing at them. European powers cooperated in the Hague Conference agreements, results of meetings in 1899 and 1907, which seemed likely both to lessen the brutality of future war and through cooperation perhaps make it more avoidable, and in any case set up an international court of arbitration designed to referee international disputes. If we take the Europe of 1914 to have been *only* a maelstrom of nationalist passions and hatreds, we will misunderstand the world which plunged into war.

Yet the war came nonetheless, the direct result of the diplomatic crisis of July 1914. We have seen above the very significant linkage of Germany and Austria-Hungary and Russia and France by the last decade of the nineteenth century. We must now turn to the formation of the great alliance that came to stand opposed to Germany and Austria-Hungary.

Though Britain and France certainly enjoyed closer relations in the nineteenth century than in the eighteenth, it was still the case that British did not go out of their way to remove France from its predicament of international isolation after 1871. Indeed, the increased pace of imperialism brought Britain and France into direct conflict in North Africa and other areas by the 1880s. In 1898 the two powers almost went to war over the Sudan, but the Fashoda Crisis ended with the French backing down, faced as they were with a domestic problem of much greater enormity, the Dreyfus Affair.

The Dreyfus Affair, which crashed into French public consciousness in late 1897, was both symbol and result of many of the tendencies of European life which contributed to the coming of the war. The scandal broke out after the top-ranking Jew in the French army – Captain Alfred Dreyfus – had been found guilty of espionage for the Germans, court-martialed and sent to Devil's Island. The circumstances were quite hazy, and the captain's family enlisted the help of others to find out that Dreyfus had been railroaded. By the time of the Fashoda Crisis in 1898, the real turning point in Anglo-French relations, the Affair was creating opposing camps within French public life. On the one hand were the *anti-Dreyfusards* – Catholic, conservative, pro-monarchy, and anti-Revolution elements – and on the other the *Dreyfusards* – anti-clerical, liberal (or Radical, in the French nomenclature of the day), pro-republic, and pro-Revolution elements.

This was a crisis which convulsed France not just for months, but for years, revealing a fissure far more fundamental to French culture than a mere political squabble. It revealed heightened antisemitism, distrust, political hatred, and frequently violence. In later years, those who had stood up for Dreyfus were proud of their civil courage, and indeed many of them would be around to make hard decisions before and during World War I, including the political journalist Georges Clemenceau, who would finish the war as France's prime minister. Consequences for military affairs were significant: before the war French officers tended to be chosen based on the great cultural divide, and this political influence often held back competent and even brilliant officers of the wrong persuasion. In the years before the war, the republicans were in the ascendancy, and hence the "wrong persuasion" was that of officers who were from the conservative/Catholic/monarchist group.[36]

The scandal also had a direct, and quite immediate, effect on the international origins of World War I. Imperial rivalries tended to emphasize national clashes and struggles. Yet when France found itself facing Britain in the Sudan, the French simply deemed the domestic situation too unstable to risk engaging in foreign hostilities. Indeed, France appeared amenable to some kind of colonial agreement. The British, moreover, found German naval construction increasingly alarming and aggressive. Hence, the two powers put their colonial disputes on the negotiating table in 1904 and reached an amicable agreement, the *entente cordiale*. In the wake of this understanding, British and French military planners began to meet for "conversations," and these conversations, especially after Major General Henry Wilson – an outspoken advocate of military alliance with the French – became British director of operations in 1910, were extraordinarily frank. There was no question in the "talks" who the mutual enemy would be.[37]

Yet forging the third side of the triangle of powers seemed an impossibility. If France and England had a tradition of being opponents, from the Congress of Vienna onward, Britons had tended to feel about the Russians something like the Americans felt about the Soviets during the Cold War a century later. And colonial clashes likewise fueled this long-standing mutual animosity. One aspect of the enormous popularity of the writer Rudyard Kipling was his ability to cast the Russian "Bear" as a sinister force in the world and correspondingly to demonstrate the essential hard-nosed benevolence of the British Empire.[38] The clash was especially clear on the northern borders of India, the centerpiece of this empire.

And it was quite clear that Russia's imperial ambitions were expansive. Indeed, it was expansion in Asia, east of Siberia and north of Japan, that brought the Russians into the clash of war with Japan in 1904. Under their brilliant admiral, Togo, the Japanese navy defeated two Russian fleets, and the land war which raged in the Amur River region approximated the kind of fighting which would characterize World War I.

It was this clash which would reorient Russian attitudes toward Britain, for though the war ended with negotiations umpired by the President of the United States, the Russians had clearly had the worst of it. Moreover, the strains of modern industrial war had impacted Russia as fundamentally as they had in 1855 or would in 1917: shortages in the cities led to major worker unrest and extensive strikes while widespread revolt eventually broke out in the countryside. With social revolution in progress, the parties and individuals who had been fighting for an even incipient liberalism seized the opportunity to revolt politically. In essence, vacillating Tsar Nicholas II was forced to grant Russia's first constitution and its first "parliament," the Duma, fighting the liberals at every step of the way, but conceding at last the points of a limited parliamentary regime under the threat of true revolution from below. In exchange, the constitutionalist politicians agreed to and facilitated the suppression of the urban and rural insurrections and the return of social order.

Much like the Dreyfus Affair which had so shaken France as to lead to conciliation toward Britain, so the Russian Revolution of 1905 weakened Russian imperial capabilities and led Russia to engage in conciliatory talks with the British over the most irritating colonial rivalries of the moment, especially that over Persia. In fact, the two powers – encouraged by their mutual ally, France – agreed in 1907 to divide Persia into spheres of influence, in the same way that Britain and France had made agreements to stay out of each other's way in North Africa.[39] This agreement signaled a real diplomatic change and an alliance that overcame animosities dating back at least 100 years. It also signaled the admittance of Russia into the "understanding" that now came to be called the Triple Entente.

In fact the configuration of powers in the upcoming war had already made its first appearance a few months earlier at a conference in Algeciras, Spain, an international meeting to settle the first of the great "crises" which led to World War I. The crisis derived from the aggressive diplomacy of both Germany and France in seeking the economic domination of Morocco. Seeing a chance to test the strength of the new *entente cordiale*, the German foreign office arranged for Kaiser Wilhelm to visit Tangier and make an inflammatory speech, an assignment well suited to him. There was talk of war, but instead the powers met at Algeciras in January 1907. There the Germans found to their surprise not only that they were unable to split apart the new Franco-British Entente, but also that the whole community of powers, with the exception of the Austrians, lined up in support of France. This array included Germany's putative ally Italy, as well as Russia and the United States. Hence, from Algeciras onward, the two armed camps may be viewed as forming opposing entities.

With one exception – that of the Second Moroccan Crisis of 1911 – the great diplomatic clashes which punctuated the seven years before the outbreak of the Great War had to do with the Balkans. The background takes us far afield from our themes and can only be outlined here. The disintegration of the Ottoman Empire in the nineteenth century led to instability among the emerging powers in the Balkans and those neighbors who hoped to fish in these troubled waters. The key to the series of crises which led up to the war was the so-called Young Turk Revolution of 1908.

Attacking the sanctity of the Ottoman sultan, a group of modernizing nationalist leaders called the Young Turks took power in 1908. On Balkan borders, the Russian and Austro-Hungarian empires saw a good chance to use Turkey's disruption to gain territory or influence. These competitors met together at the end of the summer to discuss an idea originating with the Russian Foreign Minister, Alexander Izvolsky. An orderly division of influence in the Balkans would satisfy the long-standing desires of Russia and Austria. On the one hand, Izvolsky proposed, the Russians would agree to the Austrian annexation of Bosnia-Herzegovina (a region occupied but not owned by Austria since 1878); on the other hand, the Austrians would agree to the use of the Dardanelles Strait by Russian warships under specific conditions. The Russians would gain access to the world's oceans year round and a shipping outlet for Russian wheat; Austria would solidify its South Slav holdings and lay some of the groundwork for a more equitable and stable governance, perhaps a federal reform, of the Empire as a whole. The arrangement would end cherished Serbian hopes of acquiring Bosnia-Herzegovina.

The Austrian Foreign Minister, Aloys von Aehrenthal, agreed to support Izvolsky's plan, but the two ministers planned to introduce the idea gradually and take it up at an international conference, the groundwork for which the Russian would lay in a whirlwind tour of European capitals. Over the next days Izvolsky gained the tentative cooperation of the Italians and Germans, but he arrived in Paris to discover that Aehrenthal had announced the annexation of Bosnia-Herzegovina unilaterally. Without a multilateral process, Britain would never allow the Dardanelles to go to Russia. Izvolsky's plan was foiled.

The Serbians and Turks were enraged, but in Russia – where it was unknown that Izvolsky had originated the idea – Pan-Slav nationalists were beside themselves. It was probably not Aehrenthal's intent to double-cross Izvolsky. Yet more than any other single event before the assassination of the Archduke, the Bosnian crisis redirected international energies and hardened the loose camps which had been forming. Henceforth, Austria and Russia each regarded the other as the principal enemy in the Balkans. Russia took up the cause of Serbia, and the Austrians were soon mixed up deeply

in the politics of the volatile region. Before long the chief of the
Austrian general staff would propose a war to decide which power
would be master in the Balkans.[40]

The next six years saw the working-out of these tensions. In October
1912 the independent Balkan states tried to drive the Ottomans out of
Europe and divide up the territory left over. In May 1913 the war was
stopped chiefly by the intervention of the Great Powers, who managed
to create a new state, Albania, out of the conquests. The anti-Ottoman
Balkan states really won the war but fell out among themselves almost
immediately when Serbia, frustrated at not getting Albania, attempted
to take compensation from the lands that Bulgaria had gained.
A Second Balkan War ensued with a reshuffled deck, and the Serbians
ended up in Albania. Austria managed to get the Serbs out of Albania by
international agreement – anything to cut down on the power of Serbia.
The Serbs were now more dissatisfied than they had been before, and
they too were focused on how to expand their state and settle old scores.
From the spring of 1914 onward, Europe – and even southeastern
Europe – was outwardly peaceful, but all interested parties were
maneuvering for position against the appearance of the next crisis.

The July Crisis

The immediate crisis of the war came at the end of June 1914, when the
heir to the Austrian throne, Franz Ferdinand, was shot dead along with
his wife during a parade in his honor in the Bosnian capital Sarajevo.
Franz Ferdinand, nephew of old Franz Josef, was a complicated man
who consorted regularly with Austrian liberals and who had thought a
great deal about how to maintain the Habsburg Empire while sharing
out the political power to the various nationality groups. However they
might have looked, rejuvenating reforms would probably have
emerged had Franz Ferdinand succeeded to the throne. Instead, he
was assassinated on June 28.

His assassin was Gavrilo Princip, one of several young Bosnian
nationalist terrorists in Sarajevo aiming to do the job, seeking to strike
a blow for Bosnian independence. In their cause they had made
contacts with a secret Serbian ultra-nationalist organization, known as
the Black Hand, which had close ties with Serbian military intelligence.
Though some of the circumstances remain hazy to this day, it is clear
that the planning and equipment (guns, bombs, poison to be taken

after the assassination) came from the Black Hand. It is also clear
that at least several Serbian government officials were aware of the
conspiracy and did nothing to warn the Austrians.[41]

Though observers could not know all the facts, it was clear to all that
the heir to the Austrian throne had been assassinated on Austro-
Hungarian territory by young men probably connected to high levels
of the Serbian government. To the Austrians, who viewed Serbia as an
aggressive state bent on acquiring Slavic lands belonging to the
Habsburg Empire, the act seemed to be the final straw in a long series
of provocations. Having already discussed the possibility of ending the
Serbian irritant by war, Austrian statesmen made the decision to use
the assassination to pressure the Serbians, either for wide-ranging
concessions that would end Serbian ambitions, or for war. Indeed, in
Vienna, the assassination crystallized forces which had long been
calling for war with Serbia. Yet the Austrians did not necessarily have
a free hand in the matter, since Russia had, we have seen, taken up the
cause of Serbia. Hence, the Austrians had to consult with Berlin to
ascertain the extent to which they could count on German support
against Serbia (and potentially Russia).

During the sleepless month of July 1914, European statesmen
struggled with a truly amazing list of particulars as they tried to
balance their countries' interests against international pressure. Far
from international anarchy, the diplomacy of the July Crisis reflected
the stated interests of all the European states. If all the cards were not
played, the players at least knew what was still held in each hand. The
July Crisis has been the subject of thousands of books and articles.
From 1914 to the present, participants and historians have discussed
the most immediate "causes" of the war in terms of the roles that
various actors played during the crisis. The Fischer school, as noted
above, emphasized the "blank check," that is, the go-ahead which the
Germans gave to Austria-Hungary when the Austrians turned to
Berlin for back-up. In this view, the Germans "caused" the war. On the
other hand, many historians, and recently Samuel Williamson, have
pointed out that the Austrians fully understood the nature of their
pressure on Serbia in the midst of the crisis, and fully knew that this
pressure would result in war, though perhaps not in a general one.[42]
Further research continues to expand the historiography of these
difficult questions. The Russians mobilized in support of Serbians
who had been less than open about the Serbian connections to the
assassination. The British, by prolonged silence, particularly that of the

Foreign Secretary, Sir Edward Grey, missed an opportunity to make the Germans understand that Britain would not stand by during another attack on France. The French, perhaps least guilty of all, can nonetheless be seen urging the Russians to mobilize (enormous investments by the French middle class seem to have played a role), a move which precipitated the final crisis. During the aftermath of the Fischer debate, Joachim Remak made the point that all sinned and all were sinned against; he suggested that one might as well regard the Great War as the "Third Balkan" War. Indeed, in a thoughtful comment in the early 1970s, Paul Schroeder suggested that the hunt for the "one true cause," the *causa causans*, is futile in any case. Indeed, even the assertion that the international system broke down is suspect, since war was an accepted part of the international system.[43]

Though statesmen made many attempts to head off war, by the end of July, sleep-deprived European diplomats began to weaken in their conviction that war could be avoided or even contained as a regional conflict. As a result both of long-standing Austro-Serbian animosities and of the German backing (the "blank check"), on July 23 the Austrians issued an ultimatum to the Serbians, an ultimatum designed perhaps to be turned down. It demanded full cooperation in investigating the murders and stopping anti-Austrian propaganda and arms smuggling. It also demanded that certain Serbian officers be delivered up to Austria for trial.

The Serbs agreed to as many of the demands as possible, but they stopped short of allowing Austria-Hungary a free hand in investigating the conspiracy in Serbia itself and in other internal matters. In retrospect, from the vantage point of the other end of a violent and brutal century, the assassination of the Austrian archduke still seems startling, the Serbian insistence on legal propriety somewhat disingenuous. The heir to the Habsburg throne had been murdered, and the Serbian government had been implicated. Even if the Austrian ultimatum was blunt and harsh and the Serbian reply two days later conciliatory in many respects, the Serbian government demonstrated only mild concern that the future head of a neighboring state had been shot dead with Serbian bullets.

Meanwhile, on hearing the terms of the Austrian ultimatum, the Russians proved more decisive than was their habit and let the Serbians know that Russian backing was available. According to Luigi Albertini, author of one of the classic histories of war origins, without these Russian assurances, the Serbs would likely have come to terms with Austria.[44]

Instead, two days after the Austrians issued the ultimatum, the Russians instituted a compromise measure of partial mobilization, the first move toward a military solution to the problem. In light of the military factors which lie at the heart of this study, the Russian move was a decisive point in the genesis of the war. It is clear that many European statesmen, including Bethmann Hollweg and even Wilhelm II in the wake of the Serbian reply, and including many Russian statesmen, still hoped for and worked for a peaceful solution, but mobilization now brought Europe to the brink of war.

In spite of a number of proposals for negotiating a settlement between Austria and Serbia, the war party in Vienna won out. Austria-Hungary declared war on Serbia on July 28, and Austrian forces shelled the Serbian capital, Belgrade, the next day. Even now, however, both Britain and Germany pushed the Austrians to occupy Belgrade as the opening to international talks regarding the Serbian reply, but the Russians declared full mobilization on July 30.

The Germans now found themselves prisoner to the Schlieffen Plan. Since their whole response would be contingent on the timing of Russian mobilization, the German high command demanded action. Indeed, the other powers involved were little behind the Germans in interpreting mobilization as the signal for war. On the afternoon of August 2, 1914, France and then Germany ordered mobilization. A few hours later Germany declared war on Russia. German troops were already crossing into Luxembourg, just south of Belgium, by August 3, and the Germans found reasons to declare war on France the next day, simultaneously sending the vanguard of the vast right wing of the "Schlieffen" army into Belgium.

London had a more difficult time entering the war from the outset of the July Crisis. Indeed, in London the assassination had aroused much sympathy for the Austrians. Still, it was clear that British leaders would not allow the Germans to challenge British naval supremacy, or indeed, to dominate the Continent. Clearly, the naval rivalry between the Tirpitz navy and the great sea power of the British was decisive, involving as it did financial and economic power, and much else. In the aftermath of war, historians sometimes pointed out that British statesmen were ambiguous as to what they would do in the event of a continental war. In retrospect, however, it is clear that only a great deal of wishful thinking and positive mental outlook kept the Germans from recognizing that in spite of intermittent friendliness and periodic British attempts to make relations bearable, Britain's creation of a Triple Entente with a military component could have only one meaning for the Germans. The high commands of the French and British armies had been making joint plans, including the landing of as many as two British corps, should Britain and France go to war with Germany.

It was not so easy for the British government to translate its long-range goals and national interests into reasons for war which might satisfy the public. To have argued that Britain must join a war because Austria had invaded Serbia would have been the height of absurdity. Many Britons had little idea where Serbia was. Britain had its own internal problems, in particular the crisis in Ireland, and anything short of a direct attack by Germany or perhaps a highly emotional issue which could be sold to the public would risk the disaffection of that public and hence potential disaster. The first German footfall in Belgium salvaged this situation for the British.

Treaty obligations can generally provide a sufficient legal justification for entering the war,[45] and the protection of little Belgium – long considered a strategic extension of Britain – was tailor-made for the kind of public support needed to justify the war. Britain's interpretation of its guarantor role vis-à-vis Belgium had been public knowledge for decades. Sir Edward Grey referred to this interpretation at least twice on August 2, 1914. German behavior toward Belgian civilians once the Schlieffen Plan was in progress would of course be of tremendous assistance in bolstering public enthusiasm for the war, but we must look at this phenomenon in later chapters.

The British government had long since decided to frustrate German expansion in any way possible. The naval plans of Germany, the falling British share of world commerce, the German desire to become in some sense hegemon of the Continent; all these factors pushed Britain toward participation in August 1914. For the Germans' part, their government was in effect overtaken by the swiftness of the crisis, and by the Austrians' insistence on the Serbian invasion in spite of a partially conciliatory Serbian reply (Wilhelm II and others were horrified at the Austrian action). Still, the Kaiser and many German leaders were convinced that the British were determined to strangle the new Germany. Hemmed in such a way, German leaders reasoned, no dynamic power would do otherwise than go to war. As for the remaining Western Front power, the French never blinked as war approached. Bolstered by powerful allies, they were ready to take back both the pride and the territory which the Germans had taken in 1871.

Hence, on August 4, Britain declared war on Germany. Two days later Austria-Hungary declared war on Russia, and the principal actors of the war's first stage were all firmly registered as belligerents. The most famous quotation from these days comes from the British Secretary for Foreign Affairs, Edward Grey, who said: "The lamps are going out all over Europe; we shall not see them lit again in our lifetime."[46] In Europe's capitals, however, crowds flooded the squares to cheer.

2

MOBILITY AND UNITY

The extraordinary events of August, September, and October 1914 offer crucial insights into the interconnections between battle front and home front. The horror of fighting itself was unknown to the belligerent publics, but the mediated (or euphemized) version of battle-front events exercised its own influence on the dynamics of war, governance, culture, and society. In this sense, the first months of the Western Front give us a look into the formation of both home and battle fronts. It cannot be surprising that the fronts would influence, constrain, and shape each other.

In spite of Sir Edward Grey's grim forecast of impending darkness, public enthusiasm, even ecstasy, seemed to break out in all the belligerent countries. On the announcement of war declarations and even early war news, jubilant people gathered in the great squares of European cities by the hundreds of thousands to experience a sense of community which class-bound, materialistic European societies had rarely offered. Troops departed for the front by train, and for weeks crowds cheered and sang them off.

Recent research suggests that this enthusiasm for war may not have been as extensive as the excited crowds suggest. Indeed, it may have been chiefly an urban phenomenon in an age when half of the populations involved lived in small towns and villages. The traditional supplier of human material for European armies, the countryside, appears to have adopted a more sober attitude when war broke out in 1914. Nonetheless, we have today hundreds of written accounts and photographs which demonstrate the pitch of enthusiasm and joy which many Europeans felt. Soldiers – the enlistees had months of training ahead, but reservists were integrated immediately into

fighting units – were equally enthusiastic, painting on their railroad
cars slogans full of national pride and bravado. Singing German
troops, marching or riding, rushed to Belgium, where the attack was in
progress, and to Alsace, where the French threatened. French soldiers
rode troop trains "bedecked as if by magic" with flowers, singing the
Marseillaise and other martial tunes. The British Expeditionary Force
(BEF) suffered a ferry ride but found euphoria once landed: after the
tremendous effort of packing over a hundred thousand men, their
weapons, horses for transport, and supplies onto ferries, they landed
the whole array in Le Havre, Rouen, and Boulogne to the cheers of
celebratory crowds. This was, in effect, a northwestern European
moment, and the scene was drenched in sunshine, a rare enough commodity in the region. When a young French officer tried to describe
his trip to the front, words failed him, but the sunshine colored everything: "Sunshine cannot be reproduced on canvas." The tail-end of
a fabulously beautiful summer, the sunshine colors all accounts of the
war's outbreak, and it certainly colored the mood of the time, belying
Lord Grey's predictions of encroaching darkness.[1]

Standing and looking back at the twentieth century's wars and
brutality, indeed, looking back at the slaughter that the Great War
became, our comprehension may well give way before this mood of
August 1914. Yet though we can only go so far in trying to make sense
of any historical episode, one can begin to make sense of August 1914
by thinking about the predominantly peaceful century which served as
a preface. For most Europeans, Britons in particular, wars tended to be
fought far away and with much "valour." Many young Europeans welcomed the chance to do their "duty," even making the "sacrifice" for
their country by "falling" on the field of battle. For a continent steeped
in escapist fiction, and for whom the knowledge of wars had generally
been disseminated through sensationalist newspapers which read like
such fiction, the war would be potentially deadly, but still a grand
"show." After the international politics of compromise upon compromise, the vision of a short but horrific war seemed more decisive, more
vigorous, almost purifying.[2]

One might take into account the statements of counterparts in
Germany and France in the first days of the war. When the French officer quoted above, Alphonse Grasset, contemplated the almost mystic
way in which crowds broke into national songs and bedecked troop
trains with flowers, he wrote: "During forty years of peace, we had
been taught, in France, to consider such shows of emotion vulgar and

ridiculous. But their time had come again, and to all of us who were there, they gave a feeling both grand and sublime; our eyes filled with tears." A German counterpart, Ernst Gläser, conceptualized the war's outbreak in nearly identical terms: "At last life had regained an ideal significance. The great virtues of humanity . . . fidelity, patriotism, readiness to die for an ideal . . . were triumphing over the trading and shopkeeping spirit. . . . This was the providential lightning flash that would clear the air. . . . The war would cleanse mankind from all its impurities."[3]

We close off our own understanding if we consider the long lines of sun-dappled soldiers at recruiting stations and cheering crowds as simply quaint and foolish. Europeans were quite aware that many young men would lose their lives (though no one imagined the extent of what was to come); in 1914 "making the sacrifice" by dying on the battlefield was not considered a waste or a sham, but something that could give a life meaning, even perhaps a kind of salvation. In the brilliant sunlight of August 1914, Europeans discovered a sense of awe.

Even while the crowds cheered, the European leaders who had brought their countries into war were anything but ecstatic; indeed, they lacked almost entirely the kind of vacuous, optimistic attitude which would later characterize the total war states of the twentieth century. Britain's Foreign Secretary was not the only statesman with profound misgivings. Germany's Chancellor, Bethmann-Hollweg, would make enthusiastic speeches to the Reichstag in support of the war, but privately – and more in keeping with his morose personality – he thought of Germany's participation as a fatalistic "leap in the dark." Likewise, leaders from all political sectors saw, like France's great socialist elder statesman, Jean Jaurès, that war meant calamity. Strange to say, the generals themselves were no less disturbed and depressed by the outbreak of war than the civilian leaders. Or perhaps it is not strange, since they had some idea of the potential consequences.

Perhaps most paradoxical of all, the commander who presided over the aggressive Schlieffen Plan was, by 1914, anything but the bold and bluff leader one might expect. Chief of the general staff since 1905, Helmuth von Moltke was the antithesis of the hardworking Schlieffen. The nephew of the great Helmuth von Moltke and, through him, a friend of Kaiser Wilhelm II, Moltke had played the role of courtier-officer, with little staff experience and none as a commander. Yet when Schlieffen retired, Wilhelm's wish prevailed, and

Moltke took over. In one sense, his contributions to war planning were slight, since he had little patience for detailed work, but his personality would turn out to be one of the most important factors in the way events unfolded during the first month of the war. Of average intelligence and well read, the aristocrat Moltke was much influenced in the decade before 1914 by the Theosophy movement of Rudolf Steiner. This mystical bent went hand in hand with his wife's enthusiasm for spirit mediums and trying to contact the dead. It was also related to pessimistic, and Social-Darwinist, visions of a future of worldwide conflict and catastrophic racial conflict. In the short term, by 1914 Moltke had developed serious worries about the ability of Germany to fight the next war.

These worries may have contributed to a deterioration in the mental or physical health of the 67-year-old field marshal. During mobilization, Moltke apparently broke down emotionally at least twice, crying uncontrollably. One of these breakdowns occurred less than 48 hours before hostilities opened, when the Kaiser called Moltke, Tirpitz, and the War Minister Falkenhayn together to consider dropping the Schlieffen Plan and proceeding only against the Russians. Considering the complexity of the Schlieffen mobilization requirements, Moltke's negative was understandable. Yet when the Kaiser replied, "Your uncle would have given me a different answer," Moltke seemed shattered emotionally and thereafter displayed symptoms of nervous trauma and severe depression, perhaps what modern psychologists would call a "transient psychotic episode." Once the invasion of Belgium began, Moltke secluded himself far from the fronts in a small brick schoolhouse in Luxembourg, giving little direction or coordination to his army commanders. Plagued by sickness, self-doubt, and bad relations with the Kaiser, Moltke would prove to be more important to the success or failure than many accounts of the "automatic" nature of the Schlieffen Plan would have us believe. But his worried attitude was not far from the norm among German leaders.[4]

The Battle of the Frontiers

For all the misgivings in high places, the battle fronts seemed almost as brilliant as the sunshine at first, especially to the German soldiers walking and riding into Belgium. The Schlieffen Plan called for a quick passage through Belgium, then exploitation of a thinly guarded

Franco-Belgian border to sweep around to the north and west of the French forces (and Paris itself) and complete the encirclement by crushing the bulk of the French armies facing eastward toward Germany, the whole plan to be completed in about six weeks, the period thought to be required for Russian mobilization.

Hence, when the troops of General Otto von Emmich – commander of the X Corps of Bülow's Second Army – crossed into Belgium on August 3, they set ticking a six-week clock against which their armies had to work; by mid-September the French component of the campaign had to be more or less completed. Unfortunately for them, the first slowdowns had occurred by the time German troops set foot in Belgium. Schlieffen had planned to tread upon Belgian soil without so much as an ultimatum, hoping that mere mobilization on the border would bring the French to enter Belgium first to meet the threat. Instead, the nervous military and civilian leaders of Germany presented Belgium with an ugly ultimatum on August 2, and the French actually had too little time to react before the Germans attacked. This earlier desire to pin some of the blame on France was reflected in Chancellor Bethmann-Hollweg's weak speech of justification to the German parliament on the day of the border violation:

> Our troops have occupied Luxemburg and have perhaps already entered Belgium. This is contrary to the dictates of international law. . . . we knew that France was ready to invade Belgium. France could wait; we could not. . . . We were, therefore, compelled to ride roughshod over the legitimate protests of the Governments of Luxemburg and Belgium. For the wrong which we are thus doing, we will make reparation as soon as our military object is attained.[5]

In the field, German troops knew nothing about such squalid moral calculations. Trained to a fever pitch of pride in Germany and aggression against others, on the fighting fronts the Germans – from field officers down – found the early stages of the plan exhilarating. The mobilized German forces in the West consisted of five armies lined up north to south. Beginning at Metz, the German Fifth Army stood ready in the middle of the Lorraine gap, through which the opposing French units intended to attack in accordance with Plan XVII. On its right, to the north, the Fourth Army was prepared to help occupy Luxembourg to its immediate north and to push westward toward Longwy. Behind hilly and forested Luxembourg, the German Third Army was posted to occupy little Luxembourg and break through the Ardennes into France.

These three armies, concentrated in the space of a little over 50 miles, were essentially the holding elements of the Schlieffen Plan. The southernmost, the Fifth Army, constituted the pivot of forces containing nearly one and a half million men stretching across about 150 miles. The northernmost armies were the First (commanded by General von Kluck) and the Second (commanded by General von Bülow), the real attacking wing of the plan. Kluck and Bülow – commanding together just under 600,000 men – had the task of threading these men and their equipment through a dense but still too limited road network in the narrow corridor between the southern tip of the Netherlands and the northern reaches of the rough Ardennes country, about 40 miles wide.

As noted above, nervousness had marked Moltke's tenure as army head. Instead of Schlieffen's bold scheme of robbing Peter to pay Paul by keeping Germany's contingents in Alsace and on the Russian border ridiculously weak in order to keep the knockout blow through Belgium ridiculously strong, Moltke had slowly weakened the right wing to hedge his bets in Alsace. Later, two weeks into the war, when the Russians managed against expectations to invade German territory, Moltke sent two army corps to reinforce the beleaguered German army in East Prussia. Along with the two corps bottling up a small Belgian and British force in Antwerp and several other divisions tied up elsewhere in Belgium, the total strike force of the Schlieffen army was only two-thirds that of the original plan.

If the Germans had hoped that Belgium could be bullied into acquiescence, the Belgian government was probably putting too much faith in the force of international agreements in preventing the Germans from invading the neutral country. Counting on protection from Britain, the Belgians had only recently decided to upgrade their small army and modernize it somewhat. Even at that, the planned reorganization would take several more years. Hence, though Belgium had a professional army of 117,000 men, it was only partially mobilized by the evening of August 3, when the first German troops set foot on Belgian soil, making for Liège.[6] Still, the first fighting of the war would teach a number of lessons. Schlieffen had hoped to bypass the Belgian fortress city of Liège, allowing plenty of leeway simply by invading the Netherlands as well. But by changing Schlieffen's plan to avoid the Netherlands, Moltke narrowed the pathway into Belgium, necessitating an attack aimed directly at Liège.

Liège had been fortified by a ring of a dozen large and small forts constructed with the most advanced fortress designs of the 1890s. Looking like giant mushrooms, these reinforced concrete forts – filled with rooms, vaults, machinery, and supplies and reaching several stories below ground – were built to withstand the new, more powerful artillery developed in recent decades. The ring of forts, connected at least in theory with entrenched infantry in between, extended for 30 miles and made the passage through Belgium much more dangerous than casual students of World War I might suppose. Liège was a formidable obstacle: the desperate defence of Verdun two years later from the same kind of forts would become one of the most significant episodes of the war. In the hands of a determined commander – like Belgian General Gérard Leman – such forts were powerful military tools.

Outside of Liège, hostilities broke out on August 4 in the form of artillery exchanges with the Germans. The German troops did not appear until they emerged in the old-fashioned columnar attack formation at daybreak on August 5, undoubtedly because the German commanders were little inclined to offer up troops to real fire without the reassurance of being in a tightly packed group. The result of the attack was that the Belgian units facing the Germans east of Liège not only withstood the assault but counterattacked and won the first engagement of the war. Not a single fort was taken.

Yet the odds were overwhelming, and General Leman determined to send most of his division west to the River Dyle, before Brussels, where the Belgian army was gathering. He himself would remain to direct a small group in holding the eastern forts, as a delaying action. The troops left, and the city fathers of Liège surrendered to the Germans the next day, August 7, after a well-known general staff officer, Erich von Ludendorff, led a group of Germans into Liège to effect the spectacular capture of the garrison.

Still, the forts themselves were untouched. The Germans brought up heavier guns and continued the attack, but the defenders held on, tying up or delaying both the First and Second German Armies. Throughout Belgium, and in a sense throughout the Western world, these days were tense, expectant, even hopeful. Not knowing the script, Belgians in Brussels and Namur, in Mons and Antwerp, went about their business in a kind of frenetic torpor. The queen saw to the setting-up of hospital beds in the state apartments of the royal palace in Brussels; children decorated the empty beds with miniature Belgian flags. The French Republic conferred the Légion d' Honneur on the city of Liège. As the American ambassador to Belgium described those days of waiting, "Men met each other on the streets and said ecstatically: "Les forts tiennent toujours," 'The forts are still holding out!'"[7]

Knowing the weak state of the army, many Belgians acted on this enthusiasm by rushing out to arm themselves in the defense of their country; as one foreign observer commented, "emptying the museums" of antiquated firearms. And in the public sphere, in Belgium, in micro-cosm to what would happen among all the Western Front powers, all parties loudly determined to fight together to repel the invader, even the antimilitarist Labour Party calling for workers to flock to the colors. Resistance and defense were in the air, and the forts still held, but increasingly after August 12, German advance units of cavalry began working their way to the west, past the still-holding forts. Meanwhile, the German government had repeated its ultimatum of August 2, thinking, it seems, that the military resistance so far offered would satisfy Belgian national honor. The Belgians refused, and the Germans intensified the bombardment of the Liège forts.[8]

In the event, the battle for Liège lasted from August 6 to 17. Leman, one of relatively few "front-line generals" of the war, personally directed the defence of the forts and experienced the tremendous four-day bombardment. On August 15, the climax of the shelling of Fort Loncin, one of the last forts holding out, Leman was nearly asphyxiated after a terrific explosion, but came to in the hands of the Germans. Most of the Fort Loncin garrison was killed in the shelling, and the Germans took possession while Leman was unconscious, a point he was anxious to have verified by his old friend, General Emmich, commander of the German forces to whom Leman tendered his personal surrender. Emmich took the surrender while compliment-ing Leman on his defense and insisting gallantly that he keep his sword. The first capitulation of the war thus combined the chivalries of military tradition with the vastly increased explosiveness of modern artillery.[9] The chivalry would not last long, except in some eccentric corners of the fighting forces.

Ten days from jump-off and still in the middle of Belgium, the Germans now had a month to defeat France and were behind schedule by no more than a few days, a delay the great military theorist Clausewitz might have ascribed to the "frictions of war." Brussels fell on August 21, but German forces were about to encounter still further "frictions" in Belgium.

As these early engagements were being fought, Belgian civilians – many of whom, it has been seen, were mobilizing themselves for defense – surprised German troops by firing on them and otherwise behaving as guerrillas, or *francs-tireurs*. In retrospect, it seems that the

Belgians were acting out some version of what the Germans dreaded. In these first days of the war, German officers and men tended to see treachery in many civilian acts, in eastern France as well as Belgium. And this fear was not limited to the army. Within a day or two after the invasion, German newspapers were already reporting terrible atrocities committed by roving bands of Belgian guerrillas, some of them led by priests. The German enthusiasm for guerrilla fighting by the Boers against the British 15 years previously did not, it seems, extend to similar behavior by ill-armed Belgians.

Germans reacted rapidly and harshly to any such resistance or suspected resistance. When they could not find the suspects, they simply chose other civilians to shoot in reprisal. Sometimes they burned the closest village or town. Overall, the German military shot over 5,000 civilians in reprisal or as spies and burned almost 16,000 houses and buildings, almost all of this during the first month of the war (strangely, the Russian armies which invaded East Prussia a few days later would behave in exactly the same way and kill about the same number, though property damage was much greater). The most atrocious single stroke of reprisal came in Louvain (Leuven), occupied on August 20 by the Germans. Here, persistent rumors of sniping led to extensive shootings of civilians and on August 22 the systematic burning of parts of the city. In the end, the destruction included one of the great libraries of Europe, that of the University of Louvain. Though the German government steadfastly contended that the Belgian *francs-tireurs* had started this irregular kind of war, and even published and circulated abroad a White Book of documents to support its assertions, there were probably very few *francs-tireurs*. German soldiers, on the other hand, were probably much influenced by journalistic stories of "*franc-tireur* atrocities" in the Franco-Prussian war. Some scholars have suggested that the German army was carrying out a specific policy of brutality (*Schrecklichkeit*, or "frightfulness"), and even German memoirs demonstrate that the Germans were overly ready to shoot civilians as spies and partisans (the invading Russians were about equally ready to do so). Evidence seems to indicate that much of the brutality in Belgium and France in the first weeks of the war came more from the bottom up than from official policy. It may well be that the *franc-tireur* pot shots which occasioned most of the reprisals came from nervous German soldiers.[10]

In any case, with the fall of the Liège forts, the German First and Second Armies could finally gain access to central Belgium. The

Belgian army now executed what might be called a two-pronged retreat. One section fell back to central Belgium to cover Brussels, the other to the northwest, to cover Antwerp. Brussels fell within four days, and General von der Goltz assumed duties as occupational governor of Belgium.

Though it was clear that most of Belgium would fall to the Germans at this stage, the importance of the war in Belgium remained undiminished. It was clear that Antwerp possessed tremendous significance as a port for supplying the Allied Forces. Moreover, the Belgian army remained intact and ready to fight. The army had fallen back on Antwerp, one of the most strongly fortified cities in Europe, but threatened German forces by a series of sorties from the fortified lines south of the city. Volunteers filled up the rolls of the army again, and General de Moranville launched a counteroffensive on August 23, pushing the Germans out of Malines on the River Dyle, more than halfway to Brussels. Seesaw battles destroyed Malines, but German General Beseler was forced to maintain pressure on an army which would not give up, in spite of the first aerial bombardment of the war, which took place when a German dirigible floated over Antwerp on August 25 and dropped ten bombs on the city, killing about 50 people, all of them civilians. One can well say that "Gallant Little Belgium," in the phrase of the day, had presented a number of Clausewitzian frictions to the Schlieffen attack.[11]

Perhaps as important a source of "friction" was the army which the British hurried to French ports and hustled northeastward toward the Germans. Though Anglo-German tensions rose after the establishment of the German high-seas fleet in 1898, Schlieffen and his planners did not worry much about British intervention in their plan, apparently assuming that any intervention would be too little and too late to make much difference to the massive right wing of the attack. Here German intelligence failed, for the army that the British fielded in France and Belgium in August 1914 was, if small, the most efficient and dangerous fighting force of its size in the world at that moment.

"The Old Contemptibles," as the BEF came to be nicknamed (a reference to a supposed insult by the Kaiser), consisted of long-term professional soldiers with much experience, a substantial percentage of them the sort of soldier immortalized in Rudyard Kipling's poems. What made this force unique in the war was its sense of collective identity, discipline, and tradition. It was remarkably well suited to its task for a number of reasons. The tradition and values of the "Old Contemptibles" hearkened back to Rorke's Drift, Waterloo, and beyond, to the great defensive victories of the "thin red line." So powerful was this tradition that Foch, in his theoretical writings, had offered the idea that the English were by temperament naturally suited to the calm, dogged defense (a temperament he thought entirely lacking in French soldiers).[12] What made its contribution so great was that it proved to be the delaying line of defense after the defeat of Belgium itself.

Since the Anglo-French military talks had begun in the years before 1914, the British army had worked out careful plans (the War Book) for many contingencies. In case of German attack in Western Europe, these plans provided for mobilizing enough reserves to double the standing army to 120,000, gather work animals and supplies, and get the army to appropriate ports. Moreover, the divisions of the army alternated years in holding a practice mobilization, which was scheduled in 1914 for July 27. Hence, when Field Marshal Kitchener gave the order, the BEF, comprising eventually nearly 104,000 men, 40,000 horses, and about 470 artillery pieces, moved with the rapidity that professionalism, training, and good luck could produce. By August 16 (Britain had been at war for only 12 days) the BEF had landed at Boulogne and Le Havre – as seen – amidst local euphoria. The Liège forts would not fall for another day, and the Germans were just fanning out across the Maas, or Meuse, into central Belgium. The British divisions quickly took their prearranged place on the left of French General Lanzerac's troops and had extended their army in front of the Germans by August 20.

The situation was critical. The British force fielded five infantry divisions and a cavalry division. The Belgian army of 117,000 was now partly engaged, killed, or captured; partly in retreat; and partly forming the garrison for Antwerp. The French forces on the Franco-Belgian border consisted of 12 infantry and 4 cavalry divisions under Lanzerac. All told, something over 400,000 men in three loosely coordinated armies now faced the German right wing of nearly 600,000.

The British were only just in position when Brussels fell, and the first German assault on the Anglo-French forces struck the French at Charleroi (August 21) and the British at Mons (August 23). Lanzerac managed to escape total disaster only by rapid retreat. To the immediate west of the French, at Mons, Sir John French's BEF held off repeated German attacks for a day, but when Lanzerac fell back, leaving the British unprotected, the BEF quickly executed a "gradual withdrawal," in the venerable argot of the army, turning at Le Cateau on August 26 to engage in a furious defensive battle with Kluck's huge army, which was now in the open and moving at breakneck speed. A battle right out of British military tradition, Le Cateau represented only a brief delay for the Schlieffen juggernaut, but one which added to the mounting "frictions" of the German army.

It had taken some time for the French to comprehend the significance of the German attack in Belgium. In command of the French army since 1911 was Joseph Joffre, war-college instructor, military theorist, and veteran of French imperial clashes in many parts of the world, now in his early sixties. Joffre had presided over prewar strategic planning and had played an important role in creating the attack-oriented Plan XVII. Yet when hostilities opened, the Plan XVII strike through the Lorraine gap did not materialize, luckily enough for Joffre. French army organization was probably inferior to both German and British, and mobilization slower. In any case, the spectacular element of the Schlieffen Plan was precisely its early and rapid jump-off. As for Plan XVII, the French made a few tentative attacks along the German border in Alsace in the first days of the war, but in most places they were not only repulsed by the inner (southern) armies of the swinging Schlieffen line, they were pushed back. As will be seen, had the French found themselves far advanced into Alsace when the German right wing swung southward, Joffre might have faced disaster.

Given their careful strategic plan, there was little chance that the Germans would launch any major campaign westward through the gap, since the bulk of the French army was blocking the way, and since, as Joffre put it, the French countryside opposite the Germans "fairly bristled with fortresses," and the French could ultimately fall back to these great concrete mushrooms.[13] Once the German right (under General von Kluck) had turned south, Joffre began to transfer units from southeast to northwest to reinforce the Belgian border. As this happened, the German high command ordered the southernmost armies to press the French divisions ahead of them, so as to hold French troops away from the real German strike force in the northwest. But instead of standing and fighting in the "open," the First and Second French Armies fell back as part of a general French retreat. The Germans drove into the Lorraine, but the French forces there were neither destroyed or used as a pivot. As one of the German generals wrote in his diary, "If the enemy really wishes to retreat, not even God Almighty could stop him. Everywhere we are up against fortifications. The enemy is in a position, even with an inferior fighting force, to hold all fortified sectors long enough to enable the mass to get away."[14]

Joffre contended after the war that his order for a general Allied retreat on 25 August was part of a far-seeing plan to set up the First Battle of the Marne and the final disruption of the Schlieffen Plan.[15] Whether or not he understood all the ramifications at this early stage, it is certainly true that by retreating to Verdun in the south and by pulling his armies southward through the Champagne, east of Paris, he both broke away from the Battle of the Frontiers and drew the Germans into a trap in the region of the River Marne.

At the same time, Moltke's actions took the force out of the Schlieffen advance. The problem was the Russian attack on East Prussia. Counter to all expectations, the Russians mounted an invasion of northeastern Germany, in the province of East Prussia, on August 17. Since the Schlieffen Plan had been predicated on the inability of the Russians to carry out this attack, the Germans were shocked. Two Russian armies quickly pushed back Prittwitz's defending army and occupied part of the province. The hero of Liège, Erich von Ludendorff, was rushed eastward to direct the army as chief of staff, and retired general Paul von Hindenburg was called upon to oversee the army. We will learn much more about these leaders below, but the decisive point to make here is that they were soon joined by two army corps (around 60,000 men) from the Western Front. These corps departed the west at the precise moment of decision there. Whether the Schlieffen Plan might have worked with these men and the other contingents which Moltke had directed toward other duties is of course impossible to say. Historians have pointed out that of all the "frictions" encountered by the right wing, logistics – just getting men and supplies to the points needed along the insufficient network of roads – was as important as any. Still, it seems clear that 60,000 more men on the strong right wing would have altered the dynamics of the battle.[16]

Joffre's retreat ended momentarily the furious, mobile engagements that had taken place along the international line of frontiers running in a great arc from the Franco-Belgian border starting at the Channel, across the Luxembourg border and then the Franco-German frontier all the way to Switzerland. Casualties were dreadful compared with any stage of the war. During August 1914, the losses (killed, wounded, captured, missing) of the Belgians, French, and British amounted to over 237,000 men, with the French sustaining nearly 90 percent of

these. The Germans lost about 220,000 men. Hence, the first month of
the war was one of its bloodiest, consuming nearly half a million
soldiers. By comparison, on the Western Front during the whole of
1916, about 2.5 million men would be killed, wounded, or captured.
The Western Front powers experienced losses equaling a fifth of that
grisly total within the first month of the war.

The Mobile War and the Soldiers

To envision this opening stage of the war, one must begin by thinking
of sunshine, heat, dust, and movement. The weather held beautiful
throughout most of the month, and the sunshine which "cannot be
produced on canvas" heated up the battlefields to unaccustomed levels
for northern Europeans. The uniforms worn by all soldiers were mostly
woolen and worn in heavy layers. Headwear was for the British troops
a soft or at least flexible cap. Most German troops wore the old spiked
helmet, sometimes covered with canvas. The Belgian and French troops
would soon switch to a soft cover, but for the moment still looked a
great deal like soldiers from the Franco-Prussian war, wearing rigid,
molded hats. Having disdained the drab khaki colour of the prewar
British army or the field gray of the Germans, the French showed up
for World War I in sky-blue tunics and red-striped trousers, though
they would change rapidly to a more nondescript – and less visible –
neutral colour. Boots for all were very heavy, with thick leather soles,
the tops wrapped with one form or another of cover partway up the
calf. Many troops traveled to the fronts by rail, but, once there, troop
movements were almost all on foot. The two German armies of the right
wing, 600,000 strong and built for movement, had at their disposal
a mere 162 trucks, which would have made no dent had they carried
men in any case. Hence, the armies slogged across Belgium, France,
and western Germany during a hot August, and the soldiers suffered
cruelly from heat, dehydration, heat exhaustion, and the various other
complaints that accompany vigorous activity in great heat with too little
water. That is, unless they encountered some of the thunderstorm systems that punctuated the heat from mid-August onward, in which case
troops could find their wool uniforms soaked through and themselves
shivering. The problem of finding sufficient water was compounded by
the presence, along the front, of probably a million horses used by the
four armies. The month of August 1914 saw the front's last great cavalry

activity, but most of the horses were for the transport of supplies. Though the month was a good one for provisioning these animals, they too needed water.[17]

One of the greatest intensifiers of the heat and thirst was the great weight carried by each infantry soldier. Prewar British regulations counted on 65lb. as the standard load. German and French soldiers may have carried 10 or even 20lb. more. In fact, all soldiers carried more later on in the war, as various pieces of equipment were added to the kit. And this pack weight does not include the various extra loads with which infantrymen are often burdened. Indeed, as difficult as it seems to *march* for days on end with a 70- or even 80-lb. load, one stands in awe that soldiers fought the battles of August 1914 fully loaded, and probably then some.[18]

It has been seen that war in the decades before 1914 was bloody. European military leaders were well aware of this, and they were still coming to terms with the new technologies and tactics of war in 1914. One might say that the Boer War had demonstrated that hit-and-run tactics, the conversion of whole regiments into skirmishers, and the small-team attack could indeed be effective when employed against well-equipped European armies. On the other hand, the Russo-Japanese War had seemed to indicate that while defensive positions entrenched and protected by machine guns were amazingly strong, the right kind of mass assault could overcome them.

The Western Front armies of August and September 1914 were led by officers who could not decide which of these lessons to apply. The composition of their armies played a major role in calculating for specific battles how to arrange, or deploy, their troops. In the BEF, consisting in about equal parts of full-time professionals and well-trained reserve troops, tactics were fairly well decided. Indeed, during the first weeks of the war, the BEF fought almost exclusively on the defensive, a posture at which – as seen above – the British had long excelled. The discipline of fighting tough, defensive battles, and the technical knowledge (of formations, fields of fire, volley repetitions, and the like) required to fight such battles was engrained in this professional, experienced, and (it should be noted) relatively small group. The great mobilized armies of France and Germany contained only a core of professional or regular reserve troops and officers. The standing armies of France and Germany before World War I amounted to 823,251 and 880,000, respectively. Mobilization put the French army at 3.8 million strong and the German at 4.5 million.[19]

Hence, even in the earliest phase of the war, a high percentage of soldiers on the Western Front were new recruits or lightly trained reservists. Officers were therefore loath to use newer tactical ideas of smaller-unit tactics over a large front, and indeed some were hesitant to use any formation for assaults but that of men marching or walking in a rectangular mass (called the column formation). Such Napoleonic tactics were, it was thought, better suited to raw recruits who might well falter and run during battle. The mass was supposed to give each man a sense of protection. As we have seen, some of the early German assaults on the Liège forts were made in columns, and individual commanders used the old-fashioned formation for several months. Whether it gave a sense of security, however, it provided a near-perfect target for the new weapons. Officers soon found the value in prewar proposals to spread attacking infantry out into loose "waves" (usually three separate waves advancing at a walk perhaps 50 yards apart), presenting much less of a target. Hence this form of assault came to dominate by the end of the 1914 fighting, but only after the several forms of massed assaults had brought about disastrous casualties.

In fact, perhaps the most spectacular combination of lightly trained soldiers, close-order attack, and slaughter occurred at the very end of the mobile war, in October and November 1914, when the Germans launched an assault between Ypres and the Channel with four new corps from the reserve army. About three-quarters of the manpower of these corps were war volunteers, many of them middle-class and upper-class youths who had left school or university for the front. The other quarter consisted of the various reserve elements of the army, many of them older men who manned the reserves and militia at home (British soldier Robert Graves noted a similar dichotomy in his unit during his first days at the front: very young and very old). These troops lacked nothing in *élan* and morale. Indeed, their exploits in wading across flooded plains to attack, in marching shoulder-to-shoulder into the slaughter, in regrouping for one attack after another, are famous.

After a month of high casualties on the Flanders front, the German high command deployed four elite regiments as a strike force to attack Ypres directly. In spite of their elite status and training, they too were ordered to attack in old-fashioned close order. Their casualties were fearsome. We shall see that the British would suffer an almost sociological disaster on the first day of the Somme battle in 1916, but a German equivalent of this has to be the attacks just northeast of Ypres, at

Langemarck, in late October and early November 1914, when this army of old, middle-class reservists and young, middle-class students and cadets marched in column attack into the waiting BEF. As one German staff officer, Rudolf Binding, entered in his journal on October 27, "these young fellows we have, only just trained, are too helpless, particularly when the officers have been killed . . . . In the next division, just such young souls, the intellectual flower of Germany, went singing into an attack on Langemarck, just as vain and just as costly." It may be that Binding had misunderstood exactly what happened, and some writers have recently tried to expose the "slaughter of the innocents" at Langemarck as pure myth for home-front consumption. In any case, at least a fifth of those German soldiers who died in the futile attacks on Langemarck, Bixschoote, and neighboring points were students, and a large majority were not professional soldiers but members of Germany's educated middle class.[20]

With or without the psychological crutch of the column, 1914 soldiers displayed amazing courage in advancing and defending on very lethal battlefields. Some of their nerve was, no doubt, owing to the tremendous enthusiasm and *élan* evidenced on all sides. Clearly, during the first weeks of the war, the soldiers shared with the public as a whole the zest for adventure, the disdain for the evil foe, and the whole crusading quality of the war that all governments learned to create early on. The words of a colonel giving last-minute instructions to troops can both explain the courage of the men of 1914 and give us pause: "Love each other."[21]

The Politics of Military Emergency

After all the maneuvering of July, and after the pessimistic efforts at peace in the last few days of the July Crisis, the Western Front powers found themselves at war, and with a public who had accepted, and were glorying in, their governments' declarations of the necessity of war, but still with political elites who were far from unified in the face of a large military conflict.

France was perhaps the least conflicted of the three Western Front powers during the first weeks of war, in the immediate sense because the war came to France in the form of an invasion, and German troops were on French soil before the war was many days old. In the long view, as well, France was one of the most socially homogenous countries in Europe, being characterized by small farms and small businesses, and by the middle and lower-middle classes associated with owning and working in these enterprises. The organized urban workers in France had indeed a long and periodically violent history, but the spectacular outbreaks of strikes or revolutionary activity in a few big cities tended to obscure the real condition of France as a predominantly agricultural country until just before World War I. French workers were, moreover, grouped into a number of different organizations (unions and parties) which did not necessarily cooperate, even on core questions. Statistics show, moreover, that French workers on the whole accepted the movement of their families into the middle class, whether in one generation or two. Instability entered this picture mainly from the twin transitions to an industrial society and the breakdown of regional and local customs and traditions owing to the rigorous governmental attempt to turn "peasants into Frenchmen," as Eugen Weber pointed out, through a uniform system of education.[22]

The parliamentary system of France was perhaps the most democratic in Europe, and the multi-party system led not as much to instability as to a fluidity in French politics that made long-term compromise both possible and probable. Still, the France which went to war in 1914 was crisscrossed with fissures of many kinds. It has been seen, for example, that the Dreyfus Affair revealed a deep split between the conservative traditionalists and the liberal republicans. France, the country with perhaps the most centralized government bureaucracy in Europe, was nonetheless a country of regions. And these regions – from before the French Revolution and since – have tended to resent the predominance of the metropolis in French affairs. French regions would experience the war in quite different ways, as will be seen below, and the results would be divisive.

Yet the government's greatest worry seems to have been the socialists, themselves divided, but united at least on the issue of antimilitarism. The most prominent French socialist of his day, Jean Jaurès, had spent nearly a decade decrying the building of warlike alliances and the maintenance of a vast army, proposing instead a more egalitarian militia-style establishment capable of fighting a defensive struggle should France be invaded. Anarchists and syndicalists on the extreme left even advocated sabotaging mobilization in the years before the war, and in July 1914, Jaurès had helped engineer a declared intention on the part of the socialist parties to call for a general strike in case of mobilization, at least if their counterparts in Germany would do so as well. Indeed, the police drew up a list of leftwing leaders who were to be arrested in case of war, the so-called *"Carnet B."* In fact, the whole socialist strategy had begun to come unglued on July 27, 1914, when the German socialist party (SPD) voted to support their government in the international crisis. Hence, when Jaurès was assassinated two days later, the leading voice against the war was silenced, but that voice would probably have been drowned out anyway.[23]

In any case, with the great goal of regaining Alsace in sight, and the humbling of the hated invaders of 1870, the French public as a whole showed solid support. The German declaration of war on France on August 3 silenced any doubt. The political reflection of this insubstantial unanimity was the "sacred union," or *Union sacrée*, called for by President Raymond Poincaré, a moderate republican, as the war broke out. This was in theory a sacred union of the French people, but in practical fact, the *Union sacrée* was a device to rally unified support from political parties across the spectrum and apply that support to the parliamentary passage of national defense bills which would provide funds for mobilization. These bills were passed by the French Chamber of Deputies on August 4, the day of the invasion of Belgium. Squabbling parties came together in an emotional moment celebrating the nation. Socalist Jules Guesde and Catholic conservative Albert de Mun embraced before the Chamber. Premier René Viviani called upon the women of France to go out into the fields to take up the work of their men who had gone to the front, and evidence indicates that by and large they did so. Witnesses recorded that even in regions renowned for their rugged individualism, a spirit of cooperation manifested itself immediately when the complicated problems of mobilization arose. In the countryside and towns of France, French people pulled together during the first months of the war with grim determination, if not with any flash of urban euphoria.[24]

Popular mobilization into the military itself was, one might say, led by swiftly beating hearts. Men from all classes rushed to sign up to fight the "Boche," not all of them young. The Under-Secretary of State for War, André Maginot, enlisted in the ranks, to be wounded in November, received decorations for bravery, and returned to politics after his convalescence. Still older (over 40) was the Paris intellectual, sometime socialist, and Catholic convert Charles Péguy, who enlisted immediately and died in action in September 1914 during a charge against the Germans. His poetry seemed to have prepared the way:

Blessèd are those whom a great battle leaves
Stretched out on the ground in front of God's face,
Blessèd the lives that just wars erase,
Blessèd the ripe wheat, the wheat gathered in sheaves.[25]

For all the enthusiasm and *esprit* among the French defenders, the invasion crisis endangered both the politicians and the republican form of government. Having called up 2.9 million reservists, having shut down factories, having declared martial law, Joffre took charge, taking what he needed and directing as he willed through national martial law during the great crisis. Strict censorship, which would last throughout the war, was immediately imposed. The brave session of the Deputies on August 4 was its last until December 1914. With German troops as close as 25 miles from the center of Paris, the cabinet fled west to Bordeaux on September 1, at Joffre's request, and the Bourse closed two days later.

The government would return to Paris once the first Marne battle ended, and indeed, French politicians would begin to reassert the primacy of civilian rule over the military. But one must recognize that for France, and still more for Belgium, the Western Front would become a military, political, and human catastrophe that trumped all other considerations until the Germans were expelled. It seemed certain that the French would defend their country.

In many ways, Germany's rulers displayed far less resolution. Wilhelm had made many impolitic and bellicose statements during his life, but it seems that during the last days of the July Crisis he sincerely regretted both Austria's pressure on Serbia and the promises he himself had made to back the Austrians. His chancellor, Theobald von Bethmann Hollweg, had already uttered the terrible exclamation calling the London Treaty guarantee of Belgian neutrality a "scrap of paper," but in reality, Bethmann Hollweg was hardly a fanatical Prussian warlord. Beset by many doubts about Germany's "leap in the dark," his pessimism was tempered by his Prussian sense of duty. He was in many ways unfitted to be the civilian leader of Germany's first total war.

At the war's outbreak, Germany displayed even more social and political fissures than France. The traditional home of localized politics, a strongly differentiated social system, and often quite localized regional identities, Prussia–Germany reflected these differences in its federalism, a system in which much power for local decisions remained in the hands of the federal states, of which Prussia, the largest, was the dominant one. As seen already, part of the dynamic of post-1871 Germany was the urge to put aside local and even ideological differences in deference to the new national existence, an urge reflected in the popular nationalistic song, *Deutschland über Alles*, a song whose words had nothing to do with the conquest of others, but the conquest of local pettiness and the establishment of a real national community. And it is true that regional differences had seemed less important during the mildly centralizing hegemony of Hohenzollern Prussia, a state whose growth over several hundred years had displayed a remarkable touch in achieving sufficient political centralization while maintaining sufficient local cultural autonomy. Still, though Germany had been through a serious depression by 1900, in fact, its economy was strong. Its universities formed the pinnacle of the academic world. Germany had really achieved recognition as a true European power. Hence, German unity held together in good times. Could that unity hold during bad ones?[26]

Naturally, the political and social problems of industrialization, discussed in Chapter 1, caused serious concern. In particular, the strength of the socialists in the federal parliament, the Reichstag, was unprecedented since the last election, that of 1912, in which one-third of the German electorate voted for the SPD. Germany was the birthplace of Karl Marx and the home of many firebrands prominent on the left wing of international socialism, including the brilliant revolutionist Rosa Luxemburg, who regarded all wars between nations as capitalist and imperialist plots to keep the working class in check. For her, the real war was that of the international working class against the wealth-controlling capitalists. Yet the SPD was also the party of labor unions, and the goals of German labor were much more in tune with the slow-going evolutionary socialism called Revisionism, advocated by another German socialist, Eduard Bernstein, at the end of the century. Hence, though there were numerous Germans in touch with Lenin and other radical socialists abroad, in fact, the majority of the SPD hierarchy and leadership were reformists and under certain circumstances, patriots.

And the circumstances under which they might be patriots seem to have been those in which they found themselves in 1914. Up to August 4, 1914, SPD delegates had never voted for a defense appropriation in the Reichstag. As late as July the SPD had denounced the militancy of the Austrian government. Yet the new conditions seemed to demand a different stance. In the first place, the official line of the government was that Russian mobilization had endangered Germany to the point that German mobilization could only be called defensive. What was more, should Imperial Russia – one of the most autocratic states on the face of the earth and one of the most ferocious opponents of organized international socialism – win the war, that victory would constitute a tremendous blow to the cause of socialism everywhere. Hence, German socialists were forced to a decision when the War Credits Bill came up in the Reichstag on August 4, the same day the French Chamber of Deputies considered the same issue. From liberal Progressives to the Conservatives, the rest of Germany's parties – the "bourgeois" parties, as the socialists called them – were ready to stand up and pass the bills to pay for war. Would the socialists?

Meeting in caucus, the SPD delegation split 78–14 in favor of the war credits. For the sake of unity, the party decided to cast all of its ballots for the war credits, and the Reichstag duly voted for five billion marks to be appropriated for fighting the war. This political event was a watershed in the history of German socialism, as will be seen below. For the moment, it seemed to vindicate those German academics and thinkers called "social imperialists," who had hoped for war in the name of unifying the country.[27] It certainly enabled German socialists to escape their second-class political status, to the approval of the moderate members. SPD leaders also made it clear to the government that their support was given on the assumption that Germany would engage in wide-ranging programs of social reform and democratization. But the whole episode gave real meaning to the words of the Kaiser, proclaimed on the same day: "I know no parties, only Germans." He thereby declared a *Burgfrieden*, or civil peace, in which all would cooperate together in the defense of the Fatherland. Indeed, the month of August 1914 may represent the zenith of Wilhelm II's popularity.[28]

Germans who resisted the enthusiasm of the early days of the war seem to have been in the extreme minority. Germans from all segments of society enlisted in the first waves of mobilization and war, but the middle class in particular sent its sons with great enthusiasm. Many of them had spent their youth in anti-establishment *Wandervogel* groups, trying to create a kind of mystical, antimaterialist tribal bond outside the strictures of middle-class life, which they regarded, along with Nietzsche and the Expressionist writers of the turn of the century, as mere Philistinism. Transferring this mysticism to a romanticized version of the war was not a great leap. Ernst Jünger, who would become the greatest German writer of the war, called August 1914 "the holy moment." At some universities, entire fraternities enlisted. Intellectuals and store clerks alike joined together in the heroics of the moment. When one considers the Flanders attacks of October/November 1914, the connections between the battle front and the home front seem direct indeed.[29]

In Britain, the war evoked very solid support from most sectors of the public. Upon Britain's declaration of war, opponents of the war staged several rallies and penned some appeals for peace. Some of these voices were from the women's movement, including an appeal by Millicent Garrett Fawcett, leader of the broad suffragist movement and in general an opponent of war. Some corners of the Liberal Party, the governing party, retained the old liberal attitudes against war and intervention in continental politics. A few speeches and protests came from the socialist leadership. But as historian Arthur Marwick characterized the opposition, it was "striking, but no more striking than the speed with which the bulk of it dissolved." With Asquith's August 5 declaration that Britain was fighting for the preservation of civilization itself – and with the German invasion of Belgium – the opposition rapidly disappeared.[30]

Some labor leaders remained in opposition, but the Labour Party itself and the trade unions immediately came out in support of the war. Though the Labour Party had only recently been founded (1900), and indeed founded for the most part by middle-class intellectuals, like the well-known writers and "social thinkers" of the Fabian Circle, the party had rapidly made some political gains, gaining a modest but still significant 53 seats in the parliamentary elections of 1906. The party's "constituency" of organized labor was, on the other hand, well established and enjoyed a vigorous life in the industrial cities of Britain. As mentioned, vigorous strike activity marked the prewar period and was particularly widespread just before the war (at war's outbreak, roughly 100 strikes were in progress), connected mostly with living standard issues. Indeed, though we shall see that strike activity would reemerge during the war, especially after 1916, the working class of Britain showed unity with its leaders in 1914: in all of Britain only 20 strikes remained unsettled one month into the war.[31] More than this, the unions in effect gave up the strike for the period of the war when the Trades Union Congress announced an industrial truce for the duration of the war, and the workers themselves voted with their feet, enlisting in vast numbers (through 1914, though more hesitantly after that) and making it possible for Britain to avoid conscription until the Military Service Act of January 1916.

The cabinet faced some difficulties along the road: how to finance and direct a increasingly socially active and interventionist government – and one at war – without alienating the populace by the increased rates of wealth appropriation necessary to the project. But in August 1914, the country seemed admirably behind the war. On August 6 Parliament authorized recruitment of 500,000 additional men, and the famous "Call to Arms" appeared the next day: "Your King and Country Need You." A series of emergency laws was capped on August 8 when Parliament took five minutes to pass the Defence of the Realm Act (DORA), which empowered the government to take control of economic resources, punish public criticism of the war, and imprison individuals without trial. Numerous supplementary acts would strengthen and broaden DORA throughout the war, and the act would serve as the justification for an extensive expansion of measures controlling behavior (including a prohibition of the suspicious activity of flying a kite), but the basic law went into effect from the beginning. DORA empowered the government to punish civilians for traitorous or unloyal acts without a trial. Jury trials for civilians were restored, but only provisionally, and executions in the wake of the 1916 Irish Rebellion would take place without a trial.[32]

Within days of the war's outbreak, the retail merchant community in London had adopted the phrase "business as usual," an advertising phrase really, which was to convince customers that true patriots would continue shopping at their former rate. Harrods used the phrase in an advertisement on August 13, various sectors of business adopted the slogan, and to some extent it was handed on a platter to the government, whose policy was very much in line with the idea. Though all belligerent societies would be transformed by the war, the British government hoped to weather the crisis by giving the appearance of carrying on as usual. The tension deriving from the necessity of transforming the government but the desire to go on as usual would mark war politics in Britain much more strongly than in the other Western Front countries, as we shall see.

Popular reactions in Britain have shaped ideas about how the belligerent publics felt about the war, and if recent research questions the unanimity of the somewhat superficial enthusiasms (a great social historian commented that anti-German feeling in England was "pretty spontaneous, though helped along by the popular press"), there is still much on record to show that people wanted to show solidarity and patriotism. English shops featuring sauerkraut and liver sausage renamed them "good English viands" (Americans would later go the English one better, renaming sauerkraut "Liberty Cabbage"). As thousands of men did indeed respond to early calls for recruits, some young women armed themselves with chicken feathers, presenting a white feather to all able-bodied young men they met who seemed slow in getting to the recruiting station. A wave of name changes occurred among those with German-sounding names. One survivor of the home front during this period recorded the popular mood as filtered though children: early in the war, Britons had to obtain a permit for any enemy alien in their household (maids, nannies, etc.); "a child, hearing some discussion on the subject, asked anxiously, 'Oh, mummy, *must* we kill poor Fräulein?'"[33]

Spy stories indeed abounded, as they had for some years before the war, and enemy aliens were rapidly counted. A whole genre of jokes based on the interplay between the war and German waiters in British restaurants emerged, some of these jokes durable enough to survive nearly to the end of the century. The London *Daily Mail* ran public service messages such as the following: "Refuse to be served by an Austrian or German waiter. If your waiter says he is Swiss ask to see his passport." A number of attacks and popular anti-German outbursts were relatively short-lived, since the authorities interned German waiters, barbers, and sailors in a camp on the Isle of Man.[34]

By such combinations of political and popular mobilization, and by the spontaneous enthusiasm of the urban masses, European countries found themselves engaged in the war in ways which went deep into their emotional being.

The First Battle of the Marne

Sir John French, the commander of the BEF, had started off on the wrong foot with his French counterparts, and poor communications and bad relations continued to mar Allied cooperation, to some extent throughout French's 16-month tenure as commander. Certainly, French considered his position as the left flank of the Allies to have been endangered by French failures on his right, though in truth, in a series of battles, the French Fifth and Fourth Armies under Lanzerac and Langle had had their own hands full facing long odds against the German armies hurtling into France. Indeed, retreating, Joffre bought some time by having the Fifth Army whirl about at Guise, on August 29, and fight Bülow's Second Army in a furious struggle which lasted all day and ended with a German setback. This stand gave both the British army on the left and the French army on the right a chance to retreat successfully behind the cover of the River Aisne, running east and west.[35]

Yet if the French troops were in retreat, their retreat was orderly and there were few signs of panic. This calmness may have been owing to the public image and seemingly imperturbable personality of the French commander, Joseph Joffre, who throughout a crisis which seemed to signal a collapse of France, still insisted on getting his usual full night's sleep no matter how serious the crisis, how deep the disaster; nor did he miss or postpone his prodigious meals. His war plan had crumbled, his intermediate plans came to naught, and his army was in full retreat from the borders of France, but the marshal maintained what has been called by a later French officer – and with little exaggeration – "superhuman calm," as he evaluated the daily situation, traveled to army headquarters, and conferred with the civilian leadership. He certainly provided the greatest possible contrast to the German commander, whose shattered nerves nearly paralyzed him in the moment of near-victory and confined him to his headquarters in a small schoolhouse in Luxembourg.[36]

And indeed, Joffre's counterstroke must stand as one of the great military improvisations of modern times. To envision the great retreat and the first Battle of the Marne, one must visualise four German armies roughly in line and moving southward. The line aims to sweep along Luxembourg in the east and overlap Paris in the west. The French army and the BEF stretch in front of the Germans, but as they retreat, they tend to bulge southward in the center, as the far left stabilizes and turns to face east and the French far right comes to be anchored on Verdun and forts to the south. As the Allied retreat continues, Joffre manages to create new units and put them where they will be needed (an army under General Michel Maunoury at the far left, beyond the British, and an army under General Foch in the middle). After nine days, during which the French are fighting rearguard battles, the line has bowed southward in the middle, and the closely following Germans are in the bow. Where the line comes closest to Paris on the left, German cavalry patrols probe to within 8 miles of the capital, the leading units of the main forces only 30 miles away.

Paris was, understandably, in a complete panic. The government fled secretly to Bordeaux, and thousands of Parisians likewise fled the city. Put in charge of the city's defense, General Joseph Gallieni, a 65-year-old retiree, announced to Parisians that the government had departed "to give a fresh impulse to national defence." He enjoined the public to "Endure and fight!" and told the country, "A nation which refuses to perish, and which, in order to live, does not flinch either from suffering or sacrifice, is sure of victory." Meanwhile, more prosaically, he commandeered the taxis and buses of Paris to haul as many soldiers as possible from the capital to Manoury's Sixth Army in its attempt to halt the German steamroller. Indeed, having helped build Manoury's new army on the German flank, Gallieni now calculated that Kluck's army had fought its way into a trap.

Telephoning Joffre on September 4, Gallieni convinced his commander. Yet if Joffre was to stop the retreat and go on the offensive, the British army under Field Marshal French (who opposed an offensive for the moment) would likewise have to turn about and fight, or the French attack would be useless. The usually imperturbable Joffre rushed to French and implored him to fight, telling him, "this time the honour of England is at stake." The British commander reluctantly agreed, and Joffre immediately ordered Manoury to attack. The reinforcement, by taxi and otherwise, was the beginning of the First Battle of the Marne.[37]

These efforts on the Allied side were matched by problems in the Germans' execution of their strategic plan. The whole purpose of the Schlieffen Plan was to sweep, like a swinging gate, in a broad movement encompassing Paris and outflanking the enemy. The German First Army, commanded by Kluck, was to play the significant role of being the outside army, sweeping southwestward around Paris, then turning to help crush the French from both sides. It is true that Moltke had, as seen, weakened the right wing, but some contemporaries did not think this weakening beyond repair. Indeed, it was not because his forces were weak that General von Kluck, poised just north of Paris, turned his army to the east of Paris rather than to the west.

After defeating the British at Le Cateau on August 26, Kluck had headed south, but he suddenly encountered a new French force moving toward him from the west (this was the newly formed army of General Maunoury). Successfully pushing away this force, on September 29, Kluck received a request from the Second Army commander, General von Bülow, to attack in his direction, to the southeast, so that the First Army could link up with the Second in driving the French southward. Kluck did so, and in doing so passed 40 miles to the east of Paris rather than 40 miles to the west. Many knowledgeable critics have heaped the blame for the Schlieffen Plan's failure on this decision by Kluck. Other observers have pointed out that Kluck made this decision with the admirable goal of exploiting the weakness of the French at this juncture, and that Moltke's headquarters was fully aware of Kluck's deviation and did not move to right it. Surely, had Kluck known that in turning southeast, he was offering his lightly protected flank to rapidly gathering forces, he would not have done so. Perhaps it was his business to know that, or the business of Moltke's staff to find out.[38]

Other, perhaps more important, factors were also at work in the last days of August 1914. Clearly, Joffre's retreating forces could use a coherent, connected system of roads and railways to move troops to any point on a far-flung battle line. This advantage, called "interior lines" by military analysts, allows the one who possesses it to use a compact position to force the enemy to more effort. Joffre used this situation to move troops from one end of his battle front to the other. The Germans, whose plan relied on speed, found most of the railroads destroyed in the wake of the French retreat (one disadvantage of being on the outside of an interior lines position).

One must also say, as has been hinted, that for all the vaunted staff work of the Germans, when push came to shove, the leadership on the Allied side, especially in the French army, was better than that of the Germans. Joffre would probably not rate highly on the military historian's list of technically brilliant generals, but his calmness and his refusal to panic allowed him to judge the generalship of his subordinates (and replace some) and to move troops and supplies to the vital areas. His counterpart, Moltke, might be faulted for decisive failures at several points during August and September 1914. Overall, his refusal to exercise command was among his greatest failures. If one attributes these failures to his health, then one must fault the military leadership, including the "Supreme War Lord," Wilhelm II, for not replacing Moltke within days of the war's outbreak. Moltke was, it is true, replaced (by Falkenhayn), but only on September 19, when the Battle of the Marne was already lost.

In any case, if we employ the idea of the French line bent southward in the middle, almost into a U-shape, the complicated battle that resulted can be summarized quite easily. The Germans battled their way into the U, which had become a trap, and on September 5, Joffre sprang the trap: the French and British stopped retreating and attacked. Maunoury and his new Sixth Army, north of Paris (and north of the Marne), surprised the westernmost German corps at midday, and the First Battle of the Marne had begun. The next morning, the BEF and the French Fifth Army started a drive that would take them into a gap between the armies of Kluck and Bülow. Faced with the need for a decision, the Germans were ill-served. Moltke sent a staff lieutenant colonel, one Hentsch, to Kluck's headquarters to investigate the situation, but instead of hearing some decisive plan from Moltke, the German army commanders learned only that the Schlieffen Plan's sweeping movement had been officially abandoned.

The next four days saw vast, furious action in hundreds of engagements across hills and plains east of Paris. This was the Battle of the Marne in earnest. It would be confusing to recount the battle even in outline here. On September 9, the Germans began to retreat back to the north. But the French and British were exhausted enough, the Germans fresh enough, that they left behind much latitude for debate, whether the retreat was the misguided result of Lieutenant Colonel Hentsch, once again sent to the army headquarters and exercising decision-making powers, or whether the retreat occurred only a step ahead of a knockout blow by the French and British. Certainly, having failed in the Schlieffen Plan, there would have been no point in sacrificing whole armies just to be a few miles farther into France.

The Marne battle ended with the Germans falling back and, like troops in the Russo-Japanese War and the American Civil War, digging trenches and establishing defensive positions. This occurred about 40 miles east and northeast of Paris along the Aisne, where Maunoury's army kept the pressure on the German First Army. In a sense, the attack having failed for the Germans, they now had a somewhat easier task: to choose a line of defensible positions, dig trenches along those positions and defend them. The French pursuit made this job harder. Joffre was now somewhat less than imperturbable: to the government in Bordeaux, he cabled, "The Battle of the Marne is an incontestable victory for us"; to his commanders he preached only pursuit, "Victory is now in the legs of the infantry." Hence, as the Germans dug in, the French attempted to outflank them to the northwest; the Germans quickly extended their line. The French repeated this process again and again, coming up, as it was said, either a day or a division short each time, with the Germans steadily defending a lengthening position in a series of deadly battles that came to be called the "Race to the Sea."

In reality, the "Race" was a series of battles at points all along a battle front which was now beginning to show some stability.

Recent scholarly work and close attention to contemporary records have really given us a more accurate vision of the formation of the Western Front than the standard, somewhat journalistic, view which told a little narrative beginning with the sweeping – and machine-like – movements of the Schlieffen Plan, the "Race to the Sea" and, at last, stalemate. We can certainly detect a different rhythm here. First, the tactics of the Schlieffen Plan stage of the war were quite standard, and losses up to the First Battle of the Marne were roughly what one might have expected (indeed, almost exactly the same casualty levels as at Waterloo and other nineteenth-century battles).

And yet it was at the Marne that both sides encountered the first real effects of massed firepower tactics with the new weapons. But this was precisely because the conventional, even classic, plans of Kluck and the imperturbable Joffre (who cajoled and persuaded the British General French along only with difficulty) led to what Napoleon (and Clausewitz) tried to avoid: direct, expected frontal assault. Indeed, in broadest outline, the First Battle of the Marne turned out to be a Gettysburg-type battle: strength against strength. Had a few more Clausewitzian "frictions" developed in the Germans' favor, they might have won this battle. Yet given Moltke's weakening of the right wing and Kluck's decision to meet the French strength east of Paris instead of following the plan and sweeping around to the west of both British and French, it is difficult to see how he could have delivered the kind of decisive knock-out blow envisioned by the brilliant staff planners under Schlieffen 20 years before. Hence, the strategic goals were probably impossible to achieve within a few weeks of the war, but the Germans could still have won the Marne fighting. This victory would most certainly have changed the course of the war, and taking Germany's enormous sticking power during the next four years, one wonders if some successful secondary strategic plan might not have grown out of it. All such considerations aside, by any measure, the successful French and British counterassault against the Germans, which drove the main body of Kluck's army back from within 20 miles of Paris at nearest point, stands out as one of the most significant military events of the war on the Western Front. It is perhaps among the most momentous military events in modern history.

In conjunction with Joffre's continuous pressure on the retreating Germans, the Belgians launched another offensive from Antwerp in mid-September, which stalled a few days later. Hence, as the German line began to stabilize, the Germans faced the necessity of taking Antwerp – now housing the Belgian government – soon or, perhaps, never. On September 29, Beseler committed a whole army with heavy artillery to a proper siege. Having learned from the unwieldy siege of Liège, the Germans simply stayed out of the range of the Belgian guns and used heavy artillery to pulverize the forts of Antwerp. The Belgian cabinet was about to flee when the First Lord of the British Admiralty arrived with 8,000 marines, announcing "We are going to save the city." His name was Winston Churchill. In fact, his men were too few and too lightly armed to help much, and the government fled on October 6, just before the city fell. Having heard both truth and exaggeration concerning the German treatment of civilians, nearly half of the city's population of 400,000 escaped, most of them to the Netherlands. Antwerp, much damaged by the bombardments, surrendered on October 10.

The army escaped to the west, to link up with the British and French forces attempting to keep the Germans away from the English Channel coast, but the Germans dogged this retreat, in compliance with a general offensive in this region – Flanders – beginning on October 19. The Belgians flooded much of the coastal area down to Dixmuide, on the River Yser, where the German assault on French and Belgian troops was vicious: during the night of 23/24 October, defenders withstood 15 assaults by the Germans. Point-blank artillery duels marked the area with a special intensity of slaughter.

Meanwhile, the Germans put tremendous resources into a developing battle at the town of Ypres, a small Belgian city with old-style fortified walls, about 25 miles from the end of the front at the Channel. The fortifications made the city difficult to take, but the Germans attacked both north and south of it, bending the lines westward, leaving Ypres in the center of a "salient," a bulge of the line toward the enemy. The inside of a salient is known for its danger, since one can be fired on from three sides. The attacks on Ypres intensified as October wore on, and the titanic battle would last for five weeks. In this First Battle of Ypres, the future of the war began to be foreshadowed.

The German attack which petered out at Ypres in November 1914 was a quite traditional attempt at outflanking the British troops who were clinging to positions in front of the city. But it was at the same time the first of a long series of attempts at "breakthrough" which would constitute so much of the fighting on the Western Front until the spring of 1918. In these Flemish battles, both sides discovered that the old methods of storming enemy defences were ineffective – we might say suicidal – in an age of vastly greater firepower, including especially the machine gun. Following on the heels of the Marne fighting, the First Battle of Ypres likewise represents one of the real junctures of the war, certainly the end of what we might call the Schlieffen Plan phase. Stalemate and the Western Front are often viewed as synonymous, but the attitude of the opposing forces was not so much that of stand-off as that of two fighters circling each other, looking for some advantage.

In any case, surviving the German attempt to break through at Ypres, the Allies hung on, and the line stabilized on the coast at Nieuport, where a French and Belgian contingent stood. It then ran down west of Dixmuide to Ypres, where British General Douglas Haig commanded locally. The British sector, still under Sir John French's overall command, stretched southward into France, roughly to the River Somme, in Picardy. There the long French sector began and extended to Reims and Verdun and thence all the way to the Swiss border. By the end of October a continuous front of about 400 miles stretched from the Channel to Switzerland.

The problem: Once the Belgian, British, and French forces faced a more or less continuous line of Germans looking back at these Allied troops over the mounded parapet in front of their trenches, there was no flank to outflank. The only flanks of either side were in fact "anchored" on the English Channel and the Alps. The hopeful alternative that the Germans tried at the First Battle of Ypres was to manufacture flanks in the British line by driving a hole through it and turning one of the "edges" produced. They almost succeeded, but not quite. The Germans, as seen above, attacked with amazing courage, but simply could not make headway against the firepower of troops firing rifles from entrenched positions, of machine guns, and of artillery exploding in front of the attackers.

The Crown Prince of Prussia – military professional, insightful observer, and one of those involved in creating the front – wrote that trench warfare as it came to be fought on the Western Front was not inevitable, but a mistake, the result of poor generalship, the "outcome of an exhaustion brought on by a failure on both sides to develop a decisive strategy." In any case, it was a situation that no one – not the civilian leaders, not the generals – had wanted. But once the trench line was in place, Western Front leaders had to work out ways to deal with it. As the British Secretary for War, Lord Kitchener, said as the Western Front hardened into its final shape and his country faced a prospect for which it had never bargained, "We must make war as we must; not as we should like."[39]

3

STALEMATE AND MOBILIZATION, 1915/1916

The metaphor of "stalemate" is apt to mislead us as much as enlighten us if we apply it too literally to the Western Front. It was a potent concept of the era, which influenced the actions of participants, decision-makers, and bystanders, and in large measure, the history of the Western Front has been envisioned in terms of stalemate.[1] Since the 1970s, on the other hand, historians have begun to emphasize change and development rather than stasis. Yet even in light of new material emphasizing the extent to which the battle front itself changed during the four years of war, the idea of stalemate is still a useful analytical tool for thinking about the course of the war, both on the battle front and on the home front. It is necessary first, of course, to comprehend the nature of this stalemate, and we make a good start by understanding that individuals and armies in 1915 were not inactive, hamstrung, or otherwise unable to introduce new ideas and adopt clear courses of action. Indeed, in some ways, the military behaviors of the Western Front powers in the period from November 1914 to the crucial year 1916 represented sometimes frantic, sometimes fatalistic, plans in reaction to or even in fear of stalemate itself.

The Generation of Stalemate

Although the Western Front can seem a monotonous parade of failed and self-destructive offensives, some of the individuals most engaged in the actual conduct of the war – not necessarily the commanding generals – were also engaged in the design of new methods and techniques of warfare at a rate far exceeding various phases of earlier

74

military change dubbed "revolutionary" by historians. A host of special weapons and tactics emerged during this period, from new artillery techniques to the use of gas and flamethrowers to the astounding development of military aviation almost from scratch. Nearly all of these innovations related to the problems of fighting a war of entrenched positions, without flanks, across a 400-mile front – in a word, a war of stalemate.

Many commanding officers on the Western Front were unable to comprehend the significance of the new ideas and techniques. Partly because the actual warfare taking place on the battle front was techni-cally complex and hard to describe, some leaders were unable to make the immediate mental leap necessary for rapid adaptation to the new tactical realities. Moreover, high-ranking officers were steeped in the traditions of a class-bound Europe, and had little confidence in the suitability of private soldiers for the kind of complicated and indepen-dent work necessary to overcome the strange, siege-like conditions of the Western Front. As we shall see below, the colossal slaughters of 1916, the war's real turning point in many ways, resulted from the conjunction of the attempt to use new tactics and weapons with the unwillingness of commanders to trust either their lower-level subordinates or the other ranks, or private soldiers, who made up their armies. There were of course exceptions.

On the home fronts, the metaphor of stalemate only came to predominate in the middle stages of the war, since the conditions of the Western Front were presented to the public of the warring countries only in carefully crafted versions which tended to keep the war sounding more dynamic and in a sense more traditional than it actually was. The average citizen read about it in daily newspapers and tabloid periodicals, many of the latter created during the first weeks of the war and designed to cater to a mass public. With names like *The Illustrated War Chronicles*, *Illustrierte Geschichte des Weltkrieges*, and *Collier's History of the Great War*, these war periodicals were heavy with what would now be called graphics (mostly drawn or painted, since very few of the thou-sands of photographs being made could pass muster as "inspiring" in any sense) and full of stories of traditional heroism on the part of "our own" and villainy on the part of the enemy. For the moment, say before the second Christmas of the war, the public seemed satisfied with official pronouncements of unity by their own governments, with tales of brav-ery and sacrifice from the front, and with the relative plenty which still characterized all the economies.

Yet at the top of the warring societies, among the elites of business, government, and to some extent education (though the reality levels of intellectuals and academics during this period seem, in retrospect, painfully low), it soon became clear that stalemate on the battle front could simply not be survived if stalemate prevailed at home: that is, if liberal parliamentarism and the relatively open and free societies were allowed to stand in the way of the management machinery needed to prosecute a long (stalemate) war of staggering expense.

As the Allied and German armies settled into the stalemate conditions, a new kind of warfare, immediately dubbed trench warfare, became the most important feature of both the Allied and Central Powers' strategies in Western Europe. Actually, we tend to assume that this central import-ance of the Western Front was inevitable, but both contemporaries and later observers have indicated that it need not have been. For one thing, the Western Front was only one of many theaters of war, and not even the first one to take shape. While the confusing Battle of the Frontiers was in progress, the Serbian front displayed a more clear-cut series of battles as the Austrians worked their way southward toward the Serbian heartland. Of vastly greater importance was the Eastern Front, which took shape with surprising rapidity and profound results in August and September 1914.

On the Eastern Front, the Russians would face the Austro-Hungarian army in the south and Germans in the north. Along this line, the Prussian province of East Prussia formed a long inroad into the Russian Empire. On the one hand East Prussia was a tempting dish for the Russians. Schlieffen had thought long and hard before shaping his plan so as to leave only a minimal defensive force in East Prussia, to hold the Russians at bay until the French were defeated. After which, of course, every energy would be devoted to fighting the Russians. And Schlieffen based his decision on the calculation that the gigantic but lumbering Russian army – with almost none of the modern military amenities such as paved roads, railroads, and telegraphy – would need a full six weeks to mount an invasion.

The early Russian mobilization (expanding from partial to full mobilization over the week before the war's outbreak) looms large when viewed in relation to the Schlieffen attack and the Western Front in general, for with a head start of a week's mobilization, the Russians were able to invade East Prussia with two armies by August 19. The German Eighth Army under General Max von Prittwitz reeled from this onslaught. The Russians occupied about half of the province, in the process killing, in a strange historical coincidence, about the same number of German civilians as the number of Belgian civilians the Germans were to kill during the same weeks (5,000 to 6,000). The battles themselves and the Russian occupation succeeded in destroying an enormous number of houses and buildings, along with livestock and other property. Though the rest of Germany knew little of these events in East Prussia, the situation was serious indeed.

At this juncture, the German high command replaced Prittwitz with two soldiers whose lives have become intertwined with the history of the modern world: as commander of forces, Paul von Hindenburg; as his quartermaster-general, Erich von Ludendorff. Promoted from colonel to general, Ludendorff was the military technician of the two. Known for his heroics in capturing Liège in August, Ludendorff had been a highly respected staff officer for many years and was intimately involved with both shaping and carrying out the Schlieffen Plan. Indeed, it was normal practice of the German general staff to appoint a younger and subordinate officer as chief of staff, with the responsibility for both planning and execution, and to name as commander an older officer to provide overall direction and to engage in morale-building. General Paul von Hindenburg was entirely suited for this role. Of an old military family, Hindenburg had just retired from a moderately distinguished career as the war broke out. He took up the role of coordinating personalities and, quite importantly, maintaining "public relations" with both army and government.

Ludendorff arrived in East Prussia with a plan for defeating the two invading armies, and his plan was similar to that of Lieutenant Colonel Max Hoffmann, Prittwitz's operations officer. Hindenburg gave them leeway to work. The result was the defeat of the Russian Second Army under Alexei Samsonov and the greatest German victory of the war, in the Battle of Tannenberg beginning on August 26, 1914. Shattered, Samsonov committed suicide on the 30th. One week later, the Russian First Army was crushed to the east of Tannenberg, in the Battle of the Masurian Lakes. The Russians were expelled, but the withdrawal of German forces to the Western Front and to the Austrians' aid to the south invited another Russian invasion of East Prussia in October. From October 1914 onward, Ludendorff – well aware of the tactical stalemate on the Western Front – urged a decisive blow in the East, but the new German chief of general staff, Erich von Falkenhayn, was already developing a strategy of victory on the Western Front by wearing down the French and British in the west. Without resources for a great offensive on the Eastern Front, Hindenburg and Ludendorff nonetheless soon pushed their sector of it well inside the borders of the Russian Empire, where it would remain for the rest of the war. Yet it was clear that the Western Front stalemate would be at the center of most of German strategic thinking for the foreseeable future.[2]

As we shall see below, the impact of these momentous events on the Western Front and the Western Front powers extended far beyond that corner of the war: one should note that Ludendorff was well on his way to becoming a "specialist" in breaking out of stalemated situations. We can find analogous instances of counter-stalemate measures shaping the dynamics of the war in other areas too. Perhaps the most obvious analog would be the activities of Winston Churchill, the unorthodox and colorful First Lord of the Admiralty since 1911. A world celebrity already – based on the happy coincidence of an adventurous early adulthood and formidable gifts as a writer – Churchill has already appeared in this book as the unorthodox would-be saviour of Antwerp early in the war. The onset of stalemate in late 1914 prompted Churchill, like Ludendorff, to look away from the Western Front in search of victory. Churchill, the old colonial soldier, found the suitable place in a vulnerable peninsula adjacent to the Dardanelles Strait. Friendly to the Central Powers but only just in the war in November 1914, the Turks possessed a strategic avenue, the passage between Russia and the British-controlled Mediterranean. If the British could gain the straits, easy supply of the Russians by Britain would be automatic, and Russian pressure on Germany would end the war. Failing this grand vision, taking the straits might knock Turkey out of the war at least. Arguing in January 1915 for an expedition to "take" the peninsula of Gallipoli and then ram a naval force all the way to Constantinople, Churchill gained the agreement of the cabinet. Naval operations aimed at forcing the Dardanelles Strait began in February and ended in failure in March, and by April the Dardanelles campaign had come down to a land attack which was attempting to hold onto a thin beachhead on the western side of Gallipoli. Commanded by Mustafa Kemal, future founder of modern Turkey, the Turks conducted as tough a defense as any in World War I. Eventually, Sir Ian Hamilton led a force of over 400,000, including French, Indian, Australian, and New Zealand troops. Only in early December 1915 did London decide to cut its losses (they had amounted in the eight months to over a quarter of a million casualties) and evacuate. What had seemed a clever run around the end had ended up as just another especially painful form of stalemate.

Yet in certain British circles, the end run still fascinated, and much of Britain's effort in the Middle East – the Mesopotamian operations in particular and later on, Allenby's offensive in Palestine and Syria, and the "Arab Revolt" – resulted not only from the long-standing British imperial design of controlling this pivotal region, but also from the desire to break up the stalemate by disrupting the Central Powers where possible.

Some of the most significant activities aimed at breaking up the stalemate took place on the oceans. Britain, of course, had long possessed the largest navy in the world, and we have seen that an important prelude to World War I was the creation of a German battle fleet beginning in 1898. Both sides had upped the ante since the turn of the century: the new *Dreadnought* class of battleship on the British side and the production of submarines ("U-boats," *Unterseeboote*) by the Germans set the stage for more unorthodox thinking about how to break up the impasse on the Western Front.

Very soon after the outbreak of the war, the British government decided enthusiastically to blockade the Germans. Blockade measures would increase month by month, until the blockade took final shape in 1915, when it included interdiction of neutral civilian shipping as well as any shipping carrying goods formally defined as contraband, including food and medicine. We will look into the "Hunger Blockade" in more detail later, but it forms the backdrop for the naval activities impacting the Western Front as well as a very direct connection between battle front and home front.[3]

On the "battle front" at sea, in spite of the heroics of the German squadron under Admiral Graf von Spee on the South American coast, the new German battle fleet was still outclassed by the British navy. But naval engagements in the first months of the war were mostly desultory, certainly not the Trafalgar-like pitched battle which was the ultimate goal of navalist strategy of most maritime powers. Surprisingly, German U-boats seemed to narrow the naval gap. On September 1, 1914, the British fleet had to flee from its main base at Scapa Flow so as not to fall prey to approaching German submarines, and Admiral Jellicoe in effect moved the fleet to the Irish coast. At the end of September U-boats sank three outdated cruisers in less than an hour, but in October, they sank the state-of-the-art battleship, *Audacious*, off the coast of Ireland. But on the whole, the submarines only evened the odds somewhat. Both the British and Germans decided that the Mahanian model of a clash of naval titans in a huge sea battle was simply too dangerous: the British because of the danger submarines posed, the Germans because the odds were simply against their new battle fleet.

Hence, the conditions on the sea were analogous to the stalemate on land. Ships were not tied down to a stationary battle line, and naval operations continued. But they continued very cautiously, with little of the risk-all attitude envisioned by the proponents of navalism before the war. British naval effort went into blockading the coast, laying mines, and later protecting supply vessels from German U-boats. The German naval commanders consciously chose a defensive *Kleinkrieg* ("small war") strategy of submarine activity and raiding and mining the British coast.[4]

German submarine warfare against Allied merchant shipping developed, like other efforts surveyed here, in late 1914 and early 1915 in the attempt to break through a stalemated situation. Interpreting the British blockade as a contravention of international law, the German navy shifted over to submarine attacks on merchant shipping.

Naval warfare had over the previous hundreds of years developed a fairly elaborate protocol for behavior in battle, but the new technology of the submarine fit ill into preexisting practices. On the surface, for example, in times of war, merchant ships – more or less unarmed – could be approached and signaled to stop and allow a search for contraband goods. If boarding was refused, then the warship was justified in attacking the merchant vessel. At the beginning of the war, German U-boats attempted similar behavior, but this was made more difficult by the necessity of surfacing. This cumbersome maneuver took many minutes and exposed the submarine either to attack from guns or from ramming.[5] By the end of 1914, some U-boat commanders were beginning to give short shrift to even modified formalities. Others were far more fastidious. U-boat commanders Arnauld de la Périère and Otto Hersing, for example, went to great lengths to give merchant ships time to evacuate to lifeboats before attacking. Indeed, both Hersing and de la Périère developed tactics which allowed them to surface safely before an engagement.

On the other hand, some commanders developed what came to be called "unlimited submarine warfare," meaning that they attacked without warning and that they attacked a much wider range of targets, including hospital ships. The German navy and government backed these aggressive tactics in February with a clear declaration:

All the waters surrounding Great Britain and Ireland, including the whole of the English Channel, are hereby declared to be a war zone. From February 18 onwards every enemy merchant vessel found within this war zone will be destroyed without it always being possible to avoid danger to the crews and passengers. . . . Neutral ships will also be exposed to danger. . . . it is impossible to avoid attacks being made on neutral ships in mistake for those of the enemy.[6]

One of the most enthusiastic practitioners of this unleashed warfare was the commander of submarine *U.20*, Walter Schwieger. Since January 1915 Schwieger had made a name for himself as a practitioner of the unlimited variety of warfare. On May 7, 1915, he came upon the passenger liner *Lusitania*, which he promptly sank with one torpedo. Nearly 2,000 passengers and crew died, among them 124 Americans.

Much controversy still swirls around the *Lusitania* sinking. Some popular historians have tried to make the case that the *Lusitania* incident was planned, so as to help bring the United States into the war. Witnesses described a huge second explosion (*U.20* fired only once), and much has been written about the extent to which the *Lusitania* may have been armed and may have been carrying munitions. It was the case that some German-American groups and the German embassy bought newspaper advertisements warning American passengers that it was dangerous to sail on a British vessel through the war zone.[7]

The German decision to wage unlimited submarine war, like the German decision to carry out the Schlieffen Plan, may have been justified in military terms, especially in light of the ruthless British blockade, but, like the Schlieffen Plan, it was a political disaster. American President Woodrow Wilson – an Anglophile of long standing – was already maintaining a lopsided neutrality: there was no chance that the United States would have entered the war on the German side. Hence, newspaper warnings in New York and arguments about the illegality of the British blockade could have little impact on American public opinion and foreign policy when American civilians were being killed by German torpedoes. Wilson warned the Germans in terms grave enough that they rescinded the policy of unlimited submarine warfare in June 1915, agreeing not to attack large passenger liners, even those sailing under enemy flags. The issue died down as the 1916 presidential campaign approached – within the voting public there was enough opposition to the war that one of Wilson's campaign slogans was "He Kept Us Out of War."[8]

Hence, a number of U-boat incidents involving the loss of American life did not bring the Americans into the war, but the desire to placate international opinion, above all that of America, led to a period of limitations on submarine warfare. One must add here that Allied losses from U-boat attacks continued to rise in 1915 and 1916, but not dramatically, as these losses (in tonnage of shipping) show: 1914 – 252,738; 1915 – 885,471; 1916 – 1,231,867. Later on, the resumption of unlimited submarine warfare would raise the 1917 total to a startling 3,660,054 tons and create pressures which we shall examine below.[9]

It is worth noting that on the seas too, the Western Front was resolving itself into something like a stalemate: the British blockade was inexorable; the U-boats were relentless; and the great battle fleets for the moment spent most of their time in safe quarters in their home bases.

The Dynamics of Stalemate

Little wonder that the vision of the stalemated front was and is so powerful, for nothing like it – at least on the scale it presented – had happened before. In physical terms, the Western Front consisted of opposing trench networks facing each other and stretching from the English Channel to Switzerland, about 400 miles. Viewed from the standpoint of military science, the Western Front presented two major problems. First, as we have seen, there were no flanks. Hence possibilities for maneuver, for feint, for any "indirect approach"[10] were *limited*, though not excluded, as we shall see. Even the new power of modern artillery shells to kill defenders and the gradual addition of other means of assault did not enable European armies as organized in 1914 to displace strongly defended, flankless forces.

Machine-gun theory was already quite advanced by the early stages of the war, though some new techniques were soon added. Machine guns were sited in positions from which their fire would hit oncoming troops roughly from the side, since a machine-gun bullet which has missed troops in front of it is likely to hit nothing, while from the side a line of men advancing – even a thin line – presents more chances of someone being hit. Machine guns are what the name says: they are machines, and they are quite adjustable, with appropriate screws and springs for locking the weapon's aim into desired directions and distances. Gunners could sight in their guns to cover a given piece of ground – still better if the ground included obstacles like barbed wire – and lock in that sighting, so that with little effort they could deny any advance over that ground. During the war the French moved away from the continuously occupied front trench altogether, presenting instead a front wall in the form of machine-gun posts several hundred yards apart, which could cover all of the space through which attackers would have to move. Infantry troops remained relatively safe in trenches several hundred yards to the rear, ready for counterattack once the enemy waves had broken on the machine-gun front. Even with new arrangements of the front lines, however, the overall density of troops only *increased* as the war went on.

To make sense of the Western Front, it is vital to understand that it was a gigantic siege operation, in which the Germans tended to play the role of fortress defenders, the Allies the role of besiegers. This situation derived directly from the military activities of August and September 1914. Once the Schlieffen Plan foundered, the Germans entrenched themselves – even fortified themselves – on Belgian and French soil. Among the most significant actors on the Western Front at this stage were the German engineering troops (*Pioniere*) and the staff officers who located strong points on which the army could fall back. Accordingly, the last step in the war of maneuver and the first step in establishing the static trench front on most of its sectors was the process of Germans defending against Allied counterattacks while building up strong points in the rear to which they could fall back. These strong points incorporated concrete shelters, pillboxes, deep dugouts, and even larger structures. Once the lines were completed, the Germans gradually fell back to them, in the end occupying the high ground across most of the front. With strong, reinforced positions sited along ridges, hills, and other high ground, the Germans could in many sectors – Ypres was a spectacular example – peer down into the Allied positions. With their fortified and entrenched positions in place, the Germans simply shifted to the defensive. Theoretically, possession of so much Belgian and French territory would give the upper hand to the Central Powers in any negotiations to end the war. Of course no one imagined that end could be more than months away at most. At the same time, this *strategic* defensive, consuming fewer troops than the offensive mode, freed Germans to fight elsewhere, eventually not just on the Eastern Front, but on the Italian and other fronts as well.

The deadly Ypres salient illustrates this whole process. Repulsed in a violent last attempt to make the Schlieffen Plan work in late October 1914, the Germans nonetheless held onto the ridges that semicircled this Flanders city on its east, north, and south. The fact that the bulge or salient in the lines allowed the Germans to pour artillery fire into the British positions and the town itself from three sides made Ypres one of the most deadly spots on the Western Front. And indeed, in spite of their general shift to the defensive, the Germans hardly gave up on the idea of breaking the British defense of this fortified Belgian city. In April 1915, they unleashed poison gas for the first time in the war, trying to break through the British in the middle of the salient at the village of St. Juliens. The German attack drove the British line back but did not achieve breakthrough.

As at Ypres, so all along the front: while their fortified positions allowed the Germans the luxury of the strategic defensive, the Germany army, now under Falkenhayn, maintained its aggressive attitude and attacked at hundreds of points on the Western Front throughout the war, and certainly throughout 1915. Indeed, like the Allies, the Germans sought both to keep pressure on the enemy and at times to break through. In doing so, they had recognized that the growing bombardments of the line would be insufficient to achieve the latter. By early 1915 the Germans had already begun to develop new technologies designed to break the deadlock, introducing the flamethrower against the French north of Belfort in February 1915. Poison gas then appeared when the Germans used it in April, and the British and French rapidly deployed their own. Other "techniques" soon followed.

Breakthrough was, naturally, even more important for the Allies, since expelling the Germans had to be the strategic goal of all Allied armies. Influenced to an even greater degree by the dictates of offensive-mindedness, the French armies practically never stopped attacking at some point on their massive sector of the Western Front, which amounted to five-sixths of the whole line during the first two years of the war. A glance at the French record of attack for 1915 demonstrates the extent to which the French commander, Joffre, was unwilling to accept stalemate. Beginning in mid-December 1914 with large-scale multidivisional assaults in the center of the front, in Artois and Champagne, French attacks continued unabated. In early January, the French introduced into the bitter struggles for the wooded hills of the Argonne forest (between Reims and Verdun) a new breakthrough technique: tunneling under the German trenches (in this case about 600 yards of the front), putting tons of high explosives under the them, and blowing them up as the preliminary to an assault. This technique soon became standard on both sides, as we shall see. The French, like all the other Western Front armies, introduced crude hand grenades during the early months of 1915, likewise in the attempt to give soldiers some way of breaking the tyranny of the fortified trenches they were attacking. On top of all this, French counterattacks against the Germans at the mountainous Vieil Armand (Hartmannswillerkopf), north of Belfort (on the southern end of the front), amounted to large-scale offensive operations. For the French, this year of probing the limits of trench stalemate cost dearly: over 340,000 Frenchmen died on the Western Front in 1915.[11]

This willingness of French commanders to hold to the prewar doctrines of furious attack and the willingness of French soldiers to continue going over the top supplies us with a crucial piece of the background in understanding the behavior of all the participants in the war. As we shall see, British, German, and later even American decisions are hardly intelligible without taking into account the fact that the war was being fought mostly on French soil and, in the French view, mostly by Frenchmen. Certainly the French launched more attacks and suffered more casualties than any other participant on the Western Front, and throughout the war – as in the first great crisis of the war in August 1914 – fellow Allies looked weak and even cowardly to French commanders who assumed without question the necessity of expending enormous numbers of troops in a struggle of survival for France. They demonstrated their devotion to this style of warfare throughout 1915 in furious attacks, chiefly in the Artois and the Champagne, with heavy losses.

The British might have fought some kind of aggressive holding operation through 1915 but for these enormous efforts of the French. Joffre's view of the British commander, Sir John French, as being too hesitant to attack was already well established. Further, the BEF of 1914 had survived the fighting of the late summer, but only as a skeleton, and the British mobilization of Western Front-sized forces was only just underway.

This mobilization was significant. By way of comparison, the peacetime German army of 1914 was 880,000 and grew by mobilization to 4.5 million. The French prewar standing force was 823,000 and grew after July 1914 to 3.78 million. The only major power not practicing peacetime conscription, Britain could count among the full-time professional regiments and "territorial" (militia) units about 255,000, of which just over 100,000 were brought to bear as the original BEF.

Mobilized, the British army of late fall could count just over 700,000 men at home and abroad, of whom less than 150,000 were in France and Belgium. Hence, in order to meet the needs of the densely populated battle fronts in Western Europe and elsewhere, Britain had to transform its whole recruiting process.

This presented fewer problems of numbers than of training, for the massive outpouring of patriotism – perhaps assisted by a substantial economic slump during the summer of 1914 – in the war's first days had led to the voluntary enlistment of 439,000 during the first five weeks of the war. The great wave of enlistments abated in September, and the House of Commons voted to raise a "second" 500,000. By December 1915 nearly 2.5 million Britons had enlisted – all without legal compulsion – in their country's military forces. Hence, numbers were no problem for the moment, but the organization and training of this mass of people (over 5 percent of a population of 46.4 million), as well as the dislocations occasioned by this great influx, probably impacted the home and battle fronts about equally.[12]

The job of training the collected human material into fighting units was overseen by Lord Kitchener. Hurriedly appointed by Asquith as War Minister on August 5, the gruff Kitchener, Britain's most revered soldier, was immediately faced with a gargantuan task. Predicting to the wondering and for once silent cabinet that the war would last for at least several years and cost millions of casualties, Kitchener revealed plans for an army far larger and more complex than the existing force.[13] His demands for many "hundred thousands" of recruits and the necessary housing and sustenance, not to mention the training, strained not only the administration of the British army, but the whole of British society as well, since the rapid creation of this army drew masses of laborers from industry and masses of goods that would have gone to the export market. The result was confusing for the army and really disastrous for the long-term health of the British economy. Moreover, as historian Gerard De Groot has put it, the Asquith government's plan of making changes slowly under the rubric "Business as Usual" was completely undermined by Kitchener's failure to follow carefully laid out prewar plans for possible expansion.[14]

The most spectacular immediate result of Kitchener's rapid expansion plans were the famous "Pals' Battalions," so called because the recruits were promised the chance to train and fight together with their pals – men from their region and often from their locality. Unforeseen was the possibility that a whole city or county might be decimated in a single battle reversal on the Western Front, or the probability that their training and performance would be lacking in some respects.[15]

The British would eventually adopt conscription of forces, though this would be only a part of the solution to the manpower problem, a problem which interconnected the battle front and home front because every soldier was an able-bodied man who was not working at home to produce something for the war effort. The Military Service Act of January 1916 provided for conscription of men of ages 18 to 41, with many exemptions: married men were exempted, as were, among others, Irishmen and clergymen. In April, however, a supplementary act broadened the pool to include married men.

Germany had always had conscription. By the time the army reached full strength in the fall, the Germans had mobilized about 4.5 million troops, or just over 7 percent of the German population of 65 million. Their recruiting effort seems to have been the smoothest among the original Western Front powers, probably because the German army's system of cantonal organization and permanent regional organization of corps only had to accelerate a system of conscription, recruiting, training, logistics, and administration that had long been in place.

French offensive planning had not envisioned the need for such a rapid mobilization. From a large peacetime army of over 823,000, the French mobilized to nearly 3.8 million, nearly 10 percent of the population. In spite of confusion, the results are difficult to argue with: the Schlieffen Plan armies ground to a halt against masses of French troops whose casualty figures in brutal counterattacks against the Germans were simply astronomical.

All of the above supplies background to what we can see as the growing necessity – militarily and politically – for "breakthrough" over the course of 1915 and early 1916. The British government was finding that "Business as Usual" was difficult to maintain in the face of a massive war. The casualties which the French were sustaining, though not publicized, began to be felt in the heartland, chipping away at the popular enthusiasm, though it seems that until well into 1916, the ebbing of enthusiasm left not discontent but simply a stoic acceptance of the war. The groundbreaking historical work of Jean-Jacques Becker has shown that discontent with the war in 1915 was centered in cities and expressed chiefly in connection with the rising prices of food and fuel. France's army was regionally recruited, and the accidents of war had thrust the regiments of some regions into more and worse battles; casualties were therefore higher, and a higher percentage of the population was actually grieving for lost kin. Yet it is clear that grieving did not translate into opposition, protest, or even much complaint. Not only were the decades-long efforts of Paris to imbue all French with intense patriotism paying off, but the economics of rising prices worked in favor of farmers and the agricultural economy. As a schoolmaster from a rural province wrote at the time: "The union sacrée is at work here as it is in the entire region." As Becker has shown, France, especially rural France, "settled down stolidly to the war."[16]

If some sectors of the population were settling down to war, it was clear to both the military and civilian leadership that a continued war of stalemate would draw on resources to an extent unprecedented in history. Leaders in all sectors therefore became intent on breaking through, if not No Man's Land, at the least the impasse of war, stagnation, higher prices, the beginnings of shortages, and the continuing tolls of death.

The Political Economy of Artillery Shells

On the battle front, in spite some short-term successes of the new "terror" weapons such as gas and flame, it was clear that reintroducing a war of maneuver would take more explosives. From the first days of the war, when artillery reduced seemingly powerful Belgian forts, there could be no doubt that artillery would be the pivotal weapon in land warfare for the foreseeable future. Artillery ranged in size from small special-use guns designed for mountain terrain and firing shells less than an inch in diameter and a few inches long, up to huge guns mounted far behind the lines on concrete platforms or railroad cars. The largest could fire a shell 16.5 inches (420 mm) in diameter. Some huge guns could hurl shells weighing nearly 2,000 lb. over ten miles. Most guns were of course smaller, but the progression of the war would be not only to increase the number of guns on the Western Front but also to increase the weight of guns and shells so as to achieve much greater explosive force on a given area. Soldiers on the Western Front developed uncanny abilities to interpret the sounds of a wide range of rocketing shells, and to name them (Whizzbangs, or Freight Cars, for example) appropriately.

Explosives, explosions, and artillery would become both symbol and motor of the war in a way unlike previous conflicts. Some "industrial" activity had been a part of European warfare as early as the Renaissance, but by and large, even with the growing artillery trains of nineteenth-century wars, the manufacture of shells was a relatively small national expenditure. This changed in part as shells themselves became more complex in the last years of the nineteenth century. Far from the "cannonballs" of primitive artillery, artillery shells had grown by 1914 into sophisticated mechanisms. In some shells, an essentially hollow projectile was filled with one of the newer "high-explosive" compounds (TNT, for example). In "shrapnel" shells the hollow tip was packed with explosives and metal balls, designed as secondary "projectiles," though most shells gave off some form of flying metal simply from the exploded hollow shell casing. Fuses had become a vital part of the explosive effect, since it would make little sense to fire an exploding shell which expended most of its force while it burrowed into the ground. Indeed, here artillery shells combined the home-front arts of proper shell design and manufacture with the battle-front science of adjusting the height at which the shell exploded and improving the margin of error in the aim and delivery of the shells.

Of the millions of explosions that churned up dirt clouds, blew men to bits, and in varying degrees shattered the nerves of most who served on the Western Front, each shell was an item that had been put together partly by hand in assembly lines at home (increasingly by female hands as time went on), carried by rail, ship, wagon, and finally by hand or handcart to battery sites at only a short remove from the front, and loaded into the artillery piece and fired by a crew of perhaps a half-dozen men, depending on the size and weight of the artillery piece. Hence, the home and battle fronts worked together. For all any artillerist knew, his wife might have helped assemble the shell he fired onto targets across No Man's Land. For all any soldier in the front lines knew, the shell screaming overhead toward the enemy had been handled by his sweetheart. In Britain, as 5.5 million men were mobilized into the armed forces, and as munitions production rose, the munitions industry rapidly recruited a female labor force that would amount to well over a million women by 1918.[17]

But the web of connections which shells created between home and battle fronts hardly ends here. In the French case, for example, prewar planning had envisioned firing off 13,000 shells a day. In the autumn of 1914, actual consumption was 120,000 shells a day. And in the battles of 1915, preparatory shelling raised consumption still higher. British factories delivered about 1.4 million shells during the first five months of the war. From January to June 1915, shell deliveries nearly doubled, to 2.3 million. During the second half of 1915, deliveries jumped to 5.3 million, and during early 1916 to 13 million. During the second half of 1916, in the Somme Offensive, the British army took delivery of over 35 million shells. Hence, the number of shells had increased by a factor of 25. Size of the average shell had also grown: total tonnage of shells increased during the same period by a factor of 36.[18] The colossal slaughters of the year 1916 would raise all these figures to similar astronomical levels.

The nexus between the firing of shells on the battle front and producing, moving, and (above all) paying for them presents a real study in battle front–home front connections. The model for war emergencies that would impact home fronts drastically was the British "Shell Scandal" of 1915. This scandal arose directly from the Battle of Neuve Chapelle, a mere three-day blip in Western Front history, but an episode which neatly demonstrates the network of relations that determined the dynamic of the war. In early 1915, Joffre launched a major offensive in the Champagne, well to the southeast of the British sector, but in so doing, he needed two of his corps that were occupying a piece of the front between the Belgians and British, north of Ypres (in turn, Joffre's offensive had the general purpose of relieving German pressure on the Russians). An important component of Joffre's offensive was to be a British "spoiling" attack (an attack designed to disrupt the enemy's response to the primary attack) north of Arras. The British forces designated to relieve Joffre's corps were delayed in the process of preparing the assault on Gallipoli in February, and Joffre was once again disappointed with the British. In March, however, Sir John French finally made his move: ringed about with critics (including Kitchener himself) and feeling the constant reproach of the French, the BEF commander gave the go-ahead to his First Army commander, Douglas Haig, to attack on a section of the front just north of La Bassée, the junction of British and French sectors at this time.

Haig organized a textbook attack, using two British divisions and two Indian divisions. The first stage of the attack would be the capture of the village of Neuve Chapelle (about 100 yards behind the German fire trench), on which the four divisions were to converge (from the north and east). The village captured, the four divisions were to face south, drive the Germans across a flat field for about a kilometer, then take the Bois de Biez, a hill which was the key to the low Aubers Ridge. The result would be possession of a strong point which would enable the British to peer into the German lines for a change.

The First Army attacked along the outer two sides of an L, across a three-kilometer front, on the morning of March 10, 1915. The Meerut Division of the Indian Corps and the British 8th division converged and took the still intact Neuve Chapelle, fighting house-to-house at the end. A few hours from jump-off, the First Army was working its way toward the Aubers Ridge, but a German machine-gun post on the British left and stiff defense (including one nineteenth-century-style counterattack) by the Germans rendered every attempt to assault the ridge a failure (Hitler, incidentally, may have been serving on that ridge).[19] A year later, artillery "preparation" would have left no village to fight through, and the Aubers Ridge – whether taken or not – would have become an exploding inferno before a single battalion attacked. But the British did not saturate the ridge with shells, in part because they had used up their supply. The attack had gained two square kilometres at the cost of about 13,000 casualties, but it had used up 15 percent of the BEF's whole stock of ammunition.[20]

Since early in the war, David Lloyd George and Lord Kitchener, both on the Shells Committee, had maintained a simmering conflict which turned on the question of whether civilian or military authorities would hold the upper hand in war planning. By February 1915, Lloyd George declared, "All the engineering works of the country ought to be turned to the production of war material. The population ought to be prepared to suffer all sorts of deprivations and even hardships whilst this process is going on." This declaration was aimed at Kitchener and the "quartermaster" mindset in the War Office, but it was likewise a pronouncement that British Liberals would no longer adhere to the traditional respect for the autonomy of individuals and the whole *laissez-faire* tradition.[21] The rigid Kitchener fought Lloyd George throughout the spring, but other problems (for example an analogous struggle between the First Sea Lord, Lord Fisher, and his political superior Winston Churchill) led to more acrimony within the cabinet. By mid-May, the Liberal cabinet was at an end, and the prime minister agreed to head a coalition government to include the conservatives, in theory a kind of equivalent to the *Union sacrée* or the *Burgfrieden*.[22]

It was in this context that the Shell Scandal broke. Though Sir John French had in fact run out of shells at Neuve Chapelle, by April he was hearing reports that Kitchener himself had publicly asserted that there was no shortage of shells. On the recommendation of the great press eminence, Lord Northcliffe, French then turned to an old friend and journalist, Charles Repington. In mid-May, Repington released a story describing the lack of shells on the front. The idea that British lads were facing long odds without even proper artillery support was too much for a public already beginning to tally the costs of the war at home. This crisis played an important role in the creation of the coalition government and in a broader sense an assault on the "Business as Usual" policy, whose demise would eventually bring a restructuring of British society. For the moment, it led to the increased influence of David Lloyd George within the warmaking establishment as he became the first head of an iconoclastic agency called the Ministry of Munitions.[23]

Within a few months of the war's outbreak, all the Western Front countries were facing "shell scandals" or "shell crises" of one kind or another. And in each case, the solutions eventually chosen and the men eventually put in charge of the solutions were calculated to introduce compulsion throughout the economy in order to see to it that the army had enough artillery shells. In a sense, therefore, to look at the shell crises is to look at both process and textbook for the broader growth of governments, or perhaps better said, the state itself during World War I. The shell scandals seemed to demonstrate to leading elites that the old order of open government and open economies was ill suited to the massive and complex structures of the twentieth-century society at war. It would call up from the ranks of government, business, and education individuals who could look through the other end of the telescope, individuals who saw the crisis not as one of having to stop the new warfare before it ate up the lives of a generation and substance of a nation, but rather as a situation which called for a solution in the form of the new organization of society and government itself. In a word, they saw the problem not as an insurmountable stalemate, but as a temporary situation in which "breakthrough" could be achieved by innovation, by rethinking the whole "management" of society.

From 1913 to 1917, British government spending rose by a factor of 14, German spending in the same period by a factor of 15. French increases rose "only" by a factor of 5 or 6 during this time. How to pay for it all?[24] Whereas European leaders since Machiavelli had pondered how to increase the revenues of the government without starting a revolt that would lead to the foundering of the state itself, the new generation of Western leaders looking at the fiscal problem felt it could be solved in part by using the exigencies of the war and war enthusiasm itself as the opportunity simply to increase the government's share of the GNP by increasing revenues. In the short term, this was done, as will be seen below, by confiscation, by tax increases, by borrowing, and above all by various inflationary measures which resulted in the silent transfer of wealth from individual to public coffers.

Actually, the question had to be qualified: how to pay for it without alienating the population, on whose motivation the whole effort hung.[25] Hence, all governments tended to shy away from outright taxation, since the obvious unpopularity of taxes would vitiate other "mobilization" efforts. Still, tax rates went up in most cases. Direct personal taxes in Australia, Canada, and Italy underwent only small increases during the war. Those of France, Germany, the United States, and especially Britain rose steeply enough to leave a permanently higher expectation of tax rates after the war. In Britain, tax rates just before the war averaged 9 percent, just after the war 27. These rates do not reflect indirect taxes, which certainly contributed much to the high increases in the cost of living experienced in all belligerent countries, increases which ranged from 250 percent to much higher.[26]

All in all, then, artillery shells and stalemate demonstrate something of the complexity of connections binding the home front to the battle front. It is clear that the shell scandals and related pressures for breakthrough led to actual breakthrough in the levels of governmental increases in tax burdens, and more generally in the French and British cases to departures from liberal economies, at least in the direction of the planned economies of the future.

Life on the Front

Let us turn to the trenches themselves, the 400-mile parallel trench system of the stalemated front where men actually did – in a kind of echo of Hobbes – live in caves. We have so far dealt with trench warfare in military terms, but in attempting to gauge the impact of the Western Front on the twentieth century, one must understand it in personal terms as well. Indeed, any study of the Western Front must include at least some kind of environmental evaluation of the trenches, and some of the best recent work on World War I starts from close examination of that environment. In the broad view, it is important to make explicit that full-scale battle was never continuous across the Western Front. Intensity of fighting moved from spot to spot, though local, small-scale aggression was always a possibility. Neither side, however, had the resources to support offensives along the whole front for any period of time, at least until the very end of the war.

Moreover, the trenches passed through many kinds of terrain. Beginning at the Channel coast near Nieuport, the "trenches" were rarely trenches at all for the first few miles, because the water table of Belgian Flanders was so high that any digging at all produced water-filled holes. It is true that some vicious fighting took place across flooded fields in 1914, and that these fields remained flooded throughout the war, but for the long term, occupying water-filled positions was simply impossible. Positions on both sides close to the Flanders coast tended to be built from the ground up, with sandbags and, occasionally, concrete.

The land in Flanders rises slowly toward the south and east, but it does rise, so that a few miles away from the coast, trenches were possible. From about Dixmuide to Loos, one finds the low-lying, poorly drained fields where mud was so much a fact of life. Around Ypres in particular, enormous amounts of shelling disrupted the natural and artificial drainage systems and created still more mud than one finds in the region today. The mud that exists in our mental depictions of the front was most prevalent on this northwestern end. Once the line crossed from Flanders into Picardy, higher and hillier (and chalky) ground meant that trenches held shape better, the land tended to drain properly, and the comfort level could be at least somewhat higher. Indeed, from Picardy onward, the line ran through first low hills, then high ones: through the Champagne and then the Argonne, on the way to the great turning of the front at Verdun. In fact, between Reims and Verdun, the hills became precipitous, the earth dark and good for trenches and tunneling.[27] South of Verdun, the lines cut through rolling land and eventually the Vosges mountains, right across really rugged terrain, like the Hartmannswillerkopf (or Vieil Armand) north of Belfort, where regular trenches were impossible to make. Still farther south the line reverted to trenches and stretched all the way to the Swiss border, ending in rolling fields and forests, much like the bulk of the front.

The Belgians, with their remnant army, manned the first 12 miles of the front, south of which they held a short stretch. The British covered 27 miles of the line during the first months, gradually extending southward to the River Somme in Picardy by 1916, to hold nearly 60 miles. The French held everything south of the British, early on about 340 miles of the front. That would gradually change as the British and, after 1917, the Americans took over previously French sectors; but even in 1918, the French still held the lion's share of the Western Front.

Though there were some important "national" differences in the trenches, for the most part they adhered to the same pattern.[28] To understand what "the front" meant in World War I, we must envision a configuration on each side of No Man's Land consisting of three roughly parallel trenches, from 50 to 500 yards apart. The front trench, or fire trench, in the Anglo-American armies, fronted the lethal No Man's Land. Some distance behind it, from 50 to 100 yards (much farther for the Germans), was a second trench line, the support trench, and beyond that, at some 100 or more yards, lay a third trench, the reserve trench. These three lines were connected front to rear with various "communications" trenches, which ultimately led far to the rear and out of the trenches. In terms of function, the fire trench, up front, represented the first defenders against any attack and was peopled by enlisted men and the most junior officers; from the next line, the support trench, the commanders at the company and battalion level could direct the defenses of the first line and keep forces for immediate reinforcement. They could, finally, call on the reserve trenches, farther back, for units and equipment.

Every trench on the Western Front was full of crooks, turns, and zig-zags. These turns served a vital practical purpose: to avoid the possibility of the enemy firing down the length of a straight trench and the possibility of shell blasts being funneled by the trench itself onto men far down the line. In fact, most trenches being used by careful units with high morale were "traversed," that is, dug with a box turn – or fire bay – at intervals, so as to isolate shell blast further. Dirt from the trenches was thrown forward, forming a hump, or parapet, sometimes held in place with sandbags.

The "front line" thus presented not simply two opposing trenches, but two opposing networks of trenches, which tended, as the war went on, to consist of more and more parallels, becoming deeper and deeper, to reflect ideas on all sides about the value of "defence in depth."

What was life like in the trenches? First and foremost, it was dangerous. Yet the danger varied greatly and depended on many variables. Though there was much firing of weapons at all times in most sectors, battle, in the sense of attacking or receiving an attack, was really an unusual event for trench fighters. The typical British soldier was unlikely to have taken a direct part in more than two or three big attacks during the war, and some veterans of the Western Front never went "over the top." Perhaps French and German soldiers would have attacked or received attacks slightly more frequently, but not much. On the other hand, speaking of the "typical" soldier can be misleading. Some units, especially those known for their aggressiveness (like the Prussian Guards, Royal Guards, or other elite units), might well be involved in many more "shows." In comparing armies, one could probably say that French soldiers, *poilus*, tended to have more experience attacking partly because French tactical doctrine relied so much on attack or counterattack, and partly because until the 1917 mutiny, French soldiers received hardly any leave time at all. Soldiers of all armies stood a good chance of leaving the front because of wounds.

Here it is important to understand that most wounds were not fatal: even in the classic head-on attack, about a third of casualties represented deaths (or "missing," which more often than not meant "dead"). Hence, most Western Front memoirs include at least one or two cycles of being wounded out and coming back when healed. Indeed, the ratios of those recovering from wounds improved throughout the war as Western Front military medical support components learned how to handle casualties, how to cut down on sepsis, and – insofar as it could be done – how to get the wounded out of No Man's Land.[29]

In times when attacks were not on, or in a quiet sector, casualties were low simply because men were in trenches, which, after all, were constructed for protection. Soldiers learned immediately that any exposed body part was likely to be fired on by snipers. For this simple reason, they tried to keep out of sight, spending their week to ten-day shifts in the front lines in a world of dirt walls and open sky. Indeed, one of the most striking aspects to trench fighters was that most soldiers saw the enemy only very rarely, even through any of a large variety of trench periscopes.

Peopled by young men from many different countries, the trenches – and the whole process leading up to their construction – produced national variations of a new kind of personality: known as the Tommy, the *poilu*, the Doughboy, and other nicknames. The comradeship of the trenches formed a powerful bond among these soldiers, who were experiencing a warfare that they regarded as indescribable at home. It was an age in which polite middle-class and even working-class young men conceptualized the feminine world of home and hearth as a sphere separate from the hard realities of "real life"(Conrad's characters in *Heart of Darkness*, for example, cover the hard facts of greed and insanity with heroic euphemisms when faced with the feminine, middle-class world). Trench fighters could hardly tell the whole truth at home, even if they wanted to horrify their families, which many clearly did not. Moreover, if the battles of World War I created nightmarish personal experiences, it is likewise clear that for many of the predominantly young men on the Western Front, the most unpleasant aspect of trench warfare was the unending nightly hard labor assignments, known in English-speaking armies as "fatigues." Indeed, when a "show" was not in the offing, life devolved into a very difficult routine of boring days and exhausting nights while in the trenches.

All these characteristics of trench existence led to a closeness on the front which defied many of the currents of modern Western life. Where individuals from different classes might not come into close contact in normal civilian life, in the trenches, classes not only intermingled but lived together. It is true that officers and "other ranks" or "enlisted men" carried out an official separation that reflected feudal vestiges in modern military practice, but even here the divisions began to fall out differently. On the front, officers at company and battalion levels, especially the subalterns or lieutenants, tended to identify more with the sufferings of their men (most of which they were undergoing themselves), while officers in the rear areas, the headquarters, the "rear echelon," became increasingly regarded as the real enemy, even in the case of lower-level staff officers who might be outranked by officers in infantry battalions. It is not true that no generals ever saw the front lines, but it is true that "red tabs" were a rarity in the trenches, that many generals and staff officers at times had little idea of true conditions and that in any case soldiers on the front *believed* that staff officers led a comfortable and even pampered life.

"Smile, Smile, Smile"

Given this Hobbesian world, where, one might say, men "lived in caves," and in which at least several times in their tenure with the army, infantry soldiers would be ordered to go "over the top" in a big "show" and cross a storm of steel (in German trench fighter Ernst Jünger's phrase) to get to the enemy, we are compelled to ask why millions of men who were ordered to engage in such a lethal activity would actually go through with it. One answer is that life was in a sense more difficult for the average person in Europe and the West in 1900 than in 2000. Trench work was hard, but perhaps not so much harder than work back home. Meals were relatively steady. Men were accustomed to doing what they were told. Indeed, if they did not, they stood a good chance of being shot for cowardice. Many, perhaps most, were also appalled at the "dishonor" involved in not following orders. The bourgeois societies of the Western Front countries, so much criticized by literary elites in their own day and by sophisticated intellectuals in ours, consisted of a high percentage of individuals with a highly developed sense of duty on the one hand and an equally developed sense of shame on the other. Hence, when soldiers were ordered to go over the top in the Great War, they usually went.

Though we have seen that the Western Front was a different world, partly kept so by the reticence of the soldiers themselves, from "Blighty," "back home," or "zu Hause." But we have also seen that nothing could prevent all kinds of connections between the battle front and the home front from being maintained and continually forged and reforged. The coherence of life on both fronts was dependent in some measure on the degree to which the warring populations were willing to pay for it all. It is clear that twentieth-century forms of mass persuasion were in the offing among the belligerent societies, even at the outset of the Great War, and the governments were not backward at all in recognizing the importance of controlling information and shaping public opinion. Censorship was part and parcel of all the societies at war, as we will examine in greater detail below.

It is, however, important to say here that not all the war enthusiasm resulted from some grand design of the warring governments. The reality was far more complex: society and culture – shaped by the emotional patriotism of the prewar period – bought into war enthusiasm in many ways and for many reasons.[30] We might scratch the surface of this vast topic with a brief look at popular songs during the war, limiting ourselves for the most part to English-language songs.

Europeans had for centuries been engaged on one end of society in singing "folk" songs, and on the other end in listening to the productions of practiced professionals. Improved standards of living through the nineteenth century had broadened the audiences at the "high" cultural end somewhat, but the emergence of the "great middle class" had also led to a process analogous to the production of the formula fiction of mass periodicals and "dime novels." This music, "popular" in all senses, expressed itself in the "polite" music of parlour playing (and the piano, and hence sheet music, were integral in middle-class culture) as well as the not so polite, and much more male-oriented, songs of the music hall, an institution which had emerged to fill the new-found leisure hours of the masses and to become one of the first "entertainment industries," bringing in profit from the increasing disposable incomes of Western workers. Moreover, Europeans sang not just in parlours and music halls, but in school, in church, at every conceivable social gathering, and on various public occasions as well. Many of the entertainers were also at this moment successfully translating their skills to the new technology of phonographic reproductions and thereby expanded potential markets to even greater segments of the public. The war broke out at a moment when Europeans still sang and still listened to live music regularly, but when phonographs had begun to become a known commodity for broader consumption.

Perhaps the most spectacular example of a song which reflected war enthusiasm and at the same time was tied into these cultural tendencies was "Tipperary," a song which came to be closely associated with the Irish tenor John McCormack, and one which became an essential war song among English-speaking troops in the war and a significant home front song as well. Written by English songwriters Harry Wills and Jack Judge four years before the war, the song had nothing to do with battle and national pride, but it is devoted to homesickness and love. It is, rather, a humorous song about the immigration of "Paddy," a young Irishman, to London, and his correspondence with his fickle love back in Tipperary. The verses are in the light vein of music-hall style, but the chorus – drawing on the effectively sentimental style of Celtic folk music – manages to resonate in a much more serious way.

> It's a long way to Tipperary,
> It's a long way to go.
> It's a long way to Tipperary
> To the sweetest girl I know.
> Good-bye Piccadilly,
> Farewell Leicester Square,
> It's a long long way to Tipperary,
> But my heart's right there.

Jack Judge, a well-known entertainer in London music halls (an Englishman of Irish background), was apparently the primary creator of the song.[31] Though the song had absolutely nothing to do with the escalating problems of Irish nationalism and British recalcitrance, in fact, the chorus seems to make some vague but conciliatory connections between Tipperary and London. When one remembers extreme tension between Ireland and England in the summer preceding the war, a song in which people are just people, and where barriers between the two sides seem less than insurmountable, was indeed timely.

Performed and published in printed form before the war, the song reached the status of immortality partly through the agency of one of the greatest singers of the century, John McCormack. In the years just before the war, the Irish McCormack had just begun to earn the enormous international reputation on the opera and concert stages which would be associated with him for the next 30 years, but the *bel canto* tenor had already devised a formula for mixing his own amazing talents at the high cultural end of music with the presentation of both folk songs (especially Irish ones) and other popular songs. Hence, McCormack's recording of "Tipperary" with RCA Victor in New York on November 23, 1914 brought together a number of powerful currents of popular culture. Both his legendary ability to express emotion musically and his work, later in the war, for the Allied war effort probably added to the intensity with which "Tipperary" was admired and adopted. It was recorded by many other artists and imitated, in frequently trivial form, many times over. On the Western Front, soldiers listened to the song, sang it, and imitated it in versions too many to count.

Like "Tipperary," many of the songs adopted by soldiers derived from the immediate prewar period and had no specific warlike connections. This was the case with the most popular French wartime song, "Quand Madelon." Like most of the other popular songs of the period, "Quand Madelon" was written by music-hall entertainers and came in the form of a compelling tune. "Madelon" is a simple but beautiful waitress, the object of every young man's affection. She doesn't succumb to anyone, but "We dream of her by night. We think of her by day." As Charles Rearick has pointed out in an excellent analysis of "Quand Madelon," the angelic waitress represented perhaps the rarefied contrast to the woman with whom the *poilus* usually trafficked: the *Rose-à-lit* ("Rose in bed"), the denizen of the army brothels whose business could consist of 60 "customers" a day. Indeed, "Quand Madelon" may have represented, especially after the mid-war demoralizations, a kind of ironic, oppositional expression that eschewed the government-sponsored songs of sacrifice and nobility, admiring instead a simple waitress. Like Tipperary, "Quand Madelon" bridged the gap between the home front and the battle front. By the last year and a half of the war (concurrent with the real crises in both army and society, as we shall see), the song was taking Paris music halls by storm, an indication that many were hearing the song, as Rearick has written, "in stark contrast to the war-sick mutineer and the sexual predator or patron of prostitutes."[32]

Similarly striking in its contrast to the violence of the war was the almost fatuously optimistic "Pack Up Your Troubles," whose enormous popularity during the war has resulted in lingering familiarity with the song more than 80 years afterwards, especially the first line: "Pack up your troubles in your old kit bag/And smile, smile, smile." Though the reference to a "kit bag" lends a soldierly mood to the song, it was written by Felix and George Henry Powell in 1912, another male-oriented, march-like music-hall tune. Ladies of the prewar period were hardly expected to respond either to the tobacco use or the tobacco slang of the first verse:

> While you've a lucifer to light your fag,
> Smile boys, that's the style.
> What's the use of worrying,
> It never was worthwhile. So:
> Pack up your troubles in your old kit bag
> And smile, smile, smile.

Indeed, the devil-may-care affectations of the music hall were likewise largely in the male domain. Still, carried into the war context and properly "edited" to bring out the more sacrificial overtones of "smile, smile, smile," the song was widely sung on both the battle front and the increasingly dreary home fronts, perhaps an earlier electronic analog of efforts during the Great Depression to produce lightweight and optimistic acceptance of the unbearable.

While John McCormack put his stamp on "Tipperary" and many other rousing songs sung by English-speaking troops, the song most frequently mentioned to him in later life as having been of special significance was the sentimental "Mother Machree." As McCormack's wife, Lily, wrote in later years: "One summer in World War II we met General Victor Odlum . . . of the Canadian Army. . . . General Odlum told John he had taken his records *Ave Maria* and *Mother Machree* everywhere with him during World War I; and neither John nor I had dry eyes when he described what these records meant to him and to his men."[33] Indeed, while soldiers and their relatives clearly sang state-promoted and state-sponsored songs and anthems like "Deutschland über Alles," "The Caissons Go Rolling Along," "Neuve Chapelle," and others, for the most part, memories of the war hang on sweet, sentimental ballads like "Mother Machree" and "There's a Long, Long Trail A-Winding." Rare is the German, or indeed even British soldier's memoir or diary that omits mention of German soldiers singing "Stille Nacht" – "Silent Night" – in the trenches; the famous Christmas Truce of 1914 began with the mutual singing of that and other Christmas songs. In fact, those songs with explicit war themes which survived both into modern consciousness and in memoirs are really less bellicose and emphasize the pathos of war. Hence, songs such as "Keep the Home Fires Burning" and "Hello Central, Give Me No Man's Land."

With the United States in the war in early 1917, Americans entered swiftly into the war culture. The British songs became American wartime favorites. Moreover, the same process of refitting older songs to suit the times took place. A popular 1908 song extolling the U.S. Army artillery was rearranged by the greatest public musician in the United States, John Philip Sousa (head of the U.S. Marine Band). Both popular musical genius and capable impresario, Sousa wrote a march into which he incorporated "The Caissons Go Rolling Along." Perhaps the quintessential American song of war reflected the intense domestic debate over whether the United States should be in the war at all and perhaps celebrated the decision for war in April 1917. "Over There" was rapidly disseminated in the usual ways: sheet music, public performance, phonograph recordings. The refrain summoned up, both in lyrics and melody, an emotional connection based on the idea that the United States had reluctantly accepted a hard job and intended to finish it, come what may.

> We'll be over; we're coming over
> And we won't come back
> 'Til it's over over there!

This discussion of wartime songs is necessarily brief, and we have to pass without comment on the thousands of ephemeral songs that gave a new lease on life to the popular sheet-music trade and the growing phonograph business. Nor have we discussed the activities of the great popular musicians who supported the war effort in various ways:

McCormack, for example, devoted much time to the cause of the war in the United States, especially in giving concerts to promote war bonds; and the great Sousa himself wrote at least nine marches directly related to World War I during this period, including the less than immortal "Liberty Loan March" (1917). Nor have we thrown into the mix the countless parodies and soldiers' songs which emerged from the trenches and almost always reflected by their ironies the knowledge of the gap between actual conditions and home-front conceptions of sacrifice and bravery. Indeed, these parodies were carried out, in seeming appropriateness with their male-oriented milieu, in the most ribald and explicitly sexual forms. This was in keeping with processes of the war we will examine below.[34]

No doubt the governments of the Western Front powers hoped to shape the attitudes of their societies through musical culture, but in the end, the official promotion of patriotic songs and entertainments for soldiers probably had only fleeting effects on wartime popular culture. It seems clear, though, that the song culture of the Western Front countries demonstrated a kind of rallying effect, and one which was undoubtedly influenced by traditional patriotism as well as the desire of conformity to what seemed to be public opinion.[35]

To sum up, songs represented *and* formed multiple emotional cultural links between the home and battle fronts. They served to help men get through physical discomfort and homesickness. They served as a religious comfort, since many of them had religious overtones that suggested life after death. They gave societies a sense of unity. They helped people endure what seemed unendurable. And in the end they help us recognize both the power of emotional and cultural bonds at that time and the extent to which such cultural bonds had become attached to the modern nation-state.

4

INNOVATION, PERSUASION, CENTRALIZATION

Maverick American intellectual Randolph Bourne wrote in the midst of the great conflict that "war is the health of the state."[1] Without question, the Western Front belligerent societies give powerful evidence of this aphorism: even the defeated would, after the war, draw on wartime behaviors and structures to fashion their new states. In fact, the governments of the defeated might fall, but their states would prove to be significantly strengthened in many ways. The victorious powers could point to their new modes of governance and management with the pride of survivors. This chapter departs from the general "narrative" of the war to examine a number of smaller "narratives" – we might look at these as subplots or different perspectives – which help us take the measure of the range of relationships between the home front and the battle front in World War I.

The Political Economy of the Stalemate War

The illusions of the short war went up in the smoke of the shell explosions of 1915. Every belligerent government now had to face the problem of long-range war planning and intervention into the national economy.

In France, for example, up to 1914, the most highly regarded French economists proudly pointed to French economic individualism as the path to an efficient and bountiful economic order. Still, as elsewhere, the nationalist policies of higher tariffs and more state intervention had begun to make substantial inroads.[2] In any case, the French government, staggered by the immediacy of the war crisis, rapidly gave

104

up what was left of the liberal economic approach. It was munitions that opened the door for structural changes. As a part of the *Union sacrée* in 1914, the coalition cabinet included a broad array of parties, including the Socialists. As Minister of Munitions, Socialist Albert Thomas soon began to take on role very similar to that which Lloyd George assumed in Britain. Thomas became Under-Secretary for Artillery and Military Equipment in May 1915 (within a few days of the creation of Lloyd George's Ministry) and in December 1916, in the wake of the Verdun battle, Minister of Armaments. Like many other war planners, Thomas saw the war crisis on the home front in very positive terms: the war would, he pointed out early, provide the chance for the government to take on a much more activist role in the French economy. Like his German counterparts, Thomas saw the key to improved efficiency of production in centralization and planning. Competition he considered "wasteful," and he organized the planning by means of supporting coordinating committees in each branch of industry.[3]

In essence, the political economy of France moved steadily toward the technocratic welfare state during the war. French labor unions and French businesses suddenly found themselves cooperating closely with the state, or rather competing for its favor, since the mechanics of planning by its nature involves the favoring of one segment of society over another. As with Britain, many of these technocratic measures emerged from the Minister of Armaments. In particular, one of his assistants, former businessman Louis Loucheur, came to the fore in reshaping the wartime economy for maximum "national efficiency."[4]

Since labor was relatively scarce, wages tended to appear high, and many "marginal" groups (in the economic sense) entered the urban labor market, women above all. Women had already taken over an even greater share of the rural work than they were already doing. Constituting nearly half of France, the rural economy was not an insignificant factor. Premier René Viviani had, in fact, made a dramatic call on the second day of the war for women to finish bringing in the harvest so that the menfolk could fight. Yet women had always worked in the French countryside. Added work tended to strain resources, but the high prices now being paid for the products of farms helped sustain the rural economy.

Labor was indeed the key. With several million men serving in uniform and some two million more dead, missing, or wounded by the end of 1915, the French war economy was in need of a workforce. During

1915 almost half a million soldiers with special working skills were withdrawn from the army and brought home to work. This was still not enough. Three other sources provided the needed workforce: neutral countries, where slowed-down economies were resulting in massive unemployment, the French Empire, and the growing pool of German prisoners of war. Completely aside from colonial troops fighting on the Western Front, France hired laborers from the colonies during the course of the war to work in its labor-intensive war economy. Hence, in addition to North African and Senegalese troops on the Western Front, we must also envision an influx of Africans, Southeast Asians, and others into France, especially in the manual-labour-intensive areas just behind the front.

In spite of relatively high demand for labor both in the cities and in the countryside, the inflationary financial regime of the war determined that prices would rise. By late 1915, some necessities of life (in particular, foodstuffs) had risen only little, but some items had tripled or quadrupled in price. The price of bread remained stable during the first year of the war and would not triple until its last. Eggs quadrupled in price in some places by the end of 1915. Potatoes did not triple in price in most places until 1917. Beans doubled in price by the end of 1915. The costs of clothing and fabric rose rapidly: by 1916 a suit of clothes cost nearly four times what it had just before the war. Fuels and metal items rose rapidly in price, quite understandably in light of the high demand for these for military use. Still, though it became more difficult to make ends meet, and though life became drab, research from a variety of sources has shown that the French people were quite patriotic throughout the first two years of the war. Only the dreadful year of 1916 would shake their equanimity, and even then not permanently.[5]

The results of French planning were impressive, especially in light of the size and economic importance of the territories either of the Western Front itself or the piece of northeastern France occupied by the Germans. About three-quarters of France's prewar coal output and over half of its steel production establishment lay behind the Western Front. Overall, of course, paying for the labor needed to keep both the consumer economy and the war economy afloat for over four years was a terrible strain, and as we shall see, the French government, and hence public finances, went into a hole attempting to pay for the war establishment. Still, in the great crisis, France held on.[6]

We have looked briefly at the activities of Lloyd George as Munitions Minister. Even apart from his ministry the emergency called forth many measures that were hardly "usual" in the traditional home of free trade. Immediately upon the outbreak of the war, the government took over the railroads and limited shareholders' profits to the level of 1913. It also prohibited the export of all materials used to make explosives. As early as January 1914, some economists were urging the government to take over the functions of buying and distributing materials to supply war goods factories. The government requisitioned sandbags when a shortage arose early in 1915. Hence, the state was intervening much more actively in the economy in various ways, but not really systematically. Asquith and many others still hoped to run the war by means of piecemeal control at home.[7]

As with the French, the lack of munitions for breakthrough created the crisis that shook the British loose from even lip service to the old liberal economy. It was the Shell Scandal in the wake of the battle of Neuve Chapelle, as described above, that moved the British economy in the direction of centralized control. The scandal ended the Liberal government and brought about a Liberal/Conservative coalition, still under Asquith, which quickly set up a Ministry of Munitions headed by David Lloyd George. This ministry began to direct the basic changes already preparing in British economic life.

If there was a certain logic in the French cabinet turning to a long-time Socialist in cooperation with a businessman-turned-technocrat (Loucheur) to reorient their economy toward central planning, the British architect of the war regime, David Lloyd George, proved, for entirely different reaons, to be suited to the role of altering the economic life of Britain. Born into a Welsh family of Nonconformist religious connections and modest means, Lloyd George represented an outsider who seemed to scruple little at new approaches. Taking the lead in the social reformist wing of the Liberal party, Lloyd George pushed for a number of social and political reforms, and as Chancellor of the Exchequer (from 1905) he championed the Insurance Act and other measures laying the basis for a future welfare state. He was therefore one of the central figures in the creation of a prewar restructuring of liberal Britain into a socially activist state.[8]

His influence in the cabinet helped unify it in the difficult days of the July Crisis. His assessment of Britain's "war government" during the first nine months of the war was that the government was too little active and quite unimaginative. He seemed specially suited to become Minister of Munitions.

Though a number of historians have pointed out the gingerly touch with which Lloyd George and the British government had to approach the creation of a war economy and war society, in fact, wartime social policies were quite sweeping considering the widespread devotion to free trade and *laissez faire* which had remained intact even a decade before the war. Almost as soon as the war began, the Chancellor of the Exchequer had begun to point out the centrality of the economic and financial powers of the nation in the war effort. In the area of munitions supply, he found a launching spot for much more direct intervention by the government than had existed, even in this often semi-public domain. The passage of an extensive augmentation of government powers, the Defence of the Realm Act, in 1915 was important, but as R. J. Q. Adams has pointed out, Lloyd George did the heavy lifting of leading government intervention and influence into supplies, labor, and many other areas of life in which Britons were unaccustomed to seeing the coercive powers of the state.[9]

The leading elites in Germany embraced a more actively interventionist approach from the outset than either France or Britain (and certainly the United States, Canada, and Australia). It occurred to German leaders far earlier than to other Western Front powers that the engagement of the whole of society would require massive planning and control by the government. One reason for this was that the so-called "mixed" form in which German autarkic (self-sufficient) state socialism would emerge during World War I had, in fact, much precedent in the history of Prussia. A long collectivist heritage went hand in hand with escalating government intervention into the economy by means of privileging chosen industries in various ways, setting up wide-ranging protectionist policies, assisting in the building of monopolies and cartels, and maintaining direct government ownership in parts or all of many enterprises.[10]

Less than ten days after the war broke out, Walter Rathenau, industrialist and visionary author, met with the chief of the general staff, conveying the fears of one of his engineers – Wichard von Moellendorff – that metal would be in extremely short supply should the British set up a tight blockade. By August 9, 1914 Rathenau was head of a new War Raw Materials Office within the War Ministry, with Moellendorff as his assistant. The office's function was to organize raw materials production, but its influence would reach far beyond in both its direct and indirect influence. And though Rathenau resigned his position in March

1915, both he and Moellendorff proved influential at the highest levels not only throughout the war, but afterwards; in working to create the centralized social welfare system of the Weimar Republic as well.[11]

Rathenau was the son of the founder of the giant electrical company Allgemeine Elektrizitäts-Gesellschaft (AEG). While working in his father's company Rathenau had come to condemn the human alienation and inhumane competition of "machine civilization," insisting that labor and distribution problems could be solved by the kind of central decision-making which he witnessed at his father's company. Social-Darwinist overtones were clear in Rathenau's prewar books on what one might call the philosophy of the planned economy. In the decade before the war, he studiously associated himself with government officials and dollar-a-year-type missions. Hence, when he presented himself to the general staff a week after the war started, there was – as with both Thomas and Lloyd George – a certain logic in making the mystical technocrat Rathenau the head of industrial planning for war.[12]

Rathenau's most important assistant was Wichard von Moellendorff, an engineer in his company. Of aristocratic background, he had become a disciple of the American efficiency expert Frederick Winslow Taylor, Social Darwinist and environmentalist planning guru.[13] Even before the war, Moellendorf had expressed the hope that the chaos of individual wills could be controlled by a new and efficient science of management. This would best be carried out in an "autarkic" system. This term simply meant a hermetically sealed system of self-sufficiency, in which government planners would provide for the needs of the nation with the resources contained in the nation's territory. The war provided the chance to maintain this self-sufficiency, or autarky.[14]

In summing up the work of the Raw Materials Office after its first year in existence, Rathenau offered the hope that the changes made in the economy would "in all probability be destined to affect future times." "Coercive measures" were of course necessary from the beginning, since the war effort would demand priority for supplies. Yet the attachment of Germany to the rule of law was problematic to the planners: laws relating to economic and industrial life had hardly changed, Rathenau said, since the time of Frederick the Great.[15] This "defective and incomplete state of our laws," that is, those laws protecting the freedom and property of individuals, was remedied by a new regime in which old words were given new meaning:

The term "sequestration" was given a new interpretation, somewhat arbitrarily I admit, but supported by certain passages in our
martial law. . . . "Sequestration" [now] does not mean that mer-
chandise or material is seized by the state, but only that it is
restricted, i.e., that it no longer can be disposed of by the owner
at will but must be reserved for a more important purpose. . . . At
first many people found it difficult to adjust themselves to the
new doctrine.[16]

No doubt many did find this adjustment difficult. Yet neither the Raw
Materials Office nor various other economic planning units relied
solely on simple "sequestration": indeed, the planners recruited many
industrialists onto boards to coordinate their own output and prices
for the sake of the war effort. Cooperation was important for the
producers, for over time, the state used its authority to starve small
and medium industrial producers of both labor and raw materials and
then to consolidate these plants into one of the great cartelized
government-supported concerns. For example, one contemporary
observer reported that thousands of local German electrical companies disappeared, to be incorporated into the "rationalized" fold of
either AEG or Siemens. Some branches of industry were "reduced"
by half in order to "save" on labor and raw materials, according to
historian Gerald Feldman: "Of the seventeen hundred cotton-
spinning and -weaving plants operating before the war, only seventy
'high productivity' plants were functioning in 1918."[17] Under the
rubric of what would later be called industrial "rationalization," production was centralized, and control of production organized under
a fortunate few concerns.

As for results, Germany did produce enormous quantities of military
goods during the war, yet these results came at the cost of severe dislocations. One case illustrating both the complexities and the costs of
the command economy is the pig slaughter of 1915. Beginning in
November 1914, the government had put in place price ceilings on
potatoes, which made it more profitable for farmers to feed their potatoes to their hogs than to sell them, though the government also
rapidly outlawed the foddering of potatoes. The inevitable potato
shortages were immediate and severe. In the cities, outcries were
raised, but against the farmers rather than the government. Soon,
journalists and politicians were claiming that people and pigs were in
a competition for the potatoes, and that some portion of Germany's 27

million pigs must go. Beginning in March, the government therefore signed the death warrant of nine million pigs. In the end neither potatoes nor pork became more plentiful.[18]

And yet the measures taken by the *central* government do not tell the whole of it. Local authorities from the federal state downward likewise partook in the flurry of planning. A collection of documents concerning food control in the Lichtenberg section of Berlin, assembled in 1916, contains 180 separate decrees, regulations, and ordinances, and these do not even include national directives from the real central planners. Item 82 ("Ordinance on the Regulation of Meat Consumption") gives something of the flavor of this collection. Apart from the basics of regulating meat sales, such as adjusting the definition of "fat" and limiting the relative amounts of meat on and off the bone which might be purchased, there were far greater intricacies, such as the control of the Meat Card, without which no one would get meat rations. Most of the people concerned lived in rented housing, and the Meat Card was carefully policed by the building owner (dragooned into the service of the state), with the help of the Building Executive Committee. To quote directly, "Should an occupant of the building die, or if he moves to another location, the Building Executive Committee has the duty of delivering the Meat Card formerly belonging to that building occupant immediately to the Nourishment and Grocery Section of the City Council."[19] The whole scene must be viewed against a background of hunger. Such had become the fabric of life by 1916.

The crucial question for governments trying to ride out the ballooning costs of war was relatively simple: How to pay for it without alienating the population, on whose motivation the whole effort hung?[20] Governments can gain revenue in a number of ways: confiscation, conquest, taxes, loans, engaging in business enterprises, even donation. Further, the forms of collecting private wealth are not equally palatable (or unpalatable). Modern mass-based politics had made it necessary for even the most reactionary of belligerents to have relatively high mass support for the war, even though the masses were already making "sacrifices" in the form of life and limb, losing relatives, suffering shortages, and the like. Hence, governments must maximize their income from "popular" forms of revenue and minimize or hide the unpopular forms. Confiscation and taxation, being the most direct kinds of transfers of wealth, generate the greatest ill will. As we shall see, confiscation took place among Western Front powers, but it tended to be clothed in terms of punishment: for aiding the enemy, for being of "enemy" heritage, and so on. Naturally, taxes affected a much broader slice of the public. We have seen already that tax rates among the Western Front powers rose during the war by a factor of 2.5 at the very least, and in most cases much more. Still, governments tended to conceal these increases as much as possible by spreading these out, by creating indirect taxes, and by other means, avoiding large, outright tax hikes where possible.[21]

Borrowing from abroad was a more appealing source of revenue for most war governments, since its immediate impact on public morale was less damaging. Especially on the Allied side, loans from British sources to the other Allies and eventually from United States sources to the rest of the Entente powers amounted to billions of dollars. To some extent, even before the entry of the United States into the war in April 1917, America was the most important financier of the Allied effort. But it was also the most important emporium of war supplies. Some strange conjunctions resulted: J. P. Morgan & Co., for example, served both as Britain's financial agent *and* as Britain's purchasing agent. Later, the company would play a central role in loaning money to Britain as well (incidentally, the British Treasury eventually fell out with Morgan & Co., set up their own buying commission, and put the operation under the supervision of Treasury official J. M. Keynes).[22]

In a way, borrowing domestically by issuing government bonds had some advantages over old-style borrowing from foreign banking houses. Naturally, this sort of borrowing had to be made a part of the public awareness so that the public would "buy" the bonds, that is to say, loan their money to the government with the promise of being paid later with interest. But belligerent governments learned to use this apparent disadvantage to their own ends: they developed aggressive advertising campaigns which finally not only sold the bonds but gave the opportunity for motivating and mobilizing their population at the same time. Germany, cut off from the great money markets of London and New York, relied primarily on war bonds (issued in nine great campaigns) to finance the war effort. The development of war-bond propaganda in Germany is interesting here because it fits so neatly into the crisis category we are constructing. Through the first war-bond series, the Reichsbank simply used stepped-up newspaper advertising to sell the bonds. Beginning with the fifth war-loan drive, that is, during the second half of 1916, the Reichsbank set up a special office to coordinate a national war-loan advertising campaign, which, if it did not match the American Liberty Bond effort in terms of outright salesmanship, nonetheless resulted in elaborate and thoughtful drives, much of the legwork being done by volunteer committees working at regional and local level. This campaign pioneered the use of animated film for advertising purposes and used traveling cinemas to do so.[23] Actually, of course, the need for an elaborate propaganda organization with over 100,000 volunteers demonstrates as much as anything the extent to which the stresses of the war were beginning to tell.

All First World War belligerents "created" currency or money by printing it or imagining it in the form of credit. Hence, as the money supply grew, each unit of money was worth less. If money is worth less, prices go up. Expansion of credit and the lowering of the value of the currency will produce inflation.[24] The understanding that one increases prices as one increases the amount of currency in circulation was well established among Western leaders for centuries before 1914, but for growing bureaucracies hard pressed to pay their own salaries, this form of redistributing wealth has proved irresistible at many points in history. When we add to the growing bureaucracy the costs of artillery shells, horses, uniforms, and the like, it is not difficult to see why World War I governments really introduced the twentieth century to inflation as a way of life. Still, it is important that we realize that such measures by the government form a hidden tax, a secret redistribution of wealth, from the pockets of citizens to the coffers of the government, the government's debtors, and the government's favorites. Yet World War I planners also paved the way to what we might call the propaganda of inflation by ignoring the involuntary nature of this transfer of wealth and enjoining the victims of this transfer to regard it as an act of patriotism. The head of the German central bank told the bank's board as early as September 25, 1914, that the best way to cover the massive war costs to come would be "an appeal to an entire people," an appeal to "ethical values and not merely personal gain."[25]

To summarize, governments used all means of gaining wealth to pay for the war. Though taxes went up, the far greater part of belligerents' expenses was paid for by borrowing (both at home and abroad) and by printing money and expanding credit (inflation). We will need to keep these fiscal facts in mind pending our exploration of the war's consequences in our final chapter.

A Changing Military–Civilian Fabric

In France, the complexities of regime changes over the previous 130
years had shaped the relationships of French generals to the French
republic, to create the aloof, almost independent stance of the French
army command. Joffre was in this respect a typical figure. Yet an imperious outlook was not the monopoly of French soldiers. Raymond
Poincaré was in many ways as aloof as the French high command. Born
in 1860, Poincaré had gone into politics in his twenties, and had served
on several cabinets before his short tenure as premier and his election
as president in 1912. By and large, this moderate conservative had
made a career out of opposing the designs of the Germans and shoring
up gaps in French policy when aggressive instincts flagged. Some had
thought it odd that Poincaré sought the presidency, since the Third
Republic constitution invested that office with little more than ceremo-
nial functions. It is clear that Poincaré intended to rule. He was able to
do so in part by nominating weak or friendly premiers, as for example,
Viviani.

Still, though Poincaré ruled as a strong president at home, his politics had put him in the role of supporting the military leaders before
the war, it was apparently difficult for Joffre and other army leaders to
treat the civilian government – even one under the control of their old
ally – with anything but disdain. Ultimately, Poincaré would replace
Viviani in 1916 with Aristide Briand, a move which led indirectly to
Joffre's downfall, since Briand found it impossible to work with the
victor of the Marne. Yet the government's tentative, almost fawning
approach to the generals – combined with the civilian hatred of the
outspoken Pétain – contributed to a number of very poor decisions,
chief among them the government's support of General Nivelle in his
disastrous offensive in the spring of 1917. We will investigate this further below.

In Germany, generals usually imagined themselves to be "above
politics," even though the army's influence over Kaiser Wilhelm II and
even the civilian leadership was often decisive. Though Wilhelmine
Germany promoted a militaristic culture, it would be a mistake to
assume that Germany was simply a military camp. Since 1871 Germany
had had a civilian government linked to a parliament elected by
universal manhood suffrage. Though the Kaiser and his military
"advisors" intervened in both domestic and foreign affairs with some
frequency, and though Germany was certainly a society given to

militaristic display, the talkative and unrestrained Kaiser was gradually distanced from decision-making processes in the years before the war. The civilian government made the decisions. We have seen that in the July Crisis, Wilhelm felt powerless even over the military when he asked Moltke to deviate from the Schlieffen Plan and attack only the Russians.[26]

With the advent of war, the generals enjoyed much autonomy, partly the result on the Prussian–German military recruitment system which divided the country into military districts in which an army corps headquarters directed the recruitment and training of troops. In wartime, these headquarters remained intact, sending troops as needed to corps in the field. With permanent regional bases, the regional commands exercised tremendous influence on such things as civilian local affairs, local governance, and economic control, since the presence of barracks full of troops in training occasioned all kinds of contact with civilians. Hence, at the local level, mayors and county officials were in the habit of observing decrees from the local military authorities.

As for Germany's military commanders, Moltke's successor was Erich von Falkenhayn. Experienced, like his counterparts, in imperial fighting, Falkenhayn had seen field action in the Chinese Boxer Rebellion. Like the British, the Germans nursed strong strategic doubts as to whether – after the failure of the Schlieffen Plan – the main weight of their efforts should be placed on the Western or Eastern Fronts. Taking command in September 1914, Falkenhayn became a primary advocate of holding in the East and hammering away in the West, though he decided early on that no great breakthrough was possible, only an attritional war and a favorable negotiated peace. Far from promoting the annexationist schemes and total war policies of a large and influential circle of politicians and military men – notably Ludendorff – Falkenhayn variously opposed German annexationist plans in the East, opposed an excess of press censorship at home (except for cases of military necessity), and opposed unlimited submarine warfare (at least early on). He would be fired after the failure of his Verdun Offensive 1916, but Falkenhayn would deliver admirable military work in other theaters, including what some have called a textbook offensive in Romania.[27] Still, as we shall see below, the whole scheme of attrition by meatgrinder at Verdun must be laid at Falkenhayn's feet,[28] and it is certain that he paved the way for the military dictatorship during the last two years of the war, in part by his arrogant refusal to coordinate his activities and plans with the responsible civilian officials.

British tradition put the civilians unambiguously in the driver's seat. In a sense the enormous importance of the navy reduced the power and influence of the army. It has been seen above that Field Marshal Sir John French was forced to use the civilian channel of journalism to induce the government to move toward more centralized and "predictable" war production organization. At the same time, French was not so successful either at working with the French high command or at fostering creative solutions to the military problems with which the Western Front presented him. Of many ideas which French's staff tried in 1915, some were simply failures, and none proved effective in breaking up the stalemate. More attacks between Ypres and Loos were less successful than the promising Neuve Chapelle had been. Moreover, the ferocious and massive attacks by the French in the Champagne and Artois made it appear to the French – both high command and government – that Field Marshal French was dragging his feet, a confirmation of the opinion that Joffre had always held.

The massive French sacrifices in particular led to much pressure on the British to take more of the offensive burden on the Western Front by the end of 1915, and French's own subordinates began to lose faith in the field marshal: his First Army commander, Douglas Haig, by the fall of 1915 was saying privately that French had to go.[29] Haig was indeed a person whose opinion the government and the king thought worth listening to. Protégé of French in the Boer War, the well-connected Haig had been promoted to general at the outset of the war, becoming the First Army commander. Though distant and aloof in dealing with subordinates, Haig was much less averse to communicating both with the French and with his own government than Sir John French. Haig presented, moreover, a serious, martial, and vigorous appearance, an asset not without meaning as British leaders understood increasingly that public confidence was one of the central mechanisms of war leadership. French resigned on December 15, 1915, and Haig was appointed to the command of the BEF the same day. We will look more closely at him in the next chapter.

To sum up, changes in the civilian–military fabric in the warring countries during the first war years were complex and varying. Contrary perhaps to expectations, one cannot say that the military invariably gained the upper hand in Western Front societies: even by the middle of the war, it is clear that the generals were having to resort to public relations, intrigue, and propaganda to influence civilian governments, and in many cases, their measures did not work: all governments fired generals during the war. If we are looking for long-term trends for the twentieth century, we find here some interesting precedents: even in the total war states which would emerge from the Great War (Communist Russia and Nazi Germany), the military per se was furiously subordinated through policy, purges, and constant manipulation.

As a final and illustrative piece of this short consideration of military–civilian relations, we will look briefly at the wartime contributions of Fritz Haber, a civilian who impacted the battle fronts of the war perhaps as much as he influenced the home front in Germany and elsewhere, not least by becoming the model of the dollar-a-year man, to use a phrase coined two decades later and on another continent.

A German Jew and a brilliant chemist, Haber was appointed to lead Germany's most prestigious institute for research in chemistry and physics in 1912. Only in his forties, Haber had already made his most famous discovery, the means of fixing nitrogen from the air (for which he won the Nobel Prize in 1918). When the war broke out, Haber immediately devoted himself to the war effort, in particular the problem which was also worrying Rathenau and Moellendorff: How could Germany survive in light of British interdiction of supplies? Haber's work with nitrogen helped address one side of the problem: synthetic nitrates replaced imported nitrates abroad as the most vital component of high explosives. On the other hand, he addressed the problem of breakthrough by heading a crash program to develop poison gas for the battlefield. The Germans had tried out some chemical irritants "delivered" in artillery shells on the Western Front in October 1914 and again on the Eastern Front in January 1915, but neither attempt produced appreciable results.

Beginning in late 1914, Haber had his system – a stronger poison and windborne delivery – ready within a few months, working so devotedly that he even experimented on himself with chlorine gas, the first of the World War I poison gases. One of Haber's assistants headed the first gas attack, which took place on the northern part of the arc forming the Ypres salient, in the early morning of April 22, 1915. Releasing the chlorine between St. Juliens and Bikschote, against lines occupied by the French Algerian 45th Colonial Division and the Canadian 3rd Brigade, the Germans attacked immediately. Many of the Algerians suffered rapid suffocation and most of the others panic. The Canadians on their right held on, but were forced to give way because of the gap left by the 45th Colonial Division. The Germans took an important ridge and made, by Western Front standards, a considerable local advance.[30]

The British and French soon produced their own gas, and both sides went on to more accurate delivery systems and more effective poisons; the Germans nonetheless had the "distinction" of introducing this weapon to the battlefield. Haber himself was known as a moderate person, a quintessential scientist. He was aware that Article 23 of the 1907 Hague Convention outlawed "poison or poisonous weapons." Some biographers have indicated that he may have experienced some discomfort with his role in the creation of poison gas; and some have speculated that his wife's suicide was related to the horrors of it. Still, if Haber was disturbed, he was able to move ahead: he became more closely associated with a number of promoters of the total war state after 1915, including Moellendorff, Bauer, and Ludendorff. It should be made clear likewise that before the war the British government approved poison gas development in spite of the Hague strictures, "in view of indications that the subject is being pursued in other countries." The BEF immediately set to work to retaliate.[31] Indeed, no Western Front belligerent was hesitant to use poison gas, and the use of gas shells (and all other kinds of shells) reached its greatest intensity at the end of the war.

Poison gas has of course become a symbol of World War I and certainly seems in retrospect one of the real horrors in a war which was full enough of them in any case. Still dreadful as gas was, actual casualties from gas were in the long run relatively low. After the early gas attacks, Western Front fighters were increasingly supplied with defense systems – the gas mask above all – and indeed, defense against gas attacks became routine. Gas casualties on the Western Front during the whole war amounted to about half a million, of whom under 20,000 died: about 4 percent of those with gas injuries died (as opposed to 25 percent from all other kinds of injuries). On the other side of the coin, gas accounted for 3 percent of all casualties on the Western Front, but only about 0.5 percent of all deaths.[32] Hence, though gas could make for the kind of horrible suffering depicted in Wilfred Owen's famous poem, "Gas Attack," and the unquestioned symbolic role of poison gas in modern memories of World War I may be more indicative of the weapon's psychological effectiveness than its actual ability to inflict casualties; some research suggests that many Western Front fighters were not as transfixed with the horror of gas as subsequent chroniclers have been.[33]

But to go back to Fritz Haber, poison gas also represents a very straightforward example of the direct connections between battle front and home front which characterized the war to a striking degree. In this regard, Haber is highly significant, but still just one of many such personalities from science, engineering, and industry who contributed to the war effort on paths parallel to that of Haber: Guglielmo Marconi, who applied his genius in radio transmission for the British war effort; Anthony Fokker, the producer of German warplanes; Herbert Hoover, an engineer whose organizational efforts would eventually rival those of Rathenau; and many more.

Entente Mobilization and Imperial Resources

In discussing the various means of mobilization, we should not overlook the considerable mobilization of human resources from the empires of Britain and France. For the war as a whole, the French would draw on their colonies in sub-Saharan and North Africa to produce nearly 600,000 troops. Many of these worked in labor battalions, but even these activities made way for more troops to be used in combat. Overall, the number may seem larger than its relative importance: France mobilized 8.2 million men. Hence, about 7 percent of French troops were colonial natives. A smaller percentage were "colonial" in the sense that they were Frenchmen living in colonies, though most of these would not have made that qualification since Algeria, where most of the French settlers lived, was officially a part of France.[34]

The British need for troops was great, though there were times early on when so many men were enlisting that it was impossible to train and outfit them all. One must remember that "Britain" could draw on the whole of Ireland, since that country did not gain independence until 1922. Hence, Irish troops were important participants in the Great War, as were, of course troops from the other "countries" that made up Britain, Scotland, and Wales. Indeed, the Celtic element of the British army formed an important component of the BEF, both in coherent, large units like the 36th Irish Division, the 51st Highlander Division, and the Royal Welch Fusiliers, and as individual soldiers scattered into other regiments. One would miss some of the dynamics of the British dilemma if one did not know that at one time or the other most Scots and Irish troops probably either heard or uttered the sentiment that the English were ready to oppose the Germans down to the last Scot (or Irishman). It is indeed notable that so many of the elite or aggressive units in the BEF were centered on the Celtic countries. And in connection with the complaint about high casualties, it is axiomatic (and a matter of common sense) in that commanders should choose as lead elements and in tough situations those which have proven themselves tough fighting units. Still, we will miss important connections between the battle front and the home front if we pay no attention to this part of the make-up of the BEF.[35]

If the Irish, Scots, and even the Welsh thought at times about their peripheral status within the Britain for which they were fighting, the "colonials" representing British settlement in North America and the South Pacific were even more peripheral. Yet the participation of Canada, of Australia and New Zealand, and of South Africa is a vital part of the history of the Western Front.

In some ways, the largest of these former colonies were the most comparable. The status of Canada as a self-ruled dominion within the British Empire had only existed since 1867; that of Australia since 1901. In 1914, Canada's population amounted to 7.2 million, Australia's to 5 million. Both countries had seen a great deal of economic growth in the years before the war, and both had experienced much internal discussion over the extent to which they should strike out on courses independent of British desires. Continued membership of the British Commonwealth and many other close ties put Canada and Australia in a special category when it came to participation in the war: no one expected either country not to enter the war, but at the same time leaders in both countries had some goals in mind which might be accomplished by participation, especially in their own distinct military units.

With the war's outbreak, both countries immediately declared war on Germany, as did Newfoundland, still a colony of Britain, and possessing a population of a quarter of a million; New Zealand, a self-ruling dominion with a population of just over a million; and South Africa, a self-ruling dominion only since 1910, whose white population totaled 6 million. Hence, loyal dominions and colonies numbering over 13 million provided an important source of manpower, as well as sources for some needed products.

In a study of comparative participation in World War I, these five outcroppings of the British Empire provide some interesting comparative history. Each of the countries possessed a native population – Indians in

Canada and Newfoundland, Aborigines in Australia, the various African peoples in South Africa, and Maoris in New Zealand – which figured only peripherally in the war effort (except in South Africa). On the other hand, substantial divisions in the European populations of Canada (where nearly a quarter of the population was of French ancestry) and South Africa (where the hatreds expressed in the war between the Boers and the English had hardly subsided) were important calculations in the enlistment of manpower.

Neither Quebecois French nor South African Boers (predominantly of Dutch heritage) tended to be very enthusiastic about the war, since both saw it essentially as an affair of the British Empire. There was considerable pro-German sentiment among the Boers dating back to German support in the British–Boer clashes of the 1890s. French Canadians were of course not pro-German in any sense, but their connections to France were also quite tenuous. Still, the long premiership of French Canadian Wilfred Laurier from 1896 to 1911 helped to cut down on the Anglo-French frictions by means of classical liberal policies which limited the national government's interference in local issues. Economic prosperity, which likewise arose from the leadership of Wilfred Laurier and the Liberal Party, helped reduce tensions between the Anglo- and French Canadians too. Laurier was voted out in 1911, and Conservative leader Robert Borden came to power, signaling the same shift seen elsewhere in the West in the around the turn of the century, the shift from classical economic and political liberalism to policies aiming much more at the creation of a national ideal and identity. In Canada this identity would be constructed much more around the Anglo-Canadians than the French. Much more closely tied to England, Borden led Canada to an automatic declaration of war in 1914.

Borden's government immediately assumed sweeping powers by means of the War Measures Act. The War Minister called for 22,000 troops and 33,000 volunteered. Financing the war by loans from the United States and after 1917 from public war bonds, the "Victory Loan," the Canadian government managed to fight the war without increasing taxes (from a rate of 11 percent to 13 percent), though Canada's national deficit rose by a factor of five.[36]

From the opening of the war Laurier provided the important service of encouraging French Canadians to enlist and to support the war effort. Laurier – blamed by later separatists as being far too helpful to the Anglo-Canadians during the war – would split with the war government only in 1917, over the quintessentially anti-liberal issue of conscription. Indeed, in October 1917, Borden would announce a Union government, consisting only of "Canadians" and not of mere party members. This would seem to be a kind of belated *Union sacrée*, but in fact the "Canadians" in the government represented British Canada only.[37] One result would be the great Anglo-French antagonism that has characterized Canadian politics ever since.[38]

In considering imperial resources, one must keep in mind that not all imperial appendages were able to contribute equally to the war effort in material terms. South Africa's gold and diamonds were not of much direct use in waging World War I. Canada provided, hands down, the most important material support, not only through supplying food but through the large munitions industry that came into being. Canada's shipping industry, too, flourished during the war, raising its capacity by a factor of eight.

But Canada likewise supplied a strong fighting force which carved out an important historical niche for itself, important both for the history of World War I, and for the history and identity of Canada itself. Eventually, Canadian forces numbering 630,000 would serve in the Canadian Expeditionary Force and the Canadian Navy. Sixty thousand Canadians would die in the war.

By 1918 Australia had mobilized 416,000, and also lost 60,000 dead; South Africa mobilized 136,000 (most of whom served in southern Africa) and lost 9,000 dead; New Zealand would send about 129,000 to war and lose 17,000 dead; and Newfoundland mobilized 12,000 troops and lost 1,100 dead, a substantial number of those on the first day of the Somme battle in 1916.[39] The level at which these appendages to the United Kingdom participated is impressive indeed. Britain mobilized 12.5 percent of its population, and in turn about 12.7 percent of those mobilized would die during the war. The figures for the Dominions are comparable, except for the case of South Africa, which mobilized just over 2 percent of its population, of whom 6 percent died. But Canada mobilized 8.7 percent of its population, of whom 9.5 percent died; Newfoundland mobilized 4.8 percent, of whom 9.2 percent died; Australia mobilized 8.3 percent, of whom 14.4 percent died; and New Zealand mobilized 13 percent, of whom 13.2 percent died. Hence, New Zealand actually raised a greater number of troops per capita than Great Britain (though not much greater), and both New Zealand and Australia suffered higher death rates in the war. By way of comparison, it is useful to note, both France and Germany mobilized more soldiers per capita than Great Britain (20 percent of the population in both cases), and both France and Germany suffered more deaths among those soldiers (16.3 percent for France, 13.7 percent for Germany).[40]

The shape of the participation of these Dominions is seen throughout this book, but it is worth taking a short moment to contemplate the role played by these forces who conceived it to be their job to help the mother country. Canadians and Australians/New Zealanders (ANZACs) were known on the Western Front as the equals of the toughest veteran units. The Canadian 3rd Brigade was one of two units engulfed in the first gas attack of the war at Ypres in March 1915. The brigade's problem was compounded when the French Algerian Division to its left broke, leaving the Canadians unprotected. The Canadians stood up against repeated German attacks centered on the village of St. Juliens, two platoons fighting until the last man was killed or wounded. Whatever one thinks of counterfactual history, we have to say that here the Canadians prevented the Germans from breaking through in a highly important sector at an important moment of the war. Two years later, after many other actions in which Canadian units proved their worth, the Canadian Corps attacked what was at that moment probably the strongest German position in northern France, on Vimy Ridge. In a two-day battle, completely under Canadian direction, the Corps took the ridge, inflicting 20,000 casualties and sustaining half that number.

The ANZACs likewise contributed substantially to the British effort. Originally sent to Egypt for training, they formed the core of the attempt to shake the Turkish hold on the Dardanelles Strait by attacking Gallipoli. Over the months after April 1915, the ANZACs lost over 30,000 men, killed, wounded, and captured. Once the Allied force slipped away from Gallipoli, the Australian Light Horse served in the Middle East, while the bulk of the Australian Imperial Force was sent to the Western Front, where, like the Canadian army, it made a name for itself, on which more below.[41]

One point to be made here is that soldiers from six continents fought on the Western Front. Their experience is not only an important component story of the war, but vital in understanding the global nature of World War I. Indeed, the Western Front powers very rapidly integrated soldiers from the peripheries of their empires into the battle front and hence drew them into a storm in many ways unrelated to their own homelands.

Mass and Elite Mobilization

Since modern wars have tended to take place over issues far removed from most of the lives destroyed in these wars, governments of modern pluralistic societies must "sell" the war to the people. Even before the war, the sharpening nationalism of the late nineteenth century and the expansion of European imperialism in the same period contributed to the tendency in both the public and private spheres to sway sections of the public with heroic and nationalistic themes. It was an easy step in 1914 for all belligerents to create public relations machinery which would promote enthusiasm for the war and vilify the enemy.

German propaganda for the war was marked by technical and even artistic innovation. Coming from a disorganized but vast array of public agencies and some private sources, German propaganda in the form of the printed word shaped the German public perception of the war from the outset. The poster art of Germany, a country with a highly developed sense of communication by poster already, was likewise a constant in delivering propaganda to the public. The Germans also led the way in the use of film in propaganda, producing documentaries and even feature films. Indeed, by the end of the war, the "mobile cinema," including open-air showings, had become a normal medium of political information. All of these media of course conveyed a message. For the Germans, the message tended to revolve around the claim that Germany had been the target of abuse, disrespect, and greed on the part of the Entente powers. A propaganda that could, and did, make the invasion of Belgium appear to be the result of direct aggression by France and even aggressive designs by Belgium (!) did indeed reflect a self-absorbed national myth. On the other hand, optimism about the course of the war had to be the major feature of daily news. German propaganda, like all other propaganda in World War I, used all imaginable rhetorical devices to raise sacrifice for the nation to the center of daily life.

But all Western Front countries egged on powerful mythmaking. Lord Kitchener, in perhaps the most famous poster of the war, told British men "Your King and Country Need You!" for the war effort. French *poilus* struggled valiantly across posters calling for collections of essentials for the war effort. In the later phases of the war, the Germans would cart around the country giant wooden statues of Field Marshal Paul von Hindenburg, so that people could hammer nails into them in a dramatic drive for metal. The war bond drives, which occurred in all Western Front countries, called forth continuous rhetoric reflecting the fiscal needs we have examined in this chapter. In an important recognition of the extent to which Great War armies consisted of individuals whose opinions mattered, all governments instituted programs of propaganda within the military as well, bolstering the troops with messsages of encouragement as well as shaping the self-image of the military in desired ways.[42]

One of the most striking things about propaganda organization on the home fronts is their disorganization. Although Sir W. Max Aitken (later Lord Beaverbrook) came to head up a Ministry of Information late in the war, Gerard De Groot has pointed out that in Britain "an ad hoc, decentralized and ultimately chaotic approach to propaganda reigned until the last year of the war." But the German situation could be described in the same words: only late in the war did the Reich Chancellery set up a single "public enlightenment" organization to coordinate propaganda, though even then this coordination was quite limited. French propaganda too, though perhaps more centralized, issued from so many different centers with many different immediate agendas. One is struck by the necessarily chaotic nature of the attempt to influence the opinions of millions of individuals.[43]

The Western Front powers all engaged in information control, propaganda, and what the "Secret Organs" of Soviet Russia would later call "disinformation." This they did first through censorship. Though there had been much room for journalistic latitude in the years before 1914, throughout Central and Western Europe, governments had censored the press in cases of "extreme" politics, pornography, libel and slander, and other matters. In the first days of World War I, all governments established much broader ranges of censorship, partly because it was so easy to give away plans to the enemy, but also because governments were beginning to habituate themselves to thinking of public opinion as a vital issue in governing, especially in times of crisis. In Britain, the Defence of the Realm Act had provided for stricter censorship from the beginning, and British newspapers could be rebuked, suppressed, or closed down as a result of disobeying official censors. The Press Bureau gave official interpretations of events to newspapers, which could publish approved stories, but not opinions. In the French republic, newspapers frequently went out with white spaces where stories had been removed. In Germany, news control and censorship had already been in place before the war. Clearly, as the war went on, control tightened here as elsewhere, though this control tended to be exercised more and more by the military authorities in the regional Army Corps headquarters.[44]

Was all this propaganda and information control effective? Did it sway people? In recent years, as the study of the "mentalities" of the masses has made headway, historians have become more hesitant to make broad assertions about the opinions of the population, especially the segments at the lower end of the socioeconomic ladder. Recent studies of propaganda have likewise emphasized variations in the reception of propaganda by men and women, or based on regional differences. For the British case, De Groot has suggested that the British public *wanted* to believe that the war was going well, and this was undoubtedly true for the other Western Front countries also. Hence, whatever their conclusions about the "reception" of propaganda during the war, most historians would present them cautiously.[45]

Still, it seems that a bundle of attitudes and "common knowledge" was for most Western Front populations the result, at least in part, of prolonged propaganda and careful control of information. The "advertising" of a fairly coherent set of wartime views and values was so pervasive that most individuals would have needed extensive and unusual means of collecting information about the world in order to make judgments which did not accord with prevailing and desired opinions. There were in fact almost no alternative news sources. As a different kind of measure of the effectiveness of emerging information control and propaganda during the First World War, we may note that *all* postwar regimes, and indeed all subsequent regimes, have been centrally concerned with information control and propaganda, so much so that all of them have set up a variety of agencies (some of them direct descendants of World War I creations) to manage information going to the press and the public. Indeed, the most "warlike" postwar regimes (the ideological regimes which would base their social programs in some sense on the idea of a permanent war footing, like the National Socialists and the Bolsheviks) were also the regimes whose concern for propaganda was most elemental.

The most influential single propaganda effort of the war was the so-called Bryce Report, an account of German atrocities in Belgium issued by the British government in the spring of 1915. Charged with heading a committee to investigate atrocities in Belgium in 1914, Lord Bryce seemed a good choice: he had a long and distinguished career as a jurist, historian, and ambassador (to the United States). In fact, Bryce had opposed what he regarded as the anti-German direction of British policy before the war. Only with the Belgian invasion did he decide that Germany had become the enemy of European civilization and must hence be exposed as such. The product of the committee's work, an important document in twentieth-century European politics, included "eyewitness" – and supposedly officially corroborated – testimony about numerous horrific atrocities in Belgium. The Bryce atrocities are horrendous even now; they must have been a great deal more so in 1914. Three excerpts give the flavor of the whole:

> Belgian Soldier: "I saw evidence of German atrocities between Malines and Hofstade. . . . I saw a woman with breasts and hands cut off. . . . I also saw the body of a youth, about 20. Both legs were cut off. The body was quite close to that of the woman. . . ."

> Belgian Non-Commissioned Officer: "When we entered Hofstade in August last, or some village near to it, a girl of about 18 or 19 years of age complained . . . that she had been violated by several German soldiers for a period of about two hours before we entered the village on the threshold of a house in full daylight and in full view of villagers. She had been stripped of all clothing but her chemise and had bled freely from the private parts.

The Bryce Report was presented to the public by a committee headed by a well-known jurist, Lord Bryce, but the committee was only the recipient of documents provided by some government agents whose identity, again, has been disputed. The origin of the "reports" handed over to Bryce is likewise not completely clear, since the original documents have never appeared, and since no one on the committee ever questioned the "witnesses" face to face. In a few cases, Bryce received warnings from investigators involved in the process who had actually tracked down some of the addresses at which "outrages" had occurred and found no evidence of them. Yet so carefully did the Bryce Committee separate itself from the origin of the documents that even critical contemporary historians of British propaganda are not able to pinpoint where the fabrications lay. Historian Trevor Wilson has judged that the committee itself made its way by avoiding any materials or actions which might disprove the charges handed to them.

The Bryce Report "documents" are fascinating from a number of aspects, not least the reportage of acts which can only be called psycho-sexual in nature. Historian Joachim Remak has pointed out that the descriptions are more reminiscent of a certain variety of English pornography than they are of atrocity accounts known to be authentic.[46] We might try to explain the whole Bryce Committee episode by reference to the British government's need to strike a deep chord in favor of the war effort. In the public mind, Britain had entered the war because the Germans invaded Belgium. We now call this the "violation" of Belgium without, perhaps, thinking much about the now somewhat archaic usage of the term "violation" as a synonym for the modern English word "rape." It may have been accidental that the word used for "violations" of borders since modern English came into being was also used (and equally far back) to indicate sexual aggression. But the conjunction was fortuitous for British propaganda. The image of a young and frightened woman, representing in effect "violated Belgium," was commonplace in Allied posters, illustrations, and cartoons.

The effect of the Bryce Report and lesser imitations was to associate the two usages of the word "violate" so closely together that one would stand for the other. The Germans did in fact behave brutally in the invasion of non-offending Belgium. German troops behaved atrociously to Belgian civilians, killing over 5,000 people in "reprisals" for irregular resistance by other Belgians. The Germans were quite open about this and reasoned, with colossally bad public relations judgment, that the only way to fight guerrilla activity – a violation of the norms of "civilized" warfare – was to carry out reprisals against the civilian population, precisely the calculation that the British army had made during the South African war only a few years before. The Germans likewise carried out reprisals against "property," the library of Louvain being only the most famous piece of destruction. The civilian refugees fleeing to Holland and England amounted to tens of thousands of displaced persons. These were terrible acts of war. And perhaps in all of this, some raping occurred. But the bizarre and clinical sadism of the Bryce Report was something else again. Indeed, as Trevor Wilson has pointed out, the committee chose to write a report which passed over the real "crimes" and instead fabricated grotesque depictions of inhuman cruelty. Some Germans in Belgium were cruel, but they were all quite human.

Released, the report was electrifying. A British public brought up on titillating murders in the darkened byways of London and other large cities could find special fascination in the German mutilations and other cruelties. But though the victims were dismembered like those of

Jack the Ripper, they were hardly prostitutes: "There was also the body of a child lying close to the other body." Could any Briton miss the message that the enemy was not only a foreigner, but a degenerate and a sadistic sexual maniac, and hence someone with whom there could be no question about fighting to the bitter end, and in particular no question about going to war with in the first place?

Fatefully for the history of the war, the Bryce Report made its way to the United States. As we shall see at the end of this chapter, the crucial diplomacy of the war would revolve around the United States. Influencing public opinion in that large and heterogeneous country would be a vital concern to the Allies in particular. In the event, the Bryce Report was successful in America beyond all British expectations. Head of British propaganda Charles Masterman wrote to Bryce a few days after the Report had been published: "Your report has *swept* America. As you probably know even the most skeptical declare themselves converted, just because it is signed by you!"[47]

The United States, in particular the less urbanized America of the Southern and Western states, was light years removed from the cosmopolitan readers of the London sensationalist press. Sexual violence was little known outside the great cities of the United States, and the standards of behavior toward women, especially away from the Northeastern cities, could make "Victorian" standards look slack. It was precisely these regions whose political support would be most needed by the Wilson administration in bringing the United States into the war in 1917. The Bryce Report appeared in the United States just after the sinking of the *Lusitania* on May 7, 1915, a disaster which claimed nearly 1,200 lives, 139 of them American. Hence, as British agents reported back to London, the Bryce Report was "sweeping" the United States and the Belgian atrocities were consistently linked with the outrage of the *Lusitania* in the press. Indeed, the *New York Tribune* pointed out that "while our own women were only slain those of Belgium were outraged." Many other press reports echoed this theme. In American popular writing, even in the postwar period, the "violations" of Belgian women frequently surface. In a 1919 novel by the famous writer of Westerns, Zane Grey, the hero, dying a lingering death from being gassed in the war, is asked why he volunteered. His reply: "To avenge Belgian womanhood."[48] If anything, the success of the Bryce Report encouraged the British propaganda office at Wellington House to put more effort into "converting" Americans. The propaganda exploitation of the German execution of nurse Edith

Cavell, who had secretly assisted a few hundred Allied prisoners to escape, was so successful that many observers considered the Cavell affair as just behind the "violation of Belgium" and the sinking of the *Lusitania* as a propaganda victory. The American public proved malleable in the face of these major propaganda sorties as well as hundreds of minor ones. Among the Bryce stories and thousands of others was the tale that the Germans were gathering the bodies of the Western Front dead and transporting them to Germany to be boiled down into soap at a special factory for that purpose.[49]

It is important here to look briefly at the mood that was developing against the background of this growing manipulation of opinion by the belligerent governments. How did the governments maintain morale at home? Coincident with the massive casualties and stalemate, it is clear that popular enthusiasms began to wane, though only to stages of somber acceptance. One signal of this change in the British case was that the wave of recruits fell off fairly rapidly. Where British recruits had come in at a rate of over 100,000 a week during the first war months, the weekly rate fell to under 22,000 by February 1915.[50] However, there is little indication that any substantial antiwar sentiment was as yet at hand. On British streets, men of military age in civilian clothes risked being handed a white chicken feather by enthusiastic young ladies.[51] Girl Scouts and other patriotic groups were ever watchful when it came to potential local enlistees, praising those who did sign up, shaming those who did not.

Still, among all the Western Front countries, whatever enthusiasms had reigned during the flush of the war's outbreak, a more sober outlook was settling in, both as death tolls mounted and as the shortages of wartime began to make themselves felt. In Germany, as we have seen, food controls were already appearing by the fall of 1914, and daily life was becoming much more difficult for most Germans. Recent research makes it clear that Germany's urban working classes were little influenced by war enthusiasm. Nor were German farmers likely to view the war with much positive feeling: unaffected by hunger like their city cousins, they were nonetheless forced both to sell their produce for mandated low prices and to pay more and more for all other items.

Rural and provincial populations in France, women now in the vast majority, had a heavy burden in replacing the labor of the millions of the mobilized who came from the countryside. In the cities of France, dating from the onset of stalemate, a number of antiwar movements emerged, some of these originating in the French and international labor movement. The closest recent scholars have concluded that these sentiments represented "a handful of supporters, a few rare tokens of opposition."[52] In a study of popular culture during the war, Charles Rearick has shown that even in the working-class quarters of French cities, serious sentiment for "holding out" remained strong well into 1916. Indeed, a recent study of French trench journals indicates that "national feeling" and self-conceptions of dignity and loyalty to the nation were in fact core motivators for enduring the war among the soldiers themselves, and part of of this dignity was the regard in which French soldiers were held at home – as protectors of the nation.[53]

On the other hand, in spite of the high demand for labor, Britain, Germany, and France continued to experience labor unrest during the war in the form of strikes, though the dislocations and enthusiasms of the war's beginning, along with the repressive powers of warring states, seem to have lowered the level of strike activity. From 1914, a year of fairly high labor unrest, strike activity abated in 1915: in France from 672 strikes in 1914 to 98 in 1915; in Germany from 1,223 strikes to 141 in 1915; in Britain from 972 strikes in 1914 to 672 in 1915. This trend would prove temporary: as we shall see below, strikes began to climb by the end of 1915 in a trend which would continue through the war and thereafter. We may also add the United States and the British Empire countries to this list. In all, a considerable part of the strike activity involved not sentiment against the war, but objections to longer hours and poor conditions, and in many industries the presence of women in increasing numbers, since union leaders and the rank and file feared that women would continue to take up a man's spot after the war.

To turn to a different segment of society, that of the intellectuals, we find very few who opposed the war. Hence, the famous case of French novelist Romain Rolland is instructive. Rolland penned from Switzerland a series of famous condemnations of nationalism, cruelty, and the war itself, publishing them in late September 1914 in a collection, *Above the Battle*. He was widely condemned in the French press, which found his essays most subversive when they called for reconciliation with the Germans and an appreciation for the high culture of Germany. His collection rallied hardly any intellectual opposition to the war, except for a few journals of the extreme left. The right wing dismissed him as a deracinated cretin. From the center of the political spectrum, however, French intellectuals – including the famous historian of the French Revolution, Alphonse Aulard – impugned Rolland's pacifism, his weakness, his "academic" Germanophilia, and even his "degenerate" eyes, which appeared to one of his literary enemies as "dull and drawn." French intellectuals were in no mood for reconciliation.[54]

In neutral America, the most spectacular intellectual opposition to war, to the war, and to American entry to the war was Randolph Bourne, a American dissident writer who opposed the war on grounds that echoed Leninist critiques in some ways but derived more from the American individualist tradition than from any utopian scheme. Only 28 when the war broke out, he wrote over 300 essays during the war, a large number of which cast the war as simply an aggrandizement, a strengthening, of the state at the expense of individual wills. "War," he wrote in a now famous essay, "is the health of the state." He meant that whatever the international dimensions of war, all kinds of individuals hope to use war to gain power over their fellow human beings and to enforce their own sort of factory discipline on their the weak-minded masses. The intellectuals were especially to blame, as he wrote just after the American entry into the war:

> it has been a bitter experience to see the unanimity with which the American intellectuals have thrown their support to the use of war-technique. . . . Socialists, college professors, publicists, new-republi-cans, practitioners of literature, have vied with each other in confirming with their intellectual faith the collapse of neutrality and the riveting of the war-mind on a hundred million more of the world's people. . . . They are now complacently asserting that it was they who effectively willed it, against the hesitation and dim percep-tions of the American democratic masses. A war made deliberately by the intellectuals![55]

Though Bourne was a former student of John Dewey at Columbia University, and to some extent a promoter of Dewey's plan for pro-gressive education, the student criticized his teacher intensely for welcoming the war. Indeed, Dewey, who welcomed World War I enthusiastically because he thought it would speed up "progressive" reforms, was in a sense Bourne's target.[56]

Not only will we fail to find most intellectuals, thinkers, scientists, and literary figures in the ranks of those opposing the war, but a large section of the intellectual classes in all belligerent countries supported it enthusiastically with their efforts. We have seen this phenomenon already in looking at the wartime activities of Fritz Haber. Many, like Haber, saw opportunities in the conflict. German historian Friedrich

Meinecke, no rabid annexationist, wrote to a friend in September 1914 that while he disliked some of the decivilizing aspects of the war, the war would "free us from a lot that troubled us until now." Though he had reservations against extensive German territorial expansion, he was ready for Germany to take up "the task that destiny has given us." Actually, during the first year of the war, much of the prewar fear of encirclement seemed to convert itself into enthusiasm for an aggressive policy of annexationist war aims. Secret meetings in the ministries had as their agendas plans for the incorporation of some of France's coal-fields (especially in Longwy-Briey, in the east), and even the takeover of Belgium and Luxembourg were on the agenda. This unrealistic enthusiasm soon extended to the broader educated elite, and it lost nothing in the retelling. In May 1915 Chancellor Bethmann Hollweg received a memorandum from major organizations representing industry and agriculture which demanded the future annexation of tens of thousands of square miles of territory in Europe, and even more from the colonial possessions of the Entente powers. A few days later, an equally bombastic "Declaration" was issued by 1,347 professors, clergymen, landowners, politicians, journalists, literary figures, and other prominent people. Even the Socialist Party, technically still Marxist and hence prone to view the war as the infighting of capitalist elites, supported the war effort by maintaining the unity of the *Burgfrieden* and voting for war credits (parliamentary approval of the war budget).[57]

The extent indeed to which even critics and opponents of the war hoped to use it for their own ends is striking. As early as March 1915, the left wing of the SPD, led by radical Marxist Karl Liebknecht, voted against the War Credits Bill, denouncing the war as imperialist, but Liebknecht proposed to use the war situation to ignite genuine class war and eventually dictatorship of the proletariat (Lenin was issuing a supernational version of the same program from Zurich). Moreover, though the mainstream socialists considered themselves good German patriots, they soon developed reservations about the annexationist aims of government and military figures. Leaders in the other parties too were not completely blinded to both the precariousness of the German military situation and to the hubris which annexationism represented. The Chancellor himself, a pessimist in any case, was never convinced that the war would empower Germany to take all the territory demanded. And other prominent figures such as sociologist Max Weber, theologian Adolf Harnack, and physicist Albert Einstein joined liberal newspaper editor Theodor Wolff in a memorandum to the Chancellor which renounced annexationist plans while still arguing for a strong Germany as a result of the future victory. Yet it is likewise clear that these individuals hoped to use the war as a means of broadening political participation in Germany and introducing liberal political reforms to the country's constitutional monarchy.[58]

Eventually, a vast array of intellectuals, scientists, writers, politicians, and artists signed on to help the war effort by supplying intellectual backing, by whipping up public enthusiasm, by inventing ideas to stymie the enemy and by validating the coercive measures of the state. Clearly the most significant optimism for war came from elite actors who hoped to use the war to effect social change.

International Mobilization: Diplomacy, the Blockade, and American Neutrality

In modern wars diplomacy must intensify once the war starts. First, as we have seen already, the very holding together of the military alliances under the stresses of battle and sometimes defeat can lead to the most intricate and difficult kind of diplomacy, carried on in fact by national leaders and military men as well as professional diplomats. Second, each side in any modern coalition war has had to set its sights on gaining more allies to its own cause and detaching allies from the enemy's coalition. Far from being a peripheral part of the war, this kind of diplomatic activity is as crucial as military successes at the front, sometimes more so. Indeed, the attempt to bring other powers into the war (meaning, in part, the wealth of other powers' citizens) and to deny their wealth to the enemy paralleled in very important ways the domestic programs of war governments. In this view of war as activity that has to be paid for, the British attempt to sway the Americans is of course the most important financial aspect of the whole war, since the United States was the richest country in the world. Hence, it will be useful here to review this diplomacy both as an important element of non-military "mobilization."

With the outbreak of the war, the opposing alliances both considered the most important immediate diplomatic goals to be the wooing of Italy and Turkey. Neither of these two powers joined them in declaring war on the Entente in 1914. Still, the Turkish situation cleared itself up soon enough. Both economic and military ties argued strongly for entering the war with Germany, especially with those nationalist associates of the War Minister, Enver Pasha, who had in fact made a secret alliance with Germany just before the war broke out. More broadly, though the Entente made some attempts to woo Turkey, in fact the most aggressive enemy of the Turks since the late seventeenth century was Russia, and Turkish nationalists harbored only slightly less animosity toward Britain, which had made enormous gains during the previous 40 years in controlling vital parts of the Middle East over the traditional Ottoman sphere of influence. Finally, the German cause made great gains as a result of two German warships being chased into the Dardanelles Strait by the British at the outbreak of the war. The German ambassador promptly presented these two ships as a gift to the Ottoman government (thereby effectively replacing two Turkish ships being constructed in British shipyards). Before long, these ships participated in the bombing of the Russian port of Odessa. Shortly afterward (November 1914), the Sultan declared a *jihad*, or holy war, against the Entente powers. Though the Ottoman Empire was a junior partner among the Central Powers, the weight which it could bring to bear against both Russia and Britain was really out of proportion to its military strength. Not only did the Ottomans keep enormous numbers of troops pinned down on Russia's southern border, but British attacks in three different theaters of battle would attest to the importance that Britain attached to the Ottoman component of the Central Powers. The Turkish declaration of war in November 1914 had been a signal diplomatic victory for the Central Powers.

It was not as clear that Italy would enter the war at all: should she do so, it was not clear which side she would choose. Long a member of the Triple Alliance, Italy had wavered in the course of the diplomatic crises leading up to the war. Her declaration of neutrality at the outbreak of the war was therefore no great surprise, and the Italian government was on firm ground in pointing out that the Austrian action against Serbia was an offensive action (whereas the Triple Alliance only obliged the members to aid each other if the others were attacked). In any case, both alliances hoped to bring that country into the war on their own side. The result was a sort of diplomatic auction, in which both sides offered territory and colonial concessions in exchange for Italian help in the war.

Without going into elaborate detail, we can mention here that Austria still held territories on Italy's northern border which the Italians considered *Italia irredenta*, unredeemed Italy. The Germans were willing to offer Austrian real estate to the Italians in exchange for entry, and at first the Austrians balked. They were especially alarmed at the Italian demand to occupy *immediately* the territories to be ceded. The Austrians gave in under much pressure from Germany, and too late in any case. In a secret agreement signed in London in April 1915, the Entente made it clear that not only these territories but also considerable stretches of the Adriatic coast, some Turkish islands in the Aegean Sea, and even a piece of Asia Minor itself would go to Italy in the event of Entente victory. The real decision that the Italians had to make was which side was more likely to win, since whatever the offer, pay-off would only materialize on the winning side. They decided for the London offer and the Entente: Italy declared war on the Central Powers on May 23, 1915.

These episodes demonstrate that diplomacy was going on at very intensive levels during the war itself. This kind of bartering continued. After the Turks came in November, the position of Bulgaria was critical to military operations in the region, so bidding started, and the upshot was that Bulgaria joined the Central Powers in September 1915 with the promise of the receipt of Macedonia after the war, and the Dobrudja (a region in Romania) should Romania enter the war. Romania did so a year later, in August 1916, on the side of the Entente, the result of Allied promises to recognize Romanian claims to substantial pieces of the Austro-Hungarian Empire.

While Spain remained neutral, Portugal was a traditional ally of the English and a colonial rival of Germany. The Portuguese parliament voted to join the war in November 1914, but an insurrection and seizure of power by a pro-German faction killed the declaration. In fact, during the first war years, Portuguese forces clashed repeatedly on the border between German East Africa and Portuguese Mozambique, and much more Portuguese "military" effort went into large-scale executions and displacement of Africans in retaliation for uprisings inspired by Germans. In May 1915, a democratic (and anti-German) revolt and an election put Bernardino Machada in the president's seat, and a number of incidents, including the seizure of some German ships in Lisbon harbor, led the Germans to declare war on Portugal in March 1916. A Portuguese expeditionary force of two divisions reached the Western Front about a year later and took over a piece of the British sector. The Portuguese effort was more than token participation. Eventually, about 50,000 Portuguese troops would serve on the Western Front, holding the fairly quiet but dangerous sector around Laventie, between Armentières and Béthune. By the spring of 1918, Haig – like his predecessor in Flanders, Wellington – doubted the loyalty of his allies and feared an attack on them. In fact, the Portuguese would be the target of a famous German breakthrough in April 1918. Portuguese casualties on the Western Front would amount to nearly 20,000. The economic strains, despite British loans, would lead to revolution and civil war immediately after the Armistice. Almost unique among the countries which entered the war after August 1914, the Portuguese expected no payment for loyalty to old allies.[59]

That the United States would enter World War I was not a forgone conclusion. As we have seen, the traditional views of American diplomats and statesmen revolved around the idea that the United States as a republic – and both for political and economic reasons – should avoid "entangling alliances" with all powers (European ones above all). Yet after its fratricidal civil war from 1861 to 1865 and an ensuing period of national consolidation, the United States began to project its power abroad. Some American statesmen from the 1880s began to envision a kind of crusading empire, in which American "principles" of freedom and self-government would be spread across the globe.

Yet anti-imperialist sentiment was clearly widespread, especially in the western and midwestern parts of the United States. Though American imperialists had already begun to label their opponents "isolationists," the United States maintained extensive relations with Britain and all European countries in business dealings, in cultural and educational matters, and of course in family matters: millions of Europeans had migrated to the United States in the course of the previous 60 years. Plenty of ties to relatives remained. Yet the multiplicity of these ties militated against taking sides in European quarrels, since the ties led to all European countries.

Indeed, this multiethnic background made it quite unclear – especially when European political configurations became clarified around 1907 – which side America would choose should she decide to enter the war. Many members of the American elites of education and wealth tended to be Anglophile, and relations between Washington and London were quite warm for the most part. Some historians have suggested that Britain's seapower provided substantial defense services to the United States: being on good terms with the world's most powerful navy surely lessened the need to keep a large, protective navy. Britain's

principal ally, France, held a very important place in American relations. France was historically an ally, friend, and cultural mentor.

But important segments of the population had ties to the German
world. The contributions of 200 years' worth of German immigrants
and general American admiration for German culture would make it
difficult to say whether Americans were "naturally" more inclined to
prefer Britain in international matters or not.[60] Moreover, the bulk of
the migrations to the United States from the mid-1890s were from
countries which were members of the Triple Alliance, Austria-Hungary
and Italy in particular. Once the war started, the substantial sympathy
for the Austria and Germany and the large reservoir of opinion that
America should tend to its own business seemed to counterbalance
sympathies for the Entente.

With American sentiment in the balance, the most important figure
in the story of American intervention in the war was President
Woodrow Wilson, Democratic winner of the presidency in 1912 (and
reelected in 1916). Son of a Presbyterian minister in the South, Wilson
became a professor of political science. At the age of 54, Wilson left his
academic career to become governor of New Jersey. Two years later he
was elected president of the United States. Perhaps because of his religious background, perhaps because of his unctuous public speeches,
perhaps because of the finely crafted interpretations by fellow professors and friends like historian Charles Seymour, Wilson has come
down to us as a "moralist" in the White House. With regard to war in
particular Wilson is often viewed as a man of peace, whose tremendous
reluctance to go to war was finally ended by the German decision to
reintroduce unlimited submarine warfare.

Yet we must remember that Wilson was not opposed to war in principle, nor to aggressive war, if by that term we mean the invasion of
other countries. During the first four years under Wilson, the United
States had intervened militarily in Nicaragua, invaded Haiti to "restore
order" (at a cost of 2,000 Haitian lives), and invaded the Dominican
Republic (also to restore order and establish a protectorate). In 1916
he intervened in the Mexican Civil War by invading Mexico with an
expeditionary force under General John G. Pershing, the former
Indian fighter and Philippines veteran. Pershing's expedition, though
its military results were meager, served as a proving ground for the
American Expeditionary Force to be created in 1917.[61]

One might see connections between the Wilson who invaded Latin
America so he could step in and "organize" it in the framework of his

Pan-American Pact and the Wilson who intervened in Europe and in the end stepped in to "organize" the Old World along the lines of the "new diplomacy" and the League of Nations. The scale of intervention into the Great War was magnitudes larger than any of the Latin American conflicts, but Wilson had certainly established a pattern by 1913 or 1914: the crusade for "democracy" was for him no pacific endeavor. And he was increasingly committed to the idea of crusading democracy as time went on. Less than a month before the assassination of the archduke, Wilson delivered a Flag Day address in which he said that in the future, the flag would stand for "the just use of undisputed national power . . . for self-possession, for dignity, for the assertion of the right of one nation to serve other nations of the world." He would, he added, "assert the rights of mankind wherever this flag is unfurled."

Only slightly less important in the decision of the United States to intervene was Edward Mandell House, who loomed large in the intervention question. As Wilson's personal representative to all the belligerent governments, House's shuttle diplomacy and reports to Wilson were vital in shaping his view of a corrupt Europe which needed his help, and above all a barbaric Germany. Wilson's Secretary of State, William Jennings Bryan, was a confirmed opponent of U.S. intervention in the war, but as Wilson's "alter ego," House was able to nudge Wilson toward the Entente more or less steadily until American entry in April 1917.[62]

We have looked briefly at the crisis occasioned by the German sinking of the _Lusitania_ in 1915. The effects of this event were, in a sense, far out of proportion even to the death and destruction caused. As a result of the sinking, the Americans forced the Germans to end unlimited submarine warfare, the flow of supplies to the Entente forces became more secure, and the British blockade against Germany became more effective. Moreover, coupled with the "rape of Belgium," the sinking of the _Lusitania_ solidified for Americans the image of the Germans as cruel and heartless barbarians. At the same time, the crusade to "make the world safe for democracy" had to remain in the future, since joining the Entente meant becoming an ally of Tsarist Russia – far and away the most autocratic of the European powers. But a trickle of American volunteers began to make their way to Canada or France to enlist in the "fight for civilization" and the fight against German "brutality."

This chapter has been an attempt to look at some of the links between the battle front and the home front in World War I. We can summarize as follows. Even during the first year of the war, the material and mental strains of the conflict set in motion significant alterations in the ways in which belligerent societies were "organized." Both "structurally" and "intentionally," the war took certain trends already well underway in Western societies and accelerated them. There is no way around it: the war ate up the material wealth of the nations involved. The expenses of artillery shells alone demonstrate this. Hence, governments took more from their citizens to pay for the carnage, a structural brake on all kinds of productive activity. On the one hand, since all the governments involved claimed in some way to be the representatives of the "people," all war governments had to turn to new means of persuasion and information control, including the production of outright falsehoods. On the other hand, Western Front governments had to adopt more aggressive techniques of intervening in their economies and societies. As Rathenau had put it blandly, "The term 'sequestration' was given a new interpretation." This kind of "redefinition" soon became part of daily life among the Western Front powers.

5

THE CRUCIBLE OF WAR: 1916

Without becoming too teleological about it, one might suggest that 1916 was one of the most significant years of the twentieth century. It was certainly the year in which the Great War changed in its character, size, and intensity. By and large, the war took on an increasingly mechanized, even automated aspect, above all in the Western Front armies, where the "automaton-like" steel helmet replaced soft caps during the last months of 1915 and early 1916. The great Western Front battles of 1916 were larger in size and scope than previous struggles, partly because commanders were pressured to "break through," but partly, as will be seen, because a whole new conception of war by "attrition," or "wearing out," came to influence the thinking of European leaders. Huge battles also took place on other fronts, expending both lives and wealth, making plain in particular the enormous costs of high-explosive artillery preparation.

On the home fronts, the soaring costs of the war helped intensify the state's intervention both into the lives of individuals and economies as a whole. The draconian Hindenburg Program of 1916 would echo throughout the century. On all home fronts the prescribed *political* specific for mastering these difficult problems was a turn to strong men who could in one way or another shore up the crumbling situation. Hence, in a period of a year and a half – beginning about mid-1916 – all of the Western Front powers had turned for leadership to "tough" individuals who were not afraid of unpopular and even brutal measures in the process of marshaling the resources of the nation.

In a sense, too, this profound alteration in the war's leadership, outlook, and nature derives from the earlier, in retrospect almost frivolous, hopes of early breakthrough. The overall change in the war was truly the realization that deeper forces must – as historian René Albrecht-Carrié put it – emerge in many forms.[1] It might not go too far to say that the script for a disastrous century was written during 1916 and 1917.

The Attritional War: The Blockade and Verdun

We usually associate the onset of attritional war with the year 1916. We have examined the various schemes and plans of 1915 to break through to the "green fields beyond." Neither the ferocious French attacks in the Champagne and Artois or the British attacks between Ypres and Arras effected any change in the stalemate. Breakthrough was indeed still on the minds of all, but by the end of 1915, it is clear that Allied leaders, military and civilian, had begun to understand that the side which lasted longest would win. By extension, in order to win, home societies must sustain war for the long term. "Attrition" was a well-known military concept, but some planners now began to conceive of the front in terms of this concept, realizing at last that the "short war" had indeed been an illusion.

This new realization led to a basic shift in strategic planning. The opening of the Verdun campaign, for example – in which, as we shall see, the German goal of the battle was not local victory but the killing of Frenchmen – demonstrates the operation of whole new categories of departures from pre-1914 norms, departures which tended to have as their goal wearing down and outlasting the enemy. Yet we should recognize that attritional thinking was already an important element of the war as early as 1914, when the British established their naval blockade of the Germans, using their fleet and their enormous mining capacities to close off Germany from the outside world. The blockade which the Admiralty ordered at the end of August 1914 and instituted in November was a contravention of some of the terms of international agreements and the norms of international law in two respects. The Declaration of Paris of 1856 had renounced "distant" blockades while allowing "close" ones, meaning that naval forces were limited to stopping ships within three miles of a port, rather than simply declaring whole seas off limits and patrolling or mining them. Britain's first declaration on the blockade was that the whole North Sea was henceforth a military area, and that neutral ships would proceed at their own peril, with similar provisions for the Channel. Second, where a number of international agreements had tried to ensure that food was "conditional contraband," that is, that food would only be treated as contraband if it was to be used to feed military forces. The Admiralty's order of August 1914 made it clear that all food headed toward Germany, even food coming through the neutral Dutch port of Rotterdam, was to be captured.

The Germans soon felt the results of this policy. Shortages crop up in wartime for many reasons, most directly because the diversion of wealth into warlike activities and goods is an assault on the capacities of society to produce goods needed by all "consumers." Governments intervened in their economies much more directly in World War I than ever before, increasing inefficiencies and setting the stage for scarcity. Still, the blockade intensified these inefficiencies and shortages.

The devastating effects of the food shortage were a constant reminder to ordinary Germans of the implacability of the Entente, the British in particular. Foods had been controlled from the beginning of the war in Germany, but bread rationing began in 1915, and by 1916 the urban working classes were in dire straits, standing in endless lines to procure increasingly expensive and increasingly scarce food. Eventually, the National Health Office in Berlin would calculate that by the time of the Armistice 763,000 Germans had died as a result of the blockade (the Allies kept it in place until the end of March 1919). Surely, the shortages generated by the consumption of war materials counted for some of the increased mortality rate, but it seems likely that the reduction of the food level of civilians to about 1,000 calories daily was in part the result of the blockade. The mortality rate among German civilians was 38 percent higher than in 1913. Tuberculosis, rickets, and edema were almost epidemic, and the weaker individuals were the ones hit: older persons, young children, the sick.[2]

The Allies ushered in the blockade with almost bloodthirsty enthusiasm. Churchill wrote that it would "starve the whole population – men, women, and children, old and young, wounded and sound – into submission." Somewhat later, several British public figures began to calculate the "physical inferiority" which the blockade would inflict on Germany for generations to come, understanding the measure in demographic terms quite closely related to the emerging understanding of attrition. And the British continued to tighten the blockade as time went on, even though the resulting frictions might irritate the United States, which was theoretically as much opposed to the blockade as it had been to unlimited submarine warfare. In February 1916, the British cabinet regularized blockade policy somewhat by creating a Blockade Ministry, headed by Lord Robert Cecil. In the larger picture, as a recent commentator has pointed out, the blockade hit hardest those groups – the elderly, children, the weak, the poor – which were least crucial to waging the war.[3]

In a world influenced by the Social Darwinist modes of thinking discussed in the first chapter, and under the pressures brought about by a stalemate, it is not difficult to see how the British and other Europeans arrived at something of a demographic view of the war by the end of 1916. This view was certainly explicit in the plans of the German commander on the Western Front, Erich von Falkenhayn, as he prepared the most massive attack since the outbreak of the war, the Verdun Offensive.

Like most Western Front commanders, Falkenhayn's previous combat experience had hardly prepared him for the stalemate war, limited as it was to uneven colonial encounters in East Asia, where the Europeans tended to meet opponents whose weapons were generations behind their own. He had been appointed Prussian Minister of War in 1913, and had received the appointment as Chief of Staff after Moltke's defeat at the Marne in 1914, overseeing what can only be regarded as a successful year of defensive war on the Western Front. Indeed, the German defense of the Western Front had succeeded in spite of decisions to send troops to the Eastern Front and to send Germans to fight with the Austrian army too. Falkenhayn remained convinced that the Western Front was the key to the war, but he was stymied: from the beginning his basic strategic assumption was that a German seizure of Antwerp on the Channel coast would force a withdrawal of the British and perhaps end the war. Yet breakthrough of this sort was proving not only unsuccessful but increasingly impossible as British human resources grew rapidly through the reservoirs of Kitchener troops, Canadians, Indians, and Australians (every group, by the way, consisting of volunteers).

Some time before the end of 1915 Falkenhayn, so it seems, came to the conclusion that breakthrough in the conventional sense would not be possible. One of the Entente allies must be knocked out of the war. Since neither the Russian nor the British forces could be defeated in a single great blow, Germany would have to move to the offensive against France, whose Western Front losses up to the end of 1915 amounted to nearly 2 million (killed, wounded, captured, and missing) compared to the German losses of "only" 1.3 million.

The means to winning the war, it became clear to Falkenhayn, would have to be based on a demographic solution: "bleed the French Army white." For all practical purposes, then, Falkenhayn gave up on breakthrough for the moment, adopting instead a strategy of "attrition," similar in fact to the British strategy of the blockade. The French had suffered massive losses in a year and a half: more sustained losses would simply deflate the war effort. At some point, the French would run out of men. Or rather, the French people and government would lose heart and become unwilling to suffer such an enormous slaughter of their countrymen. Falkenhayn needed a sector which the French were unwilling to give up, one which the French regarded as indispensable, one from which they would launch counterattack after counterattack, as was their fashion, with disregard for life and limb. He found this sector at Verdun.

The old fortress city of Verdun, on the River Meuse, represented one of many French bastions in Lorraine, guarding against attack from Germany. Verdun was itself fortified, and the French had enhanced Verdun's position by building a complicated system of forts and fortified sites in a semicircle curving around the town. The strongest were Douaumont and Vaux, but the Verdun complex ran from northwest of Verdun to northeast of the city, where it curved south, ending up at Fort Troyon, about 20 miles south. These were concrete and masonry forts for the most part, built in the late nineteenth century, and similar to those which the Germans had crushed rapidly outside of Liège in the first days of the war. The Verdun forts went many stories deep underground, could house thousands of troops and many supplies, and were outfitted with heavy guns. Little wonder that Verdun formed the great lower curve of the "S" on the Western Front: in 1914, the French lines were bent back westward on either side, but Verdun held, creating a salient into the German lines.

This is a standard telling of the story, one that came both from Falkenhayn and from more than a few historians of the battle. We should add here that some – both participants and historians – have doubted that Falkenhayn's original plan was an attritional battle, at least in the cosmic sense described above. His great opponent at Verdun, Pétain, thought that Falkenhayn's postwar disclaimers of attempted breakthrough were only post-facto justification for what actually happened. The French general thought that Falkenhayn was indeed trying to break through, take Verdun, and thereby hand the French a spectacular defeat. Pétain's biographer Stephen Ryan pointed out that the ferocious German attacks which would come in May and June certainly do not look like wearing-out battles, but something entirely different.[4] On the other hand, as Niall Ferguson's recent discussion of attritional results has made clear, Falkenhayn was in any case quite correct in his calculations that the Germans could be more efficient in killing the enemy than the Allies: remarkably, from August 1914 until the German defeats of June 1918, the Allies lost more soldiers than the Germans in every single month.[5]

The French Second Army held the Verdun sector, and the Second Army leadership reflected the whole French approach to the war. The French, as Foch had told students at the War Academy, were unsuited to the defensive posture. The supreme excellence of French arms came into the attack. In the face of enemy assault, fortresses were simply bases for launching the counterattack, and sometimes a hindrance at that. Hence, along the Verdun sector, which had been quiet throughout 1915, the Second Army proceeded to "reorganize" the garrisons and gunnery of the forts ("dismantle" would be a better word). This was part of new plan for defense, but the implementation of the plan was so confused that many officers and men in trench lines in front of and between the Verdun forts were alarmed beyond measure at the German build-up through January and the weakness of their own defenses.

Indeed, Lt. Col. Emile Driant, a former member of the National Assembly now serving on the line, went over the heads of his commanders during the last half of 1915 to write to friends in the Assembly that French defenses at Verdun were woefully inadequate. This had gained Driant only the hatred of his superiors (including the commander-in-chief, Joffre), who continued to remove the forts' guns to the rear and to drain the garrisons so as to increase the potential counterattack force.

As it happened, Driant was correct. By February 20, 1916, the Germans had amassed a million men facing 200,000 Frenchmen along about ten miles of the Western Front. The preparatory bombardment lasted only nine hours but used a million shells in pulverizing the forts and the trenches northeast of the town. At the tip of the salient, in the late afternoon, the German attackers walked into No Man's Land (here quite wide, from 600 to 1,200 yards). The van consisted of 6,000 specially trained troops, carrying, in addition to rifles and grenades, 96 flamethrowers. These troops concentrated on areas of hard resistance, especially French machine-gun placements. Following the vanguard, the standard waves emerged, as the Germans attacked relentlessly. In the center of the salient, they drove the French back to their secondary trench positions by the end of the first day, and to the third line of trenches – five miles from the city itself – on the third day. Artillery fire was incessant, and when the German attackers were not trying to get past some French strong point, they faced stiff French counterattacks.

The French defense was marked by valiant effort. In the center of this cauldron, Driant and his men, coming under attack immediately, were overwhelmed, attempted to fall back in good order, and were killed in swathes. Another politician, André Maginot, was wounded in these days. After recovery he would make his way back, eventually, to the National Assembly, where he would become an advocate of advance-design defensive posture as a replacement for the *furore francesa* of counterattack upon counterattack – surely a battle front/home front connection with wide-ranging repercussions. Within four days Joffre gave in to pressure from the government to give the command of the French Second Army to Philippe Pétain, a bitter pill for Joffre since Pétain was known not only for his criticisms of the general staff and the whole Grandmaison view of combat, but for his willingness to voice these directly and sharply.

Philippe Pétain,[6] born in 1856, was a brilliant officer, but one whose views and manner had tended to work against him in the prewar army. He was born of peasant stock, but so were Joffre and Foch: on this score the French army maintained a tradition of advancement by merit going back at least to Napoleon. Pétain's personal aloofness and his willingness to speak his mind, even give insult, lent him the reputation of being a difficult officer (an English journalist recorded of the general, "Freezing formality as usual. Pétain inspires terror except among a few of his friends"). His dim view of tactics-by-morale was an affront to the whole Foch–Grandmaison establishment. Actually, Pétain remained convinced by the French military doctrines of the 1870s, which emphasized the strength of firepower and the need for caution in the face of it, in keeping with the lessons of the Franco-Prussian War. By the turn of the century, when he began to make his name as a military theorist, Pétain reasoned that the relentless infantry attacks and counterattacks advocated by the new offensive-minded school would kill both men and morale, instead of bolstering it, as Foch believed. But the enthusiasm with which the military hierarchy embraced the Foch–Grandmaison ideas made Pétain the odd man out and his promotions slow to come.

A 60-year-old colonel of a regiment when the war broke out, Pétain gained a firsthand view of the new warfare from the battlefield itself, a view that would make him practically unique among French generals. Under the new circumstances of warfare, he became convinced, artillery should be used to capture an enemy position, while infantry should be used to take the position and hold it: hence his expression, "Artillery conquers, infantry occupies."

Still, the problems which confronted Pétain when he arrived on the scene on February 25 (very ill with pneumonia for the first week, by the way, but nonetheless operating at a high level of effectiveness) called for much more than good tactical understanding. He might have addressed all of this by giving up Verdun and falling back to some prepared line: that is, give up space for time, at the same time shortening his line of defense. Yet this was a political impossibility. The Briand government, under fire from many directions in the long term and highly criticized for allowing the defenses of Verdun to be degraded, demanded that Pétain hold onto the beleaguered town. Forced to stand and fight, the general calculated that new tactics were necessary, but also that logistical arrangements for a massive support system had to be made immediately. Finally, the ill-used *poilus* had to be convinced that their lives meant something, despite their experience from years past.

With the center of his line fighting a desperate action against the Germans, Pétain simultaneously addressed all three issues. He organized a vital supply line from Verdun southward to Bar-le-Duc. This was a single road, but he decreed that the road would be open and passable henceforth. He placed labor battalions alongside the road to shovel gravel and sand (culled continually from fields adjacent to the road) under the wheels of endless lines of trucks. He had the road carefully policed for traffic problems. Little wonder that the road was soon dubbed the Sacred Way (*la voie sacrée*), since the whole French defense of Verdun depended on it.

At the same time, he addressed both tactics and morale by issuing orders that created new conditions. He immediately instituted a more rapid rotation of divisions in and out of the line to give relief to those in the cauldron and took other measures which provided both physical and psychological relief. Pétain also spoke to his soldiers, through addresses and in fliers and written orders. The Germans would not get past, Pétain told his troops, and this would take bitter fighting, but he assured his tired *poilus* that when called upon to attack, they would have the artillery support needed for success. "Artillery conquers; infantry occupies," the teaching of the instructor Pétain, must have made good sense to the weary French soldiers. And indeed, Pétain gathered every available gun and trained them on the attacking Germans, bringing their advance to a temporary halt on February 28.

He ended his famous first message to his troops with an expression derived from the street-level Parisian which was at that moment becoming part of the national argot. Departing from the stiff and formal style of French generals to reach out to the troops, Pétain wrote, "We'll get 'em!" (*On les aura!*). The general was telling the soldiers that they were all in the struggle together, that the army was a team, that he identified with them. These concepts were not unique in the hard-charging French army, but after the senseless waste of French lives in under-supported attacks throughout 1915, they took on special meaning. Pétain told one of the shattered regiments: "You went into the assault singing the *Marseillaise*; it was magnificent. But next time you will not need to sing the *Marseillaise*. There will be a sufficient number of guns to ensure the success of your attack."[7]

If Falkenhayn's plan was to bleed France white, the German Fifth Army commander, Wilhelm, the 34-year-old Crown Prince of Prussia, seemed to be carrying it out. The first days of the attack not only brought the collapse of the French center, but massive French casualties as well. Indeed, giant Fort Douaumont, key to Verdun's defensive network, fell without a fight on the fourth day of the battle, denuded of garrison and guns by Pétain's predecessors. Yet by the second week of the attacks, the terrific artillery pounding by the French guns ended the advance in the center, leaving the lead German troops within eight kilometers of Verdun. Responding, the Crown Prince extended his attacks to the west, eventually to the northwest of Verdun, where the key to the defense was a long ridge named, in prewar times but appropriately enough for the battle, le Mort Homme ("the dead man"). Indeed, if the Germans could take the Morte Homme, they would be able to look down on much of the *voie sacrée*, the single line of supply, and shell the road, limiting the possibility that the French could hold on.

Important here is a piece of the internal history of the Verdun battle which would later emerge as quite significant. Though Pétain became a national hero overnight for defending Verdun, Joffre and the high command at Chantilly regretted immediately having appointed him. Though one might credit at least to some extent

Joffre's later explanations, it is undeniable that he withheld from Pétain supplies and troops which might have enabled the French to end the Verdun battle earlier and with less human cost. In his memoirs, Joffre contended that he was saving troops and supplies for the Somme Offensive. In any case, the high command did much to foster the rise of one of Pétain's corps commanders, Robert Nivelle. The earnest and confident Nivelle had a real charm that garnered him much behind-the-scenes support from both Paris and Chantilly, and he proved an excellent object of this kind of promotion. Nivelle was in many ways suited to the hour: he was tough and resourceful. But in terms of Pétain's overall theory, Nivelle became genuinely detrimental, since he was a true believer in the Grandmaison–Foch theories of attack. And increasingly in the late spring of 1916, in Pétain's center, Nivelle lauched ever more costly counterattacks against the Germans, with a goal of retaking Fort Douaumont.

The Germans renewed their attacks across the whole front in April, taking the Morte Homme northwest of the city at the end of May and the strongest remaining fort, Fort Vaux, in June. Pétain – nearly desperate in his communications to the imperturbable Joffre – again expressed the need to withdraw to some more manageable line, but Joffre refused. In fact, the Battle of Verdun heated up to a climax in early June, testing the French to the limit.

At this point, war diplomacy paid off as French pleas to their Russian ally produced results: on June 4, 1916 General Brusilov attacked the Austrians in the center of the Eastern Front with 40 divisions, sending the Austrians reeling and necessitating reinforcements pulled from the Western Front. Hence, as the French made a stand for what seemed the last time, that stand proved enough. Though fighting would go on into the fall, the June crisis proved to be the last great one.

By the end, when the sector settled down in December 1916, the Battle of Verdun had lasted longer than the entire Franco-Prussian War of 1870–71. Sixty-six French divisions and forty-two German divisions were eventually engaged in the battle, and the losses amounted to over 500,000 French casualties and nearly 450,000 German. Since the tactical practices of both sides turned on artillery fire at all stages of the battle, the battlefield was a particularly terrifying place. Death and wounds were at their most horrific, and also at their most impersonal. The ground was churned up as at few other places on the Western Front, the masonry forts were smashed and dissolved. As one historian pointed out, the phrase "holding the line" really misrepresents the cyclical reality that was repeated on a daily basis: (1) German bombardment and obliteration of the front lines and front-line soldiers, (2) "reinforcement" in the form of units struggling through curtains of German shell blasts toward the front, (3) the desperate struggle of the French survivors for the remaining shell craters and trench remnants that now made up the front line.[8] The ratio of deaths to casualties was probably the highest for any large sector on the Western Front: nearly half of those wounded died. Phosgene gas – much more deadly and insidious than the skin and lung irritants used previously – made its appearance in the midst of the Verdun battle, part of a last-ditch effort by the Germans to break through. In a war of horrors, Verdun deserves its special place.[9]

The course of the battle led to important changes in command in both the German and French armies. On the French side, the debacle of the early phases of the battle was bound at last to have political consequences. In spite of the vastness of the French casualty figures in the first two years of the war, the *Union sacrée*, the political truce that unified the parties behind the "war effort," began to come unglued. In mid-June 1916, the middle-class opposition to the government's handling of the war forced a secret session of the Chamber of Deputies. The session opened with the words of ex-sergeant and now Deputy André Maginot – who was still recovering from wounds at Verdun: "What might seem astonishing is that until now we have all kept quiet." Though the political leadership took many blows, the premier, Aristide Briand, managed to stay far enough in the background for the full fury of the deputies to be aimed at the high command, Joffre in particular. Still, such was the reputation of Joffre that he survived the secret meeting of June 22. Clearly, though, his days were numbered.

At a different level, Pétain was meanwhile maneuvered out of the way. Though Joffre had run the war by firing offending generals, Pétain had performed the impossible in the spring of 1916 and had won a tremendous following, both in the army and in the public at large. Yet for their own reasons Joffre and the French civilian leaders found a way to kick the prickly Pétain upstairs by promoting him to Army Group Commander. His successor as commander of the Second Army: Robert Nivelle. Now, on the one hand, both civilians and the high command could bypass Pétain to rub shoulders with the vigorous and exciting Nivelle, and on the other hand, the offensive-minded general could use the extensive logistical machinery created by Pétain to open up counterattacks which gradually pushed the Germans almost to their original positions, though at tremendous cost and for the most part after the Germans had stopped their offensive.[10]

Nivelle's counterattacks succeeded in part because of successful use of new artillery tactics in which the artillery would "walk" or "creep" forward at a given rate while the soldiers followed this moving curtain, or barrage. All armies had experimented with variations of this technique, and the British had incorporated this into their plans for the Somme Offensive, but the first high-profile successes became associated with Nivelle, who advertised the walking barrage as the breakthrough technique which could dislodge the Germans and return movement to the war. Indeed, Nivelle's optimism was infectious, and even Lloyd George would be influenced by it.

Still, domestically, the increasing unwillingness at home to accept the slaughter of still more troops in misguided offensives led to much discontent, and this discontent was concentrated by the civilian leadership on the commander. Joffre departed from the high command on December 13, 1916, and Nivelle took over at Verdun and set about demonstrating that attacks pressed home with enough fury could still win the war. The result of this whole episode would be disaster when the government, now drawing a somewhat tighter rein, permitted Nivelle to commit the French army to a vast offensive in the spring of 1917, as we shall see below.

German leadership likewise changed. Falkenhayn, who had in effect created the Western Front by overseeing the entrenchment of the German army after the departure of the broken Moltke, was relieved of command in August 1916, as Nivelle's counterattacks began to tell and as the British and French offensive on the Somme entered its second month. His replacement was even more fateful than the changes in French command. Having been heroes of the Eastern Front since their arrival in 1914, Field Marshal Hindenburg and his Quartermaster General, Ludendorff, watched the Western Front disapprovingly. The two loudly disapproved of Falkenhayn's strategy and hoped to succeed him. Supporting them was an imposing array of military men, industrialists, and government figures, the result of a subterranean "campaign" coordinated by Falkenhayn's ambitious staff officer, Max Bauer, a lieutenant colonel whose influence was so great that he had access even to the Kaiser at times. The enormous losses at Verdun and the Somme continued to fuel sentiment for Falkenhayn's dismissal, and the giant Russian Brusilov Offensive of the summer of

1916 likewise worked to the disadvantage of the army commander. The "campaign" for Hindenburg and Ludendorff now shifted into high gear.

The crucial figure here was Theobald von Bethmann-Hollweg, the Imperial Chancellor. Bethmann presented an odd visage for a war leader. Thoughtful, ponderous, pessimistic, and to many more than a little boring, Bethmann perceived the dangers of the aggressive attitude still held by many leaders in German life. Though there were many who disagreed, very significant industrial leaders, military men, and government officials clung to the annexationist dreams. These individuals still bemoaned the government's agreement to stop unlimited submarine warfare in 1915, and they still hoped to erect a kind of empire consisting of various sizes in various tellings, but at the very least Belgium, parts of France, and a large strip of East Central Europe. Bethmann himself tried to think through a postwar order which featured Germany as the central organizer of a number of European satellite states. But his pessimism that this could or should be accomplished overwhelmed him increasingly as 1916 dragged on. Much like French leaders at the same moment, Bethmann looked at the fragility of the political truce, the *Burgfrieden*, and feared that anything but a noncommittal policy on war aims would alienate either the powerful annexationists on the one side, or the middle-class moderates and Socialists on the other, neither of whom were willing to support a new German empire in Europe. By 1916, Bethmann was convinced that Germany should take advantage of its strong position in France and the East to secure a favorable peace from the Allies, one with only minimal territorial extensions, if any.[11]

Bethmann-Hollweg was not among Falkenhayn's greatest admirers, but through 1915 the army chief had supported the Chancellor as the navy (and the pressure group building around Tirpitz and the annexationists) demanded to reintroduce unlimited submarine warfare. But with the planning for the Verdun Offensive in early 1916, Falkenhayn decided that his plan of bleeding the French white would gain much by the immediate reintroduction of unlimited submarine warfare. Bethmann was appalled, being realist enough to understand the catastrophic political potential vis-à-vis the Americans. Bethmann had lost his most important supporter against the admirals. Looking about for others, he realized that the Kaiser was for most purposes now simply inert. Hence, Bethmann turned to Hindenburg and Ludendorff – though both of them were enthuasiastic supporters of a huge postwar German empire – in the hopes that they would help keep the submarine advocates in check. In part, Bethmann had fallen for the propaganda put out by Max Bauer, the *éminence grise* of the great Eastern duo. In part, Bethmann's support for the heroes of the East constituted wishful thinking on a grand scale.

Yet among Falkenhayn's remaining supporters was the Kaiser, relegated to the wings in most decision-making but still paramount in choosing the military commanders. And in order to achieve Falkenhayn's ouster, Bethmann must persuade the emperor. This became possible when Romania – the object of much courting by both Central Powers and Allies – joined the Allies in mid-August 1916. Since Falkenhayn had repeatedly and outspokenly predicted that Romania would not join the Allies, and since Romania's joining of the Entente seemed to doom the whole geographical axis of Germany–Austria–Hungary–Bulgaria–the Ottoman Empire, the dejected Kaiser now – at the end of August 1916 – felt compelled to remove Falkenhayn and put Hindenburg and Ludendorff in his place.[12] We will examine the momentous results of this change below.

The Somme

Yet Verdun was by no means the whole story of the Western Front in 1916. On July 1, the British and French attacked the strong German positions crossing the River Somme in Picardy, thereby giving history another name which still resonates as a place of particularly horrific battle.

The history of the Somme battle is intertwined with that of Verdun. Though frustrated in 1915 by the successes of the German defense, by the end of the year, the Allies saw some light at the end of the tunnel when they considered that Lloyd George's increased munitions production and Kitchener's battalions would be ready for use on the Western Front by 1916 (Kitchener himself died just after these troops began reaching the front, killed on a mission to Russia when his ship struck a mine). These encouraging developments raised the question of how these new resources might be used, and the Allies met to discuss this at a conference at Chantilly in December 1915. Joffre's voice would be the loudest in any deliberations, since France was still fighting the lion's share of the war, and since Joffre was the Allied commander in chief. He called for the Allies to exploit their new resources by launching a coordinated offensive on either side of the River Somme, which now formed the junction of the French and British armies.

Joffre's plan for an attack on the Somme, up to now a quiet area, was based in part on the fact that all sectors of the Western Front were not equal. As John Keegan pointed out in his elegant description of the Somme battle many years ago, since Joffre was still looking for breakthrough, he needed a large, relatively passable battle sector for this, rather than for the attack itself. In order to pour resources into a break in the line, those resources (men, vehicles, horses, artillery pieces, food, ammunition, engineering and entrenching supplies, etc.) must have some way to be moved forward. One or more narrow lanes would not suffice. Joffre needed a wide battle zone, and there really was none south of Verdun and few west of Verdun. The Champagne region, especially north of Reims, offered the vistas demanded, and hence the French had been attacking there already throughout 1915. Yet as Joffre pointed out, as a sector was attacked, the Germans tended to deepen and thicken their defenses, making subsequent attacks less effective at that point.

Looking at the line from the north, the British favored an attack either north of Ypres toward Antwerp or around the Ypres salient itself, but for very good domestic reasons, Joffre hoped to achieve the breakthrough in France. In the Somme sector, the vast ridges roll upward from the River Somme and the smaller River Ancre to its north, creating large sweeping battlefields with vast, exploitable, and largely treeless plains behind them. It is true that almost everywhere in the Somme sector from Arras to the River Somme, the Germans held the high ground, but this was the case across almost all of the Western Front. Hence, the Somme made sense, even if it was not the first choice of the British. Clearly, the dynamics of the Western Front itself and the shape of the Allied coalition meant that the British were going to go on the offensive in 1916 in any case.[13]

The British were apt to listen to Joffre's demands for a number of reasons. It was uppermost in the minds of British leaders that the French had done the lion's share of the fighting in 1915. They held at least three-quarters of the 400-mile front, and their casualties – partly of course the result of their aggressive tactics – made up three-quarters of the Allied losses on the Western Front (including 250,000 casualties at Gallipoli, the French tolls were still much greater: about 966,000 to the combined British losses of 546,000). Clearly, after the disaster of Gallipoli and frustrations of stalemate in Belgium and France, the

British were ready to act. And even if they were not, the massive French sacrifices led to much pressure on the British to take more of the offensive burden on the Western Front by the end of 1915. Hence, as General Haig assumed leadership of the BEF, the responsibility of producing an Allied offensive fell chiefly on him.

More than any other field officer in the First World War, Douglas Haig has provoked controversy among observers. Many of his peers thought him a great commander. Commenting on Haig's triumphant last 100 days of the war, Marshal Foch had only praise: "the victory was indeed complete, thanks to the Commanders of the Armies, Corps and Divisions and above all to the unselfishness, to the wise, loyal and energetic policy of their Commander-in-Chief."[14] The American commander, John J. Pershing, would likewise praise Haig, as did many contemporaries. Still, once the lower-level participants in the war began to issue memoirs after the war, and in particular as the "war poets" and other modernist writers began to dominate the public view of the war in the late 1920s and early 1930s, the tide of criticism turned slowly against Haig. He would become the quintessentially bluff and unthinking slaughterer of innocents: his own innocents, whom he slaughtered by ordering them into impossible attacks, obsessed by the vision of breaking through to the "green fields beyond" and exploiting the breakthrough to end the war. This view tended to prevail until a number of historians in the 1960s – concurrent with the availability and then publication of Haig's diary – began to revise the accepted view of Haig, pointing out that Haig in fact carried the knowledge of his casualties as a true burden, that he did in fact reward innovation, and that he took an essentially small, defensive force and turned it into a large offensive army that in the end defeated the Germans even though the French were able to offer only weak support. Casualties might still be held against him, but historian John Terraine countered with Haig's comment: "In the stage of the wearing-out struggle losses will necessarily be heavy on both sides, for in it the price of victory is paid. If the opposing forces are approximately equal in numbers, in courage, in morale and in equipment, there is no way of avoiding payment of the price or of eliminating this phase of the struggle."[15] On the issue of the Somme in particular, Haig's supporters admit that casualties on the first day of the battle were immense, but they point out that overall, when the battle ended six months later, most of the objectives were in British hands, and the Germans had suffered not only a terrible setback, but terrible casualties themselves.

Yet the debate is still in progress, having produced perhaps its own sort of stalemate, but it has caused both detractors and supporters to unearth much information of great use, even to those who do not necessarily stand in one camp or the other. It will be seen below that the reassessment and debate over Haig have led to a whole branch of recent Great War studies that highlight the ways in which the British army improved over time, improvement which represented a solid learning curve, since a whole new kind of warfare had to be encountered, understood, and reacted to. The controversy has certainly made some useful connections between the battle front and the home front, so that one need not be a partisan or critic of Haig to make use of innovative and insightful approaches to the history of the war.[16] Haig still has many detractors, who appear sometimes to regard the 1960s farce *Oh! What a Lovely War* as a relatively accurate portrayal of the field marshal.[17]

To the particulars, Haig was born in Edinburgh in 1861. His Scots background was of the upper-class variety, and he moved in aristocratic circles. He went up to Brasenose College, Oxford, though he did not take a degree. He was well connected with many influential friends both inside and outside the army, and his wife was a former maid of honour with the royal family. Before the war he had seen much active service in Egypt and the Boer War, and was a a highly regarded staff officer and cavalry commander. Fifty-three years old at the outbreak of the war, he led one of the Corps of the BEF and later the First Army.

Up until December 1915, Haig was in a familiar role: he had served under Sir John French in many capacities since the turn of the century. Yet French's former dash had turned to a very cautious timidity very early in the war, and he had made few friends by exploits such as his role in the Shell Scandal. Among the French, his well-known refusal to cooperate and communicate made him a diplomatic liability. The extremely poor results of the Loos battle in the autumn of 1915 led to his dismissal.

Haig, on the other hand, seemed to have the abilities which French lacked. His handling of the Neuve Chapelle battle in the spring of 1915 had been very good: the British advance, it will be remembered, was substantial in Western Front terms, and only the shortage of artillery seemed to have stood in the way of real breakthrough. Yet one might say that Haig never recovered from that battle, in that his subsequent battle planning was patterned on this near success, even when similarly favorable conditions did not prevail. In a sense, the plan for the First

Day of the Somme in 1916 would be Neuve Chapelle raised by a factor of ten and fully supported with artillery. Now in command of the whole BEF, and a BEF with full complements of the Kitchener battalions streaming to France, Haig was in a position to make a difference.

Indeed, Haig took command in time to attend the first real coordinative meeting between the Allied military forces, at Chantilly on December 6, 1915, a gathering including Russian, Serbian, and Italian leaders as well as the Western Front leadership. At the meeting, the Allied Commander-in-Chief, Joffre, tried to impress Haig and the British with the necessity of attacks on many fronts, to keep the Germans so busy that reinforcement from unthreatened sectors would be impossible. This strategy, of course, implied that the British would go on the offensive, and Haig was planning to do so, though he preferred an offensive in the north to the plans that Joffre had for the British army: an attack along both sides of the River Somme in the summer of 1916. On instructions from London, Haig cooperated with Joffre and began planning. When the Germans attacked at Verdun on February 21, the French needed a British offensive desperately so as to divert German troops away from Verdun.

The planning for the Somme required somewhat paradoxical considerations. On the one hand, the newly trained Kitchener troops now filling in the British sections of the Western Front were inexperienced. A comparison with the superb BEF of 1914 was out of the question. These young men had been civilians little more than a year before. Recruited from all classes, they had in common a desire to fight for their country. But they would hardly be able to perform complex operations. One thinks back to the original German attack on Liège in the first days of the war and the German cadets assaulting Langemarck: attacks in simple close order, with simple objectives, seemed most suitable for troops at the beginning of the learning curve. On the other hand, the British army itself had learned a great deal about fighting battles, like all other Western Front partipants. Three of the most important lessons were these: barbed wire was almost impossible for infantry to cross, especially under fire; it did not take many machine guns to command a whole battlefield; artillery used in innovative ways could solve many of the first two problems.

Hence, the British plan that emerged turned on artillery, and in two ways. First, a week-long bombardment along the whole 15-mile sector of attack would pulverize the German trenches and kill, wound, or disorient German machine-gunners. Some of the artillery fire would be directed onto No Man's Land, with the objective of cutting the German barbed wire. Next, at jump-off time (eventually decided for July 1), a different sort of artillery bombardment would start, the walking or creeping barrage, the same idea which Nivelle's soldiers had been developing at Verdun. Hence, the British soldiers would go over the top, and walk across No Man's Land with very little opposition, taking the first German trench. The barrage would continue to "walk" to the second and third German lines, and by the end of the first day, the great connecting ridges would be in British hands. To make success certain, British "sappers" (tunnelers, many of them with coal-mine experience) set about tunneling under No Man's Land and under the German first line. Underneath strong points, they loaded massive quantities of explosives, ran electrical wiring for detonation, and sealed off the "mines."

There was tremendous technical preparation. But of the soldiers the plan would require only an old-fashioned attack, over the top and a walk across, in any case. The principal preparation for the troops was a sort of enforced optimism rolling down from the high command. Negative attitudes were frowned upon. A few weeks before July 1, for example, an officer of the 9th Devonshire Battalion devised a plasticine model of the Devons' trenches and the German machine-gun post at Mametz, showing how dangerous the attack would be should the Mametz post not be neutralized by the shelling. The plasticine model actually made it up to brigade level as an instructional tool, but its implications were apparently not optimistic enough to make it higher. The officer who made the model was killed on the first day, along with 123 other members of his battalion, since the machine-gun post in question was not destroyed in the bombardment.[18] On the other hand, the most famous case of false optimism also involved a captain in the line, W. P. Nevill, a company commander of the 8th East Surrey Battalion. Before July 1, Nevill handed out a football to each of his four platoons, offering a prize to the platoon which first kicked its football all the way to the German fire trench. On the order to attack on July 1, Nevill apparently got out of the trench and kicked off the first ball, but was immediately killed.[19]

The week-long bombardment of the Germans was duly terrifying, but not deadly enough as it turned out, since the well-constructed German trenches included very deep dugouts and even underground galleries which could house troops. This is not to say that the bombardment was easy for the Germans, and this is not a bad place to pause for a moment to think about the effects of spending a week packed with dozens of men in a claustrophobic, underground, dirt cave in which the walls periodically crumbled from the enemy bombardment. Dugouts *did* cave in, and the combination of the fear of artillery with the fear of being entombed alive seems almost unbearable. We will discuss shell shock below, but we should note that it was precisely this kind of helpless waiting under bombardment that represented the worst of the war for most surviving soldiers. On the German side of the Somme attack, at a dozen strong points, the waiting was ended by the horrendous explosions of the mines, the largest of them (60,000 lb. of explosive) just outside the village of La Boiselle, which left a crater 300 feet across and over 90 feet deep and which swallowed up several hundred German soldiers in the process.

The shelling stopped at 7:30 A.M., and the mines were blown (though one was blown early). At this moment, Germans knew that the attack was coming and started scuttling out of the earth, and the British went over the top for their walk across No Man's Land. It was a race that the Germans won, in particular the machine-gun crews. In most sections of the line, the British troops met machine-gun fire before advancing more than a few yards. Survivors recorded that those leading "were practically annihilated and lay shot down in their waves." Within a few minutes, some soldiers found themselves alone in the advance. Many remembered thinking it odd how so many of their fellows could be tripping and falling, since much of the ground was still unshelled. Much of the enemy barbed wire remained intact, slowing down the soldiers so that the "walking barrage" simply walked away from them. Behind the barrage, one must also think of the subdued sound of this slaughter, since the barrage explosions must have covered the sound of distant machine guns. Men fell without being aware they were being fired upon. In a large number of survivors' accounts, men being hit simply fell without a sound. Toward the line of attack at Beaumont Hamel (close to where the mine was blown prematurely), a number of German strong points and machine-gun posts could sweep the field, and the first wave was stopped a few yards after leaving the front trench. The second wave, an hour after the first and consisting of the Newfoundland volunteer battalion (just rebuilt after a real hammering at Gallipoli), found the communications trenches leading to the front line to be glutted with wounded and dead and had to attack from the second line, in easy range of two German machine-gun posts. Without any significant support by artillery, they sustained most of their casualties before clearing the front trench. Few made it very far into No Man's Land – literally, all this occurred within a zone only a few yards deep. Of 801 attacking soldiers, only 63 survived unwounded. This all happened within half an hour.

Almost at random, some elements of the first day's attack worked. The Ulster Division took its objective and got beyond it. Some soldiers got into the German front lines and occasionally beyond, all along the front. But in most cases the hold was very tenuous, the advance stopped by exhaustion. About 21,000 British and Empire soldiers died within a few hours of zero. Total British casualties ran to about 60,000. The Germans lost some 2,000 dead and 4,000 wounded.

But this was the first day. The Somme battle, really an offensive or series of battles in various parts of a vast battlefield, lasted into November. Eventually, the first-day objectives were taken bit by bit, and the subsequent months' fighting took on the grisly aspect of attack after attack upon German strong points on the higher ground, usually on wooded knolls or in the remains of villages. Haig unveiled the highly secret new weapon, the tank, in mid-September, and perhaps prematurely. These lumbering hulks frightened German troops in spots, but the Allies had not as yet manufactured enough tanks to create a real gap in the line. By the end, the grinding misery of the Somme ordeal was shared on both sides, and the misery went on until about mid-November, when the British struggle up the chalk slopes of the battlefield ground absolutely to a halt. Their line had advanced a few hundred yards in some places, but not much more. The French part of the offensive south of the River Somme had made somewhat better headway, but nothing close to the breakthrough envisioned. Together, the British and French lost over 600,000 men. The Germans lost about 450,000. Generally, about a third of these numbers were deaths, two-thirds making up wounded, missing, and prisoners. Lloyd George summed up much current thinking in November 1916, when he called the offensive "a bloody & disastrous failure."[20] Haig loyalists and others, then and now, have called the Somme a long-term success, pointing out that the terrible losses of the first day do not tell the whole story. Though the troops were not able to do much more than charge across No Man's Land in July, by the end of the battle, the British were beginning to respond to the new warfare in many ways. Tanks had not proved a great success in September 1916, but tank men had gained the experience needed to fight the first great tank battle at Cambrai in the following year. Artillery and infantry did not coordinate well on the first day of the Somme, but by the end of the battle, the walking barrage had become standard practice, and a year later, British soldiers were following the barrage as closely as 25 yards away. Artillerists, moreover, were in the same period inventing new ways of "boxing off" the battlefield so as to seal off routes of escape and reinforcement during a specific time. Machine gunners learned new techniques of "indirect fire" over the horizon and even rapid movement of machine-gun teams forward in the midst of battle to provide more flexible support.[21]

At the same time, as we shall see below, the new recruits of the British army, including new officers, began to understand the need for more "specialization" within the infantry: by 1918, some soldiers carried only bombs (hand grenades) into battle, their special job being to clear trenches so that others could move on to the next trench. Flamethrower teams, Lewis gunners (who manned a light machine gun, highly mobile), trench-mortar teams and others became a normal part of the battle. Indeed, elaborate rehearsals for taking quite specific objectives became the norm before the attack. Hence, the British soldiers who carried out the final offensives of the war were fighting a very different kind of warfare than that of the Pals' Battalions in 1916.

Still, at the end of these considerations, one must account for much failure in the commanders of the Somme campaign. Though supporters of Haig can claim victory, German commanders then and later counted their refusal to break before the British and French onslaught as a triumph. As with the Battle of Jutland, the results were enormous but inconclusive. Clearly, commanders came to the understanding of the new warfare at different rates (their personal learning curves). The alacrity with which the generals and colonels of the Western Front saw the need for more preservation of their troops' lives was undoubtedly connected with a whole web of intellectual, social, and cultural considerations prevalent in their own time.

What made these considerations more urgent and ultimately remembered is the tremendous loss of life. On the disastrous first day of the Somme, casualties were high, but not higher than for the average battle of the nineteenth century, Waterloo, for example. Yet in the case of the Pals' Battalions which went over the top on the first day of the Somme, whole towns mourned the loss of dozens at once. In these towns, "attrition" no doubt took on its own meaning.

The Political and Social Mechanics of Attrition

On both sides of the Western Front in 1916, just over two and half million men were killed, wounded, or captured, 80 percent of these in the furious offensives of Verdun and the Somme. In fact, 1916 was the year of great battles everywhere. The only major sea battle of World War I took place in the midst of the land-based carnage. The Battle of Jutland on May 31, 1916 entailed far less loss of life – "only" about 8,000 died on both sides as a result of the battle – but the losses in shipping were substantial: Britain lost 14 ships, Germany 11. Oddly, the battle resembled most of the other battles of 1916 in that it promised breakthrough but ended inconclusively. Both sides claimed victory, both with some justification. The Germans destroyed more British ships than vice versa and killed more sailors, but when the battle was over, the British held the "battlefield" and the German fleet was scurrying home. Indeed, this scurrying represented a major development in the German war effort. Influenced by Alfred Thayer Mahan, the German admirals had hoped to use their fleet in a big showdown battle with the British. But after one try, the admirals took the fleet back to its north German bases, and there, for the most part, it stayed for the rest of the war. Hence, though Jutland was not a clear victory for either side, the British effectively ended the threat which had originated when the Germans passed the First Naval Bill in 1898.[22]

The simultaneous battles in southern and eastern Europe had less direct impact on the Western Front powers but an impact nonetheless. It was in these same months that the Trentino Offensive and other fighting on the Italian Front pitting Italians against Austrians raised total casualties to over 550,000, over four-fifths of them Italians.[23]

On the Eastern Front, the great Russian Brusilov Offensive against the Austrians opened in June, and when it ended in October, on both sides upwards of 500,000 men had died. The 1916 Russian Offensive, moreover, made an impact on several levels of the war. The expenditure of resources – including human resources – on this colossal effort really moved Russia much closer to the unraveling of sociey and government that would be symbolized by the two revolutions of 1917. The second revolution – the Bolshevik Revolution – would pull Russia out of the war and provide one of the most important backdrops for the Western Front during 1917 and 1918, and during the peace negotiations, for that matter. For our analysis of the Western Front, then, the Brusilov Offensive is highly significant. It reveals a very important pattern for the war as a whole: all-out attempt at "breakthrough" accompanied by tremendous expenditure and loss of life; resulting strains at home and on the battlefields (shortages, strikes, mutinies) which put pressure on governments and produced changes in leadership; government attempts to respond to increasingly difficult problems; some kind of new mechanisms for the governing of society.

In this interim tally for the year 1916, we should stand back momentarily and contemplate the enormity of the killing and wounding which we are describing. And we have not detailed here the losses in the "peripheral" areas of the Balkans (110,000 military casualties), Armenia (190,000 Turks and Russians), Egypt, Mesopotamia, East Africa, and even Cameroon. The year 1916 was indeed a bloody one. All told (and the numbers at this level are really only estimates), about seven million men were killed, wounded, or captured in 1916.

It was also a year in which the material costs of the war soared. The costs of explosives and munitions, artillery shells in particular, serve again as both example and internal motor of a process. We have already noted that the differences between the most inflated prewar estimates and the actual levels of wartime consumption are staggering. Of course shells do not tell the whole story, and one must add to the costs of munitions production the warmaking costs of horses, automobiles, food, transport, uniforms, weapons, chemicals, and all the rest, for even a simple calculation of what such expenditures might do within a society and a polity. The massive bloodletting of 1916 and the accompanying explosion of ammunition and destruction and consumption of goods put the war on a different footing, one which would have been beyond the imaginative powers of previous generations.

The shell scandals and accompanying "crises" in many other goods reflected so great a strain on national finances that leaders saw the need for fundamental changes in the role and size of Western governments. The government of each belligerent country had to change in such a way as to extract much more from its home society – not only more soldiers and more wealth, but greater obedience as well. Hence, the solutions eventually chosen and the men eventually put in charge of them were calculated to introduce compulsion throughout the economy in order to see to it that the army had enough artillery shells, or mortar tubes, or helmets, or whatever the need was.

Although many scholars have examined social changes in time of war, in particular World War I, fewer have studied structural changes in government. Martin Kitchen has examined the case of the German dictatorship, calling it a "silent" dictatorship and tracing the stages of increasing civil powers by the military authority. And a number of historians have touched on the various authoritarian means used to get modern countries through total war. Robert Higgs has gone farther in studying the particulars of such structural changes in the U.S. government by testing a theory of rapid change as the response to crisis – whether war crisis or some other kind. He has shown convincingly that the government of the United States grew both in size and scope in a series of great leaps during distinct times of crisis. During World War I, the United States would embrace widespread intervention into the economy, a quantum leap in the size of government, and hence the frequency and depth of government intervention into the lives of Americans.[24]

We might also apply this crisis-growth pattern in the European context, in particular with the Western Front powers. The crucial escalation of the war on both the home and battle fronts in 1916 was perhaps the defining episode of the Western Front, and in various ways it caused social upheaval both at home and among the men fighting this massive war.

The suggestion here is that World War I, and the escalations of 1916 in particular, produced a crisis in Western government, a crisis which would end in a different kind of government (certainly in much larger, more complex governments) and an essential shift away from the generally liberal conceptions of government in Europe and North America, at least since the nineteenth century. Western governments had tended, even in authoritarian regimes, to respect the person and property of individuals (one of the crucial instructions of Machiavelli to his ideal authoritarian prince). Though nineteenth-century governments had often departed from the values of classical liberalism, and though movements for governmental redistribution of wealth had long called for an activist, interventionist state, by and large European, and indeed Western, governments before World War I were not large enough and powerful enough to separate their citizens from more than a small percentage of their wealth.

A number of social historians of the Great War have seen the results of this crisis as a positive development in Western history. Some historians have described the internal dynamics of this change in governments as the beginnings of a salutary social democracy, in which the British government – after some false starts in the prewar period – owned up to its responsibility to be an activist government with responsibilities to the working class.[25] Other historians have hailed the socially activist direction that Western governments took in the midst of the Great War: the greater comfort level with unions, the encouragement in many cases of women in the marketplace, the cooperation of government and science, the forwarding of political rights for women, the increasing acceptance of parts of the social democratic premise that the state should be more than just a protector of life, liberty, and property.

This view has recently come under attack from different directions. Though such advances tended to be hailed as a success story in the past, critics now point to the destructiveness of war for the productive lower and middle classes, the increased tendency for Western parliamentary systems to become hothouses of mere "interest politics" (with all groups attempting to get as close to the public trough as possible), the damage to manners and morals done by inflationary financing, and many other problems.[26] In the same way, in the area of women's rights and status, the older analysis starts with increased employment of women during the war and their gaining of the right to vote in all of the Western Front countries afterwards. Yet the whole picture is less optimistic in recent tellings. Labor was very hard and very dangerous for lower-class women, who were sometimes called "canary girls" because they turned yellow, either from chemicals or from liver stress. Moreover, women understood clearly, and unions made it clear to them, that their employment would end after the war. Indeed, some studies have shown that much of the employment in war industries was not "new," but rather came from service employees looking for higher wages. Some historians have pointed out that the "improvements" in the employment opportunities for women were at best temporary and at worst destructive of some of the goals of the women's movement. Indeed, on the whole, considering the extraordinarily high cost of the war for women in terms of increased mortality rates, extra work because of lost male labor at home and in family businesses and farms, and increased child-rearing, historians have become much more cautious in discussing women in World War I.[27]

One may assess all these issues according to inclination, but it is clear that war worked not for the long-term well-being of people or the increase in the rights of the working class, but toward societies in which, in various ways, governments took on a kind of managerial paternalism, made possible by the manipulation of a society now clearly regimented into *groups* rather than the older liberal conception of the society of individuals. Certainly the extreme political systems emerging in the wake of World War I and explicitly owing their origins to it – Bolshevism, Italian Fascism, and Nazism – were all characterized by the rejection of the European liberal conception of the autonomy of the individual. And all emerged directly from the war.

The most dramatic and in many ways most influential of the economic approaches to the Western Front was the Hindenburg Program, which the new high command announced at the end of the summer of 1916. The Hindenburg Program itself was really the outgrowth of many of the measures of the Command Economy already discussed, but the sharp edges of the plan, its compulsory nature, and its very extensiveness give it a special place in the history of the Western Front and World War I itself.[28] The background was the intensification of the war in 1916, the result of the slaughters of Verdun and the Somme. German losses at Verdun had already mounted to massive proportions by the end of the summer, and the level of artillery shells being fired off had reached a new plateau. The British attack on the Somme as of July 1, 1916 drained German resources still more. The civilian and military leadership of Germany therefore faced a shortage of shells and, before very long, a shortage in productive capacity along a broad front of items to support the intensified war effort. Under these circumstances, at the end of August 1916, Falkenhayn was replaced by Hindenburg and Ludendorff.

Walter Goerlitz, historian of the German general staff, asserted that in essence Falkenhayn left command because he was unwilling or unprepared to effect a transformation of the economy from the "traditional profit economy" and the standing aspiration of workers for an "enhanced standard of life."[29] Falkenhayn was perhaps worried about revolutionizing the social structure of Germany, but it was nonetheless the case that previous measures of the command economy were already being discussed as a "war socialism." Hence, one wonders whether Falkenhayn's departure resulted from his own scruples, from what was perceived as strategic failure at Verdun, or from what might at that time have been termed simply "lack of energy."

Certainly the ousting of Falkenhayn had been the object of a fairly diverse coalition comprising officers from the general staff, steel producers who objected to irregular methods of general staff planning, and politicians who wanted to bring Hindenburg to supreme command in order to cash in on his public image. Coordinating these efforts was an officer on Falkenhayn's staff, Colonel Max Bauer, who was already making plans for a "total" war regime well before Hindenburg and Ludendorff came to the rudder.[30] Ludendorff had always been the workhorse and planner behind the successes of the famous team, and Bauer's long-range interest in harnessing the resources of Germany in a "total" fashion found echoes in Ludendorff's own opinions: Ludendorff had openly espoused the idea that instead of half-measures, the country ought to go on a total war footing, to correspond with unlimited submarine warfare, and eventually total victory as opposed to negotiated peace.[31]

Yet in all probability, Colonel Bauer – who would be active in the Nazi Party at a later period – actually laid out the elements of what became the Hindenburg Program. Bauer worked out his plan in conjunction with Moellendorff, with whom the general staff officer had come into contact through Fritz Haber, Nobel Laureate in Chemistry, introducer of poison gas to the battlefield, and later advocate of total government. Eventually General Wilhelm Groener, a technocratic general who in October 1916 was working as head of the army rail-transport service and as a board member of the War Food Agency, was brought into the planning elite as head of a new *Kriegsamt*, or War Bureau, with coordinating powers over the whole economy.[32] Soon, the planning elite was filled out with other industrialists, military men, and individuals from many parts of the political sprectrum who cooperated in working out the coercive details of the Hindenburg Program (and some of whom would later assume the same role in Hitler's economic and strategic planning apparatus after 1936). As Gerald Feldman has put it, Moellendorff viewed the whole program as "the institutional framework for a new economic order,"[33] and a variety of men seemed well up to the job of forming a new planning elite of very diverse origins.[34]

In any case, the program was launched almost immediately after Hindenburg and Ludendorff took over. With a distinct Stalinist air to it, but without outright expropriation of property, the Hindenburg Program called for large increases in heavy industrial output of weapons and ammunition, in some cases doubling, even tripling production. As a contemporary economist evaluated the plan, "the so-called Hindenburg Program claims the remainder of our goods of production for the use of the state, at the same time that the new demands have made the increase and extension of our current production facilities necessary."[35]

In December, moreover, the planners pushed through an acquiescent Reichstag the Patriotic Auxiliary Service Law to make every German citizen from 17 to 50 liable to involuntary wartime service. Justifying this measure, Bauer wrote in September 1916, "There are thousands of war widows who are only a burden on the government. Thousands of women and girls are either simply idle or pursuing unnecessary occupations." Trying to shore up labor shortages from other sources as well, Ludendorff oversaw the rounding-up of tens of thousands of forced laborers from Belgium and northern France to work for the German war effort.[36] Some parts of the plan were never realized before the war ended: the closing of universities, calling up all the weak and unfit so that they could heal at "suitable stations," compulsory labor for the whole population "more or less in conjunction with the distribution of food tickets." But the Patriotic Auxiliary Service Law included the bulk of the plans of Bauer and Ludendorff. As Hindenburg wrote in September 1916, "The whole German nation must live only in the service of the fatherland."[37]

The results of this massive intensification of intervention into German society might have been predicted. The various increased output quotas led to a national railroad crisis in early 1917. Working conditions in factories worsened as hours lengthened. Accident rates shot up as lesser-skilled workers were pushed into skilled jobs. Food supplies were already short as a result of the blockade, but an amazing array of substitute (ersatz) products had up to now staved off starvation. Now, as more of the country's resources went into war production, food supplies dropped dramatically. Bad weather also produced a shorter than average growing season and hence a poor harvest. The first winter of the Hindenburg Program was remembered bitterly as the Turnip Winter: the allotment of food in Berlin consisted of between 2 and 6 lb. turnips (or, if available, 2 lb. bread), less than 2 oz. butter and 1 oz. margarine, one of the many ersatz products created by war shortages. Inadequate food supplies led to strikes in Berlin, the Ruhr, and other areas in early 1917. On top of the death and destruction prevailing at the front, the human misery of Germany under the Hindenburg Program was enormous.[38]

Meanwhile, state-supported scientists held public lectures reassuring Germans that they were not really hungry. "Our nutrition," one such "scientist" put it at the end of the Turnip Winter during a lecture in Berlin, "is totally outstanding!" Indeed, the same scientist pointed out all the advantages accruing to the German wartime diet. One could hear, the professor confided to his audience, that certain ignorant classes of the population were spreading rumors about starvation, but in reality, the newly efficient diet was not only plenty for even the heaviest work, but had contributed signally to the eradication of disease: "Certain diseases . . . have almost disappeared." This positive thinker and others went from lecture to seminar spreading the happy word about the health benefits of food planning. Teachers and pastors gathered for three-day meetings, after which they could spread abroad the good news about the newly engineered diet and pass along ideas about efficient cooking and new recipes (many of them including turnips).[39]

Suffice it to say that the multifarious frictions of war and a worn-out, hungry home front made it impossible to implement all the points of the Hindenburg Program, even before the war ended in November 1918. Hence, the universities of Germany were never closed and ransacked to create labor battalions, and the compulsory mobilization of women was never fully carried out. Still, the program went far enough in the dislocation of the war-wrecked economy that it certainly prepared the way for the economic, political, and social chaos encountered by Germany's soldiers when they made their way back home.

Finally, it was not only by the famous sealed train containing Lenin and friends that the German high command would contribute to the Bolshevik Revolution and revolutionizing of Russia. The Bolsheviks also took German ideas with them, in particular the vision of the Hindenburg Program. In the midst of the revolution, Lenin exclaimed, "Yes: learn from the Germans!" Ludendorff's command economy, or war socialism, he said, embodied "the principle of discipline, or organization, of solid working together, on the basis of the most modern machinery, of strict accounting and control." In a comparison beyond the framework of this book, one would be struck by the similarities in the "war socialism" of the Hindenburg Program and the "war communism" instituted by the Bolsheviks as they fought to control Russia.[40]

By 1916/17 the war was taking more and more from the populations involved, hollowing out the economy, creating rationing, shortages, and loss of individual autonomy at many levels, creating a grim wartime home-front existence which required much "mobilization" in the forms of breathless or heroic government propaganda to counteract. To this home-front scene, we must not forget to add the physical deaths and ruin of friends and loved ones on the battle front. As supplies were diverted to military uses and to outright wastage and destruction, food production declined dramatically, as did consumer goods of all types. Shortages emerged everywhere, most seriously in Germany, where the Allied blockade kept food out and contributed to civilian death, misery, and disease. As tired, underaged, and inexperienced workers were brought into the industrial labor force, many of them by forcible recruitment, accidents and injuries increased. Inflation ravaged household economies.[41]

These blows to the resources – both physical and spiritual – of wartime populations led people to revolt in many ways. Though strike activity declined substantially from 1913 well into 1915, beginning with the crisis year of 1916, strikes rose rapidly everywhere.[42] Even in Germany, which orchestrated perhaps the most coherent wartime organization, local frictions led to the rise of regional sensitivities and discontents, even within coherent Prussia, which would emerge as centrifugal and even secessionist movements after the war.[43] Overall, a number of quiet protests emerged, even though the Western Front regimes were pioneering the repressive techniques which became the stock in trade of twentieth-century totalitarian government: concentration camps, prison, mental hospitals.

Even on the battle front, though survivors of trench warfare could still call on reservoirs of traditional patriotism to remain in place, and both military justice and to some extent psychological pressures and group dynamics tended to maintain a high degree of solidarity, things began to crack apart after the massive slaughters of 1916. The stepped-up level of warfare and the murderous tactics involved in both breakthrough sectors and relatively quiet fronts led increasingly to the practice of what soldiers called the "Live and Let Live" System. By a series of nonverbal kinds of communication, soldiers of both sides engaged in informal truces, which did not affect the strategies of the high command but did cut down on senseless killings on the Western Front. Sociologist Tony Ashworth calculated that at least half of the British sector of the Western Front – and this was in sectors where a battle was not in progress – was at any given moment engaged in some kind of "Live and Let Live" arrangement across No Man's Land, ranging from the ritualized firing of artillery during a specific time slot each day to tacit avoidance of the other side's patrols in No Man's Land. To emphasize again the importance of 1916, one can quote the British private who saw the Somme battle as having changed attitudes fundamentally: "From now on, the veterans, myself included, decided to do no more than was really necessary, following orders, but if possible keeping out of harm's way. I have the feeling that many of the officers felt the same way." Ashworth's neglected work is not about cowardice, but about trench fighters who began to take responsibility for their own lives. Naturally, the high commands worked tirelessly to root out "Live and Let Live" behavior.[44]

As we shall see below, this behavior would explode into open revolt a few months after the end of the Somme and Verdun battles: the French army mutinied at the end of April 1917, in the wake of General Nivelle's murderous Champagne Offensive.[45] This was precisely the kind of behavior which was beginning to emerge for the same reasons in the even more hard-pressed Russian army on the other side of Europe. And indeed, these kinds of strains were not far from the surface of any belligerent army after the abbatoirs of 1916.

Is it going too far to say that 1916 produced the blueprint for the twentieth century? Deeper forces did indeed emerge. Massive killing, massive expenditure, sea changes in government – all of these results came from the titanic struggles that still make thinking people shudder. Yet as we shall see, these struggles also laid the basis for the second half of the war and the emergence of still further change.

6

1917: New Strains, New War

Change, not stasis, dominated 1917. Military men responded to the battles of 1916 in ways that produced a new synthesis even as they produced new strains. Change dominated the domestic and diplomatic fronts as well. Strike activity rose sharply in the United Kingdom and Germany. The first Russian Revolution in March 1917 and the Bolshevik Revolution in the following November took Russia out of the war. The United States entered the war in April 1917. By the spring of 1917, new war leaders were in place in Germany, France, and Britain, leaders who would remain in charge until the end. A large mutiny in the French army in May altered the dynamic of Allied strategy, as did the arrival of the American commanding general, John G. Pershing. Both at home and on the battle fronts, soldiers, medics, nurses, and a host of others increasingly saw in the war an unremitting horror.

The logjam was beginning to break up. The colossal battles of 1916 led to the beginnings of "movement" among the Western Front powers in 1917; the front began to take on a different dynamic and new techniques and approaches. These adjustments would be facilitated by great changes in international relations that paralleled the new dynamic on the battle fronts. At the same time, the year 1917 required reassessment on the part of all belligerent governments.

Another, and related, way of making sense of this period brings us back to our earlier discussions of diplomacy, in particular the theory of German historian Eckart Kehr in the 1920s (and Fritz Fischer, who built on his work) that domestic politics tends to be the controlling factor in foreign policy (*Primat des Innern*). In this sense, we might try to connect the battle fronts and home fronts as well as wartime diplomacy by thinking about domestic discontents, the rising death toll that by now had affected practically all individuals in the belligerent countries, the growing sense of betrayal, the increasing costs of living and increasing shortages, and other encroachments on individual well-being. The motor of the war, we might paraphrase Kehr, was becoming life on the home front.

The United States Intervenes

The American declaration of war on Germany on April 6, 1917 carried profound meaning for the shape of World War I and its subsequent history, indeed, for the history of the twentieth century. The United States remained the largest industrialized country among the powers not in the war. With a population about equal to that of France, Britain, and Belgium combined, the United States also had the most successful industrial economy in the world. The U.S. national income was not much less than the combined incomes of all the major belligerents in the war (Britain, France, Japan, Germany, Italy, Russia, and Austria-Hungary).[1]

The German roots of a large minority of the American population led German statesmen to hope to sway the American colossus in their direction.[2] But the allegiance of German-Americans was a much more complicated thing than imagined in Berlin, and the American press, moreover, had painted such a negative picture of the Kaiser and his Germany since well before the war that, all in all, it was far from certain that German-American influence would keep the United States neutral.[3] At the same time that various British agents were exerting free and extensive influence over the American press and the American government, several legal German missions to influence the United States came to nought and were vilified in the press.[4]

Indeed, from early in the war, the "neutral" United States was sending much of the sinews of war to Britain and France. East Coast banks had worked out a $500-million war loan to Britain and France in October 1915. Before April 1917, the United States had extended a further $2.6 billion. Apart from outright loans, the United States could and did supply enormous quantities of food and other provisions to the Entente powers, delivering $3.2 billion-worth of export goods to Allied countries in 1916 alone.[5]

Public sentiment was a very close call on the issue of involvement in the war. Yet many in the intellectual, political, and business elites were enthusiastic for American intervention. Many bankers hoped to ensure that their loans would be paid back. Most of the leadership in both parties considered Britain to be in a community of interest with America. Moreover, we have seen that the "Progressives," Wilson's ideological backers, favored intervention because they thought that the wartime setting would be the perfect time to effect social and educational reforms and national homogenization. Hailing the Defence of the Realm Act as a stroke of egalitarianism and discipline, progressives lauded the war as productive of rapid reform. The progressive journal *New Republic* called the war a chance to extend collectivism, promote economic equality, and completely overhaul the educational system to make it a tool of the reforming state.[6] The American collectivist philosopher John Dewey promoted American entry explicitly because the war represented to him "a plastic juncture" in history, during which right-thinking leaders could mold the United States easily in the direction of "social possibilities" and establish "the supremacy of public need over private possessions."[7]

Wilson himself was interested in a new kind of international system based on open agreements. From 1916 onward, in speeches and letters the President put himself forward as a mediator for peace. The famous Fourteen Points of January 1918 would be only the continuation of numerous plans for peace put together by Wilson and his closest advisor, Edward Mandell House. While numerous incidents emerged regarding the thousands of tons of supplies which the United States was shipping to the Allies, Wilson seemed unable to decide between taking a hard line against Germany and playing the role of peacemaker. In the presidential campaign of 1916, one of Wilson's most prominent slogans was "He Kept Us Out of War." In December he issued a "Peace Note" to belligerents and in January 1917 further called for "a peace without victory." Yet his communications with House and others from this period might almost show that Wilson and his advisors had concluded that if Wilson was to orchestrate a new order of international peace and open covenants, the United States would have to enter the war. Certainly he had definite plans for entering the war as early as April 1916, when he called a secret conference of selected legislators to see if he had enough support to bring the United States into the war on the Allied side. When these legislators opposed the plan, Wilson backed away from it until after the election.[8] Wilson scholars have frequently pictured him as an idealist and pacifist reluctantly drawn into war. We have seen, however, that Wilson's idealism had included much military activity before 1917, most of it aimed at extending his ability to promote his ideals abroad – a kind of crusading democracy.

The United States was clearly an unneutral "neutral." Yet the Germans gambled in ways that offered ample opportunities for the United States to abandon "neutrality." The readoption of unlimited submarine warfare was in part an attempt to deal with the problem of the British blockade. Wilson had remained so adamant on the issue of unlimited submarine warfare that it makes sense to think that the German government, at least the Foreign Office and the military quasi-dictatorship of Hindenburg and Ludendorff, in essence "gave up" on the United States, calculating, as some have suggested, that the United States was a bigger problem as a neutral protecting the supply line of the Allies than it would be as a belligerent in a war with no holds barred.[9] The new submarine offensive was announced on January 31, 1917. Wilson sent the German ambassador home and determined to join the Entente side, but waited, as he said, for some overt act.

The German Foreign Office – aided by British naval intelligence – provided this act when it initiated one of the clumsiest episodes in modern diplomacy, the so-called "Zimmermann Note." The note was a short message sent to the German Ambassador in Mexico City by Foreign Office Permanent Secretary Arthur Zimmermann. Zimmermann wrote that Germany would begin unrestricted submarine warfare on February 1, with the hope of keeping the United States neutral. "If this attempt is not successful," Zimmermann continued, "we propose an alliance on the following basis with Mexico: That we shall make war together and together make peace. We shall give general financial support, and it is understood that Mexico is to reconquer the lost territory in New Mexico, Texas, and Arizona. The details are left to you for settlement." The telegram was intercepted by the British, deciphered, and handed over to Wilson, who released it for publication the next day, February 27.

This piece of foolishness and blindness strains belief, but the results were quite predictable. Resistance to intervention could not survive the blunt plans of Germany. Several sinkings by U-boats followed in the next week, with the loss of American lives.[10] The Senate ratified the declaration of war on April 6.[11]

The United States decisively tipped the balance of the war. Where the Entente powers had previously taken quite seriously the possibility of a negotiated peace, that is, peace proceedings on the basis of give and take, the overwhelming power represented by the newly energized Entente meant that the Entente would not negotiate, that the blockade would remain firm, that Germany could only win the war in the field. The tremendous wealth and productive capacity of the United States meant that the Allies, over the difficult and wrenching events which lay ahead in the next months, could always look toward some light at the end of the tunnel.

Attack!: The Nivelle Offensive and the Mutiny

The year 1917 forced a rethinking of tactics and strategy for Western Front military leaders. The colossal battles which ground to a halt at the end of 1916 would seem to have ground down the Western Front powers too, and we have seen that fundamental and profound social and cultural changes began to emerge by this time. In terms of material sustenance for both battle front and home front, the Western Front powers were moving toward exhaustion, though at different rates. By the beginning of 1917, Britain was still maintaining an industrial production level of about 90 percent of the pre-1914 level, though of course the profile of production had changed dramatically in favor of war goods. German industry began 1917 producing about three-quarters of the prewar level, France still lower. France had lost an important segment of its productive capacity in 1914 when the Germans took the textile mills and coal and steel production of northeastern France. Still, the French economy was surprisingly strong considering the body blows it had sustained, though much of the industrial effort came at the expense of the agricultural sector.[12]

For Germany, the lessons of 1916 were ambiguous. Chancellor since the beginning of the war, Theobald von Bethmann-Hollweg had stood by since August 1916 as Hindenburg and Ludendorff instituted something like a total war footing at home. Meanwhile, the failure of the Verdun Offensive to bring France to her knees, as well as the strategic defeat at Jutland, hovered behind all discussions of German strategy for 1917. Though an international – or rather, American – outcry had caused the German government to end unlimited submarine warfare in August 1915, the submarine offensive was anything but harmless for the Allies, and the German leaders decided in March 1916 to try a limited submarine offensive designed to loosen the British blockade. The campaign became "unrestricted" again, in the sense that the German submarines were ordered to fire on civilian shipping carrying goods to Britain. This second unrestricted campaign ended after the United States protested in April 1916. By the fall of 1916, Bethmann-Hollweg saw Germany's position as so imperiled that he sent a note to the American president, asking for American mediation in a peace plan that would include giving up Belgium and other occupied territories. Receiving no reply, Bethmann continued with his peace efforts, attempting in the autumn to make an international plea for a peace based on the open statement of German war aims as a basis for negotiation. These efforts would be rendered pointless when the high command and the Kaiser decided to begin unrestricted submarine warfare once more in January 1917.

Hindenburg and Ludendorff arrived on the Western Front in the midst of these discussions and were not at first opposed to peace initiatives. Yet by November, they had developed plans of their own which peace might endanger. Some top military leaders had already recognized that Ludendorff would never sacrifice his own ambitions to the achievement of a reasonable peace. As the duo took over the high command, the head of the Military Cabinet, General Lyncker, wrote that Ludendorff, "with his boundless vanity and pride will continue the war until the German people are completely exhausted."[13] A new study of the Eastern Front under Ludendorff's leadership indicates that the general's plans for a future German empire were likewise boundless.[14]

If peace was not the answer to military losses, a new unrestricted submarine offensive presented itself as a solution. Actually, Ludendorff's analysis of the military situation was in a sense parallel to the calculations of Lloyd George. Since 1916 had proven breakthrough well-nigh impossible, then Germany should try a defensive footing on the Western Front while "winning" elsewhere – for the moment in southeastern Europe and on Allied shipping lanes. German engineers and labor battalions, many of them newly rounded-up forced laborers from occupied Belgium and France (a feature of the new Hindenburg Program), constructed an excessively strong position extending behind the northern center of the Western Front, a position later known as the Hindenburg Line.

As with other innovations coming out of the first years of the war, experience showed the way to new defensive techniques. The Hindenburg Line, like most German positions, occupied ridges and other high ground and incorporated major existing features (bridges, the St. Quentin Canal) into the defensive structure. It consisted not so much of a line of trenches as an overlapping series of entrenched fortified positions with a high density of concrete pillboxes, blockhouses, and fortresses, many of them two-storied and quite elaborate and most of them "interlocking" in terms of firing angles. Artillery placements were all in a position to fire "indirectly," that is, over hills, and the area immediately in front of the new line was surveyed and marked down to the meter for the benefit of artillery crews. Though the German trench system had previously been much deeper (from the front to back) than that of its enemies, the new "line" was deeper still, in places as much as 15 kilometers from the front trench to the artillery batteries and rear communications trenches. Hindenburg later described the concept as it appeared to the high command, calling it a "network of lines and groups of strong points. In the deep zones thus formed we did not intend to dispose our troops in a rigid and continuous front but in a complex system of nuclei and distributed in breadth and depth." His troops could move out of the way of sustained bombardments and then retake evacuated positions. In February, along a 100-mile segment of the Western Front – from Arras southward to Soissons – the Germans began carrying out "Plan Alberich," an intensive devastation of the areas immediately behind their front line and subsequent withdrawal to new positions, 10 to 20 miles in the rear.[15] The Germans thus signaled that they had no intention of leaving France and Belgium any time soon.

Though many in the Allied camp counseled a similar strategy (stalemate on the Western Front and victory elsewhere), their leaders chose the opposite. Here, changes French military leadership played a crucial role. The unpopularity of Marshal Pétain among various French military and civilian politicians had, it will be remembered, led to a multiple personnel moves. In December 1916 the animosities built up against Joffre led to his being promoted to Marshal of France and "kicked upstairs" as special consultant to the government, a post of no importance from which he soon retired. As one of his last acts, Joffre made certain that Pétain would not succeed him as commander in chief, and that Robert Nivelle would jump over Pétain to replace Joffre in the top command role. Poincaré had only suffered the independence of the victor of the Marne unwillingly. Joffre had, in most minds, never recovered from his disastrous decisions before the Verdun battle. Ferdinand Foch might have been a candidate to replace Joffre, but his stock was still low from being associated with failures in the Somme operations in 1916. Pétain's promotion might have been expected too, considering his spectacular performance at Verdun, but Joffre and Poincaré considered the brusque Pétain to be too pessimistic and too slow.

Nivelle, on the other hand, had gained much favor with both Poincaré and Prime Minister Aristide Briand after his furious offensives at the end of the Verdun battle. Unlike Pétain, he was urbane, charming, and convinced of the superiority of his *attaque brusquée* methods. Moreover, where the essentially anticlerical French leadership distrusted Pétain, who was a nominal Catholic, Nivelle was a Protestant and hence perfectly acceptable. Nivelle's mother had been English, and both his charm and his ability to speak English without accent undoubtedly helped him to win over Lloyd George, who was in any case ready for any change in the French command that appeared to involve ambitious French plans for an offensive.[16] Hence, Nivelle became the new commander in chief in December 1916. "Victory," he pronounced, "is certain."

Actually, Nivelle's jaunty self-assurance was only part of his ability to gain both the high command and backing for his offensives in early 1917. In November 1916 Allied military and political leaders had met once again at Chantilly to discuss strategy for the coming year. Not yet "promoted" out of command, Joffre told the British that the French army could no longer bear the brunt of operations. He proposed a new offensive involving a massive British–French attack south of Arras and a British assault north of Ypres, with the object of collapsing the German line along the coast far enough to take the German U-boat bases at Ostend and Zeebrugge. Lloyd George distrusted a plan which relied so much on British forces, coming in the wake of the dreadful Somme campaign. To Lloyd George and the British, Nivelle's plan seemed at least an improvement over Joffre's: a powerful French offensive on a small and unexpected front and breakthrough into the "green fields beyond." Though both General Robertson, the chief of the imperial general staff, and Haig had grave reservations, they acquiesced. Upon the German decision to carry out unrestricted U-boat warfare in February 1917, Allied leaders met hurriedly at Calais to reassess, and Nivelle gained complete support for an offensive in the Chemin des Dames: the U-boats made it imperative that Germany be defeated on land before Britain could be defeated on the ocean.

"We now have a formula," the new commander declared, "We will defeat the enemy with it."[17] He insisted that his offensive would end the war in 48 hours. His plan was not without innovations: after a week-long artillery preparation, a million men would follow a walking barrage to attack the Germans on a broad front centered on a high

mass of forested hills called the Chemin des Dames, between the cathedral cities of Soissons and Reims, in the center of the Western Front.
Unlike the Somme attacks, French units would bypass strong points
and choke them off, hence penetrating to the rear of the German lines.
Nivelle's conception of flowing around strong points was in fact a real
step forward in thinking about the new kind of warfare, and the
Germans would make use of the same principle with great effect in the
Ludendorff Offensive just a year later. Indeed, this innovation would
become fundamental to subsequent warfare in the twentieth century.
Perhaps the chief reasons for Nivelle's failure were not the method of
attack, but its breadth (40 miles across), long delays, the German capture of documents, and a long artillery preparation that left nothing to
the imagination for the Germans as to when and where the French
would attack.

Well before the offensive began, military and civilian leaders were
worrying about Nivelle's plan and counseling caution: with the United
States on the verge of entering the war, simply holding on might be the
best strategy after all. Yet he had much support from the British, and
many French politicians were hesitant to put a halt to preparations
which might in fact lead to the end of the war.

Preparatory to the Nivelle Offensive would be a five-day bombardment, followed by the partly diversionary or spoiling attack of the
British before Arras. Led by tanks in some locales on either side of
Arras (north of the German withdrawals), the British infantry went
over the top on April 9. The most famous of these preparatory component attacks was that of the Canadian Corps at Vimy.

Sustaining 14,000 casualties, the Canadian Corps contributed
to their country's national identity and pride by storming up Vimy
Ridge, as many observers then and historians later have commented.
In military terms, there was much more than "storming" going on,
however. As an important study has shown, the Canadians were able to
work their way up the sweep of the ridge not on courage alone, but
with the careful tactics which their commander, Sir Arthur Currie, had
instilled in his Corps. As with all armies in 1917, the learning curve of
officers and troops had begun to change the face of battle. New platoon
organization which allowed squad-level tactics allowed platoons and
companies to advance not in blind waves, as on the Somme, but in
units which would make a dash, take cover, and fire to keep the enemy
soldiers' heads down while the next platoon or company made its dash.
Weapons were distributed with more careful thought, and in a more

specialized way, so that there were not only rifle-carrying soldiers on the field but soldiers using the Lewis gun (a portable, light machine gun), soldiers firing off rifle grenades, soldiers carrying only sacks of grenades (simple bombs) for clearing out trenches and deep dugouts once the objective was taken, and actual machine-gun crews of three men carrying heavy Vickers machine gun, tripod, water for cooling, and ammunition belts, hustling along in the wake of the attackers to set up to defend against German counterattacks. Just to the rear were officers controlling their units and further back commanders in touch with upper commands by trench phone, courier, and a large number of carrier pigeons. All of this took place with the hope of, and with much success in, keeping close behind the "creeping" or "walking" barrage, as the gunners steadily lifted their guns to move the barrage forward, spewing shrapnel (when everything worked as it should) toward the wire and the Germans in front. Each step had been rehearsed many times in advance. On the day, Allied airpower delivered much information and some tactical support, a far cry from the crude usefulness of airpower early on. Successful attacks such as the superb assault on Vimy Ridge took courage, to be sure, but commanders in all armies began to realize by 1917 that careful training and an intelligent response to technology were absolutely essential. Currie was a master of this calculus.[18]

The British First Army, to which the Canadian Corps was attached, made other gains as well, and along with the British Third and Fifth Armies in this first stage realized its task of "fixing" the reserves of the Germans, even though the attacks ground to a halt. The cost was high for the British (150,000 casualties) but actually lower than expected. A week later, after a long bombardment, Nivelle announced to his *poilus*, "Our hour has come!" and opened the main attack against the new German position on the Chemin des Dames heights, between the cathedral cities of Reims and Soissons. Nineteen French divisions duly went over the top. With even more experience than the Canadians, the French had developed their approach to the new warfare extensively. Indeed, Sir Arthur Currie brought back many of his ideas from observation of a French assault in December 1916. The French had also learned to exploit new weapons and better training. But their objectives were more difficult than those of the British to the north. The German Seventh Army commander, von Boehm, had held in his hands the French plans since they had been captured weeks before and had made every possible preparation.

Straining to the utmost, the French broke through the forward German defenses at a number of points in the first days, and a major tank attack on the right nearly punctured the whole *Stellung*. The French Fourth Army launched a successful secondary attack to the east of Reims on April 17 but was unable to proceed to second-stage objectives. The German counterattacks now began, and the pattern of attack/counterattack continued for several days. Each phase of fighting on the Western Front seems to have had its own special set of horrors and miseries. The Champagne region and the Chemin des Dames massif in particular present very high and rugged hills interspersed with long open valleys, valleys which became intense zones of killing for the defending Germans. By April 20, Nivelle had committed 1.2 million men to the battle and 7,000 guns (whose gunners never quite delivered the creeping barrages essential to Nivelle's plans). The Germans suffered substantial losses in the offensive (75,000 against the combined British and French attack), but the French losses were astronomical: in the first eight days, France lost 117,000, 32,000 of those dead.

These losses justified the worst fears of the French civilian leadership, which had extracted from Nivelle promises that he would break off the attacks if they were not successful. The government hesitated to enforce these promises because of the possible effects on the coordinated British offensive, but by April 25 Paris had decided to replace Nivelle at the first slight improvement on the front. Certainly Nivelle's vaunted 48 hours were up and the war was not won. But Nivelle reacted by ordering a new series of offensives against virtually impregnable positions, to be launched on May 1. Direct instructions from Paul Painlevé, the new War Minister, caused Nivelle to draw up more modest objectives, but the attacks went forward anyway. After delicate negotiations with the British, who distrusted Pétain's tactics as "defensive-minded," the French government secured approval for the appointment of Pétain as French commander in chief, removing Nivelle in mid-May 1917.[19]

The Nivelle Offensive looms large in any consideration of connections between the battle front, the high command, the civilian leadership, the home front, and indeed, relations among the Entente partners. Though studies have shown the immense reserves of patience and fortitude on the part of French men and women, both at home and on the battle front, during World War I, the Nivelle Offensive proved the straw that very nearly broke the camel's back.

Conditions in the French army were harsh. Officers lived like beings from another world, though many soldiers were far more educated. Legally permitted furloughs were not permitted in practice. In the French army (of all armies!) food was terrible. The Germans and British had devised means of carrying hot food to the front lines and had been doing so since 1914. French soldiers hardly got hot food when out of the line, not at all when in it. Above all, French soldiers were demoralized by the French generals' frivolous sacrifice of soldiers' lives in ill-considered attacks. The French army had long been attack-minded; Nivelle's disaster was only a new and improved form of attack. Moreover, Nivelle had been so extravagant in his predictions to officers and troops, that the crushing disappointment of surviving the terrible offensive of April 1917 only to discover that the whole offensive had been an exercise in futility was simply too much for human beings. The army began to mutiny.

The first mutinies occurred just as Nivelle ordered the new attacks, on April 29. Members of an infantry battalion refused to go to the front line, knowing that they would be ordered to attack. Over the next two weeks, other similar low-grade mutinies cropped up in other units. The mutiny began in earnest at the end of May, and for two weeks, the French army was dissolved as a fighting unit. Yet the mutiny was an excessively rational event. Most often, soldiers would refuse to occupy jumping-off positions for attacks, saying that they would remain in defensive positions ready to fight should the Germans attack. In a few cases soldiers went further and rioted, threw stones at officers, called for an end to the war, or organized soldiers' councils. For the most part, they continued to respect their officers, but units throughout the French army, on all sectors of the front, refused to attack. This included 21 chasseur battalions, the elite of the French infantry. One cavalry regiment did mutiny, but by and large the French cavalry – not much affected by attacks, since the cavalry was largely useless – stood ready to suppress the mutineers when called upon to do so.

Nivelle was dismissed just as the mutiny broke out. The new commander was the soldiers' general, Pétain. But many French generals on the front called for old-style remedies: immediate and generous shooting of mutineers. Pétain is remembered for having curbed his overzealous officers in this regard, but both Poincaré and War Minister Painlevé were watching the situation closely to make sure that the generals did not institute a terrible reprisal on the soldiers. Painlevé in particular distinguished himself as a statesman in this difficult time.

This mathematician-turned-politician stood up to the inertia of the French military tradition and insisted that Pétain and his generals regard the mutineers as Frenchmen as well as soldiers. The whole War Committee indeed supported Painlevé in restraining the soldiers, so that Pétain had ample backing for clemency in a very difficult situation.[20]

Still, he had to resort to punishment, though considering the circumstances, this was quite limited. Death sentences were handed out to several hundred "ringleaders," but most of these had their sentence commuted and were instead exiled to penal colonies. In the end, fewer than 50 soldiers were executed for a mutiny that encompassed hundreds of thousands of troops. Several thousand more suffered lesser punishments: penal colonies, penal battalions, and other sentences. On the positive side, Pétain was tireless in visiting army units and talking with officers and men. Assuring French soldiers repeatedly that unsupported frontal assaults would cease, that French attacks would henceforth have tangible objectives and full artillery preparation and support: "Artillery conquers," as Pétain had long held: "infantry occupies." Henceforward, Pétain was at last able to convince both civilian and military leaders, attacks would aim for local objectives and wearing down the enemy, not breakthrough.

He likewise addressed local concerns of the *poilus* regarding food, reliefs in the line, furloughs, rest-area accommodations, and a range of other activities. And indeed, Pétain was as good as his word. A new furlough system gave rapid relief to many; new mobile kitchens came into existence; liquor began to appear in a more regulated ration (neither too much or too little at a time); soldiers' savings accounts were set up to help the men hold onto more of their pay; special rest areas with clean facilities and good food soon made their appearance.[21]

Though the impressive study of Jean-Jacques Becker has shown that civilian France stood amazingly firm in the midst of all the war crises, the case of the mutiny demonstrates a multiplicity of home front–battle front connections, overlapping, countervailing, and sometimes contradictory. It is hard to imagine that the growing domestic unrest in France was not related to the outbreak of the mutiny, even though it was kept secret – not only from the French public at the time, but from a whole society for decades. In any case, dissatisfaction was clearly on the rise even before the first mutinous acts. Although censorship was strict, by 1917 even the least observant French citizen had to see that the war was having an enormous impact on a whole generation. A hatmaker in a small French town noticed that she and her mother had made mourning hats for practically every woman there. Particularly in the cities, where rising food prices hit hardest, people had begun to have enough – as extant systematic reports of officials show. On May 1, three days after the first tentative outbreaks of the mutiny, a growing antiwar organization, the Committee of Syndicalist Defense, drew nearly 10,000 people to a rally in Paris. Strikes broke out during the late spring, principally among women working in the clothing industry. Early 1917 also brought the end of the *Union sacrée*, the political truce declared by all parties in 1914 in support of the war effort. And it was not only French Socialists (who proposed attending an international socialist congress for peace), but bourgeois politicians as well, including many formerly staunch nationalists. Pétain in fact demanded that the government block French Socialists from attending any sort of international peace meeting, a step which the government took.[22]

If one pulls back from the sometimes arbitrary distinctions typically made between battle front and home front, the mutiny constitutes one of the most interesting and telling episodes of the war. We have examined above the analysis of sociologist Tony Ashworth, whose 1980 study of the "Live and Let Live" system examined the dynamics of trench life. Ashworth and others have demonstrated that the spatial organization of trench life led to the tendency of front-line fighters to engage in various kinds of "informal truces" with the other side. Like the famous "Christmas Truce" of 1914, the French mutiny bore much resemblance to this sort of behavior – not a rejection of defense, but a recognition by soldiers that they were in the same boat as the soldiers across the way. The larger, almost conceptual point here is that intermittently from the time of the famous Christmas Truce of 1914, front-line fighters began to identify more with the front-line fighters on the other side of No Man's Land than with the "high command," the "rear echelon," the "brass hats," all terms of increasing opprobrium. The extreme example of such behavior in the war was, perhaps, the collapse of the Russian armies in 1917 amid amorphous fraternization and even celebration with the "enemy."[23] The French mutiny differed from many examples of Ashworth's "Live and Let Live" cases in that the *poilus* do not appear to have fraternized at all, and in most cases did not break ranks at the front. They simply refused to attack. Most of the actual mutiny occurred just behind the lines, where bored soldiers used their pay to buy alcohol from the apparently omnipresent liquor salesmen, and inebriated boredom led to mutiny. On the front, more serious moods seem to have prevailed. But it is likewise clear that in the Western Front army, whose officers maintained the most glacial aloofness of all, the idea that leadership does *not* know best emerged loudly and in the end for most participants, triumphantly. The twentieth century would live with the legacy of such triumphs.

Though the mutiny crisis was over technically by June 1917, the army continued to be crippled by reverberations in military affairs until the fall. With the home front likewise in disarray, France was facing the crisis of the war in the late spring and summer of 1917. If Pétain reversed the collapse of the French army by working miracles of good sense, the Nivelle Offensives and the mutiny combined had destroyed the French army as a offensive force for the remainder of the year. One may well ask: Why did the Germans fail to exploit this amazing weakness and break through some chosen part of the French line? For three reasons. First, the French were successful in keeping the mutiny a secret from the Germans. Second, if the army could not attack in the immediate future, it could still defend, and was quite willing to do so; and the strength of the defense during World War I is central to our whole study of the war. Finally, the Germans faced other Allies on the Western Front, and the plans of the British in particular began to occupy much of the attention of the Germans.

Attack!: Passchendaele

As Nivelle had assumed command of the French army at the end of December 1916, the British commander in chief had worried that both the changing strategic ideas of the French and the hostile ideas of his new prime minister, David Lloyd George, would upset his plans for a new offensive in Flanders in 1917. His plan was indeed altered while Nivelle commanded the French army, but with the crashing failure of Nivelle, Haig was able to return to his conception and begin work on a new Flanders Offensive in May, eventually delayed until June/July.

Many older accounts of the war treat both the Nivelle disasters and the Passchendaele offensive as more of same, simple stubbornness on the part of the "red-tabbed butchers." While no recent research has done much to "revise" our view of the Nivelle Offensive, recent historians have tended to moderate their views of Passchendaele as an unmitigated disaster. For one thing, some have pointed out the strategic logic of the plan in its focus on Antwerp, a factor little noticed before. Moreover, many historians (especially those who write positively of Haig) have pointed out that the Passchendaele Offensive was, if costly, successful in the long run, and it might have been much more successful if the weather had not turned the battlefield into a near-impassable mire. Yet for all the justifications, no one can deny that Passchendaele exacted a horrific cost in human lives and human misery. How could the army that produced the first day of the Somme also produce Passchendaele, one year later?

The British commander had long nursed a plan that would coordinate more precisely with British interests than attacks against the massifs of France. The greatest threat to England – and indeed to the Allied cause since British shipping was carrying the bulk of supplies even for the Italians and Russians – remained the German submarine offensive, whether restricted or unrestricted. Since the short range of 1916/17 submarines dictated that the German U-boats launched from the Belgian channel ports, Haig thought as soon as early 1916 that the greatest chance of making substantial gains would be a major blow at Ypres, combined with an attack on the Belgian channel ports. Early on, Haig's planners, with the blessing of Asquith, put together a three-part plan: main blow at Ypres, another attack along the Channel from the extreme left flank of the Western Front, and finally (and top secret) an amphibious landing (from submarines and trawlers) in the German-held channel-port harbor of Ostend, about ten miles behind the extreme right of the German front line. These plans became more urgent in October 1916, when the Germans redoubled their restricted U-boat offensive and sank 176,000 tons of British and neutral shipping in the month.[24]

Haig was therefore the more disturbed by the developments leading to the ascendancy of Nivelle, which forced him to put his plans on hold. With the failure of the attacks and the mutiny looming, Haig pushed for his Flanders Offensive (though his amphibious landing remained known to only a few) and the Allies met to discuss options. In ways parallel to the whole Nivelle episode, the civilian leadership did its best to evaluate the situation and keep a tight rein on any offensive. Still, some reports looked favorable. Since the French had collapsed, Allied leaders decided that the British should mount an attack. On May 1, Haig wrote to the War Cabinet that his plan was now "reasonably possible . . . ; while even if a full measure of success is not gained we shall be attacking our enemy where he cannot refuse to fight."

Indeed, at worst, the attack on the Passchendaele Ridge would push the Germans back from their convenient positions overlooking Ypres. Moreover, the "wearing-down" of the Germans would be an important result. Lloyd George and the War Cabinet concurred, as did the French, in early May.[25]

It will be remembered that the Ypres salient consisted of a kind of half-saucer, with the straight chord running north and south (about seven miles), and the curved ridges making an arc from which the city of Ypres could be seen at almost all points. This jutting out of the line, the salient, had resulted from vicious fighting in 1914 (First Ypres) and 1915 (Second Ypres). The year 1916 was relatively quiet in the salient, but only relatively, since the German guns could hit practically anything that moved throughout the whole area. The plan to which Haig now introduced his commanders was the main attack – mainly the job of General Hubert Gough's Fifth Army – that of jumping off from the British lines just outside the Menin Gate, about half a mile from Ypres city center, and head straight up the long incline toward the high ridge east and north of the famous cloth city, with the objective lying on the crest of the highest ridge on the "saucer," on the crest of which sat the village of Passchendaele, exactly two miles from the gate of Ypres. Haig planned to use all the techniques which the British army had now mastered: the walking barrage, indirect fire from machine guns, a division of labor among the infantry squads, careful rehearsals of each attack for each objective. The official pronouncements to the troops were perhaps less explicit than Nivelle's guarantees of victory in two days, but British soldiers likewise thought the upcoming battle would be, as one of them called it afterwards, "the great battle to end the war – as we thought."[26]

In fact, Haig prefaced the main attack with an offensive farther south along the arc of the salient, at Messines (or Mesen) Ridge. By pushing the Germans back from this ridge, the Germans would no longer have a clear view of preparations for the attack toward Passchendaele. The task of taking the Messines Ridge he assigned to the highly capable General Sir Herbert Plumer and his Second Army. For the attack on his ridge, Plumer decided to add to the other new techniques an extensive mining operation, using the coal-mining expertise of his men to dig tunnels from behind the British lines, under No Man's Land, under the Messines Ridge, to a point just underneath the German trenches, where chambers would be filled with explosives. This technique, we have seen, was well known already, and digging at Messines Ridge had begun 18 months before, but the

Second Army was taking no chances: the miners placed 25 underground mines along about a mile of the German front lines – 957,000
pounds of ammonal high explosive.

At dawn on June 7, 1917, the British set off the charges, and 19 of
the mines exploded in what is assumed to be the biggest man-made
explosion to occur up to that time. The bang was clearly heard in
London, over 150 miles away. People within 20 or 30 miles thought
that an earthquake was occurring. Plumer's inspector of mines
watched the blast: "A violent earth tremor, then a gorgeous sheet of
flame from Spanbroekmoelen, and the same time every gun opened
fire . . . period which elapsed between first and last mine, about 30 sec-
onds . . . . The earth shake was remarkable."[27]

The attacking divisions went over the top immediately. The German
front lines were, for once, not much of a problem. Thousands of
Germans were buried in the blasts, and most of the remainder were
wounded or dazed, presenting no difficulty. German positions farther
back, toward the crest of the ridge, put up a defense, but by this time
the British (including two Irish divisions, one of nationalists, one of
Ulstermen), Australians, and New Zealanders were in full swing and
took all of Plumer's objectives with minimal casualties. Bracing for the
German counterattack, none ever really came. Plumer had gained
1,500 yards and some very useful ground. In the following six days,
Haig pushed Plumer to go beyond the limited objectives to exploit success, and the fighting resulted in 25,000 casualties. But overall, the
Battle of Messines Ridge was a victory, indeed, the first real British victory since the beginning of the war – no small achievement.

The next phase of Haig's offensive was the attack toward
Passchendaele. In contrast to Plumer's smaller offensive, Gough's attack
looked more like the mammoth plans for the Somme the year before,
and included not only his army but a coordinated effort by the French
First Army and some of Plumer's Second. His artillery pounded the
German lines for 15 days before jump-off, a bombardment of 4.3
million shells. Though planned for early dawn, the attack began in
pitch dark since the cloudy, rainy weather system that would mark the
whole campaign was already forming, and cloud cover was low. Indeed,
rain began to fall before the first day's assault was complete.

On the northern end of the attack, with plenty of artillery support,
the French took German points up to 2,500 yards within a few hours.
Both the French assaulting force and the British corps next to it found
mostly deserted front trenches as a result of the colossal artillery

bombardment. Elsewhere, the attack met with less success, though the advance was, by Western Front standards, amazing at most points, several thousand yards in most places. Yet even the first day brought some disconcerting elements that seem in retrospect to have portended ill. Seemingly on the run early, by the end of the first day, the German "flexible defense" had established well-organized defenses in front of the exhausted Allied attackers. Compared with the first day of the Somme (57,000 casualties) and the first day of the Nivelle Offensive (40,000 casualties), the British losses on the first day of Passchendaele seemed relatively low: 27,000. Still, the Germans were not dislodged from very significant strong positions, and the first of Haig's crushing blows had been on the whole weaker than expected. Moreover, the configuration of the thinly held outposts on the German side led to a new level of brutality on the battlefield. As the British troops moved quickly forward, capturing groups of pillboxes that made up the forward strong points, the units barely secured the points and moved onward. In several cases, Germans emerged from deep dugouts under the strong points, saw the British troops moving to their rear, and opened fire – on their backs. For some outraged British troops, retaliation seemed almost a pleasant necessity.

Finally, the weather system mentioned above had, by the end of the afternoon, introduced what we might call the leitmotif of the battle, the reduction of the battlefield to a quagmire of enormous proportions. Indeed, the next phase of the battle was dominated by the environment. The Flanders plain is, in any case, famous for its high water table. We have seen that closer to the coast, trenches of any depth filled with water even in dry times. A significant part of the local culture of the Low Countries has emerged from the practices of controlling and channeling water so as to use the interspersed dryness. Rivers carry out this sort of drainage naturally, and the farmers and townsfolk of Flanders had long since become adept in creating systems to enable efficient use of the drained areas. The fighting before Ypres had of course destroyed most of the natural and artificial drainage systems, and the arrival of 4.3 million British shells and a large number of German ones on an area of perhaps 50 square miles all told created an even more absorbent medium. In short, by the end of the first day, soldiers were describing being waist-deep in mud in some places. Keeping in mind that neither the rain nor the artillery shelling would stop for months, one can begin to imagine the muddy impossibility of the battlefield of Passchendaele.[28]

But the battle continued on, with the British units slogging forward from attack to attack, the Germans holding on in desperate action after desperate action, the brutalities of the first day remaining fresh in the memories of both sides, the mud becoming a demoralizing fact of life. The story of the next months was one of continual doubt by Haig whether the attacks should continue, continual bursts of optimism in favor of new attacks, continual throwing of resources into the battle by subordinate commanders, huge artillery preparations and clear advances, coordinated and effective counterattacks by the weary Germans, and gradual Allied advance. The final scene was played out in early November, when the Canadian Corps struggled up the unearthly landscape and amid torrents of rain, lead, and steel and captured the village of Passchendaele, now no village at all but something out of a nightmare, as one soldier recalled: "The buildings had been pounded and mixed with earth, and the shell exploded bodies were so thickly strewn that a fellow couldn't step without stepping on corruption."[29] Field Marshal Haig ordered the Canadians to attack again the next day; they gained 100 yards at enormous cost. The Passchendaele Offensive was over, though Haig himself wrote that the positions captured at Ypres "may be difficult and costly to hold if seriously attacked." He thought German counterattack a likelihood. It would come in a few months, and in line with Haig's predictions, not only the forward positions, but all the ground gained during the dreadful months from July 31 to November 10 would be right back in German hands. Casualties totaled about 270,000 for the British, some 70,000 of these killed outright, and about 200,000 for the Germans.

Passchendaele became, even more than the Somme, a symbol for the pointlessness of the Western Front, for its callousness and disregard for life, its futility. Yet in recent waves of historical reevaluation, Passchendaele forms an important strong point in what we might call the Battle of Haig, a battle that began in the 1960s when historian John Terraine began to rehabilitate Haig as a commander of intelligence and feeling who chose among bad alternatives and ultimately won the war. Recent supporters of Haig, in this sense, have pointed out that Passchendaele fell short of the victory it might have been, but that the British did in fact push the Germans back over a considerable distance, giving breathing space all along the northern end of the Western Front. More importantly, the Germans were unable to launch any offensive against the shattered French army during 1917, certainly a significant factor in the equation. The new position might have provided possibilities for future operations along the Channel coast, and if these operations never materialized, this is partly to blame on the weather, and partly to blame on the Bolshevik Revolution, which changed the complexion of the war and allowed Ludendorff to seize the initiative in the spring of 1918. Some revisionists have claimed that though the Third Battle of Ypres seemed to end in desultory fashion, in essence it wore out the Germans and caused such a disastrous drop in morale that we might well consider it the crucial victory of the war.[30]

Still, other recent assessments confirm earlier tellings of poor leadership in the British army, of the military's insistence on its own program, on poor coordination between the land and sea forces, and on a callous disregard for the sacrifices being made in vast numbers. Called at the time to explain the failure of his part of the assault, General Gough blamed his soldiers for not fighting hard enough. In a much discussed book, historians Robin Prior and Trevor Wilson have recently contended that the battle was eminently stoppable, and that many good reasons dictated that it should have been stopped, as the Nivelle Offensive had been.[31] In a book about connections between battle fronts and home fronts, we must ask hard questions about both the goals of the battle and about the civilian and military decisions which kept it going. It soon became clear that breakthrough was just as chimerical for Haig as it had been for Nivelle three months earlier. Yet London stuck with Haig and even granted him continued leeway in decision-making, whereas Paris had both removed Nivelle and established much tighter control of the military command.

The questions surrounding Passchendaele are far from settled, but whatever we conclude about it, it is indisputable that the terrible losses and the suffering of the British and Commonwealth forces in the battle give it a special place in the British collective memory of the war.

The Russian Revolutions and the Western Front

The cataclysm that struck the Russian Empire in 1917 was, like World War I itself, one of the fundamental events of the twentieth century. From the Russian revolutions of 1917 flowed the introduction of Marxism–Leninism as a ruling system, the implementation of Communist terror as a mode of state security, the killing of probably 100 million people in the following three-quarters of a century, and many more essential elements of twentieth-century history. The revolutions of 1917 also played an integral role in the history of World War I, and indeed the Western Front itself, since the revolutions, in particular the Bolshevik Revolution, pulled Russia out of the war and allowed the Germans to open up the great Spring Offensive of 1918.

By 1917, the Russian armies were thoroughly worn out. In the titanic Brusilov Offensive during the second half of 1916, the Germans, Austro-Hungarians, and (relatively few) Turks who faced the onslaught lost 918,000 men killed, wounded, and captured, but the Russians lost half again as many: 1,412,000 men.[32] At the same time, after a promising start, the internal organization of the war effort seemed hopeless, shot through with corruption up to the highest levels. The strange historical situation of the Tsar's family has perhaps been over-dramatized, but the presence of the charismatic, libidinous, and hairy holy man Rasputin in the entourage of the Tsarina was disastrous from the standpoint of wartime morale. Rasputin was not the empress's lover, but he was using his influence with her to try to affect the conduct of the war in some cases. His murder at the end of December 1916 repre-sented a sordid plot of effete nobles and did nothing to avert the avalanche of social discontent, political rage, and public revulsion at privation and death.[33]

As with the Western Front societies, Russian society reeled from the losses of 1916 and acted accordingly. In brief, with turmoil and revolt in the army and in the countryside in the offing, the political parties ended the reign of the tsars and established a provisional government, headed by Prince Georgii Lvov but including representatives from a variety of moderate parties. This constituted the "February Revolution." Russia might have pulled out of the war, but the men running the government understood that Russia must continue to support the Entente or face the prospect of drastic reductions of foreign investment. The provi-sional government then attempted to square the circle, staying in the war but declaring freedom of speech, assembly, and other political activity, opening the door to political exiles, including the Marxists–Leninists led by V. I. Lenin.

Lenin was the leader of the Bolshevik faction of the Russian Social Democratic Party, and like most of the principal socialist leaders, had been living in exile for years. The Bolsheviks had always denounced the war as an imperialist enterprise and advocated Russia's withdrawal, or at least its "transformation" into a civil war in Russia. For many months before the February Revolution, a number of twilight figures had tried to establish connections between Lenin and the German general staff on the assumption that the Bolsheviks and the German government shared the immediate goal of knocking Russia out of the war, even if their long-range goals were quite different. In the midst of many intrigues, it was eventually the long-time socialist theorist and conspirator, Alexander Helphand (revolutionary nickname: "Parvus"), who suggested to the Germans that they "assist" Lenin and other Russian exiles back to Russia. In March, Chancellor Bethmann-Hollweg gave his approval to a plan to send Lenin and some compatriots from Switzerland across war-torn Europe all the way to Russia. This was the famous "sealed train," though the story that the passenger cars were boarded up so as not to "infect" Germany is apparently a myth. Lenin and 31 revolutionary compatriots departed from Zurich on April 9, crossed Germany and reached the Baltic, where they took a steamer to neutral Sweden, and from there a ship to Finland and Russia, arriving in Petrograd (the renamed Russian capital) on April 16.[34] Other Bolsheviks, notably Leon Trotsky, soon arrived in one way or another, but the small sect's grandiose plans to take over Russia and pull her out of the war still seemed far-fetched.

By April 1917, however, the provisional government began to face ominous riots and other signs of social protest. Eventually, the socialist (but not Bolshevik) Minister of Justice Alexander Kerensky came to the fore to head the provisional government during its last months. The Bolsheviks meanwhile did much basic propaganda work with variations on their slogan "Land, Peace, Bread" – meaning landing redistribution, pulling out of the war, and distribution of bread to hungry urban workers. At the same time, they were the smallest of the three major socialist parties until the fall of 1917. That they succeeded nonetheless is owing to many local conditions and the multiplicity of problems in the war, to be sure, but in the context of the Western Front powers, we should also make it clear here that the original German support of the Bolsheviks did not end when the "sealed train" reached the Baltic. In December 1917 the German Foreign Minister Richard von Kühlmann described numerous activities that the Bolsheviks carried out in Russia with German support: "It was not until the Bolsheviks had received from us a steady flow of funds through various channels and under different labels that they were able to build up their main organ, *Pravda*, to conduct energetic propaganda and appreciably extend the originally narrow basis of their party." The German government apparently spent a sum far exceeding 50 to 60 million marks on the Bolsheviks (worth over $8 million in 1918 dollars).

The paralysis with which the country seemed to respond to the Bolshevik coup d'état in November (October in Russia's old-style calendar) was due in part to extensive propaganda, in part to the increasing strains of the war. The Bolsheviks were hardly in the saddle at all when they began negotiating with the Germans to get out of the war. The Germans were of course well informed about Bolshevik activities, and had intended all along to gain a quick ceasefire and then dictate a peace. Though on the fringes of these plans, Ludendorff saw their value. On learning of the Bolshevik takeover, he immediately fell to planning a giant spring offensive with the troops who would soon be idle on the Eastern Front. Ludendorff scheduled the great assault for the spring of 1918, knowing that if he waited longer, the arrival of American troops on the Western Front would alter the balance of the front dramatically.

Lenin proposed to withdraw from the war and wait for revolution to break out in one country after the other, crumbling all the war regimes. In this mood, Lenin proposed to accept any German terms whatever in order to get Russia out of the war. Still, he had to act with caution, since the rumors were widespread that he was a German agent (which, in a sense, he was). Delegations met at Brest-Litovsk in early December and negotiated an immediate armistice. For a month the Germans listened to Bolshevik pronouncements and appeals to the German workers to overthrow their government, but in the second round of negotiations, beginning on January 9, the Germans took matters in hand and dictated the peace.

The German peace aims at Brest-Litovsk represented yet another manifestation of the annexationist urge which had threaded in and out of German wartime policy and strategy. Now, as at the outbreak of the war, German industrialists, politicians, and military men collaborated in plans for the extension of German economic and political power beyond the continental power the country unquestionably possessed. Hoping to set up a kind of economic hinterland for raw materials, the Germans first hoped to dismember the Russian Empire, taking some territory in its own right and setting up a buffer zone of friendly states in the form of the Ukraine and Poland. Next, they hoped to force rump Russia to favorable, actually one-sided, trade agreements. The real controversy among the peace planners was whether the Bolsheviks, now called Communists, should be left in power because they were rendering Russia omnipotent or whether they should be removed from power because they were a danger to Germany and the world.[35]

In the event, the Germans demanded a border which chopped off about one-third of the European part of the Russian Empire. The Bolsheviks refused to sign, but when the Germans reopened hostilities on February 17, 1918 the Communist leadership of the new Soviet state finally capitulated. The Treaty of Brest-Litovsk was signed on March 14.

The very weeks of the treaty's signing produced the beginnings of the Russian Civil War: the Whites (bourgeois, conservative, and tsarist elements) against the Reds (the Bolsheviks), with various peasant bands, anarchists, Russian socialists, and other groups crossing the stage from time to time as Greens. In this period, the Soviet government met the emergency of the German renewal of hostilities with what was essentially carte blanche for the new secret police organ, the Cheka, both to round up Russian citizens, at least members of the bourgeoisie, for forced labor, or to execute Russian citizens summarily. Before very long, the same Chekists would descend on the countryside to confiscate food to be used for fighting the "imperialist" forces of the Whites. The Soviet regime also gained time by tempting the Entente powers with proposals to stay in the war in exchange for help. As localities and regions of the Russian Empire began to declare independence, the Civil War accelerated into the brutal conflict that it became.[36]

Although the Bolshevik Revolution was physically far from the Western Front, it represents an event of great importance for our analysis of the Western Front powers. Not only were the Western Front powers all involved at some level in the revolution at one point or the other, but the dynamics of the revolution itself gives to us a kind of model, one might say a *reductio ad absurdum*, in dealing with possibilities and trends among the warring countries. Where we have charted tendencies to centralize among the Western Front powers, the new Soviet leaders created a regime that arrogated *all* powers to itself. Where we have been interested in tendencies of war governments to work against the traditional autonomy of the individual under the rule of law, in the new Soviet conception the individual disappeared almost entirely: class defined personhood, and the only question for the individual would be: "How can I serve the state?" Where Western Front governments increasingly intervened in their economies and indeed exerted considerable control, the Soviet regime introduced "War Communism," a system in which all economic activity was to be regulated by the state, all property owned by the state. Where Western Front regime, as we have seen, relied heavily on propaganda and

public relations to manipulate the masses to support the war state, in
the Soviet Union, propaganda came to dominate all life; truth was
Pravda, the central propaganda news organ, and the state's propaganda came to determine not only what was truth in the present, but
what had been truth in the past.

Hence, we will do well to keep the Russian case in mind, as a kind of
platonic form of what could happen when, as historian René Albrecht-
Carrié put it, the deeper forces broke through.

Finally, and simply put, the Bolshevik Revolution would soon end
major warmaking for the Germans in the East; the plans of the
German general staff now came to fruition. Tens of thousands of
troops from the East enabled him to launch an enormous offensive,
which would become the penultimate military action of the war and
lead to German collapse.

Strains and Stresses in the West

If the Western Front powers were able to avoid the kind of total collapse which Russia experienced, it was still the case that the strains of
war increased perceptibly from 1916 onward. Britain demonstrated an
ability to bend but not break in the face of real political, regional, and
social problems. France seemed, at the very least, to be threatened in
mid-1917 with a collapse of the front, mutiny of the troops, and strikes
at home (a recipe familiar to observers of Russia). Hence, the potential
for collapse seemed to increase. Held together by the toughest and
most draconian of the Western Front powers, Germany experienced
many fewer problems of discipline on the front, but much labor unrest
at home. We shall see below that 1918, within three weeks of the
German public's learning that Germany would surrender, sailors, soldiers, and workers rose up in a revolution, and the country experienced something very close to collapse. Hence it is not out of place to
show how these countries managed to hold together under conditions
which might well have ruined them.

We have seen that growing economic intervention and increased
controls of the private sector marked the policies that allowed the
belligerents to stay in the war. Though the belligerents were able to
continue producing shells and other war goods, they did so by
reallocations of wealth within their societies, which had dramatic
impact on economy and society as a whole. These "reallocations,"

whatever else they did, redistributed the wealth of society by paying, for example, artificially high prices to farmers for food or by subsidizing certain industrialists. In general, farmers seem to have done well in the war, since demand for food during wartime was up (even though government price controls had the effect of lowering production), and since farmers could usually count on help from government subsidies. Welsh farmers, for example, received heavy subsidies through the Cultivation of Lands Order to plant wheat on fields previously used otherwise. These crops failed because of too short and too wet a growing season, as the farmers had predicted to the London planners at the outset, but large subsidies and considerable effort had been funnelled into the failed program. Selected industrialists, cooperating with the government in producing goods needed for the war effort, became wealthier, as governments tended to "assist" leading companies in taking over their smaller competitors. On the other hand, not only the smaller, independent operators in the sector of war-related manufacture, but also the small and large companies producing civilian goods suffered, constantly seeing supplies and materials diverted to "priority" industries and hard pressed to pay the inflated, subsidized wages of the war industries.[37]

In general, the middle classes in the belligerent countries lost economic ground during the war. Finding themselves paying for the war both with the lives of their young men and the increased taxation and privation, middle-class families bore much of the burden of World War I. Essentially, those persons who bought savings bonds, who worked in white-collar jobs, who saved in any form, were doomed by the inflationary monetary policies that marked all the wartime regimes.[38]

One of the most perceptible problems of wartime was manpower, which was bound to be problematic given the enormous size of the armies. From the outset, war governments tried to convince the unions to renounce strikes and tough labor negotiations for the duration of the war, but the hoped-for controlled labor harmony began to break down almost immediately. It took the losses of 1916, however, to produce real breakdowns in the system. Again, a simple economic calculus impeded total war labor mobilization: with manpower in short supply, laborers were more likely, not less, to get what they wanted. When their demands for better conditions, safer workplaces, and the like were not met, unrest occurred. The labor truce which the governments had in effect negotiated with labor foundered when the war regimes lengthened working hours, drew in non-union labor to fill gaps (particularly

women), and made accidents more likely and more serious as plants
and people worked beyond their capacities. In this regard, unions were
the greatest enemy of the movement of women into factories, since even
men at the front asked themselves if women would be expecting to take
their jobs once the war was over. Still, though the home fronts saw, perhaps surprisingly, many strikes, on the whole, the labor movement used
the need for manpower to make its position as influence broker secure
for the rest of the twentieth century.

The most extreme labor shortages came in Germany, where the blockade had also produced hunger of enormous proportions, rationing, and
still more rationing. The Auxiliary Service Law could produce only so
many male bodies, but driven by hunger, working-class and middle-class
women made up some of the labor shortages. By the end of the war, one
industrial worker out of three was a woman, and some two million
German women were working in factories with more than ten employees. Much of this increase did not represent totals of women gaining
employment outside their homes for the first time, but instead women
who had already been in the workforce moving up to higher-paying
jobs, and munitions work paid the best. Yet the conditions of these
higher wages were longer hours and more accidents, a deadly proposition indeed in munitions plants. Forty women died in a munitions factory explosion in Fürth early in 1917, and industrial accidents increased
as time went on. Still, food was the problem. Workers, both men and
women, were indeed making high wages, but inflation had already
raised the cost of living, which steadily outran wages. Occasioned also by
antiwar feeling, riots broke out in Leipzig and other major cities in 1916,
touched off by the arrest and jailing of radical socialist Karl Liebknecht,
who had publicly called for revolution and the end of the war. The
strikes began to grow not only in number, but in size and duration, and
finally in the degree to which they appeared to be motivated by antiwar
sentiment as opposed to working and living conditions alone.[39]

The sinking of the economic well-being of the middle classes was
perceptible. Hemmed in by price controls on their products, but still
rationed many of the products they themselves were producing, farmers were reaching their own boiling point. The *Mittelstand*, the old middle class of white-collar workers and middling bureaucrats, was losing
purchasing power and status from day to day. In spite of the rosy propaganda produced by government organs, by 1916 and 1917, German
society seeing the first of the unraveling which would characterize the
German social trajectory for many years.[40]

While the German case was the extreme, massive increases in the resources – both physical and spiritual – of wartime populations led people everywhere to revolt in many ways. Beginning with the crisis year of 1916, strikes rose rapidly everywhere. Other and quieter protests emerged as well, even though the garrison regimes were busily pioneering the repressive techniques which became the stock in trade of twentieth-century governments: concentration camps, prisons, mental hospitals.[41]

Even on the battle front, where both military justice and to some extent the psychological pressures tended to maintain a high degree of solidarity, things began to crack apart with the massive slaughters of 1916. The stepped-up level of warfare and the murderous tactics involved in both breakthrough sectors and relatively quiet fronts led to more elaborate forms of what English-speaking soldiers called the "Live and Let Live" system, which we have examined above. Sociologist Tony Ashworth calculated that at least half of the British sector of the Western Front – and this was in sectors where a battle was not in progress – was at any given moment engaged in some kind of "Live and Let Live" arrangement across No Man's Land, ranging from ritualized firing of artillery during a specific time slot each day to tacit avoidance of patrols of the other side in No Man's Land. To emphasize again the importance of 1916, one can quote the British private who saw the Somme battle as having changed attitudes: "From now on, the veterans, myself included, decided to do no more than was really necessary, following orders, but if possible keeping out of harm's way. I have the feeling that many of the officers felt the same way."[42]

As we have seen, this behavior intensified into mutiny in the French army in the spring of 1917. Other armies faced mutinies as well, including the British. Much of the good feeling of the waves of Kitchener troops survived, even though so many of them did not. Any disaffection seemed to be well taken care of by the range of punishments, from Field Punishment No. 1 (being lashed while spread-eagle in a public place for humiliation – a latter-day version of the old "stocks"), to death. The latter was applied in the British army for cases of refusing to fight or running away, for striking an officer, for sleeping on guard duty, and for casting away one's weapon (or as Julian Putkowski has shown, cases which could be represented as any of these). Not every death sentence given by a British military tribunal was carried out, but the handing out of these sentences present an interesting trajectory: 1914 – 85; 1915 – 591; 1916 – 856; 1917 – 904;

1918 – 515. From 1915 to 1917, the handing out of death sentences for desertion tripled. In the end, the British army would execute 3 officers and 343 soldiers and military laborers. Some of these sentences were for murder, some for mutiny. For military offenses besides murder and mutiny, some 306 were "shot at dawn." These sentences represent, comparatively, many more executions per capita than any other Western Front belligerent and, indeed, an increase in the severity of sentences from immediate prewar practice.[43]

Mere rumblings of mutiny seemed to follow the problems of desertion and discipline, in military prisons, work details, and so forth, until September 1917. This was when a genuine series of riots and mutinous behavior broke out over several days, involving many thousand British (and New Zealand and Australian) soldiers at the hated British base camp at Etaples, remembered by all soldiers for its "Bull Ring," where merciless drilling took place by the hour. Indeed, some antiwar sentiment arose, but on the whole, the Etaples "mutiny" seems to have been a spontaneous response to the brutal and demeaning discipline of the place. Still, several mutineers were shot at dawn as a result. The British were taking no chances.[44] In fact, taking no chances but also ameliorating conditions was the common Western Front response to growing disaffection among soldiers.

So, for example, in the midst of social tensions and manpower shortages in Britain (December 1916), David Lloyd George came to head a war regime which took off its gloves in handling the domestic unrest and keeping dissidents, like Siegfried Sassoon and his famous antiwar letter, out of the public eye. In France, on the front Pétain was brought in to restore order both by making conditions and tactics more bearable, and by harsh military discipline combining executions with the shipping off of thousands to the penal colonies. On the home front, the crisis brought to power the tiger Clemenceau, whose political assistant, economic advisor, and minister of munitions was the technocrat Louis Loucheur, a specialist in artillery-shell production who had advised an earlier premier that in order to get the industrialists to produce enough, "we must push people around, kick them in the pants, drag them along, incite them, show them that without it [more production] we are finished."[45] By these methods and others, the Western Front powers made it through the war.

The "nations" fighting on the Western Front were all, in reality, "countries" that called themselves "nations," but which consisted of multiple national or ethnic groups. Hence "England" was really a country encompassing English, Scottish, Irish, Welsh, Cornish, and so on. The highly nationalized French "nation" consisted of French, German-speaking Alsatians, Celtic Bretons, Catalonians, and more. The German "nation" consisted in reality of Germans of various lineages, Danes, Poles, Lithuanians, French, etc. (before the war, Jews in all of these countries usually considered themselves, and were, patriotic "Germans," "Britons," and so on). The strains of the war were likely to test this homogeneity. Such bonds were not indestructible. We have seen that at this moment in the war, the Russian Empire was beginning a kind of dissolution into a dozens of animated and armed nationalities,[46] and if this extreme case of national collapse stands as an extreme example, it still gives us a kind of yardstick as to the "worst" that could happen to national integration.

Poles and Danes fighting in the German army did their "duty" throughout the war and their relatives in Eastern and Northern Germany worked on grimly like everyone else to keep the war efforts going, though strikes in the predominantly Polish-speaking workforces of the Upper Silesian industries rose more rapidly than elsewhere after 1916. Still, though the Poles and Danes (and Sorbs and French speakers) never developed anything like coherent movements in protest of the war, postwar evidence shows much anti-German sentiment in these regions, a sign that at least parts of the German entity were coming unglued as the result of the war.[47]

An almost textbook case of the problems of national cohesion surfaced in the Canadian case of protests from Quebec, home of nearly two million French Canadians. Though some would see in the great Canadian assault on Vimy Ridge in 1917 the "creation" of a nation, the Conscription Crisis of 1916 displayed much divisive rancor between the dissatisfied French-speaking minority and the English-speaking majority in Canada. As losses in the three Western Front divisions of the Canadian Army Corps mounted in 1916, recruitment at home began to fade. By the middle of the year French Canadian units were so undermanned that many were incorporated into English Canadian outfits, a measure which irritated many French Canadians. On the other hand, some French Canadian units were shipped to Bermuda for guard duty. Desertions were on the rise in training centers, and some disturbances broke out among French Canadian units. After punishments and dismissal of French Canadian officers in the units involved, French Canadians were outraged. Calls for conscription meanwhile arose in English Canada, calls clearly aimed at drafting more French Canadians into the army. The great Canadian politician Wilfred Laurier, French Canadian leader of the Liberal Party, tried to raise the level of French Canadian support for the war, but recruiting in Quebec was slow, the more so since the recruiters tended to try to insult French Canadians into enlistment, or at least threaten them with conscription. In August one recruiting rally put on in Montreal (some might say ironically) by the Irish-Canadian Rangers was broken up by protest leaders who proclaimed: "We shall perhaps allow ourselves to be crushed, but we shall never accept conscription."[48]

Laurier continued to try to sway French Canadians to enlist, but so entangled was recruitment, the threat of conscription, and the whole question of the French Canadian identity that French Canadian enlistments fell far below the national average. The national discussion would end early in 1917, when Canada passed the Military Service Act, which would conscript over 100,000 Canadians before the end of the war. Laurier, opposed to conscription on the liberal grounds that government coercion in this matter was wrong, left the government. The nation which would, in the view of some, burst into view at Vimy Ridge in the spring of 1917 was a nation in which the French Canadian component was becoming far more self-aware and opposed to integration as a result of the war.[49]

Irish Home Fronts and Battle Fronts

The most spectacular case of ethnic centrifugalism to emerge among the Western Front powers was the Irish problem, which boiled over into open revolt in Dublin in Easter 1916. We have seen that the Irish movement for independence had a long history behind it, and that the issue was really at crisis point when the war broke out in the summer of 1914. After acrimonious political struggles, Parliament had passed the Home Rule Bill in 1911, which was to give Ireland autonomy. Protestant Irish from the northern counties feared for the Catholic regime which would be the majority government under Home Rule, and they proceeded to form a paramilitary group called the Ulster Volunteers. The Irish nationalists in the south countered with their own paramilitary groups, the Irish Republican Brotherhood and Sinn Fein ("Ourselves Alone"). The outbreak of the war seemed to put the whole dispute on hold.

Irish soldiers formed a substantial part of the British army before the war, slightly overrepresented in terms of the population of the UK: about 10 percent of the population but about 12 percent (30,000 men) of the army in 1914.[50] About 30,000 reservists were mobilized immediately after the war broke out, and 140,460 enlisted voluntarily during the war. Conscription brought the number of Irish in the British army to over half a million. There were Irish throughout the army. Some served in units with no Irish connections whatsoever; some served in Irish battalions within British regiments; some served with the three Irish divisions that were eventually raised in Ireland itself.

These three volunteer divisions present some vivid battle front–home front connections, since each division was raised on the basis of sympathies and goals. As Myles Dungan has explained, "Irish recruits filled three volunteer Divisions, the 10th (Irish) – southern but not exclusively nationalist, the 16th (Irish) – southern and almost exclusively nationalist, and the 36th (Ulster) – northern and overwhelmingly unionist."[51] It is plain to see why unionists in Ulster would raise a division to fight for Britain. Sir Edward Carson, prominent unionist and future cabinet official, had organized the Ulster Volunteers in 1912; the Volunteers indeed formed the core of the 36th Division. They were fighting for the country they intended to stay with. Less transparently, the Irish nationalists likewise had political goals in mind.

Most Irish nationalists apparently joined the army in order to weaken the Union of Ireland with Britain. John Redmond was the leader of the Irish Parliamentary Party, which had claimed victory in gaining Home Rule in 1912, but after the nascent hostilities of 1914 and the postponement of Home Rule by London when the war broke out, Redmond urged the Irish – indeed, urged the Irish Volunteers themselves – to enlist, not as Britons but as Irish, the people of an emerged European nation. He reasoned that Germany presented an enemy of Ireland which "by a most fortunate conjuncture" was also the enemy of England. Fighting in the war would prove not only the "genuine military spirit" of the Irish, but it would demonstrate that it possessed the power to exist as an independent state. "Account yourselves as men not only in Ireland," Redmond told his countrymen, "but wherever the firing line extends in defence of right, of freedom and religion in this war." [52]

Large numbers responded, including most of the Irish Volunteers themselves. The 16th Division was the center of this nationally motivated recruiting. Indeed, Redmond's brother William (universally known as Willie), a Member of Parliament in his mid-fifties, enlisted and served in the 16th Division, saying "I prefer to say to my fellow countrymen 'Come' instead of 'Go'." In worsening health, he was several times sent home and along the way appeared in the House of Commons, making several speeches in favor of the war effort and Home Rule. Indeed, his final speech came on March 7, 1917. Supporting a motion for immediate implementation of Home Rule, the very popular Redmond spoke spontaneously and eloquently. Many seated around, according to a friend of Redmond's, "sobbed and wept unabashed." Just three months later Willie Redmond died in the furious attack of the 16th Division at Messines Ridge.[53] In a book about connections between the battle front and the home front, the final months of Willie Redmond's life must represent as striking an individual example as one can find.

The existence of the two Irish divisions, one highly politicized as pro-Union Ulstermen and one highly politicized as Irish nationalists, provides a point of irony in a war in which irony abounded. Literally fighting for opposing causes, the divisions were nonetheless in the British army fighting the Germans and found themselves in close proximity to each other on more than one occasion. Both divisions fought with distinction in the Battle of the Somme. The 36th (Ulster) Division provided one of the only cases of success on the dreadful first day of the battle, July 1, 1916. Going over the top from trenches at Thiepval Wood, the Ulstermen rushed uphill through heavy machine-gun fire to take the German front trench by the village of Thiepval. They flew past the German front and fought their way far into the German trench system. They were too successful, really, since the divisions on either flank could make no headway. After a long day of fighting, the Ulsters fell back to the German front trench, which they had taken in the morning. The division suffered 5,000 casualties that day, and four Victoria Crosses – Britain's highest military decoration – were awarded to individuals in the division for bravery. A few days later and a few miles away, the 16th Division fought in the very tough Somme sub-battle for the villages of Guillemont and Ginchy in late July and early August 1916, on the Somme battlefield's right flank, one of the toughest German defensive fights of the whole campaign (in the view of some British officers, one of the toughest of the whole war).[54] In yet another battle front/home front connection, the subsequent history of Irish independence (1922) and conflict with Ulster are reflected in the ways in which Ireland and Northern Ireland later remembered and memorialized their fighting in the Somme battle. In the 1920s Northern Ireland erected on the site of the 36th Division attack a replica of Helen's Tower at Clandeboyne near Belfast. Even if it is lessened by the colossal Thiepval Memorial nearly a mile away, the 36th Division Memorial nonetheless makes a bold and proud statement about men dying for their king and country. At the scene of 16th (Irish) Division fighting, to the south, the counterpart to the castle at Thiepval is a small stone Celtic cross by the side of Guillemont church; one might drive by it without noticing its presence. The strategy of fighting so as to gain Home Rule and to forge a nation seems almost overwhelmed in the subsequent history of independence and disputes. Not least of the events which would eventually cloud the efforts of the 16th Division was the Easter Rising.[55]

Here again, the interplay between battle front and home front is dense, even when we avoid the controversies which still mark the discussion of the rising.[56] In brief, under the leadership of Patrick Pearse, Sinn Fein and the Irish Republican Brotherhood seized the main post office in Dublin on Easter Monday, April 24, 1916, proclaimed independence, and set up a provisional government. Pearse and his colleagues had planned a major rising to coincide with German deliveries of arms, but various plans went awry. Amounting to perhaps 2,000 men and women, the rebels took over several significant buildings and sections of the city. British garrison troops responded rapidly and were rapidly reinforced. A British gunboat arrived, and the shelling of the city inflicted much damage. After several days of heavy urban fighting, the rebels gave up. From the first, though, it was clear that the rising had the support of neither the majority of nationalist leaders nor the bulk of the population. The rising itself was a horror to the uninvolved population of Dublin, and the 450 dead and 2,500 wounded included many innocent bystanders. Clearly, the hope that the country would join the uprising was a chimera. Imprisoned rebels seen by the public as they were transferred from their Dublin prison were, according to eyewitnesses, railed at, particularly by women who depended on the "separation allowance" being paid to them because their husbands were at the front.

Yet in repressing the revolt, the British managed to give credence and dignity to the rising. They immediately arrested some 3,500 individuals in Ireland, freeing about 1,500 after questioning. Of the remainder, most were interned without trial in England; 170 were convicted of crimes; 90 were sentenced to death; in the end all but 15 of the death sentences were commuted. Among those shot were all those who had signed the proclamation of independence. Though these measures seem fairly mild as a response to an armed rising with connections to the enemy in the midst of a desperate war, the executions seem to have pushed many Irish people toward the camp of independence. Certainly enlistments fell. The populace soon came to think of itself on the side of the rebels rather than that of the police, as it had predominantly been.

The rising was over when the Somme battle began. The 16th Division thus seemed unaffected, certainly in its fighting capabilities. The next year, indeed, the 16th would fight alongside the 36th in an attack that was a part of the Messines Ridge battle, in April 1917. This was the battle in which 19 mines blew up and disoriented the Germans. At one of the prominent German strong points on the ridge, at the village of Wytschaete, these two Irish divisions, both of which had originated in formations raised to fight each other in civil war in 1914, lined up side by side in the attack. The two aggressive divisions followed their walking barrages, in one description, like terriers, rousting out and securing positions all the way to Wytschaete positions beyond. It was one of the most successful actions of a successful day.

Before the battle, the extremely popular Major Willie Redmond had insisted on leaving staff work to go over the top. Wounded on the way, he was picked up by stretcher-bearers from the Ulster Division who took him to their dressing station, by all accounts with great care and special handling. The Ulsters then moved him to the field ambulance station of his own division, where he died of shock from relatively minor wounds. Some observers thought that the cooperation of the two sides on Messines Ridge might provide some foundation of respect and cooperation later on. The obscurity into which the 16th (Irish) Division slipped in modern Ireland's telling of its foundation may point to the failure of such hopeful prophecies.[57]

One might say that the whole burden of 1916 fell on the second half of 1917. The horrors of Verdun, the Nivelle Spring Offensive, and the mutiny had for most purposes robbed the French army of offensive capabilities, yet the American declaration of war in April 1917 and the flux in Russia seemed pointed to a changed configuration of powers and power on the Western Front. The Americans could not be expected until early 1918 at the earliest, but both British and French generals looked with anticipation at the masses of troops the Americans would be bringing. Even so, the events of the February Revolution in Russia and the confusing situation of the Russian war effort under its new government were as disquieting to the Entente powers as they were encouraging to the Germans.

As Russia disintegrated and the United States entered the war, the contours of the international system for the twentieth century took much of their basic shape. At home, governments became more activist, less interested in – and often militantly opposed to – the autonomy of the individual. In many ways, the individual rights of the classical liberal West gave way to group identifications, group entitlements, and group politics – even group targeting. On the battlefield and at home the older verities of the loyalty and patriotism of the lower classes, the old feudal ideal, received body blows as strikes at home and huge mutinies in the field indicated that trust in the high command and the civilian leaders had been eroded. Indeed, "Live and Let Live" in the trenches carried with it the germ of mutual understanding among the poor devils in the opposite trenches, as opposed to national solidarity with upper-class officers who remained largely strangers to the fire zone. The old beliefs were not yet dead, but after Passchendaele and the Nivelle offensives, trust in government to do, ultimately, something like the right thing was weakened substantially.

7

TRANSFORMATIONS: POLITICS, CULTURE, WARFARE

Safe for Democracy?

German war aims and peace aims, their reasons for fighting the war, were many and various. They fought because they were "encircled," or because it was their responsibility, or because the Russians had threatened. Some ordinary Germans may have thought of the war as a crusade for the expansion of German culture and influence, and some German leaders undoubtedly did. But hardly any Germans at any level thought of the war as a crusade for freedom or democracy. In authoritarian Germany, such sentiments would have made little sense.[1]

Yet on the other side, the sentiment of fighting the war for "civilization," or at least some better future, was pervasive. From the start, the French could with justice argue that they were fighting for their great homeland (as could the Belgians) and against "babaric" invaders. British justifications often took more metaphysical or abstract forms, such as fighting the "beastly Hun" for civilization, decency, or, as one song had it, against the Kaiser's assault on freedom. The Americans made famous the goal of fighting the war to make the world "safe for democracy." One triumphal American book from early 1919 is entitled modestly *America's War for Humanity: Pictorial History of the World War for Liberty.*[2]

This insistence on fighting for "freedom" and "democracy" raises an important question for us as we move to the end of our study. The "silent dictatorship" gives us a fairly clear answer for the German side of the front. The Ludendorff dictatorship took Germany very far toward what we would call a "total war" state, with the subordination of individual and civil rights to the exigencies of war. How do the Entente powers, with all their talk of "freedom," compare?

Clearly, wartime regimes were less repressive in France, the United Kingdom, Australia, Canada, and the United States than in Germany. But this generalization does not take us very far. Each of these states had been less authoritarian before the war than had Germany. The more productive comparison to be made here is the comparison of freedom and repression in all the Entente societies over time. From this standpoint, we can say that all of these societies became more repressive during the war.

In political or civil life, all of the Allied countries passed repressive laws. In Britain, the Defence of the Realm Act (DORA) extended the potential for civil repression considerably, not only in economic terms – it permitted the confiscation of property and resources for the war effort – but political as well. It allowed for the executive organs to imprison individuals without trial and to censor any public expression construed as criticism of the government. During the war, Parliament many times expanded the power and extent of the act. Under DORA came the Defence of the Realm Regulations, which extended government authority into vast areas which had been considered personal business in England for many centuries. The right of assembly was abridged, and freedom to speak or express opinions dwindled. Individuals were punished for telling friends that a given military unit had been hit hard in battle. The regulations decreed that the government had the right to remove individuals in an area in which "the competent naval or military authority" deemed it "desirable" to remove them. A police officer or military sentry had the right to stop and search any vehicle using a public road and arrest its occupants on suspicion of an offense against the regulations. Indeed, among a host of prohibitions the regulations made it illegal to fly kites, loiter near railways, or keep pigeons.[3]

In Britain, as in all belligerent countries, the (rather small) movements for peace suffered search and seizure in their headquarters and press establishments as well as direct pressure from the authorities when it came to public meetings and rallies. Striking workers, and those threatening to strike, likewise felt much government pressure in the U.K. as elsewhere. Government pressure there took the form of supressing union printing presses and deporting strike activists, for the most part.[4] Britain also moved actively against "enemy aliens," eventually interning over 10,000 people with German (or sometimes Jewish or other Central European) connections, many of them the English spouses of German nationals.[5]

In the United States, home of the crusade for democracy, American Progressives praised the social controls established in European war governments. The Progressive *New Republic* judged in late 1916 that "if we wish to compete with Europe after the war we must do the same sort of thing with our production, our labor and our distribution that Europe has done with hers."[6] Indeed, in a society that most Progressives thought "dangerously diverse," in the phrase of historian David Kennedy, measures of militarization, regimentation, and efficiency from the top down seemed healthy.[7]

As Wilson told Congress in his war address, the war would require "the organization and mobilization of all the material resources of the country." Although significant organizers of the war effort, such as Herbert Hoover, would put emphasis on a "volunteerism" that seemed to coincide with freewheeling American ideas of organization and unity,[8] war measures limiting civil rights such as freedom of speech and intervening into society at all levels commenced immediately. Congress passed the Selective Service Act (conscription) five weeks after the declaration of war. The Espionage, Trading-with-the-Enemy, and Sedition Acts had already been passed by Congress by this time. The War Revenue Act increased income taxes and imposed new levies on "excess profits," while the government immediately controlled key prices and introduced rationing. The production of alcoholic beverages from food products was banned in August 1917, a measure which did double duty, saving grain and other carbohydrates for consumption and punishing the German Americans who were the ones most notably turning food products (grain) into alcoholic beverages (beer). This measure led almost directly to the eighteenth amendment – the Prohibition amendment – to the U.S. Constitution. What measures the federal government left undone, the states tended to fill out: controlling labor, rationing food, subsidizing and shaping agriculture, and more.[9]

Characteristic of the American war effort was the federal propaganda organ set up to "sell the war," as its head, Progressive journalist George Creel, put it. The dynamic Creel was appointed in 1917 and shaped the Committee on Public Information (CPI), an agency devoted to "advertising America," as he put it in his memoirs. Creel was the propaganda chief, but he went much beyond this, calling for a new kind of civic education.[10] Creel hoped to increase loyalty by indocrinating Americans in the proper democratic values: "faith in democracy," as the War Secretary described the committee, "faith in fact." Unlike many in the administration, Creel decried censorship and insisted that "no hymn of hate accompanies our message." The CPI, as Creel organized it, disseminated literature, sponsored speeches, and commissioned articles. One of his most famous tactics was the creation of a corps of "four-minute men," some 75,000 men chosen from within the community to roam public places and, wherever a crowd could be found on the spur of the moment, to give a four-minute speech on the war, on loyalty, on making the world safe for democracy.[11]

If Creel dealt in positive suasion, other administrative officials were less convinced of the need for a soft touch. In Wilson's cabinet itself, the leading scourge of disloyalty was, oddly, the Postmaster General, Albert Sidney Burleson. Authorized by the Espionage Act to ban any mail which stood in violation by advocating treason or resistance to the government, Burleson immediately began cutting off the mail service to journals he deemed disloyal, eventually extending his crusade against all whom he could discern as pacifists, radicals, or aliens. Aided by the Attorney General, Thomas Gregory, Burleson revoked mass mailing-rate privileges for any group which sought to "impugn the motives of the government and thus encourage insubordination." In a famous case of near-Orwellian irony, Burleson prohibited the sending through the mail of Thorstein Veblen's book *Imperial Germany and the Industrial Revolution* at a moment when the Creel Committee was using the book as instructional material on the evils of the German mind, morals, and culture.[12] It goes without saying that policing these policies involved searching the mail.

In this campaign, Burleson was ably backed up by the other federal departments, including a Censorship Board in which five separate federal agencies cooperated. Attorney General Thomas Gregory was unsatisfied even with his own broad interpretation of the already broad Espionage Act of June 1917 and pushed for stronger authority to root out disloyalty. He prosecuted and convicted citizens for discussing whether conscription was constitutional, for uttering socialist ideas, for pointing out that President Wilson had won the 1916 election on the slogan "He Kept Us Out of War."[13] Socialist leader Eugene V. Debs opposed the war openly, and was convicted of treason under the Espionage Act and sentenced to ten years in prison, running for the presidency from behind bars in 1920 (and garnering nearly a million votes!).

Socialist "agitation" was often thought to be an insidious German import, but Germanness alone – capitalist Germanness included – was enough to bring suspicion and persecution upon individuals in World War I America. Primed by six years of anti-German tendencies in the national press and two years of intensive and virulent messages about the barbarity of the Germans, popular opinion burst out in an orgy of anti-German hatred and pronouncements. At the head of Columbia University, President Nicholas Murray Butler fired two professors for working for peace. Against populist opposition to the war after April 6, former President Theodore Roosevelt declared that one speaker ought to be hanged. A minister at a Congregational church in Brooklyn, New York, declared that Germans were candidates for Christian forgiveness "just as soon as they are all shot. If you would give me happiness, just give the the sight of the Kaiser, von Tirpitz, and von Hindenburg hanging by a rope." Popular tunes took advantage of the moment, such as "We're Going to Hang the Kaiser Under the Linden Tree." In April 1918 Robert Prager, a registered enemy alien who had made the mistake of attending a socialist meeting and apparently had spoken against the war, was mobbed and taken into custody for "safe keeping" in Collinsville, Illinois, outside of East St. Louis. A crowd of 300 dragged him from jail, threw a rope over a branch and lynched him. Five members of the crowd were tried for the crime, but the jury delivered a non-guilty verdict, since it had to be a case of "patriotic murder."

This case was unusually brutal, but German Americans across the country found themselves targeted by super-patriotic supporters of the war and haters of Germany who loathed and feared the demonized Kaiser Wilhelm II. Numerous German Americans changed their names, or at least anglicized them. Eddie Rickenbacker, later the famous ace fighter pilot on the Western Front and in 1917 already a nationally famous racecar driver, deemed it best to alter his birth name, Rickenbacher, to Rickenbacker in 1917. Orchestra conductors were fired for playing German music, German teachers in high schools were dismissed, Boy Scouts stole bundles of German American newspapers (which flourished in the large urban German communities) and burned them.[14]

While the loyalty of various groups came into question in the United States during the war, the loyalty of the country's most notable minority, African Americans, was never in doubt. How they would be allowed to express that loyalty was another question. In essence, African American elites hoped that if the war was to make the world safe for democracy, they could use it to help their race make rapid steps toward equality in their own country. African American leaders like Booker T. Washington hoped to demonstrate the loyalty of the race to the United States. W. E. B. Du Bois, on his way to becoming an advocate of more militant strategies for civil rights and social equality, was encouraged by the war in that, like the Progressives, he saw in it the potential to reach his social goals more quickly, which included legal equality. Although the two leaders, Washington and Du Bois, were already deep into fundamental disagreements about how to achieve a better life for African Americans, they both agreed that the best strategy in the war would be a clear-cut and energetic participation of black troops in combat in Europe.[15]

African Americans had been an important component of the U.S. army since the Civil War; General Pershing had gained his sobriquet "Black Jack" early in his career when he headed a famous black cavalry unit. Black units had fought in Cuba, the Philippines, and other imperialist fields of battle. Both Wilson and many in his administration were convinced, however, that black soldiers were more useful as laborers than as combat soldiers. Their draft cards were labeled with a "C" for "colored," and they were assigned disproportionately to labor units. Black leaders hesitated to challenge these developments, but they did pressure the War Department, under Newton D. Baker, to train black soldiers for combat. Baker agreed, but training the black recruits and officer candidates was a complicated matter. Just before the war racial violence was on an upward trend, expanding into the industrial North, where large numbers of African Americans were migrating. In 1917 a number of race riots broke out, among them a vicious one on May 28 in East St. Louis, Illinois, the same locality as the "patriotic" Collinsville lynching of Robert Prager 11 months later. The causes for most of the riots were a combination of protests at African Americans taking "white" or union jobs and real or supposed sexual advances made on white females. Concentrating large numbers of young African American men for training would therefore consititute a problem, especially after the "Houston Mutiny" of August 23, 1917. On this occasion, after several clashes with police, about 100 black soldiers from the 24th Infantry, training in the area, marched into Houston and engaged in open battle with police and citizens. Four soldiers and sixteen Houston whites died in the only riot in U.S. history in which more whites than blacks died. This balance was redressed as the result of courts-martial, which sentenced 13 to hang and 40 to life imprisonment.[16]

There were higher-level difficulties. The highest-ranking black officer in the army, Lt. Col. Charles Denton Young, was an 1899 West Point graduate with extensive command experience, including serving under Pershing. Rather than appointing Young to lead a black division, the army suddenly declared Young's retirement for reasons of physical unfitness – and without irony (he was certainly physically unacceptable because of his race, but the hardy colonel was hardly feeble). Yet War Secretary Baker at last endeavored to make some concessions, appointing Booker T. Washington's former assistant (Emmett Scott) to the post of Assistant Secretary in the War Department. Baker also set up a training camp for black soldiers in Iowa and oversaw the creation of two black divisions, the 92nd, which would serve in France under white American officers, and the 93rd, which would be seconded to the French army and serve under French command. Some 42,000 African Americans served in combat units; blacks constituted a full third of the army's labor unit manpower. A number of black soldiers were decorated for bravery by the U.S. Army, and some 200 were decorated with the Croix de Guerre by the French.

At the of the war, African Americans were in large measure disappointed and disaffected at the lack of progress from their efforts and the continued racism of postwar society. The history of African Americans in the war would form a kind of repressed part of history that, as with the more immediate impact of the war in molding national identities, would contribute to the awareness of contributions to the greater community. Yet as one writer commented just after the war, describing a dreadful case of violence against a black child, "The 'German Hun' is beaten but the world is made no safer for Democracy."[17]

We have looked only briefly at the Australian home front in this study, but the country displayed variations on all the patterns we have seen on the home fronts: unity and enthusiasm, tightening economic centralization, and a very extensive period of strikes in August–September 1917 and a resultant increased presence of the state in controlling the labor force. The Labour Party premier, William Hughes, tried to push through conscription in Australia in the late summer of 1916, as the Somme Offensive wound out to its end in France, but on October 28, 1916 Australians rejected conscription by a narrow margin, a measure which ultimately led to a new coalition war government of tough-minded Labour and Nationalist politicians who didn't mind breaking the eggs in order to scramble them. Actually, the Australians continued to volunteer, eventually sending some 329,000 overseas. Yet Australian unity was in part achieved, as Gerhard Fischer has pointed out, by the creation of an "invisible home front" along which a homogenous, national, "British" majority fought against all kinds of enemies: striking workers, Irish nationalists, radical socialists, and anti-conscriptionists. In this way, especially after 1916, the Australian war government sold the war under a new banner of "Britishness" which demanded loyalty and enthusiasm.

Australia possessed a sizeable and prosperous minority of German Australians (about 100,000 of Australia's 4.4 million, about 2 percent), most of whose families had migrated in the mid-nineteenth century. In the main, they formed a prosperous and productive class of merchants and producers. A number of breweries owned by Australian Germans, like the Resch Brewery, hearkened back to German excellence in beer technology. Numerous members of the German Australian community were merchants with chains of grocery or supply stores. These Australians gave no sign of being less than loyal. Indeed, Australia's General John Monash, the son of German Jewish parents who wrote letters home to his father in German, is recognized as one of the most effective generals of the war.

Yet by 1915 popular fears of "infiltration" by Germans of Australia led to the establishment of an Anti-German League, whose members not only suspected the German Australians of disloyalty and spying, but who also decried the competition which Australians of German descent represented as against "good Australian businesses." Australia had already mirrored British repressive measures in the form of the War Precautions Regulations and eventually the Aliens Registration Order. By 1915, the government had set up a number of internment or concentration camps, with tents or open wooden shelters for housing, for German nationals who had been caught by the war in Australia and, eventually, German Australians. The Hughes coalition war government cracked down, changing German placenames, making the teaching and use of German illegal, and limiting the civil rights of Australia's German community. The program of internment seems to have concentrated on community leaders: pastors, political leaders, and prominent business people (the brewer Resch, himself, spent a year in an internment camp).

Indeed, the Australian government expanded the relatively simple "anti-German" program into a whole series of interlocking controls of the population, including registration of enemy aliens (defined broadly), censorship, police and military surveillance, and eventually expropriation, internment, and deportation. The rejection of the conscription referendum seems to have accelerated and broadened this repressive program, for the forces which reasoned that Germans and Irish Catholics were responsible for the rejection of conscription were prepared to root out these "un-British" elements. Indeed, the German connection with beer helped accelerate the Australian temperance movement, as in America.

In the end some 4,500 Australians were interned in camps because they were of German descent. Many were deported and much of their property was confiscated. This kind of ethnic expropriation, deportation, and internment did not rival the gruesome and deadly activities of the Turkish and Russian governments during the war, but the process of identifying an ethnic group as traitors or potential traitors and effectively interning and dispossessing them was a step toward the brutal ethnic politics of those countries. It was, one would think, out of place in a war to make the world safe for democracy.[18]

A New Irony? Art, Culture, and the War

American literary historian Paul Fussell has argued that the Great War was the spawning ground for the irony and sarcasm of both modernist art and modern everyday discourse. Modris Eksteins has gone further, asserting that the war represented the very birth of the modern age, or perhaps one should say, modernist age.[19] We cannot dispute the importance of the war in terms of modernist art, modern culture, and modern mores. As with most of the tendencies of World War I, we should really keep in mind that modernist art and avant-garde cultural habits were well rooted before the war. But the acceleration and even "popularization" of the modernist cultural agenda issued directly from war experience, and in particular from the trenches of the Western Front.

The clearest example of this cultural phenomenon, the one best known to the English-speaking world, is that of the famous British "war poets" and writers, above all Siegfried Sassoon, Robert Graves, Wilfred Owen, and Vera Brittain. Sassoon and Graves were already immersed in the waves of modernist culture before the war. Once they experienced the alien scenes of trench warfare, they turned their experiences into a new poetical vocabulary which tried to convey the most horrifying and shocking elements of the Western Front. In Sassoon's "Counter-Attack," a successful defense ends in the death of the subject:

And he remembered his rifle . . . rapid fire . . .
And started blazing wildly . . . then a bang
Crumpled and spun him sideways, knocked him out
To grunt and wriggle: none heeded him; he choked
And fought the flapping veils of smothering gloom . . .

Though Sassoon was an officer, and an aggressive one at that, he identified in his poems with the "other ranks" and thereby captured a real
Western Front (and modernist) contempt for the "high command"
behind the lines. In "Base Details" his contempt for the "red-tabbed
butchers" is explicit:

If I were fierce, and bald, and short of breath,
I'd live with scarlet Majors at the Base,
And speed glum heroes up the line to death.

The younger poet Wilfred Owen developed a similar style which
relied on shock and explicit and often clinical descriptions of death
and violence. Like the other "war poets" Owen was quite blunt with
his message of despair that the great age of Enlightenment progress
had been blown away. As Owen wrote in his haunting poem "Strange
Meeting," the nations would not reverse their "trek from progress."
With a kind of jaded innocence, Owen describes the aftermath of a gas
attack in "Dulce et Decorum Est," describing the dead with "the white
eyes writhing in his face,/His hanging face." Bitterness was the hall-
mark of the war poets, and this bitterness emerged in their poems, fiction, and "memoirs" such as Vera Brittain's *Testament of Youth* (1933)
and Robert Graves's *Goodbye to All That* (1929). Modernist poets and
writers everywhere were as ready to "use" the war as social theorists
and military men. Hemingway would rush to get into the war, as
would John Dos Passos and e. e. cummings. In the late 1920s, bitter
works coming from the "lost generation" began to pour forth, the
most famous being Erich Maria Remarque's *All Quiet on the Western
Front* (1929).

Developments in modernist painting and drawing were quite
analogous. French Cubist Fernand Leger served as a 35-year-old
stretcher-bearer and painted the front in stark Cubist terms. Like
Sassoon, British artist C. R. W. Nevinson was likewise a Cubist when
the war began, and his expression of the scenes of the Western Front
into geometric machines, landscapes, and people – a prime example is
his well-known painting "Machine Gun" – emphasized the impersonal,

automatic nature of the front: men as killing machines. More emotional, both George Grosz and Otto Dix created large bodies of art depicting the Western Front which retain their power both to shock and to move the viewer at the beginning of the twenty-first century. Using techniques pioneered in the Paris and Munich avant-garde, Dix's ghastly black-and-white drawings detailing fear, mutilation, death, and corruption are some of the most potent cultural productions of the war. Very much like Owen, Dix managed to display the innocence and "pity of war" (as Owen put it). Behind all of this art lies a sense of irony, as Fussell demonstrated in his classic work, *The Great War and Modern Memory*.[20]

And yet, modernist art and bitter irony were hardly the only psychological response to trench warfare. Many veterans interviewed by sociologist Tony Ashworth in the 1960s and 1970s indicated that life on the front was hard, that it was sad to lose friends to wounds and death, but that the experience of doing one's "duty" in the camaraderie of the wartime service was a great experience. Edmund Blunden was a British poet whose classic memoir of the war, *Undertones of War* (1928), figures prominently in Fussell's book, yet even Blunden, the young officer, describes many positive moments, among them the friendships, the loyalty, and the devotion found in the trenches: "Taking my meditative way along to the other extremity of our trench, I was genially desired by Corporal Worley to take cocoa with him. . . . A kinder heart there never was; a gentler spirit never. . . . Where now, Frank Worley. I should like an answer. He was for ever comforting those youngsters who were so numerous among us."[21]

American intellectual and historian S. L. A. Marshall looked back long after the war and remembered the hardships of walking mile after mile loaded down with an 80-lb. pack, not seeing a candy bar for a year, finding that the army at times left the burial of the dead to their own dead tired comrades. Still:

We were not blind to these difficulties. . . . We simply saw these things as incidental. . . .

Such was the attitude of Pershing's A. E. F. It was a crude Army by present standards, unreasonably self-confident, high-humored, boisterous, cocky, almost vulgarly so. But Man, how we loved it, and Man, how we strove to help one another! Nothing felt since has made the heart leap so.[22]

Behind the front line in 1916, Edmund Blunden waxed poetic: "We now marched in earnest. Of all the treasured romances of the world, is there anything to make the blood sing itself along, to brighten the eye, to fill the ear with unheard melodies, like a marching battalion in which one's own body is going?"[23] Blunden tells how he latched onto trench mapping and trench exploring as a real specialty. Proud of this ability, he took extraordinary chances just to find the end of a sap or the location of a deserted trench. Many other Western Front fighters remembered their ingenuity fondly, enjoying the mechanical challenges of trench warfare. Ernst Jünger, German front soldier, modernist writer, and the most famous German literary recorder of the war, described dangerous challenges with fondness: almost as a game he describes listening for the British who are undermining his trench to blow it up.[24] German trench fighter Philipp Karch showed the same enthusiasm for the simple routine of tidying up: "With the sun up we go to work, . . . cleaning out the countless drainage trenches which lead to in the direction of the enemy positions, rebuilding the shelled trenches and spending day and night in an equal rhythm between work and guarding."[25]

British New Zealander Charles Edmund Carrington wrote a famous, and early, war memoir called *A Subaltern's War* (1924). Late in life he made clear his objections to what he regarded as the "lost generation" mythology:

> I never meet an old "sweat", as we liked to describe ourselves, who accepts or enjoys the figure in which we are now presented. . . . Just smile and make an old soldier's wry joke when you see yourself on the television screen, agonized and woebegone, trudging from disaster to diaster, knee-deep in moral as well as physical mud, hesitant about your purpose, submissive to a harsh, irrelevant discipline, mistrustful of your commanders. Is it any use to assert that I was not like that, and my dead friends were not like that, and the old cronies that I meet at reunions are not like that?[26]

Like many Western Front fighters, Carrington felt a kinship with the soldiers from the other side. Of an Austrian friend Carrington met after the war, a witness of both Eastern and Western Fronts, Carrington wrote:

> When we met in later times, we never disagreed on politics or on the anomalies of a soldier's life, and his sardonic tales about staff

officers were just like mine. Whatever was the nature of the trap we had been caught in, it was the same trap, and the Germans had endured it with the same rough humor. (Not at all like that unreal civilian's fantasy of the back areas, *All Quiet on the Western Front*.)[27]

We might also take something of this mood from the trove of frontline humour:

A. "Did you hear that shell just now?"
B. "I did. Twice. Once when it passed me, and again when I passed it".[28]

In speaking of rough humor in the war as a way of dealing with everyday difficulties, the *Wipers Times*, the British soldiers' "trench journal" surely rates special mention. The original joke of British soldiers was to mispronounce the name of Ypres as "Wipers," part of a continual renaming of places all along the British sector of the front, but especially intense and often quite whimsical at Ypres. Hence, the filthy and bombed-out remains of the village of Ploegstaert became Plug Street. One might see in this behavior a kind of defusing of the vile and lethal reputation of the place by creative mispronunciation. The playing out of this joke came in the satirical journal the *Wipers Times*, which applied the satirical principle in articles, poems, songs, jokes, and drawings. Famous journalists and writers often came in for sharp lampoon: commentator Hilaire Belloc became "Belary Helloc," journalist Beach Thomas became "Teech Bomas," and so on. The bombastic Thomas did not let innocence of the front stop him from purple descriptions, and the *Wipers Times* captured his style regularly for an approving soldier audience. In the following, Bomas describes a tank battle:

How can I clearly relate what happened? All is one chaotic mingly of joy and noise. No fear! How could one fear anything in the belly of a prerambulating peripatetic progologdymythorus! Wonderful, epic, on we went . . . At last we were fairly in amongst the Huns. They were around us in millions and in millions they died.

The "Rubaiyat of a 'Line' Subaltern" begins with the elegant pentameter: "The passing whizz-bang shrieks and bullets hum."[29]

Another approach was to turn to the gentlest of all forms of literary endeavor, children's literature, and this tendency led to some of the war's most lasting, though now scarcely recognized legacies. In light of the enormous literature that now exists on the psychological connections of children's literature, it can be no surprise that many creative Western Front participants would seek to escape their surroundings by retreating to their imagination, or, after the war, to try to create a world quite apart from the traumatic chaos and brutality of the trenches. One may still be surprised at the large number of Western Front veterans who became authors of children's literary classics, as indeed at the nature of the worlds these authors created. Their biographies work in parallel (and were often quite parallel socially and in other ways) to those of the "hollow men" and "war poets," but the result is different.

Hugh Lofting (born in 1886) a struggling writer with the British Ministry of Information, joined the army in 1916 and from the trenches began to write letters to his son and daughter containing the first sketches of Dr. Doolittle. He was apparently appalled by the war in general, but the sketches really derived from his sympathy for the multitudes of wounded horses which had to be destroyed: "If we made the animals take the same chances we did ourselves, why did we not give them similar attention when wounded? But obviously to develop horse-surgery as good as that of our Casualty Clearing Station would necessitate a knowledge of horse language." Hence the doctor who "could talk to the animals." In 1917 Lofting received a "Blighty" wound and was discharged. The first "Doolittle" book, published in 1920, was immediately hailed as a classic.[30]

Another creative reaction to the Western Front lines was the world of *The Hobbit* and *The Lord of the Rings*, and this world too was related to the trenches. J. R. R. Tolkien, born in 1892, was at Oxford finishing his degree when war broke out. Already a writer of poetry with an interest in the literature of epics and myth, he finished his degree in mid-1915 and accepted a commission in the Lancashire Fusiliers, arriving on the Western Front in mid-1916. Tolkien's battalion was at the front in reserve on the first day of the Somme, and it went over the top on July 14 to attack a German strong point at Ovillers. His battalion was involved in the terrific struggle for the famous Schwaben Redoubt, near Thiepval, and other Somme actions. After a few months, serious sickness took him out of the trenches and kept him on home duty and in hospitals for the rest of the war, but service in the cauldron in the Somme campaign was as intense as anything the Western Front could offer. Tolkien found neither the front nor army life itself particularly pleasant, though he was attentive to positive aspects: like Blunden, he found contact with "lower" classes a blessing, writing later in life that one of the main characters in *The Lord of the Rings* books, "Samwise Gamgee," "is indeed a reflexion of the English soldier, of the privates and batmen I knew in the 1914 war, and recognized as so far superior to myself." In the course of a half-year he lost some of his closest friends to the Somme. Under the impact of these conditions and partly in response to them, he set out on an ambitious plan to invent a whole mythology: "in huts full of blasphemy and smut, or by candle light in bell-tents, even some down in dugouts under shell fire."[31]

Tolkien's later friend, colleague, and fellow-writer of the fantasy epic, C. S. Lewis (born in 1898), was likewise at Oxford, joining up in 1917 and arriving on the Western Front in 1917 on his nineteenth birthday. He served with the Somerset Light Infantry Regiment until he was wounded by a British shell at the Battle of Arras during Ludendorff's Offensive in April 1918. Lewis's Christianity, like that of Tolkien, might later distinguish him from most of the broken-generation intellectuals (though in 1918 he was an atheist), but the broad optimism and good humor which he displayed in letters at the time and memoirs later arose in spite of serious personal problems and a hard war:

> Everyone you met took it for granted that the whole thing was an odious necessity, a ghastly interruption of rational life. And that made all the difference. Straight tribulation is easier to bear than tribulation which advertises itself as pleasure. The one breeds camaraderie and even (when intense) a kind of love between the fellow sufferers; the other, mutual distrust, cynicism, concealed and fretting resentment.

Lewis later offered a generally optimistic view: "There were nasty people in the army; but memory fills those months with pleasant, transitory contacts. Every few days one seemed to meet a scholar, an original, a poet, a cheery buffoon, a raconteur, or at the least a man of good will." Lewis wrote much else besides the "Narnia" series and indeed, most of his work was not children's literature (he wrote seven books for children), but his career makes the point that even profound and serious intellectuals and literary men might well react in a variety of ways to the Western Front.[32]

Perhaps the longest distance from Mametz Wood or Thiepval Wood would be the distance one would have to travel to get to "100-Aker" Wood, inhabited by "Winnie-the-Pooh," but it was in the trenches of the Somme sector that the famous bear had his origin. A. A. Milne, the creator of the Winnie-the-Pooh books (Winnie first appeared in a 1924 story), served in the the Royal Warwickshire Regiment (a fellow-officer was Bernard Law Montgomery). A signaling officer and instructor in England for the first half of the war, Milne was already a writer. On the front, he experienced the same hardships as many of the "broken generation," including a bout of trench fever. He wrote during the war, like Tolkien, partly to escape the dreariness. Without doubt, the gentle, colorful, and soft world of Winnie-the-Pooh and Christopher Robin presents a profound contrast to the dreary, banal, and brutal conditions of the front. Indeed, the origin of Winnie's name may have been a bear he saw in London, one originally belonging as a mascot to the 2nd Canadian Infantry Brigade (and named "Winifred" in honour of Winnipeg, Canada), which had to be left in England when the unit shipped to France.[33]

Many other great writers of children's literature went through the filter of the war and the Western Front. A British Voluntary Aid Detachment (VAD) nurse who worked in London area hospitals, under an impact of wounds and mutilations, Enid Bagnold, would become a novelist of and author of the juvenile classic, *National Velvet* (1935).[34] The young Walt Disney, born in 1900, was too young for the army but lied about his age to get into the Red Cross Ambulance Service in 1917. He would probably have made it to Europe in time for combat conditions had he not contracted Spanish flu (another characteristic and dangerous experience of World War I). As it was, he made it to France and the front lines literally a few days after the Armistice and spent a year in and out of the war-torn Western Front zone, in his spare time decorating his ambulance with humorous, fanciful figures.[35] Jean de Brunhoff (born in 1900) reached the Western Front shortly before the war's end. He later created the "Babar" books. Austrian German Ludwig Bemelmans, who had emigrated to the United States just before the war, enlisted in the U.S. army, though he was never sent to Europe. Bemelmans created the "Madeleine" books. The author of the classic *Little Prince* (1943), Antoine du Saint-Exupéry, tried to get into the war as a flier and in the merchant marine, though the war ended before he was in the service. Erich Kästner, author of *Emil and the Detectives* (1930), served in 1917/18.[36]

If we do broaden our searchlight in studying the effects of the war on intellectuals and culture, we might well keep in mind some patterns we have seen in society, in politics, and even in military affairs: the Great War did not "create" much out of whole cloth, yet it did often accelerate preexisting tendencies so rapidly that the forms emerging from the war looked as if they were original "creations," such as women's suffrage, the bureaucratic centralized state, and a multitude of other inventions. One might argue that the "escapist" approach to mental health on the Western Front was really an avoidance of the horrors, and that the head-on acceptance of, one might say a fixation on, them like that of Remarque, or Sassoon, or Otto Dix, provides a somehow more authentic response. Yet if we only view the war through the eyes of half a dozen war poets and a few novelists, we will surely miss some of the important pieces of the picture.

Just behind the trenches, war culture was a mixture of the banal and the exciting. The gathering, regimentation, transportation, and mixing of millions of young men from many walks of life led to a homogenization of speech, behavior, and morals which clearly lent a new tone to popular culture. The American postwar song "How Ya Gonna Keep 'Em Down on the Farm, After They've Seen Paree?" contained some insights that applied to all the belligerent societies. One of the significant issues of the social mixing of the Great War hinges upon the impact of mass military life on social, regional, and religious identity. On the Western Front, farm boys from Protestant Thuringia mixed with working-class toughs from Hamburg, Catholic Bavarians, Danish-speaking "Germans" from North Schleswig, coal miners from Upper Silesia (also Catholics): similar profiling might be done, more or less, with all the belligerent societies.

Common experiences behind the trenches were many. All armies sponsored traveling plays and entertainments, in which all kinds of singing, music-hall and serious, took place. Film had already become a tremendous cultural unifier for the younger generation, and the soldiers, nurses, and various other young people in the supply towns and provincial capitals were no less hungry for films than before the war. Traveling film theaters could even take the new films close to the battle fronts, so that young men returning to Paris and London were not necessarily deprived of the latest films of Clara Bow or other stars. The most popular film figure of the time was Charlie Chaplin, whose slapstick antics (really a theater of the ironic – especially fitting for Paul Fussell's war of ironies) – made him not only the greatest box-office draw, but a potent figure of cultural change as well. Hardly vital but still of interest, moustache fashions may have changed largely as a result of Chaplin's unorthodox, squarish moustache, and this change would be parodied and echoed by other comedians – one thinks of possibly the greatest ironist of all time, Groucho Marx – as well as British,

American, and French men of all classes who adopted the same moustache style. Adolf Hitler, a Western Front fighter, appears in the Chaplinesque moustache in his earliest postwar pictures. His biographers have assumed that he was copying British "gentlemen" rather than Charlie Chaplin.

The wartime capitals for soldiers on leave, cities behind the lines, the port of Le Havre, the supply towns of Popheringhe, Armentières, and Brussels (for the Germans), transportation itself – all of the wartime experience constituted a welter of sensory impulses. A young American woman volunteering as a nurse (or "sister") in a French surgery close to the lines attempts to describe this dense sensory haze:

> Just imagine a pinwheel in motion. . . . The changing scenes of the last few hours keep dancing before my eyes like spots when one has looked at the sun . . . the arrival in a station crowded with men and munitions, our billeting each in a separate house in the village, supper off tin plates in a long dingy barrack with desperate wounded behind the partition . . . listening between rapid dreams to the booming of the guns, these are the elements.[37]

Indeed, the areas in the immediate rear of the Allied line were especially dense in human interactions. One British subaltern found "much" to do in the after-hours of training in France:

> I go down to Rouen nearly every day and mix with people. It's awfully interesting to pick up with people and talk with them for an hour or so. I have met French and Belgian officers and soldiers, English girls and French actresses and *demi-mondaines*, padres and police, and talk and drink in the cosmopolitan atmosphere of the French cafés.[38]

Middle-class women working behind the front in hospitals, aid stations, and a variety of jobs with the YMCA and many other organizations had fewer blocks of time off to experience this exhilarating atmosphere, certainly much less time than the *demi-mondaines* with whom British soldiers whiled away an hour. At Royaumont in Picardy, a whole staff of women doctors from the U.K. set up a Scottish Women's Hospital as a surgery immediately behind the lines. Working hours could be long and furious. Though the hospital's leader had to slog to the front and "recruit" casualties at first, the excellence of the hospital later cut down on French soldiers' hesitation to be treated by "women doctors." Partly because of such unremitting work, women at the front began to shorten their skirts and cut their hair to a more sensible length than the *de rigueur* prewar tresses. All the women doctors at Royaumont took up smoking, too, as many women working in the war zone did, or at least tried it.[39]

Meanwhile, Allied soldiers made their way to Paris, if they were lucky, to sample the pleasures of the city, which were specially enhanced just for soldierly enjoyments. The resulting collisions of value systems, morals, and habits echoed throughout the societies of the Western Front powers long after the war in the form of "decadent" Weimar Germany, the "Roaring Twenties" in the United States, and various versions of these phenomena in the other European capitals.

This was a chaotic human theater. Scenes such as the picture of the scholarly (and somewhat stodgy) linguist J. R. R. Tolkien listening to ragtime music on a phonograph at dull moments during training[40] may strike us as incongruous, but they represent the mixing of the disparate elements that were being blended to create "modern" culture. It is clear that this experience was of tremendous importance for European and Western culture. Indeed, as Fussell has made clear, modern popular culture is unthinkable without World War II, and World War II is unthinkable without World War I.[41]

Breakup of the Stalemate and a New Military Synthesis

Having looked at the three and half years of hostilities preceeding the great Ludendorff Offensive of March 1918, we have seen innovation on all sides. Apart from rapid-firing artillery and long-range infantry weapons, the great Schlieffen army and the Old Contemptibles were very close to being nineteenth-century formations. The French uniforms even looked like nineteenth-century accoutrements, and no Western Front soldier had a steel helmet until late 1915. The first Germans into Belgium were cavalry troopers, and the first German attack delivered at Liège was an attack in column, a formation beloved of Napoleon. Many soldiers rode part of the way to the front on railroad trains, but otherwise, soldiers walked everywhere, usually carrying supplies for the front. Perhaps the most motorized elements of the whole opening of the war was the column of "Marne taxis," which carried French troops to help fight the Battle of the Marne. Infantrymen carried one kind of weapon, the uniform rifle of their army, with a detachable bayonet. Machine-gun teams were assigned sparingly at higher levels. No one carried any sort of grenade or bomb. Infantry attacks were stand-up affairs, even those carried out by the most experienced troops who could be trusted to attack in waves rather than columns. The plan for any assault was, on the whole, to charge the position. Armies were articulated into smaller "sections," platoons, and companies, but once the parapet was cleared, this articulation did not mean very much.

If we skip ahead to 1918, things looked very different – the soldiers themselves, for one thing. Colorful markings of all sorts, and picturesque headgear, were gone. All armies wore dull colors that blended in with the earth. Everyone had worn a helmet since 1916. Perhaps the only remaining anachronism were the kilts which many Scots units persisted in sporting. Officers' field clothing, too, had ceased to be in easily distinguished form; instead, officers now looked like everyone else from a distance, and hence presented less of a target to enemy fire.

The equipage of soldiers was more varied, the result in part of "specilization" on the battlefield. Fully loaded, all soldiers carried more or less the same 80-lb. pack, entrenching tool, and the like, but in the attack, infantry soldiers were frequently differentiated. After 1916, some British individuals, indeed, some units, applied the lessons of trench raiding and carried only "bombs" in sacks. Using the experience of raids, these teams became an important element of British tactics by the end of the war, since it was their job to clear out the trenches captured while other infantrymen, mostly armed with the standard Enfield rifle and bayonet, went ahead to the next line of trenches. Naturally, another new element of warfare introduced by the British during the Somme battles came to play a major role in the war by 1918: tanks. After somewhat inconclusive results in 1916, tanks began to come into their own during 1917, especially in the great tank battle at Cambrai, and by 1918 the British, French, and Americans were all using tanks as an integral part of attack. Again, we will understand the value of the tank if we think once more of the machine gun-swept battlefield, and the protection offered to the following troops as well as the offensive power of having a mounted artillery piece and a heavy machine gun grinding away at the very front of the fire zone.

The German army was rapidly putting the pieces together as well. Applying a tactical system adapted from Western Front practice and worked out on the Eastern Front by General Oskar von Hutier to the problem of breakthrough, Ludendorff and his staff developed fully the ideas that had really been percolating in many ways in the German army since the turn of the century.[42] First and foremost were the development of small units called "storm sections," whose job was to hit an identified and relatively narrow part of the enemy front with great force using all the means of firepower and "shock" developed since the beginning of the war. This array included flamethrowers (used since 1915) and bombs or hand grenades (used since 1914). The object was for these shock troops – very much like the British system described above – to punch a hole in the enemy lines, and hold this "bridgehead" until the regular infantry could arrive to hold and expand the position while the original *Sturmabteilung* moved on rapidly to the next identified point. Indeed, in a tacit abeyance to the military tendency to view battles as drama (as in "theaters" of war, the big "show," and like expressions), these late-war German tactics, like those of the British, called for extensive rehearsals far behind the lines in very similar terrain and circumstances to the real objectives. One cannot help but compare this careful preparation to the first day of the Somme, when even the preattack study of a plasticine model by some British officers opposite Mametz Wood was thought to be subversive.

Still, as historians have focused more on the enormous fighting experience of the French in World War I, they have begun to point out that a citizen army held off a formidable invader for four years and broke only once. If the French morale was so low, why does objective information from French trench journalism, from French military reports, and from the experience of Americans training with and fighting with the French tell such a different story? In fact, the French contributions to solving the problems of the "storm of steel" battlefield help us resolve this apparent paradox. Clearly, French officers, even generals, learned from their mistakes, though the Grandmaison–Foch theories of attack exerted a powerful hold. Still, even by 1916, the French were beginning to take a lesson from their fighting up on Vieil Armand, in the Vosges mountains: they began to abandon the continuous front trench, substituting for a continuous line of rifle-shooting infantrymen a series of machine-gun posts thrust forward in front of the rear positions, with interlocking fire and supported by small groups of soldiers, not a continuous front of them. Support and command trenches were indeed in place several hundred yards behind, and indeed these were the jumping-off place for counterattack, should German attacks break through the belt of machine guns (one notices how even this defensive technique incorporated the French penchant for attack).

Increasingly as a result of the arrival of Pétain and his staff, the French also adopted a new doctrine of attack: "Artillery conquers, infantry occupies." When Pétain arrived at Verdun, it has been seen, the general assured his troops that their attacks would henceforth have full artillery support, that he would not multiply the loss of human resources when he could accomplish the same objective using material ones.[43] We have also seen that he did not convince his fellow-generals completely, and that the horrific Nivelle Offensive of 1917 was based on an opposite calculation of resources. Still, after the French mutiny of spring 1917, the French army was more open to change, in part, of course, because the tremendous losses had weakened the country and the army's morale. But one also sees a new flexibility on the part of French field commanders late in the war. Indeed, after the exemplary American victory at St. Mihiel in September 1918, they sent a group of officers to find out how the Americans had done it. Hence, we would do well to keep the French share in tactical innovation in mind.

To move from the infantry troops themselves, artillery began the war as the big killer and only increased in importance as the war progressed. By 1918 artillery pieces had not only multiplied but become bigger. Artillerists now delivered not only high-explosive and various shrapnel-type shells against enemy positions, but they also routinely fired shells filled with poison gas and various incendiary mixtures, mainly burning metals, like the substance called thermite, which was something like the firebombs of the Second World War, but fired from the tubes of artillery. The "heavy" bombardments of the early period had been intensified with each year of the war. In addition to a much higher tonnage of shells fired, artillery tactics had become much more sophisticated. The famous failed walking barrages of the first day of the Somme no longer failed by the next year, and soldiers would follow behind the curtain of explosions quite closely. Moreover, by 1917 artillerists in all Western Front armies were "boxing" off enemy movements, isolating sections of the battlefield to prevent the escape of the enemy or to prevent reinforcements and supplies from making it to specific sections of the battlefield. Commanders learned to concentrate artillery on specific areas and for shorter periods, rather than spread out their bombardments in space and time, and the composition of the shells rained onto the enemy became more varied and thought-out in terms of specific effect. The logistical feat involved in just moving the millions of tons of ammunition for these guns provides a model of problem-solving in wartime for all armies, but especially the British, so far from sources of supply.[44]

In terms of choosing and finding the right targets, artillery crews still depended on "forward observers" and on ground-level intelligence about enemy positions. Observation balloons had been used since the nineteenth century, and they were used on the Western Front, but the leap in the capabilities of airplanes to play a part on the battlefield impacted the artillery substantially. And the importance of airpower was, conversely, increased by the crucial importance of artillery as the most important weapon of the war. Airplanes provided excellent observation platforms from the beginning of the war, but the addition of cameras and even radio technology (transmitting by radioed code using a trailing antenna) provided accurate and sometimes instantaneous intelligence about enemy movements. The battlefield really gained another dimension during World War I.

Indeed, airpower generated its own expansion. Since observation of the enemy enhanced artillery effectiveness, interdiction of the enemy's observation planes became an important secondary task. Associated with pursuing and intercepting enemy observation plans were problems of mounting a heavy machine gun onto a light plane, and then arranging the mechanism in such a way that the pilot could aim the gun and fire it without shooting off his own propeller. These problems were in essence solved by mid-1915, but by the end of the war, tactics had evolved to sophisticated levels. By 1917, airplanes were not only fighting each other for the space to observe enemy armies, but taking on targets on the ground too, that is, attacking troops and positions in tactical support of the ground forces. The Germans had been bombing targets in England by dirigible since 1914, but by the end of the war, airplanes were developing effective ways to drop heavier loads of bombs more precisely on all kinds of targets.

In this air war, the aces famous in story and song caught the imagination of civilians looking for bright spots, governments looking for heroes to advertise, and soldiers slogging their way through the mud. Though much of the received popular knowledge about the war in the air perpetuates romanticized inaccuracies, it was certainly the case that the dangers of air-to-air fighting could hardly be exaggerated. The pilots and crews flying and fighting above the trenches in World War I sustained casualties at the horrendous rate of about 50 percent overall. Some 15 percent of the airmen trained for combat operations in the French air corps died. Of the great heroes of the air war, most were dead by the war's end. On the other hand, all elements of military aviation which became important in later wars – strategic bombing, aerial reconnaissance, tactical support, air-to-air pursuit and combat, and all the rest – had emerged by the end of the war.[45]

As recent work on military innovation between the two world wars has shown, there was in fact a great deal of it. It is not too much to say that the tactical synthesis which characterized the last months of the Western Front looked more like the classic weapons systems and tactics of World War II than the marching battalions of August 1914.[46]

Still, at the end of these considerations, one must account for a great deal of human failure in the command of a new warfare. Clearly, commanders came to the understanding of the new warfare at different rates (their personal learning curves). And the alacrity with which the generals and colonels saw the need for more preservation of their troops' lives was very clearly connected with a whole web of intellectual, social, and cultural considerations prevalent in their own time.

The Americans and Alliance War-Making

Until mid-1917, the military diplomacy of the Western Front consisted primarily of Anglo-French conversations which had begun in the prewar years. If the high commands and their governments did not quite get along at times, they still cooperated over the long haul. From the moment that John J. Pershing, commander of the American Expeditionary Force (AEF) arrived in Europe, the relations between the principal warring powers having to do with the waging of the war itself became much more difficult and painful. Before he left the United States, Pershing had received vague instructions to the effect that, if possible, American troops should fight in American units and under American commanders (the Canadians had, of course, faced the same issue a year before). Pershing took this somewhat flexible instruction and determined to rebuff all attempts to parcel out American troops into the line. Where in optimistic moments both the British and French high commands hoped to use the American troops individually as replacements in British or French units, Pershing simply refused. In the United States, popular support of intervention in the war was hardly a given, and what the opponents of the war might have done with a refusal to keep American troops under American command may be imagined. More than a little of the American opposition to the war came from the strongly Scots–Irish South and West, where critics noted acidly that the English were ready to fight to the last Irish or Scots soldier. Very few Americans wanted to give the English or the French a chance to fight to the last American. Pershing recognized this, perhaps more than Wilson himself, and infuriated both French and British by insisting on putting Americans only into American units with American commanders (though there were some notable exceptions). Earlier in the war, the Canadian forces had faced a similar experience, and with much less bargaining power than the Americans had, likewise resisted becoming a reservoir for British replacements.[47]

Pershing's view of tactics also irritated his counterparts. He talked briskly of offensive warfare and the warfare of movement. When the British high command suggested that the arriving American troops learn "trench warfare" under their tutelage, Pershing replied that he did not want American troops to become focused on occupying their own trenches, but on attacking the trenches of the Germans. Hence, the American forces trained more with the French than the British, and from Pershing's staff down, the Americans planned for offensive operations with an American army.

Though some historians, American and otherwise, have interpreted the Americans as somehow marginal to the conflict, it is important to say here that the United States, as we have seen, had supplied the Entente for much of the war. Though American entry did not mean that new armies would appear on the front immediately, it did mean that the Entente could expend more of its resources in the knowledge that more men and materials would be arriving soon. In the end, the United States would, in addition to its financial, manufacturing, and nutritional contributions, mobilize some 3.8 million men in less than two years of war (compared to Britain's 9.5 and France's 8.2 for over four years of war). In the end, the United States can be calculated as the third major financial contributor to the fighting of the war, and the second highest contributor on the side of the Entente, with figures as follows for the highest six belligerents, in billions of 1913 dollars: British Empire 23, Germany 19.9, United States 17.1, France 9.3, Russia 5.4, Austria-Hungary 4.7.[48]

The Americans would face a learning curve in Western Front operations, but they soon applied their own traditions and internalized the real changes in military tactics which had occurred as a result of the fighting which had gone on since 1914. Although some Entente military leaders tended to minimize the impact of the Americans on the war, German generals – including both Ludendorff and his successor,

General Wilhelm Groener – singled out the American Meuse–Argonne Offensive as a significant factor in deciding to seek an armistice.

But in the end, it was not the presence of Pershing in Allied councils which created the final organization of Allied warmaking, but the massive German Spring Offensive. As we shall see below, Ludendorff's March offensive pushed the Allies far to their rear, so far in fact that the Allies feared for their lives. It was the crisis of Ludendorff's offensive that caused the Allies to work together more closely. Pershing gave in and sent some American units to fight *intact* under British and French commanders. More importantly for overall organization, to help coordinate all forces better, the French finally persuaded the British to accept an overall commander, and indeed, a Frenchman – Ferdinand Foch.

Kaiserschlacht and Hundred Days

The Western Front produced two great offensives in the year 1918: the German Spring Offensive and the Allied offensive called the Hundred Days, which ended the war. As a result of the new technologies and techniques we have discussed, both sides were able to dislodge their opponents from their trenches, and hence end stalemate.

Though the end of 1917 had left the Gemans in a still formidable position across France and Belgium, the increasingly attritional character of the war and the coming arrival of substantial American troops made it necessary, in the eyes of Hindenburg and Ludendorff, for the German army to leave its trenches and attack. We have already learned much about the grandiose and overarching ideas of Ludendorff in this book: one would rightly expect a colossal and carefully orchestrated "total" campaign from the general now planning for the future of Germany. Aware that the Germans could add to their already extensive offensive experience the new techniques and technologies described just above, Ludendorff designed an enormous series of attacks, to be delivered two weeks apart in different sectors. "We make a hole," he said "and the rest will take care of itself."[49]

An offensive of such proportions would only be possible by the troops now freed up by the implosion of Russia and the Bolshevik Revolution. In March 1918 the Germans forced a draconian peace on the Bolshevik regime, a peace which not only rearranged the faultlines of Eastern Europe, but which also freed up substantial forces, though in the event not as many, or as high in quality, as hoped. Once the "hole" was made, would there be any reserves left to go through it? At one with many of his generation as a kind of Social-Darwinian Romantic, Ludendorff seemed to stake all on the coming climactic battle. In February 1918 Prince Max of Baden asked Ludendorff what would happen if the operation should fail. The Quartermaster General replied: "In that case Germany will go under."[50]

The first offensive, codenamed "St. Michael" and often called the Kaiser's Battle, was to "separate the French and British by a rapid advance on both sides of the Somme," as Ludendorff told the army group commanders. The attack opened at 4:40 A.M. on March 21, 1918 on a 40-mile front. Using the now set pattern for a large trench raid, the German artillery opened with a heavy and sharp shelling (in this case, five hours) of gas shells and high explosives, concentrating on supply dumps, dugouts, and strong points, and bathing the French and British lines with gas. At its climax, the bombardment hit the front trenches and positions with mortar shells, dropping of course from a high angle, and blew mines planted under heavy wire entanglements in No Man's Land. After this huge rain of fire, the artillery dropped back to start a walking barrage at selected points. Twenty-seven squadrons of specially equipped airplanes flew ahead to assault strong points, artillery units, and Allied reserves.[51]

The first troops across No Man's Land were stormtroopers, specially trained and armed with automatic rifles, flamethrowers, grenades, light machine guns and trench knives, and concentrating especially on enemy strong points. Following the storm units, regular infantry crossed over in ways they had rehearsed, supported by airplanes flying low for strafing and bombing of the French and British trenches. On the British side, Gough ordered his army to retreat, exposing General Byng's army, which was also forced to retreat. By the third day, two German armies had advanced 15 miles. General Hutier's most advanced units were dug in 40 miles from their jump-off trenches.

The Allied units facing the onslaught were battered, not broken. Moreover, Ludendorff's battle direction after the initial successes – from the third day to the seventh day – was questionable. Instead of pouring in troops while the Germans still had temporary control of the skies and while the Allies were still reeling, Ludendorff now seemed cautious and held back reserves. Moreover, in many cases the hungry, tired German troops who were exploiting the gaps cut by the elite storm units found themselves in an unexpected land of plenty – first the Allied trenches and then the booming French towns in the Allied rear – and stopped to drink and eat. Ten days into the offensive, forward progress ended, just short of the great goal of Amiens. The Germans had taken much ground and had inflicted 230,000 casualties, but at a cost of exactly the same number of killed, wounded, and captured. The British and French, moreover, were not separated, and reinforcements were hurrying to the front. For longer-run calculations, American troops were now reaching France at the rate of 125,000 per month.[52]

Ludendorff responded by launching the second tier of his offensive (code-named Georg) to the north, against the British First and Second Armies in Flanders, on April 9. The Germans gained three miles on the first day but slowed rapidly, ending up just over 20 miles from Dunkirk. With help from the Belgian army from the north and French troops from the south, Plumer's Second Army held on to Flanders.

Having lost 360,000 men in "St. Michael" and "Georg" (just 34 days of battle), Ludendorff gave his forces three weeks' respite and then on May 27 launched the final stage of the Spring Offensive, Operation – , in the area of so much previous killing, the rugged Aisne region, including the infamous Chemin des Dames. After a violent preparation from explosive shells and gas, Crown Prince Wilhelm, commander of the Army Group South, hurled 17 divisions against poorly disposed Allied troops along 15 miles of the front between Soissons and Reims. The first day saw the Allied line give way as deeply as ten miles. This Third Battle of the Aisne only increased in intensity in the following days. In the first days of June, the Germans recrossed the Marne and fought their way to within sight of the Schlieffen advance of 1914.

Yet the advance was again slowing. Lack of fuel, supplies, and troop replacements all militated against continuous fighting over more than a few days. At the same time, the Allies were throwing every resource available in the path of the Germans. The normally phlegmatic Field Marshal Haig issued an emotional appeal to his army on April 11: "Every position must be held to the last man: there must be no retirement. With our backs to the wall and believing in the justice of our cause each one of us must fight on to the end. The safety of our homes and the Freedom of mankind alike depend upon the conduct of each one of us at this critical moment."[53] By the time of the third phase, in May, American troops were reaching the line. Hastily released from the control of the French by General Pershing, the American 2nd and 3rd divisions hurried to reach the Marne just ahead of the Germans on

May 31, linking up with Senegalese troops on their right and French troops on their left. Standing in front of the extreme point of the bulge made by the Germans, at Château Thierry, 35 miles from Paris, American and French units repulsed assault after assault. Though historians comment that the attacks were losing force, the German attempts to force the River Marne and another offensives around Reims in mid-July made the German attacks violent enough. Still, the Americans seemed to energize the Allied troops somewhat, and the second division's successful counterattack on June 6 at Belleau Wood, a position equal to many another famous strong points on the Western Front, was not unnoticed by the German high command either.[54]

The crisis produced by these three great offensives did not dislodge the British from Europe, but they were not without effect, especially on French politics. Clemenceau, the tiger, fired numerous high-ranking war-department officials and transferred General Franchet d'Esperay, the loser of this third Aisne battle, to Greece. The Germans were once again nearly within sight of Paris. Foch was now appointed Allied supreme commander, since the Spring Offensive had scared both Haig and Lloyd George enough for them to cooperate fully in a more closely integrated Allied war effort. Though General Pershing had fought American integration into the British or French armies, the emergency of late May 1918 led him to place large numbers of American troops under French commanders.

Though there had been many close calls and many near misses in the German attempt to defeat the British before the Americans could get to the front, the great offensive was not quite as formidable as both the panic of the Allies and the wishful thinking of many Germans, including Ludendorff himself, made it seem. Ludendorff had asked Berlin for 200,000 more troops, but with his expansive schemes in the East, there were simply no troops to be had. Though many politicians hung their hopes on a great knockout blow against the Allies, a number of thoughtful statesmen were wondering why Germany would want to go on the offensive, given the new shot in the arm to the Allied effort which the Americans represented. The problems of the offensive were perhaps more real to the soldiers doing the fighting. One such soldier, later a famous professor of history, was serving on the front line in the Eighteenth Army, which broke through at St. Quentin, and noted the depleted nature of the German army even as the Spring Offensive opened. Doubts and anxiety, he later wrote, had to characterize the frontline soldiers in the face of the wretchedly equipped supply units, the makeshift vehicles, the dejected nags with their bones sticking out, the largely overage, poorly trained, and thoroughly weary men. Was such an army really capable of advancing swiftly across the cratered battle-field of the Somme with its elaborate trench system, to reach the sea and totally destroy the Anglo-French armies?[55]

One of the keys to assessing the whole German war effort is of course the difficult figure of Erich von Ludendorff himself. The *de facto* leader of the German military and, indirectly, of the German polity as well, Ludendorff had taken so much on himself, had constructed a system in which he retained so much responsibility, that it is well worth thinking at this point about his mental state. It is well known that the general was a volatile mixture of alternating nervousness and imperious self-confidence. Fifty-three years old, Ludendorff was experiencing not only the failure of his offensive and the loss of a great gamble, but also the pain of losing his stepson, a flier who died near the start of the Spring Offensive.[56] The general was, in addition, bent on keeping the enormous losses not only from the civilian government, but from the rest of the leadership of the German army as well. Since Ludendorff had arrogated to himself the authority for running both the war effort and German society itself, little wonder that he needed recommenda-tions for nerves and stress by the end of the summer. Indeed, numer-ous officers who worked for Ludendorff mentioned his nervous prostration, inertness, and apparent deep depression in the last days of July 1918, when he was finally forced to recognize that the offensive had failed. Modern psychologists looking at Ludendorff's behavior and symptoms during this crucial time have suggested that he was under-going a "post-traumatic stress reaction" to all of these adverse circum-stances, the same disorder now recognized as what was called "shell shock" among soldiers. Today this reaction is often associated with a compulsive personality, and from the testimony of contemporaries, Ludendorff certainly fit that diagnosis as well. It is safe to say that a stress-related nervous event was, as at the beginning of the war with Moltke, a central factor in the leadership of the German army on the Western Front at the end of the war.[57]

In the course of July 1918, the momentum on the Western Front gradually shifted to the Allied side. Some successful counterattacks in July and August turned into a continuous Hundred Days of offensive on much of the front during the last three months of the war. The

analysis of these apparently straightforward military operations have
been subject to widely varying interpretations among observers, historians, and military authorities. Just after the war, certain "national"
schools of thought tended to tout their own armies as having provided
the real heavy lifting that ended the war. Some British versions have
tried to make the American contribution seem insignificant, as if to justify British demands at the time for the use of American troops as
replacements in British units. This argument tends to run thus: the
British army had been held back by problems on the French part of the
line for long months, but during the Hundred Days, when the British
had finally mastered the tactics of attack, they pounded the enemy with
very minimal help from the French and Americans (not to mention the
Belgians, Canadians, Australians, Portuguese, and so on).

One problem with interpretations that minimize the American and
French contributions to the Hundred Days Offensive is that they must
ignore some salient facts. Pershing was forced to parcel out some
Americans at the time of the *Kaiserschlacht*. These divisional defensive
operations in the late spring of 1918 helped shore up the Western
Front against the power of the Ludendorff Offensive. American troops
arrived with several advantages over other Allied troops at this stage.
They had not undergone the kind of demoralization that had affected
the other armies. Interested in an offensive form of trench operations,
Pershing was more attentive to what the French had learned in all their
attacks than in the techniques of "trench warfare," which he hoped to
minimize. When called on unexpectedly to fight on a large scale in the
middle phase of the Spring Offensive, the Americans showed up fresh
and aggressive: in early June one observer witnessed a French officer
delivering the order to retreat to an American unit just digging in
against the German onslaught. The U.S. Marine captain replied:
"Retreat, Hell. We just got here!"[58] In larger terms, the American 3rd
Division held onto the Marne River position at Château Thierry
against tough German attacks, and just up the front, at Belleau Wood,
American troops (mostly U.S. Marines) captured the kind of wooded
German strong point that had often gone uncaptured during the first
three years of the war. One of the army commanders wrote to a political leader on August 15, "The Americans are multiplying in a way we
never dreamt of . . . . At the present time there are already thirty-one
American divisions in France."[59]

Hence, as the Ludendorff offensives petered out, Allied strength was
on the upswing, energized both by reinforcements and the ability of

the bolstered alliance to sustain the terrific blows of the German offensive. Yet the war was anything but over. In August 1918, the Allies launched one of the largest offensives in the history of warfare, putting the Germans on the defensive along most of the Western Front. On August 8, British General Sir Henry Rawlinson launched a surprise attack north of Paris across the old staging-ground of the Somme at Albert. He opened with a 2,000-gun bombardment of six miles of the German front at 4:20 A.M., an immediate tank advance which plowed into the German lines, followed by British, Canadian, and Australian infantry, whose way was further eased by an all-out aerial targeting of the German support area. The British took 16,000 prisoners and 200 guns before the day was far advanced. At some points the front advanced nine miles by the evening. Ludendorff called it the "black day of the German army." Throughout August and the first days of September, the Allies continued to arrange for limited objective attacks – not breakthroughs – with success. On September 12, the American First Army opened its first offensive as an army in a battle which removed the German salient whose center was St. Mihiel, south of Verdun. Three days later some Americans had advanced as much as 15 miles. The cost was only 7,000 casualties, making it one of the more efficient attacks of the war in terms of ground gained. Allied officers were dispatched to figure out how the Americans had done it.

The toll of American entry and Ludendorff's lost gamble began to make themselves known. Some Germans recognized the sea change in the war. As early as June, one of Ludendorff's staff members, Colonel Hans von Haeften, wrote to moderate civilian leaders in Germany a memorandum suggesting that total victory was no longer possible – a negotiated peace would be the best the Germans could get. Yet when German Foreign Secretary Richard von Kühlmann, having read the memorandum, spoke up for the opening of negotiations in the Reichstag on June 24, he was sacked as Foreign Minister a few days later. Indeed, the German annexationists used the occasion to make still more outrageous demands for a total victory which would encompass the annexation of much territory to Germany.[60] In point of fact, the knowledge of the increasing signs that Germany was losing was strictly limited to Ludendorff and his circle, who carefully controlled all information, especially bad news, coming from the Western Front. Ludendorff quite purposefully kept the truth from the civilian authorities and from the Kaiser. Certainly, the German public had heard of nothing but victories, glorious aerial combat, and German heroism

242 The Western Front

since the beginning of the war, and nothing changed now. Numerous officers around Ludendorff were by August urging him to inform Berlin of the seriousness of the war, but the "silent dictator" seemed to be hoping for a miracle.

The continuous Allied offensive opened on August 8, and German defeats mounted to disastrous proportions. On September 28, Ludendorff's staff members informed Paul von Hintze, the Foreign Secretary, that Germany was on the ropes. Ludendorff still refused to send any official messages, but that evening, he received the news that Bulgaria was leaving the Alliance by seeking a separate peace with the Entente. Ludendorff suffered what was probably another nervous breakdown. He now went to Hindenburg, telling him that Berlin must seek an armistice at once, before Germany suffered a total defeat. Three days later, his staff looked on in astonishment as the sobbing, groaning Ludendorff announced that the war was lost and that unavoidable defeat was imminent, blaming Germany's allies, Communist subversion of the army, lack of commitment at home – in short, blaming everyone except the architect of German defeat, Erich von Ludendorff. He immediately sent the same message – frantically transmitted and retransmitted – to all leading civilian offices in Berlin, demanding an immediate armistice and the formation of a new government which would make a peace offer.

At this time Ludendorff commented that Germany could not fight the whole world, and with the Austrians beginning to weaken, it looked like Germany's showdown with the world was just around the corner. Moreover, the powerful Alliance now marched against a Germany whose productive capacities had shrunk by at least a quarter and whose allies were for the most part on the ropes themselves. French production, to be sure, had fallen to about 56 percent of the prewar level, but British industrial production remained high, just below 90 percent of the prewar level. Germany, with overall industrial output at just over two-thirds of what it had been in 1914, now faced an Entente augmented by the United States, whose productive capacity was not only unimpaired, but rising to unheard-of heights.

Yet some German leaders recognized that Ludendorff was in some degree suffering from panic or hysteria. Hindenburg was convinced that "Germany, with God's help, will come through this difficult period." On the other side, all Allied leaders considered the Germans to be a still formidable force, and some thought it out of the realm of possibility, even with the wealth and the population of the

United States on the Allied side, that the war would be over before well into 1919. That its leader was suffering from intermittent, uncontrollable sobbing and other nervous symptoms was unknown beyond his staff; the German army's defense was cool and calm. As we have seen, the Germans tended to think ahead to defensive lines or positions (*Stellungen*), and at a given moment, most of the German front lines on the Western Front were backed by three or four major positions which were either fully or in part fortified and hardened. Though the enormous Allied offensive pushed the Germans back, the Western Front was still deep inside France, in many places not changed at all from the stalemate lines of 1914. Marshal Haig was perfectly justified in predicting a long, hard struggle.[61]

The Hundred Days battle belonged to both Haig and Foch, but like the Somme battle, it forms a principal point of discussion in evaluating the British war effort and Haig's leadership. Recent historians arguing in Haig's favor point out that the Hundred Days campaign included at least a dozen major British military victories, that his mastery of logistics and the new tactics allowed the Allies to push Germany back at a pace unmatched since 1914. J. P. Harris and Niall Barr have shown that the British army was now the smallest of the major armies on the Western Front, but that it took more prisoners than the French and American armies combined. Indeed, in their reassessment of the campaign, Harris and Barr give Britain the principal credit for defeating the much larger German forces on the Western Front – and the real credit must surely go to Haig. Yet as with the Battle of the Somme, discussions continue. Even in recent works devoted to a calm reappraisal of Haig's generalship, criticisms emerge that he was inflexible and unimaginative in his operational thinking, that his suspicion of and contempt for his allies – especially the French and Belgians – affected Allied efficiency overall. Historian Keith Grieves has argued recently that Haig's poor relations with Lloyd George stemmed from Haig's inability to see why Britain needed to concern itself with manpower for the home front when soldiers were needed in France and Belgium. Indeed, Grieves indicates that Haig was really unable to understand why the civilian public needed to be mobilized in any case.[62]

One reason it is so difficult to sort out praise and blame of this sort is the problem of special pleading. All the victorious powers, for example, tended to take more than ample credit for the great Allied victory at the end, and this tendency has continued, especially in sources of "history" which are more popular. A Canadian television documentary finds that that "crucial" battles of the Hundred Days were all won by the Canadian Corps, that the Canadian military contribution was "undoubtedly greater than that of the United States" and that by implication the exhausted French and British could not have managed the Hundred Days victory without the Canadians and its commander, the "authentic military genius," Arthur Currie. Some accounts have made Foch, the Allied supreme commander, the architect of victory. Americans can duly emphasize the enormous financial and, eventually, military contribution, though the latter came only during the last months of the war, indeed, during the Hundred Days campaign itself.[63]

But one way or the other, the Hundred Days ended the war. Foch and Haig laid their plans as they sensed German weakness. On July 18 Foch sent sent in 20 divisions (18 French and 2 American) saved back from defense against Ludendorff's last blow and attacked in the area of Soissons, throwing the Germans back dramatically. Newly promoted to Marshal of France, Foch met the interallied leadership at Paris and described his plan of repeating such attacks one after the other at different spots along the Western Front (very much like Ludendorff's Spring Offensive). A week later, Haig's hammering blows at Amiens with an Anglo-French army group inflicted 75,000 casualties on the Germans in three days. The August 8 jump-off and success against the Germans caused Ludendorff to dub it "a black day for the German army." German soldiers now began to surrender at unknown rates. The gigantic offensive rolled on, breaching the great Hindenburg Line.

Next came Pershing's long hoped-for attack with an American army. This came at a salient south of Verdun, St. Mihiel, an area which stood between the Allies and the Briey coalfields. Here the Germans commanded some unusually useful high ground (the commanding hill of Montsec) which had made French progress impossible for four years. On September 12, the U.S. First Army attacked at the bases of the salient while the French Colonial Corps drove directly into it. Tactically, Pershing tried out his conceptions of overwhelming but short artillery preparation with high-explosive as well as incendiary shells, extensive use of air reconnaissance and artillery coordination, tactical air support, and tanks. The battle was over in three days, and the salient was completely straightened, in spite of the novel German attempt to use elephant guns as anti-tank weapons. It was a clean and neat effort. But four days before the St. Mihiel action opened, the First

Army chief of staff, George C. Marshall, was instructed to work out plans for pulling the First Army from the line at St. Mihiel (beginning as the battle was in progress) and moving it into place for an attack up into the grim hills of the Argonne Wood, west of Verdun.

The great battle would involve an American and a French army. The attack in the Meuse–Argonne sector opened with the now practiced short storm of fire and explosions on September 26. The Americans attacked first, reducing many strong positions and moving forward several miles in places. As the Americans ran out of steam in very difficult terrain and against a determined German defense, the French attacked, making somewhat less progress. As Pershing regrouped, Clemenceau fumed, writing to Foch that he was of a mind to tell President Wilson the whole truth about Pershing's "marking time" and his obstinate refusal to fight. In fact, the American First Army had fought its way well beyond the first positions of the Argonne sector, positions which had absolutely baffled the French for four years. Foch disagreed with Clemenceau, pointing out the significance of the achievement against tough opposition and in difficult terrain. Indeed, the battle raged until the end of the war, and the two Allied armies inflicted some 100,000 casualties on the Germans.[64]

A day after the Meuse–Argonne action opened, Foch's coordinated attacks accelerated: the British attacked toward Cambrai (September 27), and the Belgian Army opened an offensive in Flanders on September 28. The British (Rawlinson's) Fourth Army, along with Canadian and American forces, carried out one of the most difficult of the Hundred Days assaults when it attacked the Hindenburg Line of German defenses on September 29. At the end of the day, the Allies had breached the line at a point regarded as one of its strongest.

The German army was no longer an offensive force. The stalemate was broken. We now turn to the end of the war on the Western Front.

8
COLLAPSE, ARMISTICE, CONCLUSIONS

Most scholarly writing about the end of World War I used to confine the discussion primarily to state-related concerns: the peace conference, the collapse of the German government, the demands of the victors, the "powerlessness" of the vanquished, and so forth. Historians now recognize that there is more to the end of World War I than the signing of some documents in the Palace of Versailles in the summer of 1919. In this closing chapter, we will look at the peace terms and the shape of the new Europe – indeed, we will really find ourselves in the midst of material which connects the battle fronts of World War I with the home fronts.

The End of the War: Allied Victory and German Revolution

Nobody would deny the extraordinary ability of the German army to fight the odds it did for four years. Yet the internal stresses of the war were telling, and not just at home. The army was drawing more on younger and overage draftees. By the summer of 1918, the desertion rate was rising, and various other acts of "insubordination" were rising too. Ludendorff reported that he was absolutely sure of only 30 percent of his divisions and that a significant number were definitely unreliable. Ultimately, the Kaiser would abdicate only when assured that the army could no longer relied upon.

Significant historical trends and events in the next 25 years would turn on the story that the German army was "stabbed in the back," the victim of liberals, Jews, and other defeatists. One basis for this pronouncement was the inclusion, in a number of postwar speeches by quite moderate, but still patriotic, politicians of the German center and left to the effect that German soldiers had not been beaten in the field, but rather let down by the home front. These comments, made in the midst of a violent revolution in the streets, are understandable but dangerous. For this idea was taken up by Ludendorff, who had no sooner finished the war than he started up a cottage industry of memoirs and booklets (based originally in Sweden, whence he had fled), assigning blame to liberals, Jews, Jesuits, and other dupes and conspirators. Ludendorff also lent his name to a number of radical nationalist groups that arose in the chaos of defeated Germany, groups like the circle of Munich crackpots which Hitler would infiltrate, join, take over, and rename – all within the first months of 1919. These groups, most of them peopled or at least salted with war veterans – such as Hitler himself – expended enormous effort in spreading the myth of the stab in the back as the explanation for German defeat.

Can we wonder at this? The war produced unparalleled opportunities for cynicism and disrespect for authority. It is clear from research on many aspects of the front that it occurred to most frontline soldiers at one time or another that they had much more in common with the mud-covered enemy beyond No Man's Land than with the sparkling and elegant red-tabbed, striped-panted generals and staff officers, whose main occupation – from the trench fighter's views – seemed to be think-ing up nightmarish scenarios to be acted out by the soldiers themselves. Even those generally patriotic and positive toward their governments could be eventually worn down and worn out. Had the French lost the war, the origins of what seemed to be the callous disregard for French lives which the generals displayed would no doubt have been examined with equal bitterness, perhaps shaping national feeling in France as much as the "stab in the back" would influence Germany. Yet one might well believe that the defeat of Germany in 1918 was psychologically more devastating to the Germans than the defeat of France in 1917 or 1918 would have been to the French, since it was clear to most Frenchmen that they had come very close to defeat more than once. The German people, on the other hand, had lived on a steady diet of optimistic assessments, heroic victories, and moralistic praise of the German soldiers' successes and superiorities, in a war which took place on the soil of other peoples. The sudden appearance of defeat was not only a shock to the masses: it was a shock to the civilian leadership, who had likewise believed the German propaganda.

The "stab in the back" theorists could get quite technical and specific. Some placed the real death blow as early as the first battle of the Marne, when various forces were supposed to have sabotaged the Schlieffen attack. Others asserted that the real treason was the sabotaging of Ludendorff's plans late in the game (October 7, 1918) to pull back the German line to stronger positions east of the River Meuse, thereby shortening the Western Front by about a third, and continuing the fight so as to influence negotiations. But here, according to this theory, the weak-kneed German government (filled with soft liberals under Prince Max of Baden) would not play the game to its end, though the army might have held out for as much as a year.

Actually, the correspondence documenting Ludendorff's demands for an immediate ceasefire is available in numerous published memoirs, and the typed and handwritten copies of his frantic telegrams to the Reich Chancellery and various other Reich offices are extant and easily available for the perusal of historians. The fierce general's multiple nervous breakdowns (and the earlier loss of his son in the war) undoubtedly contributed to the hysterical tone of his demands that Berlin arrange for an immediate armistice at various moments from late September to early October 1918. By October 1, as Gerhard Ritter later wrote, "Ludendorff was wiring [Berlin] every few hours demanding that peace be made immediately." Indeed, on October 3, Prince Max of Baden accepted the chancellorship and immediately sent a request for an armistice to Wilson, opting for a negotiated truce rather than immediate capitulation. Later in October Ludendorff regained his composure and tried to stop the negotiations for an armistice which he himself had set in motion. Yet Hindenburg and many other officers deemed the German army to be on its last legs. The last commander in chief of the Western Front, General Wilhelm Groener, wrote in his memoirs that from August 8 such a thing as offensive operations were out of the question, since the whole attentions of the army had to be, in essence, reactive: "Step by step, but inexorably, the enemy – in a decisive sector the still fresh Americans – pushed our front back."[1] As for the defensive positions on the Meuse, they existed in concept but not in reality. They represented a last gasp of the Moltkean fatalism and Social-Darwinist struggle to the death, a kind of *Götterdämmerung* approach, similar to the Wagnerian battle which the admirals ordered to be fought at the eleventh hour of the war (similar also to the future approach of the man soon to be Ludendorff's associate in radical politics, one who would command both battle front and home front in

Germany, Corporal Adolf Hitler). After a meeting of high emotions, the Kaiser accepted Ludendorff's resignation on October 25. In any case, backed by extensive parliamentary support, there was not the slightest chance that Prince Max would carry out some last-ditch effort. He was appointed chancellor to end the war.

One must pause to consider whether this legend – so close to the heart of Ludendorff – was just a piece of disinformation to cover a record of poor generalship, hypocrisy of world-historical dimensions, or a kind of self-serving self-deception (or all of the above). But legend it was in any case. At neither the First Battle of the Marne nor the Second was the German army stabbed in the back. And Ludendorff's arrogant leadership assured that no acceptable, negotiated peace would take place. He took power from the civilians, kept them from preparing for his failure, failed, and then dumped the whole thing into their lap, piously and pompously announcing that he had been betrayed. Ludendorff lost two wars: the one in the field and the one on the home front, where he was primarily responsible for introducing a version of war Communism two years before the Bolsheviks invented it. He didn't need the help of all those whom he hated to accomplish all of this.

The final passage of German war politics (and the end of the monarchy) dates to September 29. On this day, Ludendorff had regained some of his composure, but he still considered that these hammer blows had made it impossible for Germany to win outright. His call for a change of civilian government was shaped by his usual inability to blame anyone but himself for his failures: "I have asked his Majesty to bring those people into the government who are largely responsible that things have turned out as they have . . . . They must now eat the soup they have ladled out to us."[2]

In Berlin, amazed government officials, accustomed to hearing that the war was going well, appointed a south German liberal, Prince Max of Baden, to create a ministry which would be more palatable to the Allies, especially Wilson, than the ciphers who had held places during the military dictatorship. Prince Max accordingly appointed a cabinet of respectable moderates and proceeded to explore peace on the basis of Woodrow Wilson's formula, the Fourteen Points, a compendium of stipulations (revival of Poland, a League of Nations, etc.) which Wilson considered necessary for postwar Europe.

The Allies were in some measure surprised at the German offer of armistice and negotiations, and the very prospect occasioned much controversy, controversy not necessarily producing national groupings as the disputants. Pershing, for example, wanted to reject the offer and push on, getting an unconditional surrender out of the Germans. President Wilson favored accepting the German proposal for ceasefire, which did not commit the Allies to any specific measures in any case. Poincaré and Foch wanted to reject the offer and fight on to a real German surrender. The British generally wanted to accept the armistice. Whatever other factors were involved, research has shown that the European Allies could not get past the problem of the growing American military force and influence. Should the war continue on its present trajectory, by sometime in 1919 Pershing would be commanding a larger force than Haig. Hence, the Allies agreed to negotiate an armistice and built a rail line that led a German railroad car to within a few feet of Foch's special car, set up for the negotiations. The two cars were pulled next to each other in the Forest of Compiègne, behind the French lines. The Allies arranged the Armistice in such a way that the Germans would be unable to restart the war in the course of peace negotiations.

The Armistice provisions called on the Germans to leave Belgium and France within two weeks; surrender their heavy artillery, machine guns, and other heavy weapons; evacuate the army from the Rhine valley to a point 30 kilometers east of the river; renounce the Treaty of Brest-Litovsk; surrender the German navy to the Allies; return Allied prisoners of war (a non-reciprocal measure); and more. On top of these methods of ensuring that the Germans would not restart the war, the blockade would be kept in place, guaranteeing many civilian deaths from malnutrition after the war's end.

Clearly, the Germans would have fared much better had they started armistice negotiations at the various times that Wilson, the Pope, and others suggested it. Indeed, Germany might have come out tolerably well by calling for an armistice as late as May 1918, at the height of Spring Offensive gains and Allied talk of "backs to the wall," or even later. Ludendorff and the jubilant annexationists at home would never have allowed such a course, naturally; hence, the Germans were forced to go hat in hand to the Allies, who were in no mood (and whose publics were in no mood) to let the Germans off easily.

Once the government of Prince Max agreed the Armistice, on November 10 – bolstered by its genuinely honest intentions to introduce a new, moderate, open political order in Germany – the effective cessation of hostilities was set for the eleventh hour of the eleventh day of the eleventh month: 11:00 A.M., November 11, 1918.

The war ended in jubilation, though some commanders insisted on carrying out assaults up to a few minutes before eleven o'clock. As a fitting end to war in which artillery had been such a driving force, every artillerist on the Western Front wanted to fire the last shot of World War I; hence, both sides were loaded and ready. American fighter pilot Eddie Rickenbacker got into the air to see the show:

> On both sides of no-man's-land, the trenches erupted. Brown-uniformed men poured out of the American trenches, gray-green uniforms out of the German. From my observer's seat overhead, I watched them throw their helmets in the air, discard their guns, wave their hands. Then all up and down the front, the two groups of men began edging toward each other across no-man's-land . . . . Suddenly gray uniforms mixed with brown. I could see them hugging each other, dancing, jumping.

In some areas, especially where heavy fighting had occurred recently, Allied soldiers were not inclined to fraternize, but certainly the mood was celebratory across the front. Much more were there heartfelt celebrations in cities and towns all over the world. As British correspondent Philip Gibbs wrote of the moment: "The fires of hell have been put out, and I have written my last message as war correspondent. Thank God!"[3]

In the international moment of these days, home front connections once again proved vital. The German November Revolution was a complex affair which reflected the utter war-weariness of the country. It arose from disaffection, not among the hard-pressed Western Front soldiers, but among sailors. Shocked, like everyone else, at the Armistice negotiations, the German navy's high command decided to go out in a blaze of glory and meet the British in a suicidal battle in the North Sea (so ordered on October 28). The sailors of the German fleet, who had after all survived the war right up to the rumors of armistice, now faced death to no purpose (again, the "*Götterdämmerung*" maneuver), so simply fell back on the "council" idea which had gained great currency in propaganda carried out by the far left, carried to Germany from the *soviet* (council) movement in revolutionary Russia. It made a great deal of sense. Who would not prefer government from below, considering the privation and dictatorship brought about by the war and the Hindenburg Program?

The sailors formed councils in Kiel and refused to leave the harbor. There was violence. The same process then duplicated itself over the next few days at the other North German naval bases, then spread to workers' movements in the industrial cities. The professional revolutionaries then got into the act (Eisner in Munich, Liebknecht in Berlin), trying to steer this groundswell of discontent. The revolution had begun, and the Versailles Treaty would be worked out while Germany was undergoing a violent civil upheaval.

The Diplomats and the "Peace"

To clarify some terminology, though we often refer to the Versailles Treaty when we mean the Paris Peace, the peace settlement included five treaties, one with each of the Central Powers. The treaties were worked out consecutively (Versailles was the first) in five royal palaces on the periphery of Paris. Versailles, a few miles outside of the city, was the location of the formal sessions of the treaty conference between the Allies and Germany, though most of the meetings took place in locations in and around the capital. The other treaties (and their palaces) were the Treaty of St. Germain (Austria), the Treaty of Trianon (Hungary), the Treaty of Sèvres (Turkey), and the Treaty of Neuilly (Bulgaria). Speaking properly, we should say "Versailles Treaty" when we refer to issues and outcomes relating to negotiations with Germany, "Paris Peace" when we want to talk about the peace settlement as a whole. Naturally, in the context of the Western Front we will be discussing here the Versailles Treaty, with Germany (signed in June 1919), the first of the treaties made and far and away the most important, both in setting precedents for the others and in terms of its lasting impact on the history of the modern world.

The ending of World War I and the process of peacemaking were nearly as complicated as the war's beginning. In one way, they were made more so by the presence of the United States on the Allied side. Where a winning alliance made up of France, Italy, and Britain might have engaged in vigorous horse-trading in the peace settlement, the presence of Woodrow Wilson – with his Fourteen Points and his entourage of high-minded experts – had something of the effect of the parson showing up at a high-stakes poker game. Wilson extolled "open covenants openly arrived at" and hence condemned the kind of secret deals which had characterized European diplomacy. As we have seen, though the Germans finally ran out of steam, there were times during the war when Britain and France became desperate and made even more secret and more cynical deals in order to gain allies and support. Wilson's nostrums about diplomacy might have been more palatable had the United States come into the war earlier.

As it was, the Americans had lost 126,000 men dead, but the British had lost nearly a million, and the French a million and a third. Wilson seemed sometimes to be in the position of a latecomer to the game who insists on changing the rules to suit himself. We have seen that both the British and the French had met with much frustration in dealing with Pershing, but most of their problems with the AEF commander hinged on getting Pershing to do what they wanted him to. With Wilson, however, they faced a mover and shaker who had definite plans with which the Allies were supposed to conform, plans indeed which might shape and constrain their foreign policies and even position in the world for decades and generations to come. We should not wonder that Lloyd George, Clemenceau, and even Orlando – all formidable politicians in their own right – caviled at some of Wilson's schemes. Still, they were happy enough to go along with Wilson when going along gained them some other end.

The moderate politicians who came to power in Germany in October 1918 were thinking in classical European terms when they accepted Wilson's Fourteen Points as the basis for negotiations. They did not think they were surrendering unconditionally, though they realized that Germany would have to hand over some territory. Not insignificantly, among the earliest German leaders to recognize the Allies' vision of imposing a peace as they saw fit (and hence the real powerlessness of Germany) were members of leftwing branch of the German Socialist Party, as Marxists well-versed in the power of ideology and raw power. As the first revolutionary cabinet discussed whether the Allies had the right to take away and hand over to Poland a particularly valuable eastern province of Germany, leftwing socialist Emil Barth commented: "We can twist and turn as we will, but we do not have the slightest hope that we won't lose it."[4]

A second cause of German confusion during the peacemaking was the revolution that broke out, as we have seen above, just before the Armistice. A few days into the street-level riots and shootouts, the government of Prince Max of Baden simply handed over power to the two socialist parties with the explanation that only the moderate left would be able to ride out the storm of revolution in the streets. Only after extraordinary efforts did government leaders and friends of the Kaiser get him to abdicate – with the thought that the Allies would never negotiate with the demonized emperor.

Meanwhile, the leaders of the majority, or moderate, wing of the Social Democratic Party, Friedrich Ebert and Philipp Scheidemann, knew that it was politically necessary to rule along with the Independent Socialists (consisting of those leftwing socialists who had broken the *Burgfrieden* in 1917 over the issue of negotiating a peace). Many of the most revolutionary elements of the Independents meanwhile split off under Rosa Luxemburg and Karl Liebknecht to form the Spartakus League, later the Communist Party of Germany. The two firebrands took to the streets, and along with many other revolutionists attempted to channel the wrath of the hungry workers, declassed white-collar employees, and returning soldiers into a real overturning of society, like the one which had occurred a year earlier in Russia. The Bolsheviks indeed had "observers" on the ground to report on the progress of world revolution and lend a hand when needed.

The joint socialist government oversaw the end of the monarchy in November, after declaring Germany a republic and removing the possibility of a more acceptable Hohenzollern taking the throne. The moderate, or Majority, Socialists Ebert and Scheidemann saw themselves rid of the radical Independents in late December. Moreover, the Majority Socialists concluded a deal with the military for tacit cooperation while the revolution in the streets was being put down by "volunteers," many of them just back from the front and well able to handle the tactics of urban warfare. Bloody confrontations were not confined to Berlin. "Volunteer units" (*Freikorps*) and some existing army units fought with "Reds" in the Ruhr, Saxony, and other regions as the treaty was being crafted, in 1919. A national election in mid-January produced a majority for a coalition of the three parties which might be deemed to support a new democratic republic: the Majority socialists (SPD), the Catholic Center Party, and the democratic-liberal German Democratic Party (DDP). This grouping came to be known as the Weimar Coalition, since the constitution-making assembly which followed the election was moved to the small city of Weimar for safety (violence still threatened in Berlin and other big cities). The Weimar constitution followed by June 1919, hence the term Weimar Republic.

This German revolution was the background to the gathering of the Allied delegates at Paris and the opening of the Paris Peace Conference. It created a kind of political disjunction. Moderate German politicians were busy creating what they would call "the most democratic constitution in the world" while the Allies met at Versailles to consider what sort of peace to impose on the Kaiser's Germany. Although the revolution in

Germany had not brought down the old "aristocratic" and "captitalist" order, it nonetheless produced genuine changes. For one thing, the opponents of the Kaiser were in power. On the whole, few of the "annexationists" played leading roles in the first Weimar governments, though of course the new regime did not automatically fire all imperial and state officials. Still, it can still give one pause to think that Wilson – son of a Virginia Presbyterian minister – spent much time and effort at Versailles arguing that Germany was run by corrupt aristocratic elites when the president of the new democratic republic was Friedrich Ebert, son of a Heidelberg saddlemaker.

This disjunction also led to a kind of unreality in the Germans' approach to the "peace negotiations." But this air was quickly dispelled. War propaganda had made the Germans "jackbooted Prussians" and "pitiless Huns" to the Allied public. The French public especially had suffered directly from the German invasion of 1914. Lloyd George and many other British politicians had made it clear, especially in the "Khaki Election" of December 1918 (so called because of the potential votes of demobilized, in the vernacular "demobbed" soldiers), that the Germans would "pay." Americans and Britons wanted to "hang the Kaiser." Any sort of real negotiations, as at the end of the Thirty Years War or the Napoleonic Wars, for example, would have been extremely disappointing to these emotions and mass goals.

The Allies and Associated Powers met in Paris in January 1919 to organize the peace, and they tried to handle a volatile situation first by excluding the Germans, not from the negotiations, but from France itself (by the simple mechanism of refusing visas to all Germans).[5] At the conference the British, French, and Americans, respectively, were represented by Lloyd George, Clemenceau, and Wilson, whom we know well. The remaining Allied great power was Italy, whose prime minister also came to Paris. This was Vittorio Orlando, who had much in common with the others as a tough, "whatever it takes" war leader who distinguished himself in war leadership in August 1917, when as Minister of Justice he cracked down on the growing antiwar movement and met strikes and riots with the full force of state suppression. Of course, if the four men shared many tendencies as tough war leaders, their goals were nonetheless divergent.

In general, the Allies imposed as punitive a treaty as they dared upon the Germans. Should the screws be turned too tightly, all the diplomats realized at one time or another, the Germans would simply balk, whether or not their society exploded in the process. On the other hand, this insight seemed to occur to different Allies on different issues. With his tremendous prestige, and after a triumphal European tour, Wilson was at Versailles to take a hand in reforming Europe. He therefore wanted to see the territorial settlements he had outlined in the Fourteen Points and other documents, and he did indeed want to punish the Germans, but his real desire was to set up the League of Nations, a kind of parliament of mankind. Lloyd George was bound by campaign promises as well as whole chests full of hidden agendas: in his view Germany should pay very high reparation sums, but it was unnecessary for the Allies to give huge tracts of Germany to Poland. The French had some incipient dealings with the Germans in the form of joint ventures of various kinds, some aboveboard, some not. In any case, the long-suffering French public and a large share of French parliamentarians of all parties who were accustomed to playing to the masses could hardly accept any settlement which seemed to go easy on the Germans. Even "the tiger" was accused of being soft on the Germans during the negotiations.

In some ways, the end of a war is never the best time to negotiate a peace, especially a war in which mass democracies have been mobilized. The Treaty was negotiated among the victors; the Germans were called to Paris in May to receive the draft. They were told to bring it back with comments a few weeks later. The Germans were astounded that they would have no chance to do any negotiating, only commenting, but the Allies remained firm. After the comments were returned, the Allies made a few changes, but on the whole, the draft treaty was very close to the final version. The terms were strict. Germany was to disarm. Alsace-Lorraine went back to France; a large slice of eastern Germany went to the newly revived state of Poland; a small piece of land went to Belgium, and a larger strip went to Denmark. Unification with the now tiny German state of Austria was forbidden. In a strip of German territory in the west, no German military presence would be permitted. The Allies would remain in occupation of much of western Germany. Germany was to pay an undisclosed amount of "reparation" beginning immediately, the total amount to be determined later. In order to make the eventual categories of payment and reparation make sense, Germany was to assume unlimited liability for having started the war (the so-called "war guilt" clause).[6]

Far from the elegant balls of Vienna in 1814 or the blunt horse-trading of the World War II summits, the Paris Peace Conference was driven by committees, 56 of them, and herds of experts on a thousand technical questions. We might say that Paris was the most "positivist," or even technocratic, settlement of all the major European peaces. That is to say, experts piled up mountains of data on every question from the linguistic origins of placenames in disputed territories to the counting of dead horses among Allied armies. Harold Nicolson left a vivid account of this atmosphere in a famous memoir.[7]

The "peace" that emerged from the various treaties concluded in 1919 and 1920, the Paris Peace, was a tenuous and unsatisfactory new order, whatever the occasional modern historian seeking to revise older views might say. First, and foremost, it was not built to last. Further, in a technical sense, most historians and scholars of international relations would probably agree that the Paris Peace did not redistribute power in a realistic way, based on the actual potential of the countries involved. We might add that such a calculation is more art than science, depending on a thousand factors relating to internal and world politics, geography, economic trends, technology, and many more areas. Yet the subtle imaginations of a Mazarin in 1648 or a Castlereagh in 1814 enabled them (and their counterparts) to produce a European *system* which was appropriate for the times, which did not give the winners too much, which did not take too much from the losers, which recognized that in the end all must agree on the peace in some sense. For the Paris Peace, and for the Western Front part of it, the Treaty of Versailles, one could not make these claims.

In any case, in the summer of 1919, the Allies gave the Germans the choice of signing or continuing the war and the blockade. The Social Democrat head of government, Philipp Scheidemann, who had spent a lifetime opposing the imperial edifice of the Kaiser's Germany, resigned, saying, "The hand that signs this treaty will wither." Yet the Social Democrats ultimately led Germany in signing it. In fact, the peacemaking parties in Germany (the Weimar Coalition of SPD, Center, and DDP) were all tarred with having signed the shameful treaty. These, along with many others – Jews, bankers, etc. – were added to the "stab in the back" narrative as the "November Criminals." Without Scheidemann, the German cabinet, under the leadership of the impressive SPD leader Friedrich Ebert, discussed every possibility but in the end, and after consulting the military leadership repeatedly, decided to sign, with a statement to the Allies that the Versailles Treaty represented "injustice without example."

Repairing the Damage

Having spent so much time thinking about the war on the ground, we should think now about the condition of Western Europe, the front area in particular – towns, roads, fields, people. Belgium and France sustained enormous physical losses as a result of the war and the German occupation. This occupation had exhibited many of the features which would make the German occupation after 1940 so onerous: military police presence, requisitions, confiscations, forced labor recruitment. Factories behind the lines – particularly in important textile centers like Lille, Cambrai, and Douai – were taken over to assist in German war production, the owners shunted aside, many arrested. Naturally, all local commerce was controlled and ransacked, the local people experiencing rationing and, especially in the harsh winters, genuine privation. This region behind the lines amounted to practically all of Belgium, though unlike the occupation of World War II, a triangle of western Belgium from Nieuport in the north to Armentières and back up to the Channel coast remained precariously in the hands of the Allies.[8]

One way to get some answers about the damages and the costs of war is to look at the costs and complexities of reconstruction – physical reconstruction of landscapes and property, as in other senses. This comparison tells a good deal. Both Germany and France were invaded (Germany by two Russian armies), and destruction took place in both countries, though of course on a vastly greater scale in France. Still, we can profitably compare the German approach to reconstruction with the French program.

Compared with the invasions of France and Belgium, the Russian incursions into East Prussia produced less drastic damage, but in absolute terms this damage was grim enough. Several different short-lived invasions from August 1914 to April 1915 cost 6,000 civilians their lives, and about 80,000 families lost their homes as some 33,500 buildings were destroyed. Avoiding the Russians, more than half a million Germans left their homes, and their feeding and housing produced a real strain on a now thinly stretched German economy. The Kaiser had in fact made a moving announcement as early as August 1914 that all possible national resources would be used to restore the region to normalcy, following the announcement a few weeks later with the founding of a royal commission for war refugee and reconstruction matters. Most of the refugees were back at home by

April 1915, but the government had provided sustenance for nearly 200,000 of them over the months of displacement. Moreover, by the end of 1915, both combinations of local taxes, federal money, and private contributions (of both money and labor, especially by architects) had begun to work toward reconstruction; indeed, by 1915 the reconstruction of East Prussia was a topic known to all, as one contemporary put it, "from short pieces in the daily press and longer articles in the technical journals." Indeed, even as the strains of total war led to the near-totalitarian strictures of the Hindenburg Program, reconstruction in East Prussia went on, continuing evidence of the "thankfulness of the Fatherland," as Wilhelm II phrased it. The governor of the province estimated that a full half of all possible reconstruction – buildings, countryside, agricultural animals – had been accomplished by the end of the war.[9]

Unlike the Russian invaders, the Germans of the Schlieffen army poured into France and stayed for four years. France behind the lines, as we have seen, suffered from forced labor, privation, confiscations, lack of fuel, and more, but the worst destruction was in the long strip of the Western Front. Some of the territory wrecked in the early fighting ended up, after the First Battle of the Marne, on the French side of the line, as the Germans dropped back to their fortified positions in the fall of 1914. And again, as the Germans retreated slowly after June 1918, more French farmers, those whose lives were most altered by the destruction visited on rural France, tried to make their way back to their property to save what they could. In both cases, as far as possible, functionaries of the French government kept the refugees away, apparently on the assumption that government officials could more efficiently help reclaim the torn-up lands and buildings than the farmers.

As Hugh Clout has shown in his haunting book on the reconstruction of the French countryside, the bureaucratic shifts, duplications, and shortcomings were so massive that the agencies involved could not even preserve the records of this fiasco, something at which bureaucracies normally excel. The story of this reconstruction activity begins as early as 1914 and ends long after the war, with changes in agencies, hordes of offices and office workers, constant attempts to centralize what was by nature an individual or family-sized activity of restoring property (though families might better have used the army of demobilized soldiers who ended in the French government bureaucracy as laborers to help restore and recultivate their lands). The process was marked by haggling in high places over who would be responsible for the work, and the knowledge on the ground that the requisite supplies and materials were not forthcoming.[10] As one British observer wrote: "the volume of laws, decrees, and official pronouncements was out of all proportion to the work actually accomplished, and the array of functionaries was excessive in comparison with the record of their achievement."[11]

Yet, as with an apparently more efficient rebuilding of East Prussia in the wake of Russian invasion, the French state could be satisfied with this work, since it managed to appear as the real organizer of relief in a time of crisis, though judging from the results, individuals and localities could have made decisions at least as efficient and effective on their own. As with so many aspects of the growth of government into unaccustomed spheres during the Great War, a war which the great European states had, in a manner of speaking, invited to be inflicted on their populations, they offered the solution of state control at the cost of real relief.

The two cases of German and French reconstruction offer some commonalities. The Germans seem to have been enormously efficient with resources, but successful even in the midst of the war. The French seem to have been ineffective both during and after the war. In execution, French authorities seemed to put the premium on bureaucracy, and, one might say, haughtiness. Yet in both cases, as noted above, the governments took public credit for all reconstruction "success," though the Germans seem to have done a better job of advertising the government and bringing in volunteers and private money to help. Indeed, where the old technocratic French tendencies made themselves painfully felt, and among citizens who had sacrificed greatly for the fatherland, the German government used the case from the outset to demonstrate sympathy for the calamities suffered. Indeed, where the French case sometimes resulted in public outrage, the German authorities created a moment of community: collection points sprang up all over the country, and individuals became a part of the process of comforting and helping the refugees and victims. Considering the colossal material destruction wrought by modern warfare since 1914, the issue of reconstruction is far from insignificant. Great War reconstruction enhanced the power and reach of modern government into a few more areas of the lives of its citizens. We see in these cases something of the genesis of twentieth-century technocratic governmental "reconstruction," in matters from war to storms to public health, to the variety of modern social programs. Indeed, the patterns of reconstruction these cases show are now so familiar that we must take a step back even to recognize them.

To bring back some of the reality of these times of "reconstruction" and the real losses suffered by French and Belgian civilians, we should examine in some detail the front itself, the scene of the concentrated devastation. Ninety percent of it was on French soil. And the soil in question was a particularly valuable soil. The zone of the Western Front had covered one-fourteenth of national French territory, but the occupants of the land it covered had paid one-fifth of tax revenues before World War I. In this area of rich agricultural production and industrial activity, home to about five million people, an American city planner wrote in the wake of the war: "so stupendous is the destruction in the devastated regions of France that no-one can begin to realize what it means." Natural and artificial drainage systems were completely ruined. Topsoil was churned under or washed away. Much of the ground was impregnated with metal of all descriptions: barbed wire and stakes, concrete reinforcement bars, tools and implements, corrugated iron, weapons, all the detritus of masses of people. The presence of so many men and so much uncontrolled human waste over so small an area had the potential to impact upon the basic microbial makeup of the soil over large areas. This is not to mention the bodies or body parts of the missing, the greater number of which remain missing today, though they continue, over 80 years later, to work their way to the surface by erosion and other means. In fact, the sheer volume of this organic material, the metals degrading in the earth, the chemicals (nitrates, aluminum, and other compounds in artillery shells) would have, in today's terms, the potential for an ecological disaster, the more so since drainage systems were disrupted and so many of these substances could enter the water supply.[12]

In fact, by the end of the war, the French government had developed a classification system for the war zone, giving areas a Blue designation if they could be used after simple clearing of debris. Yellow shading on government maps meant that the land or structures could only be used after considerable expenditure. The Red zones were jagged and bombed areas that were too polluted with bodies, mines, shells, metal, and microbes to reclaim. Clearly, this was a calculation that involved careful judgment. The industrial city of Lens, for example, was more or less completely damaged but rebuilt with much effort. With lesser towns or villages, or with more complications, it might not be worth it. The site of the village of Vauquois, in the Ardennes, was physically altered by the enormous mines that the French and Germans exploded under each other in that stationary sector. Moreover, tunnels still crisscrossed each other underneath. The village moved a few hundred yards away and rebuilt itself. The village of Fleury, in the eye of the storm on the battlefield of Verdun, disappeared apart from a few stone doorsteps and a some foundations. Many villages left not even those traces. Hundreds of villages and towns faced the problem of destruction, though it must be said that French farmers, not the least persistent people on earth, tended to complain that too much had been Red-zoned, that more could have been reclaimed with a more efficient process.[13]

Above all, artillery shells remained, both exploded and unexploded. Shrapnel and shell fragments, shell casings, the roughly 20 percent of shells that did not go off when originally fired. In the immediate postwar period, more injuries were sustained from unexploded grenades simply because they were harder to see. At a later period, especially during the depression, enterprising Belgians and Frenchmen worked the Western Front to salvage steel and iron, a dangerous proposition, but in the rearming of Europe in the 1930s, a profitable one. On the other, it was quite dangerous. Eighty-three were killed and 203 injured in the Pas-de-Calais during the three years after the war. In the same area, another 13 farmworkers were killed accidentally. The unexploded shells had to be detonated by qualified personnel, eventually teams set up by the French army, and local people were understandably opposed to detonations near their farms. Hence, these munitions were carried to dumps, where they were exploded.[14]

Less profitable but still a paying job, many Belgians and French could join up the labor gangs used immediately after the war to flatten out the infinite number of shell holes, trenches, mine craters, though a few of the latter were so deep and so wide that no one bothered to fill them in. The work of leveling the front was as labor-intensive as the work of making it had been, if much less dangerous. Within 13 months of the Armistice, 180 million cubic metres of trenches had been filled in, though later subsidence in the soil made this work incomplete. This may have represented as much as half of the trenches on the front, perhaps less. In the year and a month following November 1918, workers cleared 222,480,000 square metres of land of barbed-wire entanglements. This clearing work was still going on over a decade after the war.[15]

Even on cleared land, the regeneration of agriculture posed another problem. Disruptions abounded. Weeds grew everywhere. Drainage systems were disrupted and topsoil had washed away. The ground was filled with iron and steel, and high concentrations of nitrates and heavy metals may have resulted from existing conditions. The groundwater was likewise subject to environmental disruptions not yet studied.[16] Needless to say, production was low in the postwar years. The *départements* of the Western Front were able to produce wheat at about a third of the prewar level, and the region was up to the prewar level of production by 1922. Sugar beet, a vital cash crop, suffered more. In 1921, beet production was still only a quarter of the prewar harvest. The vineyards of the Marne had suffered tremendous damage, which required millions of new grafts. It was the mid-1920s before anything like normal production had been reached.[17]

We should pause to think that the great warmaking apparatus of modern governance – parliaments, cabinets, the military leadership, the bureaucracy, and all the rest – rarely pay much of a price for the wars in which they engage. It is the individuals who die on the battle-field or from typhus or from starvation at home, or the lonely and penurious widows of dead soldiers, or the grieving parents of a son or sons, or the mutilated and disabled, or the farmers plowing up shells and body parts – these in particular shoulder the costs of modern war.

Mere Statistics

It is somewhat surprising that one finds some disagreement among calculations of death tolls and casualty figures for World War I, even among the advanced bureaucratic societies of the Western Front powers. About 50 million men worldwide were mobilized for military service in World War I. For the whole war, modern estimates of military deaths range from just under 10 million to about 12 million, with wounded amounting to about 20 million overall. Germany suffered the greatest death toll of the Western Front powers: 1.77 million (Russian death tolls are highest considering all fronts). France lost 1.375 million and, with a smaller population, had the highest ratio of battle deaths per capita of population – 3.5 percent. British and Empire troop deaths amounted to 950,000. Belgium suffered 13,716 military deaths, the United States 126,000. Canada lost 59,544 dead; Australia 59,330; New Zealand 16,645. Portugal lost 8,145 men on the Western Front. The total of battle deaths in World War I was greater than all the deaths in all the wars for the 100 years before 1914. Contemporary observers had no difficulty in pronouncing it the bloodiest war ever fought.[18] Perhaps four million men died in the battles of the Western Front.

In other categories of death, civilian losses are more difficult to calculate. Western Front powers suffered civilian deaths from accidents of battle, from losses at sea (both passengers and civilian seamen), from starvation at home (in the case of Germany, where apparently from half a million to 700,000 civilians died from malnutrition or its effects), and from various other circumstances related directly to the war, such as the Belgians and French shot in reprisal or as spies in the first months of the war. An indirect result of the war, the influenza epidemic of 1918–19 carried off many more civilians (and more people worldwide than the entire death toll of the Great War). The influenza was another of those battle front–home front connections, a virus that was able to adapt apparently because large numbers of men in American training camps in the Midwest, where it seems to have broken out, provided a sufficient medium. In fact, though the United States was hit hard (with some 675,000 deaths, including 43,000 soldiers and sailors), the virus seems to have made another adaptation in August 1918 that allowed it to move around the globe. Europeans died in like numbers, but the enormous total of deaths in India put the worldwide total as high as 40 million, about three times the number of dead from the whole of World War I.[19]

We have not begun to tally the wounded, some eight million, more or less, from the Western Front. Many recovered completely, but thousands were mutilated permanently. The strains on medicine produced positive results, since physicians solved numerous problems of infection, blood transfusion, and other medical techniques. The enormous number of facial wounds touched off heroic efforts by physicians in Britain and the United States in particular to develop plastic surgery, skin and tissue regrowth techniques, and many more components of modern plastic surgical work. Many thousands of the "facially wounded" could never regain a normal life, as with so many other kinds of wounds, but the numbers of men who regained something approximating a normal appearance after several years of surgeries and procedures were a testimony to the hard and persistent work of physicians and dentists during and after World War I.

To move from human losses to material losses, though some popular economists have spoken about the ways in which wars help economies, the grim truth is that war is destructive and expensive, that war goods tend to be consumed to no good purpose except destruction, that in the end certain groups may profit from war, but at the expense of other, usually larger, groups. We have seen this process at work: business concentration during the war came about with government laws which put on pressure for concentration and government (public) financial support aimed at rewarding certain industries at the expense of others. In point of fact, in the long term the war was horrifyingly expensive. Calculations of this sort are always only approximations, but it is roughly accurate to say that the Allies paid something like U.S. $57.7 billion (1913 – pre-inflation – value), the Central powers about $24.7 billion.[20] These figures point up a number of very interesting features of the war, but they tell us above all that from 1914 to 1918, $82.4 billion went to (1) produce goods which were for the most part consumed to no real productive purpose, and (2) make profits for belligerent governments and for those businesses canny enough to get contracts with governments for war-related goods. One must remember, as well, that money from a "government" is by definition money which has been transferred to the government in the form of taxes, confiscations, inflationary processes, and the like. Hence, $82.4 billion which might have been invested in creating new goods, in research, in other public projects, or indeed in making fuller the lives of the individuals who had originally earned it and those around them, was instead fired off from artillery pieces on the Western Front or other battlefields.

This financial story might well be followed briefly through the postwar period. The United States had invested much, but with the end of the war Wilson stood at the pinnacle of world politics and America stood to reap the payments from the Allies to whom the American government and American international lenders had made war loans. The U.S. Senate rejected the Treaty and the League of Nations, but American lenders did not forget the money they had loaned. France owed much, Britain (before the war the banker of the world) owed more. At the peace conference, the U.S. delegates could afford to be magnanimous on the issue of reparation, but the American delegation definitely saw the need for hefty German payments to go to France and Britain – how, otherwise, would those countries pay the Americans back? Hence, the Americans supported a high level of reparation: 132 billion gold marks. Without the reparation payments, Britain and France would not only be unable to pay their war debts, but they would be unable to rebuild (France) and pay for war pensions for the dead, and take care of other measures of demobilization. On the other hand, as seen above, the French especially were loath to take too much from the Germans, lest the Germans simply refuse to pay any – they certainly dragged their feet in paying during the first years after the war. Hence, the War Guilt Clause, and hence the financial issues which vexed international relations for the whole interwar period. The United States would step in to "save" the situation in 1924 with the Dawes Plan and in 1929 with the Young Plan, which provided palliatives consisting of a large loan to Germany from the United States (so that the Germans could pay the Allies and the Allies could pay their war debt) and an extension of the payment terms for German reparations. In essence, treasure was circulating from Britain and France to the United States (war debts), from the United States to Germany (Dawes and Young Plan loans), from Germany to Britain and France, and so forth. As American historian Carroll Quigley commented, in this bizarre cycle, the real winners were the American financial agents, who took a healthy percentage in interest and handling fees each time the money came their way.[21]

In terms of its meaning for the rest of the world, these financial patterns, the war's destruction, and the enormous financial losses involved in the war helped destabilize postwar economies and, indeed, the international financial system. Many scholars have begun to turn to American economist Murray Rothbard's explanation of the Great Depression as the end of an inflationary business cycle begun with wartime inflation which continued beyond the end of the war (Germany's hyperinflation did not reach its peak until 1923), and the three-way cycle fueled an artificially heated investment wave, until 1929/30, when the whole structure crashed. In any case, most economic historians would probably agree that the war increased financial and economic instability dramatically.[22]

In taking stock of the aftermath of the Great War and the Western Front in particular, one really must take careful stock of the fundamental changes in what French historians have called "mentalities" of the Western populations. As with the many political and social changes, and even changes in military behavior and technology, we must recognize at the outset that the war tended more to accelerate existing trends than to invent them. Hence, though we will discern a great many different "mentalities" in the postwar world of the West, it is clear that significant changes had occurred in the habits of thought and behavior, most clearly with the various elites, but perhaps even more fundamentally in the everyday lives of "normal" people. Though one of course discerns national and regional differences, socioeconomic gradients, variables based on religion and other factors, clearly, twentieth-century cynicism and irony in almost every manifestation traces its origins back to World War I. In 1975 Paul Fussell pointed out in *The Great War and Modern Memory* that the Great War created, or intensified, a great shift in mood and attitude, from the romantic and high-minded rhetoric of the nineteenth century, and not just among modernist artists and literary figures. Irony has been the mark of twentieth-century discourse, whether high or low, and one misses important aspects of the modern popular "mentality" if one fails to see the extension of urban sarcasm and working-class irony both to the still equally large rural populations of the West and to other social classes as well.

The twentieth century, taken all in all, was a century in which Marxism, Leninism, Nazism, and other ideologies along with their ideologues restricted freedom, limited self-development, controlled populations, and killed off substantial parts of those populations. We will find that these techniques of repression lead us back to the First World War. In the midst of a dreadful war between the most advanced technological societies on earth, some deeper forces did indeed break through. But it is clear that these forces were channeled and managed in specific ways. If the twentieth century became the century of managerial control, of the prioritizing of group goals and group efficiency over the autonomies of individuals, families, and regions, then we will find in World War I the accelerator of processes which were emerging before then, as we have seen in countless examples in so many areas of life. In military terms, the war transformed modern armies, and modern armies in effect transformed the modern state. The war shaped the culture of the West in ways too many to enumerate. It may not have been a "trek from progress," as war poet Wilfred Owen called it, but it was certainly a change in the course of progress. Yet the modernist culture of bitter irony and blasted landscapes was not the only worldview to emerge from the war. As Jacques Barzun put it, the "mind control" of the war regimes "broke down soonest and oftenest in the trenches, where fine words could not compete with physical and moral sensations."[23] Perhaps that home front–battle front disjuncture is among the most important meanings of the war.

NOTES

1 ORIGINS, PRECONDITIONS, OUTBREAK

1 See, among a whole library of books and articles devoted to this topic, the revisionist treatment by Harry Elmer Barnes, *The Genesis of the World War* (New York, 1926) and the magisterial study, Sidney Bradshaw Fay, *Origins of the World War* (New York, 1928).

2 The two great examples are Hans Gatzke, *Germany's Drive to the West: A Study of Germany's Western War Aims During the First World War* (Baltimore, MD, 1950) and Luigi Albertini, *The Origins of the War of 1914* (London, 1952).

3 See for example, Chester V. Easum, *Half-Century of Conflict* (New York, 1952), 3–20.

4 The literature of the controversy is enormous. See of course Fritz Fischer, *Germany's Aims in the First World War* (London, 1961), and for a good summary of the debate, James Joll, "The 1914 Debate Continues: Fritz Fischer and His Critics," in H. W. Koch (ed.), *The Origins of the First World War: Great Power Rivalry and German War Aims*, 2nd ed. (London, 1984).

5 Paul M. Kennedy (ed.), *The War Plans of the Great Powers 1880–1914* (Boston, 1979).

6 A good start would be James Joll, *The Origins of the First World War* (London, 1984) and the essays in Koch (ed.), *The Origins of the First World War*.

7 Norman Rich, *Great Power Diplomacy 1814–1914* (New York, 1992), 218–250.

8 For a good summary of recent work, see Gerd Krumeich, "The Military and Society in France and Germany between 1870 and 1914," in Klaus-Jürgen Müller (ed.), *The Military in Politics and Society in France and Germany in the Twentieth Century* (Oxford, 1995), 28–30.

9 See Carlton J. H. Hayes, *A Generation of Materialism, 1871–1900* (New York, 1941), 18–33.

10 For an excellent summary of the economic side, see David MacKenzie and Michael W. Curran, *A History of Russia, the Soviet Union, and Beyond*, 4th ed. (Belmont, CA, 1993), 419–424. The basic work on the alliance is still William L. Langer, *The Franco-Russian Alliance, 1890–1894* (London, 1929).

11 Paul Kennedy, *The Rise and Fall of the Great Powers* (New York, 1987), 194–248; William R. Keylor, *The Twentieth Century World: An International History*, 2nd ed. (New York, 1992), 34–40.
12 On construction of class during the 1960s, see Peter N. Stearns, *European Society in Upheaval* (New York, 1967). A view based on the crisis of modernization is Edward R. Tannenbaum, *1900: The Generation Before the Great War* (New York, 1976).
13 A good introduction to the new work in social history is Frans Coetzee and Marilyn Shevin-Coetzee (eds.), *Authority, Identity and the Social History of the Great War* (Providence, RI, 1995).
14 B. R. Mitchell, *European Historical Statistics 1750–1970*, abr. ed. (New York, 1978), 1–43; see the essays in John M. Merriman (ed.), *Consciousness and Class Experience in Nineteenth-Century Europe* (New York, 1979), esp. Lynn Hollen Lees, "Getting and Spending: The Family Budgets of English Industrial Workers in 1890," 169–186.
15 The literature of the socialist movements is vast, and much of it takes a more sympathetic, insider's view than the formulation above. For a general introduction, see Martin Gilbert, *The End of the European Era* (New York, 1970), 8–18; for an introduction to Jaurès, see Gordon Wright, *Insiders and Outliers* (Oxford, 1980).
16 Kennedy, *The Rise and Fall of the Great Powers*, 198–203; J. M. Roberts, *Europe 1880–1945*, 2nd ed. (London, 1989), 38–39.
17 See Perry D. Jamieson, *Crossing the Deadly Ground: United States Army Tactics, 1865–1899* (Tuscaloosa, AL, 1994); Frank Vandiver, *Black Jack: The Life and Times of John J. Pershing*, 2 vols. (College Station, TX, 1977), 1: 219–258.
18 Mitchell, *European Historical Statistics*, 3–8, 370–380.
19 Hayes, *Generation of Materialism*, 74–87, 196–241. See also Eugen Weber, *Peasants into Frenchmen: The Modernization of Rural France, 1870–1914* (Stanford, CA, 1976).
20 See John Dewey, *The Influence of Darwin on Philosophy and Other Essays* (New York, 1910); as well as H. W. Koch, "Social Darwinism as a Factor in the 'New Imperialism'," in Koch (ed.), *The Origins of the First World War*, 319–342; and Gillis J. Harp, *Positivist Republic: Auguste Comte and the Reconstruction of American Liberalism, 1865–1920* (University Park, PA, 1995), 64–75.
21 William McNeill, *The Pursuit of Power: Technology, Armed Force, and Society Since A.D. 1000* (Chicago, 1982), 223–306.
22 See Archer Jones, *The Art of War in the Western World* (New York, 1987), 419–433.
23 Ferdinand Foch, *The Principles of War* (New York, 1918) repr. New York, 1970, 310–313; Michael Howard, "Men Against Fire: The Doctrine of the Offensive 1914," in Peter Paret (ed.), *Makers of Modern Strategy from Machiavelli to the Nuclear Age* (Princeton, NJ, 1986), 510–526.
24 Paddy Griffith, *Battle Tactics of the Western Front* (New Haven, CT, 1994), ix–xii.
25 On the generational idea, Robert Wohl, *The Generation of 1914* (Cambridge, MA, 1979).

26 See, for example, the case of industrial violence in France in the prewar period, and the reaction of the authorities in David S. Newhall, *Clemenceau: A Life at War* (Lewiston, NY, 1991), 243–268.

27 See Andrew Rosen, *Rise Up, Women!* (London, 1974); and Lisa Tucker, *The Spectacle of Women: Imagery of the Suffrage Campaign, 1907–1914* (London, 1987).

28 Paul Fussell, *The Great War and Modern Memory* (London, 1975), 24–25.

29 See Theodore Ropp, *War in the Modern World*, rev. ed. (New York, 1985), 215–230; and L. L. Farrar, Jr., *The Short-War Illusion* (Santa Barbara, CA, 1973).

30 Michael Howard, "British Grand Strategy in World War I," in Paul Kennedy (ed.), *Grand Strategies in War and Peace* (New Haven, CT, 1991), 32; Laurence Lafore, *The Long Fuse* (Prospect Heights, IL, 1997 [1971]), 229–230.

31 Gerhard Ritter, *The Schlieffen Plan* (1958); Arden Buchholz, *Moltke, Schlieffen and Prussian War Planning* (Providence, RI, 1991).

32 Philip Crowl, "Alfred Thayer Mahan: The Naval Historian," in Paret (ed.), *Makers of Modern Strategy from Machiavelli to the Nuclear Age*, 444–477.

33 Jonathan Steinberg, *Yesterday's Deterrent: Tirpitz and the Birth of the German Battle Fleet* (New York, 1966); Paul Kennedy, *The Rise of Anglo-German Antagonism, 1860–1914* (London, 1980).

34 Ropp, *War in the Modern World*, 209–213.

35 See Samuel R. Williamson, Jr., *The Politics of Grand Strategy: Britain and France Prepare for War, 1904–1914* (Cambridge, MA, 1969); Kennedy (ed.), *The War Plans of the Great Powers, 1880–1914*; Marc Trachtenberg, *History and Strategy* (Princeton, NJ, 1991), esp. 47–99.

36 A number of works have recently reexamined the Dreyfus Affair. See especially Pierre Birnbaum and Jean-Marc Berlière (eds.), *La France de l'affaire Dreyfus* (Paris, 1994); Martin P. Johnson, *The Dreyfus Affair: Honour and Politics in the Belle Epoque* (Basingstoke, 1999); Pierre Birnbaum, *The Jews of the Republic* (Stanford, CA, 1996); Robert Tombs, "'Lesser Breeds Without the Law': The British Establishment and the Dreyfus Affair, 1894–1899," *Historical Journal*, 41 (June 1998): 495–510. See also the interesting military connections explored by Robert Kaplan, "Making Sense of the Rennes Verdict: The Military Dimension of the Dreyfus Affair," *Journal of Contemporary History*, 34, no. 4 (October 1999), 499–515.

37 On the *entente cordiale*, see Oron J. Hale, *The Great Illusion, 1900–1914* (New York, 1971), 240–249.

38 See his exciting spy novel, *Kim* (1901).

39 Great Britain, *Parliamentary Papers* (1908), Vol CXXV, Cmd. 3750.

40 Roberts, *Europe 1880–1945*, 266–269. See a different summary of the Bosnian Crisis in C. J. Bartlett, *Peace, War and the European Powers, 1814–1914* (New York, 1996), 144–45.

41 Joachim Remak, *Sarajevo: Story of a Political Murder* (London, 1959).

42 Samuel R. Williamson, *Austria-Hungary and the Origins of the First World War* (London, 1991). At the expense of being present-minded, one might point out that the parts of the ultimatum which Serbia rejected are quite similar

to those elements of the United States ultimatum to Afghanistan in the wake of the September 11, 2001 terrorist attack.

43 Joachim Remak, "1914 – The Third Balkan War: Origins Reconsidered," *Journal of Modern History*, 43 (1971): 353–366.

44 On the Serbs and the Russian guarantee, see Albertini, *The Origins of the War of 1914*.

45 See the text of the Treaty of London in Michael Hurst (ed.), *Key Treaties of the Great Powers 1814–1914*, 2 vols. (New York, 1972), 1: 237–253. The British interpretation had always been that the treaty imparted an obligation for Britain to intervene should any third party invade Belgium. See Lord McNair, *The Law of Treaties* (London, 1961), 239–244.

46 Edward Grey, *Twenty-Five Years*, 2 vols. (New York, 1925), vol. 2, ch. 18. Grey's pessimism is similarly described by his friend, American Ambassador Walter H. Page, in Burton J. Hendrick (ed.), *The Life and Letters of Walter H. Page* (New York, 1922), chs. 10 and 11.

2 MOBILITY AND UNITY

1 Lyn McDonald, *1914* (London, 1987), 66–68; the officer mentioned was Alphonse Grasset, quoted in Joachim Remak (ed.), *The First World War: Causes, Conduct, Consequences* (New York, 1971), 32–34.

2 Fussell, *The Great War and Modern Memory*.

3 Gläser is quoted in Gordon Craig, *Germany 1866–1945* (New York, 1978), 340.

4 On Moltke, see Buchholz, *Moltke, Schlieffen and Prussian War Planning*, 214–226; Gerhard Ritter, *The Sword and the Scepter*, (Coral Gables, FL, 1970), 2: 267–271; see the Crown Prince's evaluation in *The Two Battles of the Marne* (New York, 1927), 77–91.

5 *The Belgian Grey Book: Diplomatic Correspondence Respecting the War (July 24–August 29, 1914)* (London, 1915), doc. no. 35, Baron Beyens, Belgian Minister at Berlin, to M. Davignon, Belgian Minister for Foreign Affairs, Berlin, August 4, 1914.

6 Robert L. Rothstein, *Alliances and Small Powers* (New York, 1968), 65–68.

7 Brand Whitlock, *Belgium: A Personal Narrative* (New York, 1919), 92–107.

8 *The Belgian Grey Book: Diplomatic Correspondence Respecting the War (July 24–August 29, 1914)*, Doc. No. 70.

9 *The Story of the Great War* (New York, P. F. Collier), vol. III (1916), 641–654.

10 The most recent work on the subject is John Horne and Alan Kramer, *German Atrocities, 1914: A History of Denial* (New Haven, CT, 2001). See also E. H. Kossmann, *The Low Countries 1780–1940* (New York, 1978), 522–523; Robert B. Asprey, *The German High Command at War* (New York, 1991), 52. An example of casual readiness to shoot civilians is in Otto von Gottberg, *Als Adjutant durch Frankreich und Belgien* (Berlin, 1915), 27–31.

11 A number of older, mostly journalistic, sources are quite useful on the details of the early battles of the war. See, for example, *Ridpath's History of the World* (Cincinnati, OH, 1923), 8: 3472–3473.

12   Foch, *The Principles of War*, 24–47, 310–318. See also Howard, "Men Against Fire: The Doctrine of the Offensive in 1914," in Paret (ed.), *Makers of Modern Strategy from Machiavelli to the Nuclear Age*, 510–526. On the tradition of the professional British army, see McDonald, *1914*.

13   From Joffre's account in *The Two Battles of the Marne*, 4–5.

14   Ibid., 89.

15   Ibid., 3–6.

16   On the logistics issue, see the opinion of Bruce I. Gudmundsson, *Stormtroop Tactics: Innovation in the German Army, 1914–1918* (Westport, CT, 1995). On the transfer of troops to the east, see Jones, *The Art of War in the Western World*, 441.

17   McDonald, *1914*, 65–109.

18   Denis Winter, *Death's Men: Soldiers of the Great War* (London, 1978), 77–78; John Ellis, *Eye-Deep in Hell: Trench Warfare in World War I* (New York, 1976).

19   Randall Gray (with Christopher Argyle), *Chronicle of the First World War*, 2 vols. (Oxford and New York, 1990–91), 1: 281 (hereafter cited as Gray, *Chronicle*).

20   Robert Cowley, "Massacre of the Innocents," *Military History Quarterly* (Spring 1998). See also Gudmundsson, *Stormtroop Tactics*, 7ff.

21   Remak (ed.), *The First World War*, 33.

22   Jeremy D. Popkin, *A History of Modern France* (Englewood Cliffs, NJ, 1994), 169–179; Weber, *Peasants into Frenchmen*.

23   Popkin, *History of Modern France*, 219–223.

24   Jean-Jacques Becker, *The Great War and the French People*, trans. Arnold Pomerans (New York, 1985), 7–17.

25   Robert Royal, "The Mystery of the Passion of Charles Péguy," *Crisis Magazine*, 14, no. 11 (Dec. 1996) (online edition, http://www.crisis magazine.com/); on Péguy, see also Hans A. Schmitt, *Charles Péguy: Decline of an Idealist* (Baton Rouge, LA, 1967).

26   A good survey is Matthew S. Seligman and Roderick R. McLean, *Germany from Reich to Republic, 1871–1918* (New York, 2000); a more thematic approach is Jack R. Dukes and Joachim Remak, *Another Germany: A Reconsideration of the Imperial Era* (Boulder, CO, 1988).

27   Dietrich Orlow, *A History of Modern Germany, 1871 to the Present*, 2nd ed. (Upper Saddle River, NJ, 1991), 70, 109.

28   A. J. Ryder, *Twentieth-Century Germany* (New York, 1973), 109–113; Craig, *Germany 1866–1945*, 340–341.

29   Asprey, *The German High Command at War*, 50–52.

30   Arthur Marwick, *The Deluge: British Society and the First World War* (New York and London, 1965), 31–33.

31   Gerard De Groot, *Blighty: British Society in the Era of the Great War* (London, 1996), 109–110.

32   For good short descriptions, see Stephen Pope and Elizabeth-Anne Wheal, *The Dictionary of the First World War* (New York, 1995) 130; and Marwick, *The Deluge*, 36–39. A more detailed examination is in K. D. Ewing and C. A. Gearty, *The Struggle for Civil Liberties: Political Freedom and the Rule of Law in Britain, 1914–1945* (New York, 2000), 36–93.

33 Mrs. C. S. Peel, O.B.E., *How We Lived Then, 1914–1918: A Sketch of Social and Domestic Life in England During the War* 4 (London, 1929), 39.
34 Marwick, *The Deluge*, 44–53, 50; E. S. Turner, *Dear Old Blighty* (London, 1980), 18.
35 Gray, *Chronicle*, 1: 28, *The Story of the Great War*, 3: 714–715; McDonald, *1914*, 90–92.
36 For an excellent short introduction to Joffre, see General André Beaufre, "Marshal Joseph Joffre," in Field Marshal Sir Michael Carver (ed.), *The War Lords: Military Commanders of the Twentieth Century* (Boston, 1976), 13–22.
37 Marc Ferro, *The Great War 1914–1918* (London, 1973), 52–53; Popkin, *History of Modern France*, 223–224.
38 *The Two Battles of the Marne*, 98–101; Cyril Falls, *The Great War* (New York, 1959), 63; Theodor Ropp, *War in the Modern World*, rev. ed. (New York, 1962), 240–241.
39 The Crown Prince gives his opinion *in The Two Battles of the Marne*, 91; Kitchener is quoted in Philip Magnus, *Kitchener: Portrait of an Imperialist* (New York, 1958), 349. See also Howard, "British Grand Strategy in World War I," in Kennedy (ed.), *Grand Strategies in War and Peace*.

3 STALEMATE AND MOBILIZATION, 1915/1916

1 An electronic search of recent encyclopedias indicates that the term "stalemate" is used mostly in connection with World War I. Upwards of 80 percent of the occurrences of the word in the most recent version of the electronically searchable *Encyclopedia Britannica* were in reference to the Great War.
2 Vejas Gabriel Liulevicius, *War Land on the Eastern Front: Culture, National Identity and German Occupation in World War I* (Cambridge and New York, 2000); Asprey, *The German High Command at War*, 73–116, 151–170.
3 See Paul C. Vincent, *The Politics of Hunger: The Allied Blockade of Germany, 1915–1919* (Athens, OH, 1985). For a substantial summary, see Ralph Raico, "The Politics of Hunger: A Review," *Review of Austrian Economics*, 3 (1989): 253–259.
4 Paul G. Halpern, *A Naval History of World War I* (Annapolis, MD, 1994), 21–41; a good summary is in Neil M. Heyman, *World War I* (Westport, CT, 1997), 49–53.
5 As an example, the sister ship of the *Titanic*, RMS *Olympic*, rammed a U-boat in the English Channel in May 1918, long after German submarines had stopped surfacing to signal. The *Olympic* sustained some moderate but quickly reparable damage; the U-boat sank immediately.
6 *Reichsanzeiger*, February 4, 1915.
7 The best example is Colin Simpson, *The Lusitania* (Boston, 1972). Simpson's work has been highly criticized and even dismissed by mainstream and academic historians, though parts of his argument are based on evidence which seems quite solid.

8 Halpern, *A Naval History of World War I*, 297–302.
9 J. A. Salter, *Allied Shipping Control* (Oxford, 1921), 355–359.
10 One of the twentieth century's most influential military theorists and military historians, Sir Basil Liddell Hart, used the concept of "indirect approach" to analyze practically the whole of Western military history and attributed much of the success of history's great commanders to the use of the various forms of indirection, by which he meant essentially the avoidance of frontal assault against the strong points of the enemy line. See his work *Strategy*. It should not surprise us that Liddell Hart was a veteran, and one should also say critic, of the war on the Western Front.
11 See Gray, *Chronicle*, 1: 281–287.
12 De Groot, *Blighty*, 31–53. See also the excellent short discussion in John Keegan, *The Face of Battle* (New York: Viking, 1976), 215–225.
13 For a brief but authoritative description of the evolution of the British militia forces, see William Spencer, *Records of the Militia and Volunteer Forces 1757–1945*, rev. ed. (London, 1997).
14 De Groot, *Blighty*, 62–64.
15 A number of histories of the individual pals' battalions have appeared recently, among them two by Michael Stedman, *The Salford Pals* (London, 1993) and *The Manchester Pals* (London, 1994). For a short but lively description of the recruitment of the "pals," see Keegan, *The Face of Battle*, 215–225.
16 Becker, *The Great War and the French People*, 130–140. Quotations are from pp. 130 and 131.
17 Angela Woollacott, *On Her Their Lives Depend: Munitions Workers in the Great War* (Berkeley, CA, 1994), 17–19.
18 R. J. Q. Adams, *Arms and the Wizard: Lloyd George and the Ministry of Munitions, 1915–1916* (College Station, TX, 1978), 240–244.
19 I am relying entirely on the excellent account of the battle in J. C. H. Corrigan, *Sepoys in the Trenches, the Indian Corps on the Western Front 1914–1915* (London, 1999), 146–172.
20 "Neuve Chapelle," in Pope and Wheal, *The Dictionary of the First World War*, 338–339.
21 Adams, *Arms and the Wizard*, 20–23.
22 Ibid., 30–33.
23 Ibid., 35–37.
24 Gray, *Chronicle*, 2: 293.
25 See, for example, precisely this kind of debate in the British case, in Adams, *Arms and the Wizard*, 15–37.
26 Gray, *Chronicle*, 2: 293.
27 In these regions, many of the trenches still hold their shape today, after 80 years of erosion.
28 See especially the vital work on the trenches, Tony Ashworth, *Trench Warfare 1914–1918: The Live and Let Live System* (London, 1980); among many other good investigations of trench life, especially noteworthy are Winter, *Death's Men*, and Ellis, *Eye-Deep in Hell*.
29 See Winter, *Death's Men*; see also Eileen Crofton, *The Women of Royaumont: A Scottish Women's Hospital on the Western Front* (East Linton, UK, 1997).

30 A number of recent works take up this theme. See John Horne, "Remobilizing for Total War: Britain and France, 1917–1918," in Horne (ed.), *State, Society, and Mobilization in Europe during the First World War* (Cambridge, 1997), 195–211; Jay Winter, "Popular Culture in Wartime Britain," in Aviel Roshwald and Richard Stites (eds.), *European Culture in the Great War: The Arts, Entertainment, and Propaganda, 1914–1918* (Cambridge, 1999), 330–348 (see also the other essays in this work).

31 Verna Hale, *Jack Judge: The Tipperary Man* was written by Verna Hale Gibbons and is published by the Sandwell Metropolitan Borough Council Library Service (UK). I am indebted to Tom Morgan for information on the song, along with a citation for Verna Hale's book.

32 Charles Rearick, *The French in Love and War* (New Haven, CT, 1997), 21–28.

33 Lily McCormack, *I Hear You Calling Me* (Milwaukee, WI, 1949), 109. The sentimental Odlum may have been the officer who designed the first "trench raid," in 1915, according to *The Online Encyclopedia of British Columbia* (http://www.knowbc.com/).

34 A good compendium of English-language songs is Jerry Silverman, *Ballads and Songs of World War I* (Pacific, MO, 1997).

35 See Rearick, *The French in Love and War*, who has shown how the requirements of the French government were in a sense prefigured in the characteristics of at least the blander variety of music hall tunes. See esp. pp. 15–36.

4 INNOVATION, PERSUASION, CENTRALIZATION

1 Randolph S. Bourne, "The State," in Carl Resek (ed.), *War and the Intellectuals* (New York, 1964), 71.

2 Richard Kuisel, *Capitalism and the State in Modern France* (Cambridge, 1981), 8–10.

3 Pope and Wheal, *The Dictionary of the First World War*, 466.

4 On Loucheur, see the important work by Stephen D. Carls, *Louis Loucheur and the Shaping of Modern France, 1916–1931* (Baton Rouge, LA, 1993).

5 Becker, *The Great War and the French People*, 121–128.

6 Popkin, *History of Modern France*, 227–229; Pierre Renouvin, *The Forms of War Government in France* (New Haven, CT and London, 1927).

7 Marwick, *The Deluge*, 41–44.

8 De Groot, *Blighty*, 54–58.

9 Adams, *Arms and the Wizard*, 16–18, 71–82.

10 A good description of "Prussian Mercantilism" and state socialism before 1914 can be found in W. F. Bruck, *Social and Economic History of Germany from William II to Hitler 1888–1938* (New York, 1962), 35–60.

11 Gerald D. Feldman, *Army, Industry, and Labor in Germany, 1914–1918* (Princeton, NJ, 1966), 45–50; Arnold Brecht, *Aus nächster Nähe:*

Lebenserinnerungen eines beteiligten Beobachters 1884–1927 (Stuttgart, 1966), 272–274.

12   Henry Pachter, "Walther Rathenau: Musil's Arnheim or Mann's Naphtha?," in Pachter, *Weimar Etudes* (New York, 1982), 171–188; Count Harry Kessler, *Walther Rathenau: His Life and Work* (New York, 1930); James Joll, *Three Intellectuals in Politics* (New York, 1960).

13   See Frederick Winslow Taylor, *The Principles of Scientific Management* [1911] (New York, 1967). Taylor deplored the "wastes of human effort" as it existed in his own "blundering, ill-directed, or inefficient" society. And he proposed extending his principles of scientific management to every sphere of life to achieve "national efficiency."

14   Feldman, *Army, Industry, and Labour*, 46–47; Bruck, *Social and Economic History of Germany*, 136–141.

15   Frederick the Great, for all his own statist economic enterprises, did in fact try to blend the old Prussian respect for law with the Enlightenment respect for the individual. The circulation of the story of "the Miller of Sans Souci" – a story in which the miller stands up to the young king by pointing to the power of law – demonstrates something of this devotion, whether the story is apocryphal or not. Rathenau's reference to Frederick the Great here is quite specific.

16   See "Address of Wather Rathenau on Germany's Provision for Raw Materials," December 20, 1915, printed in Ralph H. Lutz (ed.), *The Fall of the German Empire, 1914–1918* (Stanford, CA, 1932), 2: 77–90 (Hoover War Library Publications, No. 2).

17   In *Army, Industry, and Labour*, Feldman's view of their work is fairly positive. A conservative observer writing from the vantage point of 1918, however, saw things a good deal differently; see Walther Lambach, *Diktator Rathenau* (Hamburg-Leipzig, 1918), 20–32 (a copy of this polemical booklet is in the "Krieg 1914" Collection of the Preussische Staatsbibliothek, Berlin). For the figures and quotation at the end of the paragraph, see Gerald Feldman, *The Great Disorder: Politics, Economics, and Society in the German Inflation 1914–1924* (New York, 1993), 78–80.

18   Belinda Davis, *Home Fires Burning: Food, Politics, and Everyday Life in World War I Berlin* (Chapel Hill, NC, 2000); Joe Lee, "Administrators and Agriculture: Aspects of German Agricultural Policy in the First World War," in J. M. Winter (ed.), *War and Economic Development* (Cambridge, 1975), 229–238.

19   *Lebensmittelversorgung in Lichtenberg* (mimeo, Berlin, 1916). A copy is in the "Krieg 1914" Collection of the Preussische Staatsbibliothek, Berlin.

20   See, for example, precisely this kind of debate in the British case, in Adams, *Arms and the Wizard*, 15–37.

21   Gray, *Chronicle*, 2: 293.

22   Kathleen Burk, *Britain, America and the Sinews of War 1914–1918* (Boston, 1985), 7.

23   Feldman, *The Great Disorder*, 38–44.

24   Murray N. Rothbard, *Man, Economy, and State* (1-vol. ed.) (Los Angeles, CA, 1970), 850–863.

25   Feldman, *The Great Disorder*, 864.

26 Many sources are available on German civil–military relations before the war. See especially Gordon Craig, *The Politics of the Prussian Army, 1640–1945* (New York, 1955).

27 Craig, *Germany 1866–1945*, 346–349.

28 Ritter, *The Sword and the Scepter*, 3: 99, 179–187.

29 Gray, *Chronicle*, 1: 154.

30 Toni and Valmai Holt, *Battlefields of the First World War* (London, 1993), 38–42.

31 L. F. Haber, *The Poisonous Cloud: Chemical Warfare in the First World War* (Oxford, 1986), 21; Donald Richter, *Chemical Soldiers: British Gas Warfare in World War I* (Lawrence, KS, 1992), 15–21.

32 Haber, *The Poisonous Cloud*, 259–284; Gray, Chronicle, 2: 288–291.

33 See Richter, *Chemical Soldiers*, 215–220.

34 *Les Armées Françaises d'Outre-Mer: Les troupes coloniales pendant la guerre 1914–1918* (Paris, 1931).

35 See the Great War classic by Rudyard Kipling, *The Irish Guards in the Great War* (London, 1923). A strain of modern Scots opinion has traced the present "insecurity and insignificance" of modern Scotland within the UK directly to the Great War; see Christopher Harvie, *No Gods and Precious Few Heroes: Scotland Since 1914* (Edinburgh, 1981), vii–x.

36 *The Canadian Encyclopedia* (Edmonton, 1985), 1972–75.

37 Kathryn M. Bindon, *More than Patriotism: Canada at War 1914–1918* (Toronto, 1979), 147–155.

38 Ibid., 6–8.

39 Figures are taken from *Gray, Chronicle*, 2: 288.

40 Ibid.; Mitchell, *European Historical Statistics 1750–1970*, 4–8; B. R. Mitchell, *International Historical Statistics – Africa, Asia, and Oceania 1750–1993*, 3rd ed. (London, 1998), 5, 11, 77.

41 A good place to start is still Alan Moorehead, *Gallipoli* (New York, 1956).

42 See Horne (ed.), *State, Society, and Mobilization in Europe during the First World War*, especially the essays in section III.

43 De Groot, *Blighty*, 175; Johannes Karl Richter, *Die Reichszentrale für Heimatdienst* (Berlin, 1963), 29–37; George Creel, *How We Advertised America* (New York, 1920).

44 Renouvin discusses censorship extensively in *The Forms of War Government in France*.

45 Messinger, *British Propaganda and the State in the First World War* (Manchester, 1992), 9–10; De Groot, *Blighty*, 175.

46 Remak (ed.), *The First World War*, 63–66.

47 Trevor Wilson, "Lord Bryce's Investigation into Alleged German Atrocities in Belgium, 1914–1915," *Journal of Contemporary History*, 14, no. 3 (July 1979), 370.

48 Zane Grey, *Day of the Beast* (New York, 1922).

49 H. C. Peterson, *Propaganda for War: The Campaign Against American Neutrality, 1914–1917* (Norman, OK, 1939), 45–70. Nine women spies were condemned to death by the French.

50 De Groot, *Blighty*, 92–93.

51 Increasingly, by 1915 war wounded and other "worthy" young men who were at home received protection from white feathers and other

signs of opprobrium by wearing a uniform designed for men in this situation.

52 Becker, *The Great War and the French People*, 77–85.
53 Rearick, *The French in Love and War*, 1–25; Stéphane Audoin-Rouzeau, *Men at War 1914–1918: National Sentiment and Trench Journalism in France during the First World War* (Oxford, 1992).
54 Becker, *The Great War and the French People*, 85–93.
55 "War and the Intellectuals," *The Seven Arts*, 2 (June 1917), 133–146. See also the introduction and essays in Resek (ed.), *War and the Intellectuals*.
56 David M. Kennedy, *Over Here: The First World War and American Society* (Oxford, 1980), 50–51.
57 Dietrich Orlow, *A History of Modern Germany, 1871 to the Present*, 2nd ed. (Upper Saddle River, NJ, 1991), 117–122.
58 Ryder, *Twentieth-Century Germany*, 134, 234–6.
59 Filipe Ribeiro de Meneses, "Too Serious a Matter to be Left to the Generals? Parliament and the Army in Wartime Portugal, 1914–1918," *Journal of Contemporary History*, 33, no. 1 (Jan. 1998), 85–96; Pope and Wheal, *The Dictionary of the First World War*, 370–371; John Toland, *No Man's Land* (New York, 1980), 144–148.
60 Hans W. Gatzke, *Germany and the United States: A "Special Relationship?"* (Cambridge, MA, 1980), 27–51.
61 See the early chapters of Vandiver, *Black Jack*. For a more sympathetic view of Wilson, see Lloyd E. Ambrosius, *Woodrow Wilson and the American Diplomatic Tradition: The Treaty Fight in Perspective* (New York, 1987).
62 Charles Seymour, *The Intimate Papers of Colonel House* (New York, 1926; on Bryan, see for example vol. 1, 282.

5   THE CRUCIBLE OF WAR: 1916

1 René Albrecht-Carrié, *The Meaning of the First World War* (Englewood Cliffs, NJ, 1965), 60–89.
2 C. Paul Vincent, *The Politics of Hunger: The Allied Blockade of Germany, 1914–1919* (Athens, OH, 1985). See also Ralph Raico, "World War I: The Turning Point," in John V. Denson (ed.), *The Costs of War: America's Pyrrhic Victories*, 2nd expanded ed. (New Brunswick, NJ and London, 1999), 221–230; and Raico, "The Politics of Hunger: A Review," 253–259.
3 Niall Ferguson, *The Pity of War* (London, 1999), 291.
4 Stephen Ryan, *Pétain the Soldier* (South Brunswick, NJ, 1969), 98–99.
5 Ferguson, *The Pity of War*, 298–303.
6 One often sees Pétain styled "Henri" or "Henri-Philippe." His full name was Henri-Philippe Benoni Omer Joseph Pétain, but he himself simplified his name to "Philippe." Ryan, *Pétain the Soldier*, 14. For the following section, see especially Ryan's biography and the classic account of the battle, Alistair Horne, *The Price of Glory* (New York, 1962), esp. ch. 11.

7   Horne, *The Price of Glory*, 139. See also the extensive discussion of Pétain and his approach to tactics and strategy in Alistair Horne, "Marshal Philippe Pétain," in Carver (ed.), *The War Lords*, 55–72.
8   Ryan, *Pétain the Soldier*, 91.
9   On casualties there is some dispute. See Gray, *Chronicle*, 1: 287; and Pope and Wheal, *The Dictionary of the First World War*, 494–496. Even at the lowest estimates, casualties on both sides were colossal.
10 Horne, *The Price of Glory*, 228–289.
11 Craig, *Germany 1866–1945*, 364–365.
12 Asprey, *The German High Command at War*, 245–252; Craig, *Germany 1866–1945*, 368–374.
13 See the excellent discussion of the plan in the classic book by John Keegan, *The Face of Battle*, 213–215.
14 John Terraine, *Douglas Haig: The Educated Soldier* (London, 1963), xviii.
15 John Terraine, "Field Marshal The Earl Haig," in Carver (ed.), *The War Lords*, 42.
16 See the excellent discussion and bibliography by Fred R. Van Hartesveldt, *The Battle of the Somme, 1916: Historiography and Annotated Bibliography* (Westport, CT, 1996).
17 See, for an example of the condemnatory genre, Alan Clark, *The Donkeys* (London, 1961), which is to be used with caution, since recent research has shown that some of its central arguments are based on inaccuracies.
18 See Martin Middlebrook, *The Somme Battlefields* (Penguin, 1994), 145–147.
19 Fussell, *The Great War and Modern Memory*, 27. It seems that the football idea had been around since 1915, and that it was also used elsewhere after the Somme.
20 The Lloyd George quotation is from Gray, *Chronicle*, 2: 265.
21 Not everyone learned these lessons at once. A fascinating document, printed in booklet form and issued by General Headquarters just after the opening of the Somme battle, instructs training units that recent events have confirmed the efficicacy of training for attack, artillery preparation, etc.; General Staff, General HQR, "Preliminary Notes on the Tactical Lessons of the Recent Offensive," July 1916, MS 17701, Manuscript Section, Guildhall Library, London. A coherent and detailed account of a model "learning curve" is Bill Rawling, *Surviving Trench Warfare: Technology and the Canadian Corps, 1914–1918* (Toronto, 1992).
22 Reinhard Scheer, *Germany's High Sea Fleet in the World War* (London, 1920); John Jellicoe, *The Grand Fleet* (London, 1919).
23 Gray, *Chronicle*, 1: 287–288.
24 Martin Kitchen, *The Silent Dictatorship: The Politics of the German High Command under Hindenburg and Ludendorff, 1916–1918* (London, 1976); Robert Higgs, *Crisis and Leviathan: Critical Episodes in the Growth of American Government* (New York, 1987), esp. ch. 7. On the United States during the war, see also Murray Rothbard, "War Collectivism in World War I," in Ronald Radosh and Murray Rothbard (eds.), *A New History of Leviathan* (New York, 1972), 66–110.
25 See, for example, Marwick, *The Deluge*.
26 Schaffer, *America in the Great War*; Raico, "World War I: The Turning Point," in Denson (ed.), *The Costs of War*, 203–247; David Beito, *From Mutual Aid to the Welfare State* (Chapel Hill, NC, 2000).

27 See a good summary of this critique for the German home front in Roger
    Chickering, *Imperial Germany and the Great War, 1914–1918* (Cambridge,
    1998), 114–117. See also Jay Winter, "Surviving the War: Life Expectation,
    Illness, and Mortality Rates in Paris, London, and Berlin, 1914–1919," in
    Winter and Jean-Louis Robert (eds.), *Capital Cities at War: Paris, London,
    Berlin 1914–1919* (Cambridge, 1997), 487–523.

28 The following discussion is adapted from the author's article on the
    Hindenburg Program: H. Tooley, "The Hindenburg Program of 1916: A
    Central Experiment in Wartime Planning," *Quarterly Journal of Austrian
    Economics*, 2 (Summer 1999): 51–62.

29 Walter Goerlitz, *History of the German General Staff 1657–1945*, trans. Brian
    Battleshaw (New York, 1953), 172–173.

30 Ritter, *The Sword and the Scepter*, 3: 179–206, 346–347; John G. Williamson,
    Karl Helfferich 1872–1924: Economist, Financier, Politician (Princeton, NJ,
    1971), 172–173.

31 On Ludendorff's ideas, see Arthur Rosenberg, *The Birth of the German
    Republic 1871–1918*, trans. Ian F. D. Morrow (New York, 1962), 123–137.

32 Ritter, *The Sword and the Scepter*, 3: 351–2.

33 Feldman, *The Great Disorder*, 66–68; Fritz Stern, "Fritz Haber: The Scientist
    in Power and in Exile," in *Dreams and Delusions* (New York, 1987), 51–76.

34 A very similar configuration of planners from diverse sectors – a good many
    of them actually the same individuals – worked together in a kind of eco-
    nomic planning elite under Hitler after the mid-1930s. Hermann Schmitz of
    I. G. Farbenindustrie, planner under both the Hindenburg Program and
    the Four Year Plan (1936), provides a study in this kind of continuity. See
    especially Berenice A. Carroll, *Design for Total War: Arms and Economics in the
    Third Reich* (The Hague, 1968); Dietmar Petzina, *Autarkiepolitik im dritten
    Reich, der nationalsozialistische Vierjahresplan* (Stuttgart, 1968); and Georg
    Richard Thomas, *Geschichte der deutschen Wehr- und Rüstungswirtschaft
    (1918–1943/45)*, ed. Wolfgang Birkenfeld (Boppard/Rhein, 1966).

35 Much of the official documentation is published and available in English in
    Erich von Ludendorff, *The General Staff and Its Problems*, trans. F. H. Holt
    (Freeport, NY, 1971), 1: 70–201. See also the contemporary analysis, Kurt
    Wiedenfeld, *Staatliche Preisfestsetzung: ein Beitrag zur Kriegs-Preispolitik*
    (Bonn, 1918), 16.

36 Hindenburg is quoted in Asprey, *The German High Command at War*,
    284–286; see also Ritter, *The Sword and the Scepter*, 3: 348–372.

37 The proposals were sent over Hindenburg's signature to Bethmann
    Hollweg, September 13, 1916; printed in Ludendorff, *The General Staff and
    Its Problems*, 1: 77–81. The quotation comes from p. 79.

38 See Davis, *Home Fires Burning*; Feldman, *Army, Industry, and Labour*,
    325–327.

39 Professor Dr. Emil Abderhalden, *Ernährungswissenschaft: Vortrag, gehalten
    am 21. April in Berlin* (Berlin, 1917). A copy of this pamphlet is in the
    Preussische Staatsbibliothek, Berlin, as is a repetorium of cooking and gar-
    dening tips designed for community leaders, teachers, etc.: Erich Deleiter,
    *Verzeichnis aller in der Kriegszeit erschienenen Volksliteratur über Ernährung,
    Hauswirtschaft, Kleintierzucht, Garten-, Gemüse und Obstbau* (Dresden, 1917).

40 Liulevicius, *War Land on the Eastern Front*, 216. See also the discussion of the same episode in Paul Johnson, *Modern Times: The World from the Twenties to the Nineties*, rev. ed. (New York, 1991), 90.
41 See, for a start, Albrecht Mendelssohn-Bartholdy, *The War and German Society: The Testament of a Liberal* (New Haven, CT and London, 1937), and the other volumes of the Carnegie Endowment for International Peace volumes on the war.
42 Ferro, *The Great War 1914–1918*, 178–179.
43 See, for example, my book *National Identity and Weimar Germany: Upper Silesia and the Eastern Border, 1918–1922* (Lincoln, NE, 1997), 20–23.
44 Ashworth, *Trench Warfare 1914–1918*. The quotation is from Ellis, *Eye-Deep in Hell*, 178.
45 See Ellis, *Eye-Deep in Hell*, 179–185.

6 1917: NEW STRAINS, NEW WAR

1 Kennedy, *The Rise and Fall of the Great Powers*, 243.
2 For an intensive discussion of the relationship between Germany and the United States, see Gatzke, *Germany and the United States*.
3 Frederick C. Luebke, *Bonds of Loyalty: German Americans and World War I* (Dekalb, IL, 1974), 67–78.
4 Brecht, *Aus nächster Nähe*, 269–271.
5 Burk, *Britain, America and the Sinews of War*, 7; Pope and Wheal, *Dictionary of the First World War*, 486.
6 John A. Thompson, *Reformers and War: American Progressive Publicists and the First World War* (Cambridge, 1987), 108, 117–155.
7 Kennedy, *Over Here*, 50–51.
8 The issue of an intervention engaged in for the purpose of controlling the peace is discussed in Seymour, *The Intimate Papers of Colonel House*, 2: 205–242. The statement by House is from Harry Elmer Barnes, "The World War of 1914–1918," in Willard Waller (ed.), *War in the Twentieth Century* (New York, 1940), 71–82. Barnes gives in this article a classic statement of the American "revisionists" of the 1920s and 1930s, who decried American entry into the war and showed the extent to which American entry was orchestrated by Wilson, House, and others. For a more recent statement of this thesis, see Raico, "World War I: The Turning Point," in Denson (ed.), *The Costs of War*, 203–247.
9 The classic "submarine thesis" of American intervention is the essay by Charles Seymour, associate of Woodrow Wilson, "American Neutrality: The Experience of 1914–1917," *Foreign Affairs* (October 1935): 26–36. The literature on intervention representing Wilson as an idealist who was forced into the war is very large. A good start would be the works of Arthur S. Link, in particular *Wilson the Diplomatist* (Baltimore, MD, 1957), and more recently the work of Lloyd E. Ambrosius, *Wilsonian Statecraft: The Theory and Practice of Liberal Internationalism during World War I* (Wilmington, DE, 1991). Ambrosius sees Wilson at once as an

American nationalist and idealist, who was reluctantly drawn into the war.

10 Gatzke, *Germany and the United States*, 61–69.

11 For a dramatic firsthand rendering, see Seymour, *The Intimate Papers of Colonel House*, 2: 387–472.

12 Kennedy, *The Rise and Fall of the Great Powers*, 256–271; Ferguson, *The Pity of War*, 248–254; Mitchell, *European Historical Statistics 1750–1970*, 179–183.

13 Craig, *Germany 1866–1945*, 373.

14 Liulevicius, *War Land on the Eastern Front*, 92–108.

15 See the description by Pope and Wheal, *Dictionary of the First World War*, 229–230; see also Asprey, *The German High Command at War*, 304. Civilians in the area given up (over 100,000) were transported to Belgium.

16 Ryan, *Pétain the Soldier*, 100–102; Michael Lyons, *World War I: A Short History*, 2nd ed. (Upper Saddle River, NJ, 2000), 240.

17 Ryan, *Pétain the Soldier*, 102.

18 Rawling, *Surviving Trench Warfare*, 87–142.

19 Ryan, *Pétain the Soldier*, 114–121.

20 The standard work on the Mutiny is Guy Pedroncini, *Les Mutineries de 1917* (Paris, 1967); but see also the more recent work by Leonard V. Smith, *Between Mutiny and Obedience: The Case of the Fifth French Infantry Division during World War I* (Princeton, NJ, 1994) as well as the same author's careful article, "Remobilizing the Citizen-soldier through the French Army Mutinies of 1917," in Horne (ed.), *State, Society and Mobilization in Europe during the First World War*, 144–159.

21 Ryan, *Pétain the Soldier*, 133–135.

22 Popkin, *A History of Modern France*, 232–234.

23 Ashworth, *Trench Warfare 1914–1918*.

24 Andrew Wiest, *Passchendaele and the Royal Navy* (Westport, CT, 1995), 41–62.

25 Ibid., 91–118.

26 Wiest, *Passchendaele and the Royal Navy*, 150, quoting Sgt. Major J. S. Handley.

27 The quotation is from the comprehensive guidebook to Western Front battlefields, Rose E. B. Coombs, *Before Endeavors Fade*, updated ed. (London, 1994), 57. Nineteen of the mines blew at dawn on June 7, 1917; a number were detonated safely. Two remained after the war, their locations largely forgotten, and the location and neutralization too dangerous in any case. One exploded during a severe thunderstorm in the summer of 1955 (there were no casualties). One mine remains as of the date of writing. See also Tony Spagnoly and Ted Smith, *Cameos of the Western Front: Salient Points One, Ypres Sector 1914–1918* (Barnsley, UK, 1995), 42–49.

28 Lyn McDonald tells the story through eyewitness descriptions of participants in *They Called it Passchendaele* (London, 1978).

29 Robin Prior and Trevor Wilson, *Passchendaele: The Untold Story* (New Haven, CT, 1996), 179.

30 A good introduction to the reevaluation of the battle is Peter H. Liddle (ed.), *Passchendaele in Perspective: The Third Battle of Ypres* (London, 1997).

31 Prior and Wilson, *Passchendaele: The Untold Story*.

32 Gray, *Chronicle*, 1: 282, 287.
33 Richard Pipes, *The Russian Revolution* (New York, 1990), 256–271.
34 Z. A. B. Zeman and W. B. Scharlau, *The Merchant of Revolution: The Life of Alexander Israel Helphand (Parvus) 1867–1924* (New York, 1965), 206–248.
35 Pipes, *The Russian Revolution*, 389–411, 572–576.
36 See John Wheeler-Bennett, *Brest-Litovsk: The Forgotten Peace, March 1918* (London, 1938).
37 A good summary of the rural situation in Germany is Robert G. Moeller, *German Peasants and Agrarian Politics, 1914–1924* (Chapel Hill, NC, 1986), 44–51. On the Cultivation of Lands Order and the Welsh wheat in particular, see J. K. Montgomery, *The Maintenance of the Agricultural Labour Supply in England and Wales during the War* ([International Institute of Agriculture] Rome, 1922).
38 For a description of this broad process, see Jürgen Kocka, *Facing Total War: German Society 1914–1918* (Cambridge, MA, 1984).
39 Chickering, *Imperial Germany and the Great War*, 108–119, 156–157; Elizabeth H. Tobin, "War and the Working Class: The Case of Düsseldorf, 1914–1918," *Central European History*, 17 (1985): 257–298.
40 Feldman, *The Great Disorder*, 60–64.
41 Ferro, *The Great War 1914–1918*, 178–179.
42 Ashworth, *Trench Warfare 1914–1918*; the quotation is from Ellis, *Eye-Deep in Hell*, 178.
43 Julian Putkowski and Julian Sykes, *Shot at Dawn: Executions in World War I by Authority of the British Army Act* (Barnsley, UK, 1992); Gerard Oram, *Worthless Men: Race, Eugenics and the Death Penalty in the British Army during the First World War* (London, 1998).
44 Lawrence James, *Mutiny in the British and Commonwealth Forces, 1797–1956* (London, 1987), 77–92.
45 Kuisel, *Capitalism and the State in Modern France*, 48–49.
46 Chamberlain emphasizes the territorial aspects of the Bolshevik Revolution in William Henry Chamberlain, *The Russian Revolution*, 2 vols. (New York, 1935); see especially 2: 278–334.
47 See T. Hunt Tooley, "The Internal Dynamics of Changing Frontiers: The Plebiscites on Germany's Borders, 1919–1921," in Christian Baechler and Carole Fink (eds.), *The Establishment of European Frontiers After the Two World Wars* (Bern, 1996), 149–165.
48 Mason Wade, *The French Canadians 1760–1967*, 2 vols., rev. ed. (Toronto, 1968), 2: 708–716.
49 See ibid., 730–779; Robert Bothwell, Ian Drummond, and John English, *Canada, 1900–1945* (Toronto, 1987), 142–147.
50 Population figures are from Mitchell, *European Historical Statistics*, 5–9; army figures are from Myles Dungan, *They Shall Grow Not Old: Irish Soldiers in the Great War* (Dublin, 1997), 25.
51 Dungan, *They Shall Grow Not Old*, 15.
52 Ibid., 16–18.
53 Spagnoly and Smith, *Cameos of the Western Front*, 29.
54 Martin and Mary Middlebrook, *The Somme Battlefields* (London, 1991), 107–112, 179–187.

55 I am indebted to Major Gordon Corrigan, who pointed out this contrast to me.
56 Of the many available accounts, two recent and readable ones are Peter de Rosa, *Rebels: The Irish Rising of 1916* (Dublin, 1990); and Tim Pat Coogan, *1916: The Easter Rising* (London, 2001).
57 On both Redmond and the 16th Division, see the two works by Terence Denman, *"A Lonely Grave": The Life and Death of William Redmond* (Dublin, 1995) and *Ireland's Unknown Soldiers: The 16th (Irish) Division in the Great War* (Dublin, 1992).

7 TRANSFORMATIONS: POLITICS, CULTURE, WARFARE

1 See especially Volker Rolf Berghahn and Martin Kitchen (eds.), *Germany in the Age of Total War* (London, 1981).
2 Thomas H. Russell, *America's War for Humanity*, "Victory Edition" (n.p., 1919).
3 Ewing and Gearty, *The Struggle for Civil Liberties*, 36–62; a useful brief summary is in Pope and Wheal, *The Dictionary of the First World War*, 130.
4 De Groot, *Blighty*, 143–153; Marwick, *The Deluge*, 68–76; Ewing and Gearty, *The Struggle for Civil Liberties*, 71–80.
5 Panikos Panayi, *The Enemy in Our Midst: Germans in Britain During the First World War* (Oxford, 1991); Panayi, "An Intolerant Act by an Intolerant Society: The Internment of Germans in Britain During the First World War," *Immigrants and Minorities*, 11 (1993): 53–75.
6 Thompson, *Reformers and War*, 111.
7 The classic account of home front in the United States during the war is Kennedy, *Over Here*; see also the more recent work, Ronald Schaffer, *America in the Great War* (New York, 1991).
8 Robert D. Cuff, "Herbert Hoover, the Ideology of Volunteerism and War Organization During the Great War," in Lawrence Gelfand (ed.), *Herbert Hoover: The Great War and Its Aftermath* (West Branch, IA, 1974), 23–39.
9 William J. Breen, *Uncle Sam at Home: Civilian Mobilization, Wartime Federalism, and the Council of National Defense, 1917–1919* (Westport, CT, 1984).
10 Across the Atlantic and across the Western Front, individuals in a number of German ministries were cooperating in a number of similar initiatives, which resulted in "Center" for civic education and propaganda in mid-1918. Richter, *Die Reichszentrale für Heimatdienst*.
11 Creel, *How We Advertised America*.
12 Kennedy, *Over Here*, 74–79.
13 James R. Mock, *Censorship 1917* (Princeton, NJ, 1941), 190–212; Kennedy, *Over Here*, 76–81.
14 Luebke, *Bonds of Loyalty*, 242–263; Eddie Rickenbacker, *Rickenbacker* (Englewood Cliffs, NJ, 1967), 77–82.
15 Jacqueline M. Moore, *Booker T. Washington, W. E. B. Du Bois, and the Debate over Racial Uplift* (Wilmington, DE, forthcoming).

16 Robert V. Haynes, *A Night of Violence: The Houston Riot of 1917* (Baton Rouge, LA, 1976).

17 See Schaffer, *America in the Great War*, 75–90; Kennedy, *Over Here*, 279–284; Nina Mjagkij, "Behind the Lines: The Social Experience of Black Soldiers During World War I," M.A. thesis, University of Cincinnati, 1986.

18 Gerhard Fischer, *Enemy Aliens: Internment and the Homefront Experience in Australia, 1914–1920* (St. Lucia, Australia, 1989); Michael McKernan, *The Australian People and the Great War* (Sydney, 1984), esp. ch. 7; Gerhard Fischer, "Fighting the War at Home: The Campaign Against Enemy Aliens in Australia during the First World War," in Panikos Panayi (ed.), *Minorities in Wartime* (Oxford, 1993), 263–286.

19 Fussell, *The Great War and Modern Memory*, 18–24.

20 This is the central thesis of Fussell's book; for a concise statement of it, see ibid., 29–35.

21 Edmund Blunden, *Undertones of War* (London, 1928), 62–63.

22 S. L. A. Marshall, "Introduction," in Gene Smith, *Still Quiet on the Western Front: 50 Years Later* (New York, 1965), ix–xvi.

23 Blunden, *Undertones of War*, 152.

24 Ernst Jünger, *The Storm of Steel* (published in English, New York, H. Fertig, 1929).

25 Philipp Karch, *Mit der Pfälzer Division in Flandern* (Kaiserslautern, 1918), 7.

26 Charles Edmund Carrington, "Some Soldiers," in George A. Panichas (ed.), *Promise of Greatness: The War of 1914–1918* (New York, 1968), 155–166 (quotation from p. 157).

27 Ibid., 164–165. Whatever Carrington meant or knew about Remarque, it is still the case that Remarque was wounded by a shell splinter on the Western Front.

28 Blunden, *Undertones of War*, 271; Georges Gaudy, "Our Old Front," in Panichas (ed.), *Promise of Greatness*, 88.

29 For photos of the *Wipers Times* itself as well as useful commentary, see John Ivelaw-Chapman, *The Riddles of Wipers: An Appreciation of the Trench Journal "The Wipers Times"* (London, 1997).

30 Humphrey Carpenter and Mari Prichard (eds.), *The Oxford Companion to Children's Literature* (Oxford, 1984), 324. For a highly critical discussion of the now controversial Lofting, see Donnarae MacCann, "Hugh Lofting," in Jane M. Bingham (ed.), *Writers for Children* (New York, 1988), 365–371.

31 Humphrey Carpenter, *Tolkien: A Biography* (Boston, 1977), 31–85; Humphrey Carpenter and Christopher Tolkien, *Letters of J. R. R. Tolkien: A Selection* (London, 1990), No. 66.

32 C. S. Lewis, *Surprised by Joy: The Shape of My Early Life* (New York, 1955), 183–197; the title of Lewis's chapter on the war years is "Guns and Good Company." See also Margaret Patterson Pannay, *C. S. Lewis* (New York, 1981), 8–11.

33 Carpenter and Prichard (eds.), *Oxford Companion to Children's Literature*, 350–353.

34 I am indebted to Nancy Nygaard for information on Enid Bagnold and her VAD career.

35 See Bob Thomas, *Walt Disney: An American Original* (New York, 1994).
36 See articles on de Brunhoff and Erich Kästner in Bingham (ed.), *Writers for Children*.
37 "Mademoiselle Miss": Letters from an American Girl . . . (pamphlet, n.p., 1916); text made available online by Dr. Geoffrey Miller and the web-based *World War I Document Archive*.
38 Edwin Campion Vaughan, *Some Desperate Glory: The World War I Diary of a British Officer, 1917* (New York, 1981), 5.
39 Crofton, *The Women of Royaumont*, 15–47.
40 Carpenter, *Tolkien*, 84.
41 For fuller investigations of this and related themes, see the excellent volume, Roshwald and Stites (eds.), *European Culture in the Great War*, especially the essays by Jay Winter, Peter Jelavich, Marc Ferro, and Roshwald and Stites. For a commentary on the German equivalents to these experiences and trends, see Chickering, *Imperial Germany and the Great War*, 132–140.
42 Asprey, *The German High Command at War*, 368.
43 Horne, *The Price of Glory*, 135–137.
44 A recent, and model, study is Ian Malcolm Brown, *British Logistics on the Western Front 1914–1919* (Westport, CT and London, 1998).
45 See John Buckley, *Air Power in the Age of Total War* (Bloomington, IN, 1999); the figures are from pp. 42–55.
46 See Williamson Murray and Allan R. Millet (eds.), *Military Innovation in the Interwar Period* (Cambridge, 1996).
47 On these issues, see the second volume of Vandiver, *Black Jack*, and the first volume of Pershing's memoir, *My Experience in the World War*, 2 vols. (New York, 1931). See also Donald Smythe, "Pershing," in Carver (ed.), *The War Lords*, 160–175.
48 Kennedy, *The Rise and Fall of the Great Powers*, 274.
49 Asprey, *The German High Command at War*, 361–367.
50 Ibid., 367.
51 James S. Corum, "The Lufwaffe's Army Support Doctrine, 1918–1941," *Journal of Military History*, 59 (Jan. 1995): 56.
52 Asprey, *The German High Command at War*, 363–399.
53 Haig's "backs to the wall" message, April 11, 1918.
54 American Battle Monuments Commission, *A Guide to the American Battle Fields in Europe* (Washington, DC, 1927), 22.
55 Ritter, *The Sword and the Scepter*, 4: 229.
56 See the story told in Herbert Sulzbach, *With the German Guns: Four Years on the Western Front, 1914–1918* (London, 1973), ch. 5.
57 Asprey, *The German High Command At War*, 441–443, 463–64. The post-mortem psychological opinion I have given here is the result of a conversation with two of my very patient and perceptive colleagues at Austin College, Professors Jane Ellington and Howard Starr, to whom I am indebted for their help, and who offered a number of ideas on the basis of the contemporary descriptions. Ludendorff's case seemed especially clear to Professor Starr in light of his work with post-traumatic reactions.
58 Ibid., 423.

59 Crown Prince Rupprecht to Prince Max of Baden, August 15, 1918, quoted in Asprey, *The German High Command at War*, 460.
60 Craig, *Germany 1866–1945*, 394.
61 Ibid., 394–395; *Asprey, The German High Command at War*, 462–468.
62 J. P. Harris and Niall Barr, *Amiens to the Armistice* (London, 1998); Hubert C. Johnson, *Breakthrough! Tactics, Technology, and the Search for Victory on the Western Front in World War I* (Novato, CA, 1994); Brian Bond and Nigel Cave (eds.), *Haig: A Reappraisal 70 Years On* (Barnsley, UK, 1999).
63 Richard Nielsen, Producer, "Far From Home," Canadian Broadcasting Corporation, 2001 (Richard Nielsen and James Wallen, Writers); see online notes at http://www.cbc.ca/onair/shows/farfromhome/page/last.html, accessed October 2002. For current views, see Peter Simkins, "Lions led by donkeys?," BBC News—BBC Online Network, November 2, 1998 (http://news.bbc.co.uk/hi/english/special_report/1998/10/98/world_war_i/ne wsid_197000/197586.stm).
64 Spencer C. Tucker, *The Great War 1914–1918* (Bloomington, IN, 1998), 169–172; Holt, *Battlefields of the First World War*, 143–159.

8 COLLAPSE, ARMISTICE, CONCLUSIONS

1 Gerhard Ritter, *The Sword and the Scepter*, 4: 345; Wilhelm von Groener, *Lebenserinnerungen* (Göttingen, 1957), 436.
2 Quoted in Tucker, *The Great War*, 173.
3 Rickenbacker, *Rickenbacker*, 135.
4 Hunt Tooley, *National Identity and Weimar Germany: Upper Silesia and the Eastern Border, 1918–1922* (Lincoln, NE, 1997), 34.
5 On details of conference arrangements, see Alma Luckau, *The German Delegation at the Paris Peace Conference* (New York, 1941).
6 What could, a few years ago, be a complicated matter is now quite simple. One can find the full text of the Versailles Treaty in numerous locations on the Internet – and in paper form in certain libraries as well.
7 Harold Nicolson, *Peacemaking* 1919 (Boston and New York, 1933).
8 Richard Cobb, *French and Germans, Germans and French* (Hanover, NH, 1983); Helen McPhail, *The Long Silence: Civilian Life under the German Occupation of Northern France, 1914–1918* (London, 1999).
9 This short summary of East Prussian reconstruction is based on contemporary published materials now held by the Preussiches Staatsbibliothek in Berlin. See Erich Göttgen (ed.), *Der Wiederaufbau Ostpreussens: eine kulturelle, verwaltungstechnische und baukünstlerische Leistung (Königsberg, 1928)*; Christian Krollmann, *Der Wiederaufbau Ostpreussens durch anerkannte Meister der Bauenkunst* (35-page pamphlet of the Gesellschaft für deutsche Bankkunst-Berlin) (Berlin-Grünewald, 1915); Kurt Hager, *Der Wiederaufbau Ostpreussens als wirtschaftspolitischer und kulturelles Siedlungsproblem* (Königsberg, 1916).
10 Hugh Clout, *After the Ruins: Restoring the Countryside of Northern France After the Great War* (Exeter, UK, 1996), 59–109.
11 William McDonald quoted in Clout, *After the Ruins*, 63.

12 With thanks to Dr. Kelly Reed, Austin College, for suggesting some possible effects on microbial activity. Dr Reed, a specialist in eukaryotic pathogens, suggests that the microbial activity from this amount of matter could last for decades.

13 Clout, *After the Ruins*, 23–29.

14 Smith, *Still Quiet on the Western Front*, 81–86; Clout, *After the Ruins*, 157.

15 Clout, *After the Ruins*, 154–160.

16 I am indebted to Professor Peter Schulze of the Biology Department at Austin College, Sherman, Texas, for making suggestions as to potential environmental developments, given the conditions on the Western Front.

17 Clout, *After the Ruins*, 160–163.

18 Leonard P. Ayers, *The War With Germany: A Statistical Summary* (Washington, DC, 1919).

19 For a short summary, see Pope and Wheal, *Dictionary of the First World War*, 104; see also Fred R. Van Hartesveldt, *The 1918–1919 Pandemic of Influenza: The Urban Impact in the Western World* (New York, 1992); and for a recent scientific assessment, Jeffrey K. Taubenberger, "Seeking the 1918 Spanish Influenza Virus," *American Society for Microbiology News*, 65, no. 7 (1999): 473–478.

20 Kennedy, *The Rise and Fall of the Great Powers*, 274.

21 Carroll Quigley, *Tragedy and Hope: A History of the World in Our Time* (London, 1966).

22 Murray N. Rothbard, *America's Great Depression* (New York, 1972); see also Charles P. Kindleberger, *The World in Depression 1929–1939* (Berkeley, CA, 1973). On this vast topic, see also Charles Maier, *Recasting Bourgeois Europe: Stabilization in France, Germany and Italy in the Decade after World War I* (Princeton, NJ, 1975) and Feldman, *The Great Disorder*.

23 Jacques Barzun, *From Dawn to Decadence: 500 Years of Western Cultural Life* (New York, 2000), 710.

SUGGESTED READING

The literature on World War I is enormous, and it has been growing at an accelerated pace since a revival of interest in the 1970s. The notes throughout this book are intended in part to indicate available readings. The suggestions here, in more concentrated form, represent a highly subjective selection, but they can at least give interested students some ideas of ways to plunge into this great stream of historical writing, at least the English-language channels of it.

General Narratives and Reference Works

There are dozens of good general accounts of the war, and the listing of the following books is suggestive, not prescriptive. René Albrecht-Carrié wrote an account both classic and brief: *The Meaning of the First World War* (Englewood Cliffs, NJ, 1965). Recent larger syntheses are also to be recommended, especially Martin Gilbert, *The First World War: A Complete History* (New York, 1994) and John Keegan, *The First World War* (New York, 1999). A shorter recent synthesis is that of Gerard De Groot, *The First World War* (Basingstoke, 2001).

Numerous generalized reference works provide excellent reading and good fixed points for learning more. *Chronicle of the First World War*, by Randal Gray, with Christopher Argyle (Oxford and New York, 1990–91), is one of these, as is the excellent *Dictionary of the First World War*, by Stephen Pope and Elizabeth-Anne Wheal (New York, 1995). Spencer Tucker's *The European Powers in the First World War: An Encyclopedia* (New York, 1996) also provides an informed entrance to reading on the First World War.

Origins of the War

Sidney Bradshaw Fay, *Origins of the World War* (New York, 1928) and
Harry Elmer Barnes, *The Genesis of the World War* (New York, 1926)
are still well worth reading, as is Luigi Albertini's *The Origins of the
War of 1914* (New York, 1952–57), originally published in Milan in
1942. The great Fischer controversy of the 1960s reopened and
widened the discussion. An easy entrée to the literature of this con-
troversy is the collection *The Origins of the First World War: Great
Power Rivalry and German War Aims*, edited by H. W. Koch (2nd ed.,
London, 1984), which includes, among other pieces, a reprint of
Joachim Remak's classic statement on war origins, "1914 – The Third
Balkan War: Origins Reconsidered." Samuel R. Williamson's work
also provides an excellent way into the writings on origins: see *The
Politics of Grand Strategy: Britain and France Prepare for War, 1904–1914*
(Cambridge, MA, 1969). A solid and detailed summary from the
1980s is James Joll, *The Origins of the First World War* (London, 1984).
The outstanding diplomatic history textbook by Norman Rich, *Great
Power Diplomacy 1814–1914* (New York, 1922), ends with chapters
that give a lucid, coherent, and up-to-date account of the origins of
the war. Students will also find Laurence Lafore's excellent summary,
The Long Fuse: An Interpretation of the Origins of World War I
(Philadelphia, 1965) to be useful and full of good sense.

Technical Military Aspects

Many books have elucidated the technical aspects of the front, far
too many to list here. The primary studies of the Schlieffen Plan are
by Gerhard Ritter: *The Schlieffen Plan: Critique of a Myth* (New York,
1958) and Arden Bucholz: (*Moltke, Schlieffen, and Prussian War
Planning* (New York, 1991). Two very good general introductions
are John Ellis, *Eye-Deep in Hell: Trench Warfare in World War I*
(Baltimore, MD, 1976) and Denis Winter, *Death's Men: Soldiers of the
Great War* (London, 1978). Among the more specific studies, one
might start with Tony Ashworth, *Trench Warfare: The Live and Let
Live System* (New York, 1980). Many historians have reexamined battle technology and tactics: Paddy Griffith, *Battle Tactics of the Western
Front: The British Army's Art of Attack, 1916–18* (New Haven, CT,
1994); Timothy Travers, *The Killing Ground: The British Army, the*

Western Front, and the Emergence of Modern Warfare, 1900–1918 (London, 1987); Bruce Gudmundsson, *Stormtroop Tactics: Innovation in the German Army, 1914–1918* (New York, 1989). One may also consult the many books and articles on the technologies of the war, such as gas, tanks, artillery, etc.

Apart from land warfare, expert works on other aspects of the war have been abundant. See Paul Halpern, *A Naval History of World War I* (Annapolis, MD, 1994) on naval issues. John Buckley, *Air Power in the Age of Total War* (Bloomington, IN, 1999) provides an excellent short introduction to the complexities of the invention of air warfare in World War I, as does Robin Higham's *A Concise History of Airpower* (London, 1972).

Spencer Tucker's *The Great War 1914–1918* (Bloomington, IN, 1998) incorporates much of the recent research on the military history of the war.

A handy collection for beginning the study of war leaders is *The War Lords: Military Commanders of the Twentieth Century* (Boston, 1976), edited by Field Marshal Sir Michael Carver. On Haig, see John Terraine, *Douglas Haig: The Educated Soldier* (London, 1963). On Pétain, see Stephen Ryan, *Pétain the Soldier* (South Brunswick, NJ, 1969). On the American side, nothing matches Frank Vandiver's study *Black Jack: The Life and Times of John J. Pershing*, 2 vols. (College Station, TX, 1977). Most of the war's generals left memoirs, many of which are highly interesting and most of which should be read alongside other sources, as a check for accuracy and fairness.

Politics, Economics, and Society on the Home Front

Indispensable, but – like the generals' memoirs – not always totally balanced, are the war memoirs of civilian leaders such as those of Winston Churchill, David Lloyd George, George Creel, and others.

A few classic analyses dominated for a long time, especially Pierre Renouvin, *The Forms of War Government in France* (New Haven, CT and London, 1927); Albrecht Mendelssohn-Bartholdy, *The War and German Society: The Testament of a Liberal* (New Haven, CT and London, 1937); and Ludwig von Mises, *Omnipotent Government* (New Haven, CT, 1944).

Newer works reexamining social, economic, and political issues of the home front are too many to mention, but the following provide a start. On France, the best beginning is Jean-Jacques Becker, *The Great*

War and the French People, trans. Arnold Pomerans (New York, 1985). On Britain, the works of Arthur Marwick are extensive and useful, especially his classic history, *The Deluge: British Society and the First World War* (New York and London, 1965). A more recent treatment is a good accompaniment: Gerard De Groot, *Blighty: British Society in the Era of the Great War* (London, 1996). On Germany, one can look at Holger H. Herwig, *The First World War: Germany and Austria-Hungary, 1914–1918* (London, 1997) and Roger Chickering, *Imperial Germany and the Great War, 1914–1918* (Cambridge, 1998). See also the important recent collection edited by Roger Chickering and Stig Förster, *Great War, Total War: Combat and Mobilization on the Western Front, 1914–1918* (Washington, DC, 2000). David M. Kennedy, *Over Here: The First World War and American Society* (Oxford, 1980) became the standard work on its appearance. The collection edited by John V. Denson, ed., *The Costs of War: America's Pyhrric Victories*, 2nd expanded ed. (New Brunswick, NJ and London, 1999) contains several important essays critiquing the war's tendency to expand the powers of the state and other aspects of relationships between battle front and home front; see especially those by Ralph Raico and Murray N. Rothbard.

  R. J. Q. Adams reopened the question of civilian war leadership in his outstanding work *Arms and the Wizard: Lloyd George and the Ministry of Munitions, 1915–1916* (College Station, TX, 1978). A parallel study for France in many ways is Stephen Douglas Carls, *Louis Loucheur and the Shaping of Modern France, 1916–1931* (Baton Rouge, LA, 1993).

  One can follow many recent approaches to investigating the home front in Jay Winter and Jean-Louis Robert, eds., *Capital Cities at War: Paris, London, Berlin 1914–1919* (Cambridge, 1997); R. J. Q. Adams, ed., *The Great War, 1914–18: Essays on the Military, Political, and Social History of the First World War* (College Station, TX, 1990); Belinda Davis, *Home Fires Burning: Food, Politics, and Everyday Life in World War I Berlin* (Chapel Hill, NC, 2000); and John Horne, ed., *State, Society, and Mobilization in Europe during the First World War* (Cambridge, 1997).

Women in the War

A very extensive and careful literature on women in the war emerged in the 1990s. An approach to this literature could start with the following works: Susan Grayzel, *Women's Identities at War: Gender,*

Motherhood, and Politics in Britain and France during the First World War
(Chapel Hill, NC, 1999); Margaret Darrow, *French Women and the First
World War: War Stories of the Home Front* (Oxford, 2000); Gail
Braybon, *Women Workers in the First World War: The British Experience*
(London, 1981); Angela Woollacott, *On Her Their Lives Depend:
Munitions Workers in the Great War* (Berkeley, CA, 1994). A wealth of
memoir literature by women is available, both by women on the
home front and by those who served in hundreds of capacities in the
war services, and this literature includes Vera Brittain's classic
writings, mentioned below. An especially interesting look at a specific
case of women active on the war front is Eileen Crofton, *The Women
of Royaumont: A Scottish Women's Hospital on the Western Front* (East
Linton, UK, 1997).

Memoirs

Highly recommended as a compendium of memoirs that came out
50 years after World War I is the large collection edited by George
Panichas, *Promise of Greatness: The War of 1914–1918* (New York, 1968).
    The classic British memoirs include the very literary works by Robert
Graves (*Goodbye to All That*, 1929) and Siegfried Sassoon (see, of his
many versions and titles, *The Memoirs of George Sherston*, 1929–37). An
equally classic, though sometimes overlooked, memoir by a literary
man is the thoughtful memoir by Edmund Blunden, *Undertones of War*
(London, 1928). Almost a memoir and based on many memories of sol-
diers is the classic British unit history by Rudyard Kipling, *The Irish
Guards in the Great War* (London: Macmillan, 1923; Staplehurst, UK,
1997). Vera Brittain's *Testament of Youth* (New York, 1933) is classic
account. See also *Letters from a Lost Generation: The First World War
Letters of Vera Brittain and Four Friends: Roland Leighton, Edward Brittain,
Victor Richardson, Geoffrey Thurlow*, ed. Alan Bishop and Mark Bostridge
(Boston, 1999).
    Ernst Jünger, *The Storm of Steel* (published in English, New York:
H. Fertig, 1929) and *Copse 125: A Chronicle from the Trench Warfare of 1918*
(London: Chatto & Windus, 1930). Even better known is Erich Maria
Remarque's *All Quiet on the Western Front* (Boston: Little, Brown, 1930).
A memoir from the German side published only much later is Herbert
Sulzbach, *With the German Guns: Four Years on the Western Front, 1914–1918*
(Hamden, CT, 1981).

Many diaries and journals from the war have been published and more are appearing all the time. One published with no embellishment but only generations later by the family has also become a classic. The diary of Edwin Campion Vaughan, released by his family only in the 1980s, appeared as *Some Desperate Glory: The World War I Diary of a British Officer, 1917* (New York, 1981); it was an instant success.

One of the best recent collections of primary materials is *American Voices of World War I: Primary Source Documents, 1917–1920*, edited by Martin Marix Evans (London and Chicago, 2001). One of the more significant American memoirs is e. e. cummings, *The Enormous Room* (New York, 1922).

Literature

Not to be overlooked is the superb study of the cultural and literary impact of the war by Robert Wohl, *The Generation of 1914* (Cambridge, MA, 1979). Two well-known anthologies really make the British literature much more accessible than the war literature of other countries: see Jon Silkin, *Out of Battle: The Poetry of the Great War* (London, 1972); and Jon Glover and Jon Silkin, eds., *The Penguin Book of First World War Prose* (London, Viking, 1989). A full listing of signficant literary works dealing with the war would run to many pages, but the following participants wrote fiction that became classics of war literature. In particular see the poetry or prose of Siegfried Sassoon, Rupert Brooke, Wilfred Owen, Robert Graves, Edmund Blunden, Isaac Rosenberg, Ford Madox Ford, Richard Aldington, Herbert Read, George Duhamel, Henri Barbusse, Guillaume Apollinaire, John McCrae, Erich Maria Remarque, Joyce Kilmer, John Dos Passos, and Alan Seeger.

The Peace Settlement

For an excellent, brief introduction, see William L. Keylor's "reader" on the war, *The Legacy of the Great War: Peacemaking 1919* (Boston, 1998). The literature on the peace alone is large, and most of the pertinent documents are now in print in English. One of the most intensive sources of information among printed documents is the record of the discussions of Wilson, Lloyd George, and Clemenceau, in print most recently as Paul Mantoux, *The Deliberations of the Council of Four (March 24–June 28, 1919)*, edited by Arthur S. Link and Manfred F. Boemeke (Princeton, NJ, 1992). Among memoirs here, the real classic is Harold Nicolson, *Peacemaking 1919* (Boston and New York, 1933). On the American role, a good place to start is Lloyd E. Ambrosius, *Woodrow Wilson and the American Diplomatic Tradition: The Treaty Fight in Perspective* (New York, 1987). Notable for its readability and its perspective on the peacemaking from an unusual corner is Sally Marks, *Innocent Abroad: Belgium at the Paris Peace Conference of 1919* (Chapel Hill, NC, 1981).

The "Memory" of the War

One of the great classics of historical literature on the war is Paul Fussell's *The Great War and Modern Memory* (London, 1975). Also recommended are Jay (J. M.) Winter, *Sites of Memory, Sites of Mourning: The Great War in European Cultural History* (Cambridge, 1996); Jonathan Vance, *Death So Noble: Memory, Meaning, and the First World War* (Vancouver, 1997); and Robert Wohl's *Generation of 1914*, mentioned above.

INDEX